Taxes and People in Israel

Harvard Law School
International Tax Program

Taxes and People in Israel

Harold C. Wilkenfeld

Harvard University Press
Cambridge, Massachusetts
1973

© Copyright 1973 by the President and Fellows of Harvard College
All rights reserved
Library of Congress Catalog Card Number 72–76562
SBN 674–86850–1
Printed in the United States of America

To Sarah:

Proverbs 31:10–31

Contents

Foreword

There are few critical, historical studies of the administration of an entire tax system of a country. The one by Doris [1] on the United States system is largely descriptive and contains little analysis or criticism, perhaps because it was not written by a tax expert. The useful, recent book by Chommie, a professor of tax law, is one of a series describing the federal agencies of the United States Government and focusing on current practice.[2] Sir Alexander Johnston's book [3] on the British Board of Inland Revenue is a thorough study done by a long-time official in the administration. The present study of the Israeli system was written by a tax professional, long a tax lawyer and administrator in the United States Government. He served as an adviser to the Israeli Ministry of Finance for three years, from 1954 to 1957, and has had a long-time interest in the affairs of Israel, but sees the administration as a critical observer rather than as a participant.

A study of tax administration in Israel is particularly revealing because Israel has been in a period of continuing transition and repeated crises during its short life. Moreover, it is a country for which the tax system has almost from the beginning been much more than a device to raise money. It has been used consciously, often experimentally, as a means of facilitating or accomplishing economic and social ends. These tax policy objectives have meant that the system has changed frequently with respect to technical structure and distribution of tax burden. While these changes are not the subject of the present study, they are a crucial part of the background which is briefly set forth in Chapter 2.

In a relatively short period of time Israel has had to deal with the full panoply of problems that tax administrators must face. Perhaps uniquely in modern history — that is, since World War II — it has not only faced all these problems but there have been sufficient records kept in memoranda and published in journals to make Mr. Wilkenfeld's study possible. Moreover, most of the participants are still alive, and some of them have been able to cooperate with the author in amplifying the written record. The records, the author's extended stay in Israel, his continuing research thereafter, his recent visits to Israel, and his continuing direct

---

1. Lillian Doris, *The American Way in Taxation: Internal Revenue 1862–1963* (Englewood Cliffs, N.J.: Prentice-Hall, Inc., 1963).
2. John C. Chommie, *The Internal Revenue Service* (New York: Praeger 1970)
3. Sir Alexander Johnston, *The Inland Revenue* (London: Geo. Allen and Unwin, 1965)

communication with many Israelis, plus his own dedication to this work and his scholarly interests, have all combined to yield this study.

There are many episodes in the development of the Israeli tax administration which serve as noteworthy examples for those in other countries to follow or to beware of. The property tax and compulsory payment chapters, Chapters 9 and 10, contain a fine example of interaction between the design of tax laws, on the one hand, and the organization and operation of their administration, on the other.

Particularly illuminating episodes appear in the experiment with public lists of taxpayers and their assessments. Israeli experience with these lists brought out the public's abhorrence of informers and demonstrated how this enforcement device can backfire when plagued with the twin problems of delay and errors in their publication. Why it is that experience with such lists in Sweden and Japan, for example, has been devoid of such problems is a useful question to pursue. Perhaps the answer is that in Japan no attempt is made to identify the precise amount of the taxpayer's tax liability in the public list. Instead, the Japanese lists include only the names of those whose liabilities are in excess of a certain amount. In Sweden, private concerns publish the names and assessed incomes of taxpayers above a certain level, from official assessment lists. Apocryphal or not, tales from Japan describe taxpayers who overstate their income in order to get on the list, which in turn qualifies them for government contracts and, perhaps, higher status in the community. In Sweden it is said that advertisers anxiously await the annual publication of the taxpayers list in order to prepare their own mailing lists of select customers.

The discussion of amnesties in several places throughout the volume is, perhaps, the fullest discussion of that subject in recent times. Once again, the conclusion emerges, as it has so often in other countries, that amnesties produce little revenue and are poor substitutes for the reform of tax administration. Amnesties reflect a mood of desperation and are an admission of administrative ineffectiveness.

Much of the volume, but especially Chapter 8, deals with Israeli efforts in tackling tax evasion. Years of widespread and increasing tax evasion were followed by high-level determination to stop it. This meant expanded staff and relentless prosecution. The fight against tax evasion seems to have been successful. Many of the Israeli administration's anti-evasion tactics may be transplantable to other countries, but the political will to solve the problem reflects widespread public support of a kind not yet discernible in many developing countries.

The material provided in Chapter 7 on the resolution of disputes between taxpayers and the administration, especially the development and use of lay boards, provides much in the way of useful guidelines to others who may consider experimenting with similar approaches. At the heart of the Israeli appeal process is a judicial system staffed with skilled, sensitive, and incorruptible judges. Such a judiciary is unfortunately not always available in developing countries as the essential underpinning for effective tax administration. How important it was to the orderly development of the Israeli administration clearly emerges in this study.

Are the lessons from the Israeli tax administration experience useful for all the developing countries, or are they solely of use to those countries which are either fully developed or very close to joining the ranks of the developed countries? Few developing countries appear to have as sophisticated and as broadly based a political structure as has Israel. This must affect decisions made by governments with respect to many issues of tax policy and enforcement of tax laws. On the other hand, with respect to administrative problems of both direct and indirect taxes, a number of the technical solutions which have been set forth in this book can certainly and readily be adapted to conditions in a number of developing countries. The result can be substantial advance in effectiveness of tax administration.

The book will be of direct use and considerable interest to tax administrators; it is a study that ought to be read by every new head of a tax administration. It should also prove a valuable resource to public administrators, lawyers, economists, and anyone concerned with giving fiscal advice to the developing countries. In addition, those interested in the progress of Israel will find that its history through the eyes of a tax administrator provides a specialized but valuable perspective from which to observe change and development.

This book has been partially financed by the International Tax Program, which in turn has enjoyed support from the Ford Foundation and many business firms engaged in international activity. The book is a part of the Program's continuing research which focuses attention on the tax systems and problems of the developing countries.

Oliver Oldman
Professor of Law and
Director, International
Tax Program

Harvard Law School
Cambridge, Massachusetts
July 1972

Preface

The political and social sciences have come into their own in the twentieth century. As governments have become more complex, and as reliance upon administrative agencies has proliferated, public administration has emerged as a separate science. Although tax collection is one of the most ancient, and intimate, of governmental functions, there is amazingly little to be found about tax administration in works dealing with public administration. There is also a dearth of in-depth studies of principles of revenue administration by specialists in that field. Yet in some countries the tax administration is recognized as one of the most efficiently operated agencies of government. This is so in Israel. This book is a case study of how the Israeli tax administration developed: the crises which it faced shortly after the State achieved its independence, the problems which had to be solved — how administrative policy was formulated, the interplay of a developing civil service, and a developing citizenry — all in the context of a developing economy and a continuing external conflict.

As a lawyer, trained in dealing with facts and evidence, I have tried to present the story of the development of Israel's revenue administration objectively, accurately, and understandably. Fortunately, many of the individuals who participated in developing administrative policy were available to help me. My own term of service as adviser on tax law and administration in the Israeli Ministry of Finance for three years, from 1954 to 1957, gave me many insights, sharpened my knowledge of Hebrew, and enabled me to follow subsequent developments with greater understanding.

For the opportunity to serve within the Israeli tax administration I am indebted to Mr. Ze'ev Sharef, who was then Director of State Revenue, later Minister of Finance and Minister of Commerce and Industry, and now Minister of Housing. For the opportunity to keep in touch with further developments within the administration, I am also indebted to the former Director of State Revenue, Mr. Simha Gafni, and to the present Director, Mr. Moshe Neudorfer. In particular, I must thank Mr. David Bar-Haim, Director of Public Information in the revenue administration, who assisted me immeasurably in assembling data for this study. The research facilities of the Library of Congress, especially the extensive collection of Israeli materials in the Hebraic Section, were made available to me unstintingly.

I am also greatly indebted to the many individuals in Israel who assisted me in the preparation of this work. They include judges, government officials of all ranks, academicians, lawyers, accountants, economists, financiers, and many taxpayers. Their number is so great that I must beg the indulgence of each of them for not mentioning them separately here. My debt to many of them is reflected in the bibliography.

From 1954 onward I was encouraged in this work by officials of the Fiscal Division (now the Division of Public Finance and Financial Institutions) of the United Nations. The former director of that Division, Dr. Henry Bloch, had served on three occasions as a technical assistance expert in Israel. His successor, the late Dr. Karl Lachmann, also recognized the importance of Israel's unique experience. The relevance of that experience to the furthering of efficient tax administration in other countries has been of continuing interest to the United Nations. The International Monetary Fund, also, through Dr. Richard Goode and members of the staff of the Fiscal Affairs Department, gave me initial assistance in choosing the areas of Israeli experience which would be of greatest interest to students and officials in other countries.

The opportunity to do this work while serving as an official in the Tax Division of the United States Department of Justice was a uniquely rewarding experience. It made me realize that, in the field of tax administration, the customary distinctions between developed and developing countries do not apply. In tax administration all countries can learn from each other.

The necessary research and writing could not have been done without the help of a generous grant from the International Tax Program at Harvard Law School. Even more, I must thank Professor Oliver Oldman, Director of the program. His wise counsel, continuing interest, and gentle urgings-on, constantly sustained me when my energies lagged.

As can be seen, many have shared in the preparation of this book. Still, the views and opinions here expressed are my own, and if I have erred in reporting or interpreting the facts of this case, the error is solely mine. Certainly, nothing herein can or should be construed as reflecting the position of the United States government, or any department or agency thereof.

The only person with whom I can share every word and punctuation mark of this book is my dear wife, Sarah. During our thirty-five years together she has participated in all my extracurricular writing. As Ecclesiastes said (12:12), "of making books there is no end," and so we shall continue.

H. C. W.

Washington, D.C.
July 1972

Taxes and People in Israel

1 / Introduction: The Administrative Crisis

The Burden of Taxation

For years, the individual Israeli taxpayer has been among the most heavily taxed in the world and, since 1970, he may have achieved the dubious distinction of being *the* most heavily taxed.[1] Since its establishment in May 1948, the State of Israel has been engaged in an ambitious program of economic development, while absorbing a mass of new immigrants at a rate which has far exceeded the experience of any other modern state. Simultaneously it has been compelled to equip and maintain a military establishment which has fought three wars, in 1948, 1956, and 1967. The heavy revenue needs have been met by ever-increasing demands upon the taxpaying public, in the form of steady increases in the rates of existing taxes and in the enactment of additional revenue measures.

Although the burden of taxation has been high, the declared policy from the inception of the State has been that taxes should be democratically enacted, equitably distributed, and fairly administered. The first statute enacted by the State of Israel was the Law and Administration Ordinance, 1948,[2] which is one of the basic "constitutional" enactments of the State.[3] It retained in force (sec. 11) those laws which were in effect on May 14, 1948, the last day of the League of Nations Mandate for Palestine, and provided (sec. 21) that taxes which had not been paid to the government of Palestine by May 14, 1948, should be paid to the government of the State of Israel.

1. Budget estimates for the 1971–72 fiscal year, which began April 1, 1971, give anticipated gross national product as IL.19.265 billion. Revenue collections (taxes and compulsory loans) are estimated at IL. 7.750, or 40.2 percent of gross national product. National income is estimated at IL. 17.125 billion, of which taxes will comprise 54.2 percent. *Background Data for Consideration by the Finance Committee on Estimated Tax Receipts for 1971–72* (Hebrew, mimeographed), Table 5 (Jerusalem: Ministry of Finance, 1971). Taxes have risen sharply since the Six-Day War of June 1967, primarily to finance increased defense needs, although also to curb inflation. See Josef Gabai, "Comparative Levels of Taxation in Israel and Other Countries" (Hebrew) 4 *Rivon le-Inyanei Misim* [Quarterly Tax Journal] 176 (April 1969); and compare Amotz Morag, *Mimun Hamemshalah be-Yisrael* [Public Finance in Israel], pp. 52–56.
2. Enacted May 19, 1948, 1 Laws of the State of Israel 3. The English text also appears in the 1950 *Israel Government Yearbook*, p. 247.
3. Israel does not have a formal, written constitution. See Emanuel Rackman, *Israel's Emerging Constitution, 1948–51* (New York: Columbia University Press, 1955); Yehezkel Dror, "Constitutional Trends in States That Recently Have Become Independent — Israel," Report to the Sixth International Congress of Comparative Law, (1962), 77; David M. Sassoon, "The Israel Legal System," 16 *American Journal of Comparative Law* 405 (1968).

The principle that taxes should thereafter be levied only by the elected representatives of the people was also declared by the Law and Administration Ordinance. Section 6 provides:

No government taxes or other obligatory payments to government the imposition whereof has not yet been authorized by law may be imposed, and no government taxes or obligatory payments to government the imposition of which is authorized by law may be increased, save in accordance with an Ordinance of the Provisional Council of State.[4]

Further principles of fiscal policy were incorporated in the basic outline of the policy of the government, as presented to the Knesset by Prime Minister David Ben Gurion in October 1951. The outline of policy stated, in part:

14. The following principles will be established as the foundation of the fiscal system:
(i) Equitable distribution of the burden of taxation according to the ability of the taxpayer to bear it.
(ii) Avoidance of excessive taxes calculated to harm production for export, or to be detrimental to the improvement and expansion of production or to the raising of output and the productivity of labor.
(iii) Efficiency in collection through improvement in staffing and through prevention of tax evasion by means of thorough examination of genuine accounts and profits.
(iv) Reduction of the tax in respect of income derived from the increase of output or from overtime work in essential undertakings and services.
(v) Lowering of income tax for working women.[5]

Similar expressions of governmental fiscal policy, emphasizing taxation in accordance with ability to pay, the relation between the level of taxation and incentive, and the interaction between fiscal policy and efficient administration, were contained in subsequent programs adopted by successive Knessets.[6]

4. The Provisional Council of State was the first representative body of the State of Israel. A Constituent Assembly was elected in January 1949 and transformed itself, by statute, into the First Knesset (Parliament) in March 1949. For details, see Oscar Kraines, *Government and Politics in Israel,* (Boston: Houghton Mifflin, 1961), pp. 13–27. Enactments by the mandatory government and of the Provisional Council of State are entitled Ordinances. Enactments of the Knesset are called Laws.
5. *Israel Government Yearbook, 5712 (1951–52),* pp. LI–LII (Hebrew — Jerusalem: Government Printer, 1952).
6. Elections to the Knesset are held every four years.

Buildup of Taxpayer Resistance, 1948–1954

Although the principle of taxation in accordance with ability to pay underlies the numerous tax laws in effect in Israel, those laws are not self-executing. Taxpayers must not only be able but also willing to pay. Principles can break down in the face of taxpayer resistance, and particularly during the period 1951–1955 resistance to the payment of taxes had increased to an alarming extent. This growing resistance was already apparent early in 1951 when Israel's first Minister of Finance, the late Eliezer Kaplan, said in delivering his budget message to the Knesset for the fiscal year 1951/52:

The question confronting us is how to reach all persons who are liable to tax, and how to bring it to its true level. Tax evasion does enormous harm to the State and leads to grave demoralization not only in the Ministry of Finance but throughout the whole national administration.

Although awareness of a problem is an important prerequisite to its solution, years of hard work were needed before the situation recognized in 1951 was brought under control. Meanwhile, for several years it continued to get worse.

It is paradoxical that tax evasion could have reached such alarming proportions so soon after the State of Israel came into being. Establishment of the State in 1948 was the culmination of many years of concerted devotion by those who became its first citizens. There was hardly any sacrifice which the Jewish population was unwilling to make in order to achieve this end — for which they and their ancestors had prayed for almost 2000 years. Yet the same people whose patriotic fervor at times reached the highest pitch of willingness to sacrifice themselves and their wealth for the common good, at other times seemed to have no compunction about engaging in tax evasion on a large scale. Since the willingness of taxpayers to meet their tax burden is a factor which determines the ability of the administration to perform its functions with maximum effectiveness, it would be useful to analyze some of the elements which affected the willingness of Israeli citizens to pay taxes from about 1939 to 1954, when taxpayer morale was at its lowest ebb.

For some years prior to 1939 the *Yishuv* (the organized Jewish community in the British Mandate for Palestine) depended upon both internal and external contributions to maintain communal services and institutions which were not financed out of the mandatory budget. This was an extension of customary Jewish practices for the financing of Jewish religious, educational, and other communal and charitable activities. By 1939, however, the need for funds, particularly for self-defense against increasing Arab attacks, made it necessary for a more organized system of self-imposed taxes to be collected from the Jewish community. As a result, an unofficial system of direct and indirect taxes was devised, parallel to but completely independent of the official taxes levied by the mandatory government. Under this system, which was staffed largely by volunteer workers, large sums of money were raised annually to finance the underground defense forces, illegal immigration, and the numerous institutions of the Jewish community. This unofficial system of taxation continued until the State of Israel was established. Meanwhile, evasion of the official taxes was encouraged.

In 1948 the voluntary system of taxation which had been functioning during the ten or more preceding years was supplanted by the official system of taxation taken over from the mandatory government. Immediately, the State of Israel found itself at war with its neighbors and, even before the armistice agreements with several of them had been signed, a flood of new immigrants from the European concentration camps and from the Arab countries began which, within less than four years, more than doubled the population of the country. The financial burden involved in maintaining a defense establishment [7] and at the same time absorbing about 900,000 penniless immigrants was tremendous. Yet, both obligations were accepted as entirely in accord with the national dream of establishing an independent Jewish State to which all Jews would be welcome.

The period from 1948 to 1952 was one of extreme austerity.[8] Food was in short supply and had to be rationed. World War II emergency controls on foreign exchange, rents and other items were maintained, restored, or strengthened, and other new controls were imposed. Imports were severely restricted. New taxes were enacted, and the rates of existing taxes were also substantially raised.

Underlying the strict control measures and the increases in taxes was an idealistic assumption that the population would acknowledge the need for these measures and would comply. Perhaps this was a permissible assumption in the first several years but, as conditions began to stabilize, resistance to economic controls and to high taxes began to manifest itself.

---

7. It has been suggested that "the financial burden of defense in Israel is similar to that of the developed NATO countries and far heavier than in most undeveloped countries" (Nadav Halevi and Ruth Klinov-Malul, *The Economic Development of Israel* p. 193). In his budget message for 1971–72, p. 6, the Minister of Finance stated that defense expenditures exceeded 90 percent of tax revenues (excluding compulsory loans); or more than 25 percent of gross national product.

8. For a description of the economic situation during this period, see Don Patinkin, *The Israel Economy: The First Decade*, chap. 4, "The Inflationary Process," pp. 108–125, (Jerusalem: Falk Institute, 1967).

Black and grey markets developed in food, goods, and currency.[9] Tax evasion also began to increase. It became apparent that the public administrators were unable to cope with the task. In turn, laxity of enforcement encouraged even more widespread evasion.

By 1951 it was generally known that income tax evasion had reached large proportions. Exact statistics are not available, but there seems little doubt that official concern with the problem was well justified. Various circumstances had led to this condition. In large part it reflected negative attitudes toward taxation on the part of the general public. Those taxpayers who had been in the country during the period of the British mandate had increasingly come to look upon the mandatory government with disdain. By many of them it had been considered meritorious to evade payment of the official taxes so that more could be contributed to the unofficial system of taxes and contributions supported by the Jewish population of Palestine. For some of these, it appears, the adjustment to a positive attitude toward payment of taxes to one's own government was not easy.[10] It was even more difficult for the new settlers who came to the country during and after 1948, when the bars to immigration long enforced by the British were finally lifted. The new immigrants, who doubled the population of the country in less than four years, came almost entirely from the concentration camps of Europe or from the developing societies of the Middle East. Few of them had had any experience of living as free citizens in a democratic society, and the sophisticated concepts of an income tax were a mystery to them.[11]

For those who became employees no particular problem was raised, so long as their taxes were deducted at the source from their wages. But, as the economy began to develop, many ceased to be employees and became small shopkeepers or self-employed artisans. And, even though their income levels were low, particularly during the early years, the income tax base had also broadened since 1948, so that many of these "self-employed" became subject to the income tax — perhaps for the first time in their lives. Understandably, few if any of them volunteered to file income tax returns. They waited to be asked, but (under the system then prevailing) they would not be asked to file a return unless they were already on the list of taxpayers, and they would not be included on the list unless in some way they were swept into the taxpayer "network."

9. Patinkin, pp. 109, 111, 122; Halevi and Klinov-Malul, pp. 258–260, 264–266.

10. There are indications that internal political differences within the newly established state may have encouraged some political opponents of the controlling parties to refrain from cooperating with the tax authorities. See, e.g., S. N. Eisenstadt, *Israeli Society*, (New York: Basic Books, 1967), p. 361.

11. See remarks of Income Tax Commissioner A. Givoni in 10 *Roeh Haheshbon* 136–137 (April–June 1960).

Perhaps the situation would not have been too bad if the tax administration had been able to keep pace. However, during the first few years the government was so beset with emergencies that tax administration was neglected, while attention was diverted to more pressing problems. Meanwhile, the income tax administration itself became an emergency.

By 1951 the situation was that many taxpayers had failed to file returns for past years, and many returns which had in fact been filed remained to be assessed. Of the latter, many were unacceptable, either because they understated income, overstated deductions, or both. Also, the system of withholding of the tax on wages at the source began to show signs of breaking down, partially as a by-product of the anti-inflationary "new economic policy" which was introduced in 1952. Some employers were found to be falling behind seriously in transferring to the Treasury the amounts which they had withheld from the wages of their employees. Instead, they were using the money for their own needs. Also, "under-the-table" payments of wages, without withholding of tax, were suspected to be on the increase — for they permitted the employer to pay his workers a "net" wage.

By 1952 the hostile borders had temporarily become relatively stable and the flow of new immigrants had slowed down. A new economic policy was adopted in the hope that inflation could be checked. As food and other commodities became more available, rationing and some other controls were partially relaxed. The concept of a planned economy was retained, however, and this meant the continuation of controls on imports and on currency. Since the new economic policy was only slowly accompanied by improvements in administration, it could not do away immediately with the black market in foreign currency, imported foods, and in other goods subject to import controls. Smuggling reached a peak.

Although until 1956 emergency conditions continued to prevail, they were not as drastic as before. The glow of idealism began to wear off with the passage of time. The downswing in taxpayer compliance continued, particularly with respect to the income tax, which by its nature requires a maximum level of voluntary compliance. Perhaps the income tax administration was no weaker than the other administrations concerned with enforcing the whole spectrum of economic controls. The fact is that they all were weak, largely because of shortages of sufficiently qualified personnel. Those who profited from violations of economic controls ignored the income tax as well. Many transactions were conducted in cash or in forms which could not be traced. This tendency was given added impetus by the imposition in 1952 and 1953 of compulsory loans measured by bank balances and property. This may have given even further encouragement to "off-the-record" transactions.

Efforts to Improve Administration

The fact that the tax administration was facing a critical increase in taxpayer resistance did not go unnoticed. As reflected in the 1951 statement by the Minister of Finance quoted above, there was general awareness of increased tax evasion. Moreover, it began to be recognized that the existing revenue administration was unequipped to cope with the situation. Advice was sought and obtained at this time from the United Nations Technical Assistance Administration, which appointed the Director of the Fiscal Division of the Department of Economic Affairs of the United Nations Secretariat as an expert in the field of fiscal administration and policy. His study, which covered about four months in Israel in the latter half of 1951, resulted in a number of recommendations for administrative and legislative changes. Most of these concentrated upon the income tax, which was in deepest trouble; and many of the recommendations of the United Nations expert were implemented within a relatively short time — particularly those which proposed changes in the law.[12]

While steps were under way to improve the quality of the tax administration, taxpayer morale continued to worsen. Although by 1952 a number of defects in the administration had already been recognized and although procedures to improve them were then initiated, these could not move forward very rapidly. Under the leadership of a new Income Tax Commissioner, appointed in 1952, vigorous efforts were made to clean up the backlog of unassessed income tax returns, some going back further than 1948. But as this work progressed it encountered even more taxpayer resistance.

In September 1953 the Minister of Finance appointed a special commission, under the chairmanship of the Secretary of the Cabinet (who had also formerly served as Civil Service Commissioner), to examine the methods of assessing and collecting the income tax. Other members of the Commission included one of the Supreme Court justices, the Deputy Director General of the Ministry of Finance, the Assistant Commissioner of Income Tax, and a number of officials who were co-opted to serve on various subcommittees. The Commission (frequently called the Sharef Commission, after its chairman, Mr. Zeev Sharef, submitted a detailed and comprehensive report at the beginning of 1954

---

12. United Nations Technical Assistance Programme, *Revenue Administration and Policy in Israel* (New York: United Nations 1953 ST/TAA/K/Israel/1), pp. 97–105. The same expert, Dr. Henry S. Bloch, made two more visits to Israel in 1955 and 1957 and submitted two further reports: *Revenue Administration and Policy in Israel* (*Second Report*), (ST/TAA/K/Israel/4, New York, 1955) and, same title, *Third Report* (ST/TAA/K/Israel/5, New York, 1958). These reports are referred to hereafter at I, II, and III Bloch, respectively.

which was to serve as a blueprint for many subsequent improvements in the organization and procedures of the income tax administration.[13]

Shortly after the publication of this report there were several major changes in the top personnel of the revenue administration. The chairman of the commission was appointed Director of State Revenue. The former Director of State Revenue, who had also been serving as Director of Customs and Excises, was replaced in the latter post by appointment from within of an official who had begun his customs career almost thirty years before under the British mandate.[14] The Income Tax Commissioner also resigned in mid-1954 and was succeeded by the Assistant Income Tax Commissioner,[15] who had begun his government career at the inception of the income tax in 1941. Other changes in major positions in the several other tax administrations also took place at or about this time.

Given a new and vigorous administration, with full backing of the government, the signs augured well for the ready implementation of the recommendations for administrative reforms proposed by the United Nations expert and by the Sharef Commission. But 1954 proved to be a year of crisis, with the worst still to come. Much of the difficulty was politically inspired — but forces erupted which might have completely destroyed the integrity of the tax administration. These events substantially influenced subsequent development of the revenue administration.

Political Factors in 1954

In a coalition government such as Israel's it may be expected that the differing economic policies of the political parties making up the coalition will have some influence on fiscal policy. The effect of this influence was particularly apparent during 1954. In that year the coalition included the General Zionists (a middle-class, right-of-center party).[16] As before, the Mapai Party (Israel Workers Party, with a moderate socialist platform) remained the principal party in the government although it did not have a majority. Mr. David Ben Gurion, who had been leader of Mapai for many years, and Prime Minister since the inception of the State, had left the government in November 1953 and was re-

13. This report has been translated into English under the auspices of the Harvard Law School International Tax Program. See *Report of the Commission for Examining the Methods of Assessment and Collection of the Income Tax*, ed. Martin Norr, (Cambridge: Harvard International Tax Program, mimeographed, 1962). It is referred to herein as the Sharef Report.

14. Mr. Simha Gafni, who later was Director of Revenue.

15. Dr. Theodor Brosh, since retired.

16. For background on the Israel political system and its political parties see Marver H. Bernstein, *The Politics of Israel*; Leonard J. Fein, *Israel: Politics and People*; and Oscar Kraines, *Government and Politics in Israel*.

placed by the late Mr. Moshe Sharett. Perhaps in anticipation of the elections to the Knesset, which were to take place in 1955, there was considerable internal strife in almost all of the numerous political parties.

The Herut Party (extreme right),[17] which sought to appeal to many of the same people who were attracted by the General Zionists, was not in the government. Thus, the General Zionists sometimes had to take positions parallel to those taken by Herut in order to protect themselves against possible loss of votes to Herut in the forthcoming election. The result was that even though the General Zionists were within the government they at times played the part of an opposition party. This was particularly apparent in the area of taxation, where Herut had embarked on a campaign of stirring up resistance among artisans and shopkeepers.[18] This activity came to a head in 1954.

The labor parties were understandably more concerned with the tax welfare of employees, while the right-wing parties were more interested in the self-employed. During 1954 there was considerable mutual recrimination between these groups. There was seeming justification for the contentions of the parties on both sides. Because of the breakdown in the income tax administration in past years, assessments of self-employed persons were far in arrears. On the other hand, because of the relative efficiency of the pay-as-you-go system of withholding taxes from wages, collections from employees were substantially current, even though assessments were not. It was generally surmised that there was a considerable degree of tax evasion among the self-employed.[19] However, because this had been going on for a number of years, the income tax administration found itself unable to cope with the situation when it tried to eliminate the backlog of unassessed returns and to step up collections.

Several tax issues debated in 1954 had a political flavor. The income tax rate structure was attacked as bearing so heavily upon the self-employed as to compel them to seek relief in tax evasion. The rates were to some extent alleviated by a 1954 amendment granting a partial cost-of-living allowance to self-employed individuals, paralleling a 1953

17. The Herut Party traced its origin to the Irgun Zvai Leumi (Etzel), one of the extremist underground military organizations during the British Mandate for Palestine. See Jonathan Wilkenfeld, "The Irgun Zvai Leumi in the Israeli Independence Movement," unpub. diss., George Washington University, Washington, D.C., 1966, pp. 113–128. The Herut Party has since merged with the General Zionists and the Liberals, forming the Gahal group. Gahal was part of the coalition government from 1957 to August 1970.

18. Opposition to high taxes by the right wing parties was related to their opposition in 1952 to the then open immigration policy of the government. Entry of the General Zionists into the cabinet was perhaps only coincidentally followed by a slowing down in immigration as well as by tax concessions to the middle class. Kraines, 62.

19. *Haaretz*, November 7, 1954, p. 2.

amendment exempting from income tax cost-of-living supplements received by employees.[20]

The 1954 Tax Amnesty

An illustration of the low regard which the taxpaying public held for the tax administration was the experience with the 1954 tax amnesty. In accord with the recommendations of the United Nations expert and of the Sharef Commission, the 1954 Income Tax Amendment Bill contained provisions sharpening the penalties for tax evasion and for failure to pay the tax when due. Anticipating the passage of these heavier penalties, a tax amnesty was announced for the month of April 1954. It was stated that any taxpayer who voluntarily cleared up his past omissions would be subjected to tax without penalty. It was even implied that those who showed a willingness to correct false returns would be treated relatively easily in terms of the assessments to which they would be subjected.

The results were disappointing. Very few taxpayers accepted the invitation. An extension of the amnesty through May 15, 1954, did not produce any more satisfactory results. It was obvious that taxpayers did not take very seriously the threat that they would be punished for their past evasions. The attitude, one may judge, was one of wait and see. Many were willing to take the chance, first, of not being caught; second, of being able to settle for less than the true liability; and, third, of not being penalized. There was comfort in the knowledge that so many taxpayers had violated the law that not all of them could be sent to prison even if they were caught.

Unintended support for this wait-and-see attitude may have been supplied by the Sharef Commission Report, which was published in March 1954. As noted earlier, the report proposed far-reaching improvements in the methods of assessing and collecting income taxes. The proposals themselves, by clear implication, made it doubtful that the income tax administration would be in any position in the near future to enforce any of the penalty provisions incorporated in the new law. Meanwhile, taxpayers undoubtedly comforted themselves with the ancient Hebrew saying, *"dai letzara besha'atah"* — we will worry about that calamity when it comes. Publication of the report shifted attention away from the deficiencies of taxpayers to those of the administration. The effect, at least temporarily, may have been that programs already under way for the improvement of the income tax administration were not taken as seriously by the taxpaying public as they otherwise might have been.

20. But see I. Lipavsky-Halifi, "The Self-Employed and Income Tax" (Hebrew), 7 *Roeh Haheshbon* [The Certified Public Accountant] 87; (November–December 1956).

Problems of Assessing the Self-employed

As the income tax administration attempted to clean up the backlog of unassessed returns of the self-employed, it encountered considerable difficulty in assessing the incomes of small shopkeepers and artisans, which was largely a matter of guesswork. Many of them had become prospective taxpayers for the first time after establishment of the State, but they had either filed no income tax returns or had filed unacceptable returns. Few of them had any records and, even if they did, they were generally inadequate to serve as the basis for an accurate assessment.

Since the income tax administration had not yet laid down accurate guidelines for the assessment of these small businessmen, the tax inspectors, who in those years were often without adequate technical knowledge or experience, had to guess at the amount of taxable income. Naturally, the tendency was to guess high. A bargaining process then began, with the taxpayer objecting to the initial assessment. Then some intermediate figure, which itself might have no relationship to the actual facts, was ultimately agreed upon. Even then, the taxpayer found himself obliged to pay several years of tax liability at once.[21] Many of these small taxpayers lived from hand to mouth and did not have the means to pay these accumulated liabilities. The result was that they ignored the demands for payment even after they had agreed to the liability. This meant that many of these unpaid liabilities had to be collected by the issuance of warning notices, levies on personal property, seizures of property, and threats of sale or actual sale.

As this process continued, pressures on the small, self-employed taxpayers continued to mount. By the middle of 1954 the situation reached explosive proportions. Taxpayers' strikes were threatened and held. Charges and countercharges made by members of the government as well as by representatives of the opposition parties on the left and right merely made the situation more critical.

Meanwhile, the proposed changes in the penalty provisions of the law also took on a political flavor. Explanations that these provisions were necessary in order to discourage tax evasion, when coupled with allegations that evasion had been taking place chiefly among self-employed taxpayers, were readily interpreted as a declaration of tax war against the middle class. The most vocal among the protesters were the small business men. Perhaps encouraged by the Poujade movement in France, they began to organize into pressure groups. As 1954 progressed, an increasing number of them were being assessed for past years, and de-

---

21. This was true with respect to years in which the procedure for current payments by self-employed individuals had not yet come into effect, although, even after it did so, the fact that current payments were based upon the last previous assessment still resulted in the accumulation of deficiencies.

mands were being made for payment of their arrears. Many were being over-assessed (at least in their judgment) and, in any event, they were unwilling or unable to pay. They began to resort to public demonstrations and organized demands on the tax administration for changes in the methods of assessment and for various reliefs. Some concessions were made but instead of quieting the situation these stimulated demands for more.

The Sinai Affair — 1954

An event which might have caused the complete breakdown of the tax administration occurred early in October 1954 when a Jerusalem baker named Sinai committed suicide. He left a note, addressed to the Solicitor General and Minister of Police, which implied that his suicide was due to his inability to bear his tax burden any longer. This released an avalanche of protest. Artisans' and shopkeepers' organizations throughout the country, encouraged by the opposition press, held memorial meetings in which the tax administration was castigated. A general strike was called for the thirtieth day after Sinai's death.

To meet the charges levied against the income tax administration as having been responsible for Sinai's suicide, the contents of his income tax file were made public. The new Director of State Revenue, Mr. Ze'ev Sharef, disclosed that Sinai had first been assessed for the fiscal year 1948–49 but that this assessment had been canceled on his showing that he had first come to the country in October 1948. Assessments had been made for several succeeding years, but each of these had been reduced substantially after Sinai had objected to their size. Even after the reduced assessments had been agreed to, he had not paid them until he had been pressed to do so by threats of seizure and sale of his property. Assessments for the last two years had been made, but objections filed by Sinai were still under consideration, so that the payment of tax for those years had been deferred pending their outcome. A demand had been made for payment of current advances for the year, and since Sinai had objected on the ground that his income for the year was substantially lower than that of previous years, the matter was still under consideration at the time of his suicide.[22] Thus, though it was apparent that Sinai was a small taxpayer who had been a problem to the Jerusalem income tax office, his treatment, it was alleged, was entirely in order.

This explanation did not satisfy the public, and the general strike was called. The Prime Minister then appointed a three-man special investigating commission under the chairmanship of Dr. Alfred Witkon, a

22. As to current payments, filing of an objection did not relieve the taxpayer of the obligation to pay. If his objection prevailed, he would then get a refund. Thus, Sinai was still being pressured to make the current payments.

justice of the Supreme Court who had specialized in tax matters. The commission promptly held a series of hearings at which testimony was taken from tax officials and interested members of the public. Representatives of the various merchants' associations appeared and attempted to use the hearings as a forum for widespread criticism of the tax administration.

The Witkon Commission, in order to have its report available before the date set for the general strike, accelerated its hearings and publication of its report. The report dealt only with the Sinai affair and did not go into the other criticisms of the tax administration which representatives of the small taxpayers' groups had attempted to raise. Generally, the commission absolved the income tax administration of having contributed to Mr. Sinai's death, at least with respect to the charges that it may have treated him unfairly. Among other things, it was found that Sinai had suicidal tendencies.

Not unexpectedly, the charge was made that the commission's report was a whitewash of the tax administration, but considering the caliber of the members of the commission and the objectivity with which they had approached the matter, the charge was clearly unwarranted. Nevertheless, one of the points emphasized in the report was that the file of this taxpayer showed a tendency on the part of the administration to resort to bargaining procedures in assessing the income of small taxpayers, and the need was demonstrated for the use of more accurate methods of determining income by both taxpayers and the administration.

Post-Crisis Administrative Improvements

The scare which the Sinai affair gave the administration was reflected in several changes in administrative policy and procedure that followed not too long thereafter. When the Director of State Revenue met with newspapermen immediately after Sinai's suicide, even before appointment of the Witkon Commission, he announced, after disclosing the contents of Sinai's income tax file, that he intended to put into effect immediately a procedure whereby objections to assessments would be heard by public Advisory Committees.[23]

The provision authorizing the establishment of Advisory Committees had been incorporated into the law in 1952 but had lain dormant since

23. The Sinai affair naturally caused a sensation and was widely covered in the press. Its chronicle can be traced through the following editions of *Haaretz*: October 3, 1954, p. 4 (suicide note); October 11, pp. 1–2 (Sharef statement); October 13, p. 2 (general strike called); October 11, p. 1, October 13, p. 2 (organization of Advisory Committees); October 20, p. 4 (appointment of investigating commission); October 25, p. 4, October 26, p. 4, October 28, p. 4 (reports of hearings); October 28, p. 4 (intervention by other committee); November 1, pp. 1–2 (report of commission).

then. Administrative hesitation in establishing Advisory Committees reflected recognition that many assessments were based on exaggerated estimates which required negotiation.[24] Once an Advisory Committee was called in to review assessments, such arbitrary methods no longer could be used. Accordingly, the changeover which began in December 1954 to the Advisory Committee procedure had to be accompanied by the establishment of more accurate guidelines for making "best judgment" assessments in those instances where taxpayers did not keep books or where their books were unreliable. This, in turn, resulted in a rapid move toward the creation of standard assessment guides (*Tahshivim*), on the basis of the income characteristics of particular classes of business at particular times.

Another important development was increased emphasis upon the assessment of companies and other large enterprises. These assessments had also fallen into arrears. Unlike the small businessmen, who had been subjected to assessment procedures under the guesswork techniques of 1952 through 1954, the larger enterprises had to be assessed on the basis of examination of their books and records. This required more highly skilled professional staffs than those required to put assessments of smaller businessmen on a technically acceptable level. The pressure which had previously been placed on the self-employed smaller businessmen may have produced a large number of assessments but it also evoked considerable opposition, with relatively small increase in collections. On the other hand, the large enterprises, although relatively few in number, were potential sources of large amounts of revenue. The problem, however, was how to assess them.

The shift from arbitrary assessments and from bargaining processes of settlement to assessments based on technical approaches required major improvements in the qualifications of the inspectorial staff. This was in turn reflected in the vigorous efforts made to improve procedures for recruitment and training of personnel.

Another indication of the sensitivity of the administration to reactions of the small businessmen is the procedure followed in 1955 when it was decided to issue a regulation requiring additional groups of taxpayers to keep books and records.[25] Obviously, to the extent that a taxpayer submits a return based upon books and records, problems of assessment are simplified. However, reactions to the issuance of prior regulations requiring the keeping of books had already indicated that the situation was very delicate. Extension of these requirements to taxpayers included in

24. S. Fromer, "Reasonable Cause," (Hebrew) 6 *Roeh Haheshbon*, 288 (July–August 1956).

25. Representatives of the Merchants Association had admitted in 1954 that about 95 percent of their members did not keep books (*Haaretz*, October 29, 1954, p. 2).

the groups who had been most vociferous in criticizing the administration in 1954 was an even more delicate matter. Of interest here is the fact that efforts were made to involve the various taxpayers' organizations in the process of determining what types of records would be most appropriate for particular businesses. This was partly in response to contentions by some groups of small taxpayers that they could not afford to engage an accountant or bookkeeper to keep proper books for them.[26] The administration tried to simplify the types of records required in order to overcome this objection.

Perhaps one of the most significant results of the critical events of 1954 was the emphasis thereafter placed upon the public relations aspects of tax administration. Given the explosive atmosphere which surrounded the administration at the end of 1954, it was essential that transactions between taxpayers and the administration be conducted with a minimum of friction. Among other things, the procedures were reviewed so as to reduce the number of personal contacts required between taxpayers and tax officials, to simplify reporting, to improve office conditions, to impress on personnel the need for politeness, to speed up replies to letters from taxpayers, to furnish information to taxpayers with regard to the basis upon which assessments were made, and numerous other administrative improvements.

In retrospect, the events of 1954 were frightening to all concerned. Even the most extreme partisans realized that they had unleashed forces which shook the foundations of the newly established State. As it became clear that politics and tax administration could not mix, the tax authorities were given a freer hand to establish a sound administration, based upon technical ability.

26. *Haaretz*, October 26, 1954, p. 4; see also editorials, ibid., October 29, 1954, p. 2 and November 1, 1954, p. 2.

2 / The Tax System of Israel

Introduction

The Israeli tax system incorporates almost every form of tax which the ingenuity of man can devise. Although Israel has to some extent resisted the tendency toward fiscal experimentation which has caused headaches in some countries (the net-worth tax in Japan, for example, and the expenditures tax in India), it is not averse to changing its tax structure when some possible advantage can be seen. In fact, the Minister of Finance announced in his budget message for 1971–72, that enactment of a value-added tax, effective for the fiscal year 1972–73, was under serious consideration. A gift tax is also being considered, more as a potential aid in administering the income and estate taxes than as a source of revenue. There are indications that if a value-added tax is enacted, there may be a "tax reform" in which some other taxes (particularly the purchase tax and stamp duties) may be eliminated or reduced.

Many of the taxes now in force in Israel had their origins in statutes enacted during the British mandatory regime; and some of the mandatory taxes, in turn, can be traced back to those which were in force when the British military government displaced the Ottoman Empire in Palestine after World War I. The course of development of the present system is covered in this chapter. Tax rates and their frequent changes, however, are not discussed except to the extent that rate changes may have affected administration. Generally, the trend of the rates has been steadily upward, although there have been occasional rate reductions (often balanced by increases elsewhere).

Taxation under the British Mandate for Palestine

The British Mandate for Palestine began in 1920 under the aegis of the League of Nations and ended in 1948. During the twenty-eight years of British administration the tax system, which had been inherited from the former Turkish regime, was phased out and a somewhat more modern system was introduced.

To a considerable extent the tax system, as it stood in 1948, reflected the years of internal conflict which preceded establishment of the State of Israel.[1] It also reflected certain of the political and economic con-

---

1. For a history of the mandate and the events leading up to establishment of the State of Israel see Government of Palestine, *A Survey of Palestine*, 3 vols.; Christopher Sykes, *Crossroads to Israel*; Norman Bentwich, *England in Palestine*; Albert M. Hyamson, *Palestine under the Mandate, 1920–1948*; Jacob Coleman

ceptions of the mandatory government, and efforts to accommodate the antagonistic viewpoints of the Jewish and Arab populations. The result was that the tax system was imperfect and still in transition when the mandate terminated.[2]

The tax system inherited by the British administration from the Turkish regime was based mainly on an agricultural economy. The principal Turkish taxes consisted of those on land, customs, excises, and fees for conducting various businesses. These were continued in force by the British military administration in Palestine after the First World War. Since all of these taxes, in their original form, were abolished or replaced during the mandatory period, they may be passed over rather quickly. From the administrative point of view, the predominant aspect of the Turkish system was its reliance upon extortionate tax farming as the characteristic method of tax collection.[3] This method was promptly abolished by the British.

The fiscal policy of the mandatory administration was a reflection of the political policy of the mandatory power. The initial commitment to establish a Jewish homeland in Palestine became the subject of reinterpretation and redefinition as British colonial administrators took over from the statesmen. The dynamic Jewish community, which sought to energize the economy through the development of commerce and industry, found itself frustrated by a hardening attitude of the regime, which, in an apparent effort to keep Jews and Arabs under control, had, from 1939, placed severe strictures upon further Jewish immigration. This eliminated a possible haven for Jews attempting to flee from the Nazi holocaust and its aftermath.

In the field of taxation, modernization of the taxing statutes and improvements in administration had resulted, by the mid-1930's, in revenue collections which produced budget surpluses. Another result of modernization was a shift of the tax burden from agricultural areas (largely Arab) to the cities and towns (largely Jewish). Resentment against the policies of the government, expressed by both the Jewish and Arab communities, deterred any further efforts to reform the tax structure.

Accordingly, the fiscal pattern introduced early in the mandatory period remained substantially unchanged throughout, the only significant exception being the introduction of the income tax in 1941. The princi-

---

Hurewitz, *The Road to Partition*; Bernard Joseph, *The Faithful City*; and *British Rule in Palestine*; Harry Sacher, *Israel: The Establishment of a State*.

2. II *A Survey of Palestine*, p. 543; Robert R. Nathan, Oscar Gass and Daniel Creamer, *Palestine: Problem and Promise*, pp. 342–346.

3. A. Granovsky (Granott), *The Fiscal System of Palestine*, pp. 19, 142–144. This volume has much valuable information about the transition from the Ottoman to the mandatory systems of taxation. Tax farming consisted of the sale of the authority to collect taxes in a particular region to the highest bidder. The latter's profit depended upon oppressing the taxpayers.

pal characteristic of the mandatory tax system was that it was regressive.[4] Only the income tax was progressive. However, the latter was set at such low rates that it remained a minor source of revenue until the end of the mandate.

Customs Duties

Customs Duties under the Mandate

Under the Ottoman Empire, of which Palestine had been a part, ad valorem duties had been imposed upon all imports. There were also ad valorem export, transit, and municipal duties. Administration was weak, however, and collections were low.

The Ottoman customs duties were continued for a short time under the post-World War I British administration but soon the export, transit, and municipal duties were abolished. Then, in response to changes in the economic structure of the country, the mandatory government began to reorganize the customs schedules, to adjust the rates so as to afford some measure of protection to developing local industry, and to shift to a mixture of ad valorem and specific duties.

Conceptually, the customs duties were regarded throughout the mandatory regime as revenue measures and they were, in fact, the principal source of revenue. As local industry began to develop, the authorities were urged to raise the import duties on goods competing with those manufactured locally, so that the customs would be converted into a protective tariff. The mandatory authorities acceded to these requests only partially and with reluctance.

The principal statutes under which customs duties were imposed during the mandatory period were the Customs Boundaries Ordinance –1924, the Customs Ordinance–1929, the Customs Tariff and Exemptions Ordinance–1937, and numerous expository regulations and amendatory ordinances. The Customs Ordinance of 1929 contains the executory and administrative provisions relating to procedures, controls, warehousing, computation and payment of duties, drawback and conditional entry procedures, and numerous other details relating to the activities of the customs authorities. The Customs Boundaries Ordinance of 1924 authorized the British High Commissioner for Palestine to prescribe the borders for customs purposes, these not necessarily being required to coincide with the political boundaries of the State. The Customs Tariff and Exemptions Ordinance of 1927 replaced a series of prior ordinances which had, in turn, replaced the Ottoman system of

4. Amotz Morag, *Mimun Hamemshalah be-Yisrael* (Public Finance in Israel), p. 10; Nathan, Gass, and Creamer, p. 363.

customs. The principal characteristic of the 1927 Ordinance was its adoption, in large part, of the system of customs tariff classification and nomenclature recommended by the League of Nations.

Over the years the mandatory customs reflected an increasing resort to protective tariffs, although the customs continued to be regarded until the end of the British mandate mainly as a source of revenue. However, the importance of the customs as revenue measures was diminished in the last several years of the mandate as income tax collections began to rise.

Customs Duties in Israel

Unlike the mandatory period, when customs duties were regarded simplistically as revenue measures, customs duties have been manipulated in Israel (along with the purchase tax, excises, and other measures) as means of regulating the economy or contributing to its development. Revenue has continued to be an important purpose of the customs, but in addition they have been utilized to protect and encourage infant local industries, to improve the balance of payments, and to control prices. These purposes have been complicated by inflation and periodic adjustments to the official rate of exchange of the Israeli pound.

Utilization of the customs as an economic weapon has required numerous and frequent changes in tariffs and rates. These have generally been effected *pari passu* with controls on imports and exports, subsidies, and other measures within the competence of the Ministry of Trade and Industry and divisions of the Ministry of Finance outside of the revenue administration. As new economic plans and policies have been adopted (principally in 1952, 1962, and 1970), or in conjunction with devaluations in the official rate of exchange, adjustments in the rate structure are achieved by order of the Minister of Finance, generally without prior notice. Such orders are subject to rejection by the Knesset within three months after issuance.[5]

Unlike other tax rates, which with few exceptions have steadily tended to rise, there have been occasions when customs rates have been substantially reduced. This was particularly evident in 1962 and several years thereafter, when as a deliberate matter of economic policy some tariffs were reduced in order to compel local producers to compete with imported goods both in quality and price.

As in some other developing countries, the tendency during the early years of the State had been to encourage the development of almost any industry which came along. This haphazard approach reflected an early

5. Customs and Excise Duties (Variation of Tariff) Law, 5709–1949, III Laws of the State of Israel 69, as amended.

and obviously mistaken hope that the country could eventually become almost completely self-sufficient, coupled with a desire to provide as many jobs as possible. Later, after some unhappy experiences, the officials concerned became more selective, and emphasis was placed upon viable industries which were essential to the well-being of the country or would help to achieve a better balance of payments. The 1962 customs rate reductions put many businesses to the test of whether they could survive without protective tariffs. Generally, however, customs rates have tended to be high, both to provide revenue and to protect those developing industries which fit in with the economic policy prevailing at the particular time. Inflation control and exchange-rate policies have also been factors.

The pattern of the rate structure has been changed. The mandatory system relied heavily upon specific duties — fixed sums per unit of merchandise. The Israeli system is based principally upon ad valorem duties, which are more sensitive to adjustments in the value of the Israeli pound. The mandatory customs tariffs, which had followed the system proposed by the League of Nations, were gradually replaced, starting in 1958, by the Brussels nomenclature, which is more comprehensive, detailed, and better organized. In 1961, the prior tariff was completely replaced by new schedules based entirely upon the Brussels nomenclature.

Some goods, although incorporated in the tariffs, are effectively exempt because taxed at a zero rate. Others, although taxable, are exempted if imported by specified persons. These include immigrants, tourists, and enterprises approved under the Law for the Encouragement of Capital Investments.

Starting back in Ottoman days, and through the British Mandate for Palestine, imports by the government and by a long list of charitable institutions had been exempt from customs. The latter exemptions were abrogated by the Customs, Excises and Purchase Tax (Abolition of Special Exemption) Law of 1957. Abolition of this exemption was in part intended to prevent imports by these institutions from finding their way into the open market without being taxed. It was also considered that to require government departments to pay customs on their imports would tend to compel them to reduce their purchases of foreign goods.

However, abolition of the exemption created more problems than it solved. For the government it has meant providing additional sums in the budget to cover the customs. This requires a great deal of additional bookkeeping. Some government imports may not be reflected in the customs collections figures, thus frustrating efforts at statistical analysis. Imports by charities and other eleemosynary bodies, although technically taxable, were effectively relieved of the tax burden by the establishment of an official fund out of which the import duties are paid. Thus, what had been intended as a means of preventing evasion of customs duties has produced a system of subterfuges to afford relief from the law eliminating the exemptions. This is somewhat anomalous, in view of the fact that many businesses which qualify as approved enterprises under the Law for the Encouragement of Capital Investments could import foreign goods customs-free, or at reduced rates.

Excise Duties

At the termination of the British mandate there were in effect a series of excise duties on tobacco, alcoholic beverages, methylated spirits, salt, matches, playing cards, and cement. The excises on tobacco and salt were instituted in 1925 and 1927, respectively. During the Ottoman régime these items had been controlled by a state monopoly under the Ottoman Public Debt Administration. That administration had also controlled the alcoholic beverage taxes, which were replaced under the mandate by 1927 and 1930 ordinances imposing an excise, license requirements, and administrative controls. Later, when the manufacture of matches, playing cards, and cement commenced in Palestine, these items were also subjected to excises, in 1927, 1938, and 1944, respectively.

Of the mandatory excises, those on salt, matches, and playing cards have since been abolished. The first to go was the salt excise, which was abolished in 1949. The excises on matches and playing cards were abolished in 1968, the former having first become a minimal source of revenue because of substantial reductions in rates and the latter having become a dead letter due to the failure of the sole manufacturer. Collection of the excise tax on cement was temporarily discontinued from 1949 to 1953 to encourage construction of housing for the flood of new immigrants. Since its restoration it has become a major source of revenue. Cement plants have steadily expanded operations to meet the demand.

Two new excises, those on tires and tubes and on sugar, were imposed in 1953 and 1957, respectively, when local manufacture of these products commenced. With the abolition of certain quasi-extraterritorial privileges which the mandatory regime had conferred upon the oil refineries at Haifa, the customs duties which had previously been imposed upon gasoline produced at the Haifa refineries were converted into an excise in 1958. Excises have also been imposed upon other petroleum products.

From their inception, the various excises have been administered by the Customs and Excise Administration. Some of the problems encountered in their administration are discussed in the chapters which follow.

Stamp Duties

The Ottoman stamp duties in effect at the outset of the British Mandate for Palestine had their origin in a 1906 statute, which in turn had been modeled after the British stamp duties. Almost every form of document was subjected to tax, some at a fixed rate, some measured by the value of the instrument or the amount involved in the transaction which it represented.

The Ottoman stamp duties continued to be collected until 1927, when the Stamp Duty Ordinance of 1927 was enacted. This considerably simplified the imposition and determination of the tax and reduced the number of taxable documents. Duplicate stamping, which was possible under the Ottoman law, was eliminated. Some rates were reduced, particularly on bank checks, receipts, and contracts; others were increased, as on leases and policies of insurance. The mandatory Stamp Duty Ordinance of 1927 remained in force (with occasional amendments and rate changes) until it was superseded in 1961 by a new statute.

The idea of a tax in the form of a documentary revenue stamp was well entrenched during the British mandate. It was paralleled by a variety of stamps which the Jewish community had used to raise funds for charitable and other communal purposes. Accordingly, in spite of the fact that hardly any document was exempt, the stamp duty has had considerable acceptance. This is illustrated by the fact that emergency levies, notably the Defense Stamp, have been expressed in these familiar terms.

With few exceptions, almost every form of document having some intrinsic or probative value remains subject to stamp duty. Aside from rate changes, which, like other Israeli taxes, have tended steadily upward, the most important changes in the law have produced improvements in administration. Noteworthy among these was the trend away from adhesive stamps toward impression stamps. This single change eliminated much evasion and produced a substantial increase in collections in 1961 and later years. Another trend has been toward the elimination of tax stamps in any form and reliance upon books of account as the basis for measuring the tax. Taken together with the trend toward broadening the imposition of the stamp duty on receipts given for payments on account of goods and services, some aspects of the stamp duty begin to appear more like a gross receipts tax or a turnover tax.

Real Property Taxes

Turkish Taxes on Land

The Turkish land taxes were the *Osher*, the *Werko*, and the *Mussaq-qafat*. The *Osher*, or tithe, represented more than one-tenth of the gross yield of land in Palestine during the Turkish regime. The crop was assessed on the threshing floor or in the field, and it could not be sold until it had been assessed. Annual assessment of the crops was inconvenient to the farmer and from the administrative standpoint was cumbersome and tended to foster corruption.

In 1927 the mandatory government began to commute the tithes, which in 1925 had been reduced to the traditional 10 percent. The commuted tithe for a village, settlement, or Bedouin tribe was a fixed aggregate amount to be paid annually, based upon the average amount paid by the local group of farmers in the previous four years. The portion of the aggregate to be paid by the individual farmer was allocated by a village committee, under official supervision, on the basis of the productivity of the land farmed by him. The commuted tithe was introduced experimentally in a few villages in 1927 and later gradually extended throughout the country.

The commuted tithe had been intended as a temporary measure until a more scientific rural property tax, to be based upon a cadastral survey, could be introduced. But nature played havoc with the assumptions upon which the system of commutation was based, for in the seven years which followed adoption of the commuted tithe the farmers of Palestine were plagued by locusts, field mice, drought, early frosts, and, generally, reduced crops. The result was that the commuted tithe, which had been based upon past good years rather than upon current low yields, required larger tax payments than would have been due under the discontinued *Osher*. Thus, what was originally intended as a tax reform proved to be a calamity to the peasants, and the government had to remit almost all of the taxes. The tithe was superseded by the rural property tax, in 1935.

The Turkish *Werko* was a house and land tax, varying in rate and applicable to both rural (*miri*) and town (*mulk*) land. It had many defects since, in the absence of a reliable land survey, identification and assessment of each property was difficult. Furthermore, at the time of the British military occupation in 1918 no general reassessment had been made for twenty-five years, and most of the records had been lost, destroyed, or removed by the departing Turks. Reliance had therefore to be placed upon the memories of the tax collectors who had been in the employ of the Ottoman government and upon the village elders. Understandably, their memories produced conveniently low values. By

contrast, if land was sold (generally to Jewish purchasers) the transaction would have to be recorded in the land registry, which had been
reopened in 1920. Such sales were generally at high prices, which then
served as the basis for assessment of the *Werko*. The frequent result
was that two adjacent tracts of land, identical in all respects, would be
taxed at widely differing amounts.

The *Musaqqafat*, a tax on roofed buildings, had been adopted by the
Ottoman government in 1910 and provided for a new registration of all
built-on land. Thereafter, such improved properties were to be taxed on
the basis of their gross income rather than capital value. Assessments
were to be made at ten-year intervals. This tax, which was to replace
the *Werko* as it applied to buildings, was not put into effect because of
the First World War, but in 1921 was imposed by the British in Haifa,
Acre, and Shfaram.

Mandatory Taxes on Land

The Turkish *Osher, Werko*, and *Musaqqafat* were replaced by the
urban property tax in 1928 and by the rural property tax in 1935. These
taxes, as subsequently amended, were still in force in 1948.

The essential prerequisites to the mandatory system of land taxes were
the registration of land titles, the survey and fixing of boundaries, and
the assessment of land values. In 1928 two steps were taken in this
direction with the enactment of the Land Settlement Ordinance and the
Urban Property Tax Ordinance.

The Land Settlement Ordinance of 1928 introduced a system of registration of titles of land, to be based upon a cadastral survey. Settlement
officers determined title to land on application of the owner and registered it under a method similar to the Torrens system.[6] Like many of
the mandatory fiscal measures, the registration fee which was imposed
under this law bore most heavily upon the Jewish segment of the population, and it emerged in the 1930's as the most important single land
tax.

The Urban Property Tax Ordinance of 1928 replaced the *Werko* and
the *Musaqqafat*, insofar as these taxes had applied to urban properties.
The 1928 ordinance was repealed by the Urban Property Tax Ordinance
of 1940, which was amended in 1942 and 1944. The urban property
tax was applied, by order of the High Commissioner for Palestine, town
by town. The land within each urban area was divided into blocks and

---

6. Bernard Joseph, "Palestine Legislation under the British," in 164 *Annals
of the American Academy of Political and Social Science* (Philadelphia, November
1932) pp. 39, 45; I *A Survey of Palestine*, pp. 233–241. For a description of the
chaos which prevailed before, and to some extent since, adoption of the Land
Settlement Ordinance of 1928, see Granovsky, chap. v.

subdivided into parcels, the latter being the unit of taxation. The tax payable by the owner was at a percentage of the "net annual value" of land and building, the rate being fixed annually by order. The net annual value was reckoned according to the rent which the property produced, or was considered capable of producing, after deduction of allowances for repairs and other charges. Vacant land was assessed at 6 percent of its estimated capital value.

Valuations for urban property tax purposes were made by assessment committees composed of two official and two nonofficial members, the latter selected from a list of at least six names of taxpayers submitted by the local governing body. Rather complex appeal procedures were provided. Reassessments were to be made at least every five years.

In 1935 the *Osher* and *Werko*, insofar as they applied to rural land, were repealed by the Rural Property Tax Ordinance of 1935. Ultimate adoption of a more rational system of taxation of rural land had been contemplated when the Commuted Tithes Ordinance had been passed in 1928, but adoption of a tax on rural land had been deferred until a cadastral survey could be undertaken. The survey involved the determination and marking of boundary lines, based upon a general survey of the whole country by triangulation. The next step was classification of each piece of land according to its economic use — with respect to agricultural land, for example, the variety of crops it produced or was capable of producing. The third step was the assessment of the land in accordance with the quality of the soil and the estimated crop yield. Accordingly, the cadaster would determine the location of each plot, its size and exact boundaries, name of owner, quality of soil, assessment category, net yield, and amount of tax.

By 1935, when the Rural Property Tax Ordinance was enacted, the task of land settlement and the cadastral survey had made considerable progress. Parts of the work were not completed, however, until about thirty years later, under the Israeli administration. The incomplete state of the cadaster, as well as breakdowns in valuations and assessments toward the end of the mandate, contributed to the problems which the Collections and Property Tax Division faced in the early years of the State of Israel.

Israeli Property Taxes

When the mandate terminated, the principal existing taxes on real property were the urban property tax and the rural property tax. These were imposed upon the ownership or possession of urban or rural property, the areas to which one or the other tax applied having been prescribed by order of the British High Commissioner

In 1948 there were 28 areas subject to the urban property tax which remained within the boundaries of the State of Israel. Thereafter, as the population increased, additional areas were built up, both as extensions of existing urban areas and as newly created towns. To keep up with this development, the Minister of Finance (who had succeeded to the powers of the High Commissioner in this regard) periodically issued orders defining the taxable boundaries of new urban areas and expanding the boundaries of those already existing.[7] Property which thereby became subject to the urban property tax was thereafter no longer subject to the rural property tax.

Both the urban and rural property tax ordinances have since been supplanted by new legislation which has combined them with other taxes on property, such as the local property rates and the war damage compensation levy. Their administration has also undergone a number of significant changes. (See Chapter 9.)

Income Tax

The Mandatory Income Tax

A proposal for the introduction of an income tax in Palestine was first made in 1930 by an official committee, which made the recommendation in order to "permit the rectification of present inequalities of taxation between urban and rural areas."[8] The premise of the proposal — that the Arab farmers were being overtaxed — was successfully refuted by representatives of the largely Jewish urban population.[9] The issue continued to be discussed, but political and economic conditions during the ensuing ten years put a damper on further efforts to enact an income tax. Instead, emphasis was placed upon regressive indirect taxation as the principal source of revenue.[10]

The conditions which had stood in the way of adoption of an income tax law changed drastically with the Second World War. Shipping difficulties resulted in a drop in the import of goods subject to customs duties and also reduced drastically exports of Palestinian citrus fruits. As the Middle East became a battleground, Palestine was largely iso-

7. The boundaries thus defined for urban property tax purposes did not necessarily coincide with the political boundaries of the municipality or town. Prescription of the political boundaries is within the jurisdiction of the Ministry of Interior. Fixing the boundaries for political purposes might take into account anticipated future development, whereas imposition of the urban property tax would be tied, for practical reasons, to actual urbanization. Accordingly, the urban boundaries set by the Ministry of Finance were frequently more constricted than those set by the Ministry of Interior.

8. Report of a Committee on the Economic Condition of Agriculturists, p. 50, quoted in Granovsky, p. 305.

9. See, e.g., Granovsky, pp. 305–316.

10. II *A Survey of Palestine*, pp. 543–544; see also David Horowitz and Rita Hinden, *Economic Survey of Palestine*, pp. 157–159.

lated from the rest of the free world and was in danger of being overrun by the German thrust, under General Rommel, across North Africa. Palestinian industry expanded rapidly in order to supply the needs of the Allied forces in the area and to meet civilian demand for goods which could not be imported. Resistance to imposition of an income tax under these circumstances disappeared and as a result the first Palestinian Income Tax Ordinance was enacted in September 1941.

The men who drafted the Income Tax Ordinance of 1941 derived the language and pattern of the law from several sources. Principal among these was a "model ordinance" which had been drafted in 1922 by an "Interdepartmental Committee on Income Tax in the Colonies not Possessing Responsible Government." [11] This model was based essentially upon British income tax concepts, which were considered to have been sufficiently simplified to be suitable for adoption by those British colonies which might want to introduce an income tax. The model ordinance had in fact served as the basis for income tax laws adopted by several colonies, among them Kenya and Cyprus, which thereafter served as a guide to the Palestinian draftsmen. Another principal source of the Palestinian Ordinance was the Indian income tax law, which was also derived from British sources.[12]

Frequent and substantial amendments to the original 1941 law were required to meet increasing revenue requirements as World War II continued. The basic rates, which had initially been quite modest, were increased. A surtax was imposed in 1943, and a company profits tax was imposed in 1945, in addition to the original company income tax. Amendments were also required to remedy drafting deficiencies in the original text and to adapt the law to the special conditions of the country. These numerous amendments required a complete overhaul of the original statute, and in 1947 the Income Tax Ordinance of 1941, as amended, was supplanted by the Income Tax Ordinance of 1947. This was the law which was in effect when the British Mandate for Palestine came to an end in 1948 and the State of Israel was established.

From the administrative standpoint the mandatory income tax was in trouble almost from the start. The modest administrative structure, consisting of a small headquarters staff and three field offices, had barely got under way when it was faced, immediately after World War II, with

11. S. Moses, *The Income Tax Ordinance of Palestine*, (Jerusalem: Tarshish Books, 1942), pp. 9–10. For a description of the adaptation of the same "model ordinance" to the requirements of another country, see William M. Wedderspoon, "Simplifying Taxes in East Africa," 6 *Finance and Development* 51 (March 1969).

12. Harvard Law School, International Program in Taxation, World Tax Series, *Taxation in India*, (Boston: Little, Brown, 1960), pp. 74–75; Aryeh Lapidoth, *Evasion and Avoidance of Income Tax*, pp. 20–21. The former Indian Commissioner of Income Tax was one of the main draftsmen of the 1941 Palestinian Ordinance.

the chaotic conditions which in a few short years led to the dissolution of the mandate. Meanwhile, resistance was encountered from both the Arab and Jewish populations, and tax evasion became widespread.[13] This proclivity toward evasion of the income tax, combined with laxity in administration, accounted for the relatively low collections during the mandate, when income tax collections averaged only about 15 percent of total revenue.[14]

The Israeli Income Tax

After 1948 income tax revenues rose steadily, until a balance was reached at about 50 percent of total revenues. This increase in the relative importance of the income tax is in part attributable to improvements in administration. Other contributing factors have been increases in income tax rates, automatic broadening of the income tax base due to inflation and currency devaluation, and fiscal policy, which sought to achieve a balance between direct and indirect taxes.

Like all laws of its kind, Israel's Income Tax Ordinance is a complex document, although still relatively simple if compared to the income tax provisions of the United States Internal Revenue Code. On the other hand, it is considerably more complex than the Palestinian Income Tax Ordinance as first enacted in 1941 and reenacted in 1947. Amendments made annually, or even more frequently, have added to this complexity. These amendments required another major revision in 1962.[15]

Many amendments reflect the increasing sophistication of the Israeli income taxpaying public. As they have discovered loopholes, the law has been amended to plug them, but the process is a never-ending one. Other amendments reflect changes in fiscal policy, including modifications of the rate structure, increases or alterations in exemptions, special allowances, imposition of a capital gains tax, and such like. An effort to expound on these provisions would fall outside of the purpose and intent of this volume, in spite of their great interest. Nevertheless, in order to indicate the scope of the Income Tax Ordinance, its contents will be summarized briefly.

The 1962 version of the Income Tax Ordinance, as amended, contains 244 sections. The Ordinance is divided into twelve parts, some containing several chapters, these being, respectively:

13. Nathan, Gass, and Creamer, p. 346; Hyamson, p. 179; Arnold, "Taxes and Morals," *Jerusalem Post*, January 9, 1953, p. 5.
14. Morag, 8; *Hitpathut Hamisim b'Eretz Yisrael*, [History of Taxation in Palestine and Israel] pp. 39–40 (Jerusalem: Museum of Taxes, 1968).
15. References hereafter are to the 1962 revised version of the Income Tax Ordinance, as amended, unless otherwise indicated.

Most of the provisions relating to administration of the Income Tax Ordinance are contained in Parts 8 through 12. Many of these provisions are discussed in later chapters.

Luxury Tax – Classified and Luxury Tax – Purchase Tax

In 1949, a group of three taxes were enacted — the luxury tax, the land betterment tax, and the estate tax. The Luxury Tax Ordinance of

1949 authorized the Minister of Finance to specify by order items regarded as luxuries and to fix the tax rate thereof. Consistent with the
purpose to tax only luxuries, the first such ministerial order excluded
items which affected the cost-of-living index as well as items considered
sufficiently low-priced to be available to the mass of the population. The
taxable items, upon which the rate ranged between 15 and 35 percent
of the wholesale price, included passenger automobiles, bicycles, electric
refrigerators for home use, radios, watches, musical instruments, cam-
eras, fur garments, jewelry, cosmetics, and carpets.

Administration of the luxury tax was assigned to the Director of Customs and Excise; and the purchase tax, which in time replaced the luxury tax, has continued under that administration. This is the only one
of the three taxes enacted in 1949 which has remained from the beginning under the same administration. The others wandered about before
they finally came to rest in the Income and Property Tax Branch.

On September 1, 1952, the Luxury Tax Ordinance of 1949 was supplanted by the Classified and Luxury Tax Law of 1952. This law considerably extended the scope of the tax by including items which were
not luxuries, at the same time limiting the tax on these additional items
to 7.5 percent of the wholesale price, or 5 percent of the retail price.
Thus, what had started as a tax on luxuries went far toward becoming
a general sales tax. Twenty percent of the collections from nonluxury
items was designated for distribution by the Minister of Finance to such
local authorities, and in such amounts, as he would determine, subject
to approval of the Finance Committee of the Knesset.

The first official order listing items subject to the classified tax (in
addition to those already subject to the luxury tax) was issued on October 2, 1952. It imposed a tax at the 7.5 percent rate on wholesale prices
of jars and bottles, toilet soap, shaving soap, razor blades, shaving and
cold creams, fruit and soft drinks, fountain pens, low-priced dishes, and
kerosene stoves.

The process of converting the luxury tax into a wide-ranging sales tax
was completed with the enactment, on June 3, 1954, of the Classified
and Luxury Tax (Amendment) Law. This combined the two prior
taxes into a single tax to be known thereafter as the Purchase Tax, at
the same time changing the name of the 1952 law retroactively to "Purchase Tax Law, 1952." The previous distinction between luxuries and
other taxable items was eliminated, as were the rate restrictions. Thereafter, the Minister of Finance was authorized to issue orders subjecting
items to tax and to specify the rate of tax, these orders being subject to
rejection by the Knesset within two months after their issuance. In
August 1954 a new schedule of taxable items and rates was issued,
covering 283 items within 18 groupings. Over the years, items and rates

have varied from time to time, reflecting changes in the economy of the country and in fiscal policy. Generally, these changes have paralleled similar changes in customs rates.

As the standard of living rose, expenditures for conspicuously luxurious services also increased. This led to the enactment on March 15, 1962, of the Purchase Tax (Goods and Services) Law, 1952 [sic], which replaced the original 1952 (really 1954) law and authorized the imposition of the purchase tax on various services. After a two year delay, an April 1965 order of the Minister of Finance imposed a tax on services in connection with driving lessons, catering in rented halls, and entertainment in night clubs.

As a revenue measure, the purchase tax has been the most successful of the three taxes originally enacted in 1949. In fiscal year 1954 (the first year of the purchase tax in its present form) collections were IL. 24 million. In fiscal year 1969–70 purchase tax collections amounted to IL. 636 million and it is anticipated that they will rise to IL. 856 million in fiscal year 1971–72. This will comprise 13 percent of total tax collections for 1971–72.[16]

The purchase tax may nevertheless be on its way out. In his budget message for 1971–72, delivered in January 1971, the Minister of Finance forecast the probability of enactment of a value-added tax to come into effect at the beginning of the 1972–73 fiscal year. The enactment of this tax has also been recommended by a public commission appointed in 1971 to examine the fiscal structure and to recommend "tax reforms."

If a value-added tax is enacted, other changes in the tax structure are likely to be made. As indicated, the purchase tax would be repealed, although some form of luxury tax — as on automobiles — would be retained. The compulsory loans would also be repealed, and the income tax rates, to which the compulsory loans are tied, would be reduced. Property tax rates would also be reduced and exemptions raised, thereby eliminating about 200,000 households now on the tax rolls. Stamp taxes and some other indirect taxes would also be abolished. Thus, it is anticipated, the present fiscal structure would be simplified and, perhaps more importantly, the administration of the revenue rendered more efficient because of the self-policing features of the value-added tax.

Land Betterment Tax

Whether as a source of revenue or in order to discourage land sales from Arabs to Jews, the British mandatory administration, extending

16. State Revenue Administration, *Background Data for Consideration by the Finance Committee on Estimated Tax Receipts for 1971/72* (Hebrew), Table 1 (Jerusalem, Jan. 1971).

the Ottoman *Rassem*, had early imposed high registration fees on land transfers, based on value. Although the 1941 and 1947 Income Tax Ordinances, following British tax theory (since discarded), did not tax capital gains, consideration was given in 1945 to the enactment of an ordinance which would have imposed a tax on gains from the sale of land. Opposition from the taxpaying public, both Jews and Arabs, resulted in the proposed tax being set aside for "revision." [17]

The Land Betterment Tax Law of 1949 thus carried into effect a proposal which the mandatory administration had shelved. The tax was levied on gains from the sale of real property or certain defined interests in real property at graduated rates which increased in inverse ratio to the length of time the seller owned the land and, progressively, with the increase in the rate of profit.

The essence of the law was that it taxed capital gains from the sale of land. When the law was enacted in 1949 the idea of imposing an income tax on capital gains was still abhorrent to those who were influenced by the then current British concept of income. This, in part, furnishes a clue to the reason why administration of the land betterment tax was not vested in the income tax authorities. Instead, collection of the tax as it applied to sales of land was assigned to the Land Registry and Settlement Branch in the Ministry of Justice; whereas the tax on other taxable transfers, which were not required to be recorded in the Land Registry, was collected by the Collections and Property Tax Unit.

The 1949 law was defective in several material respects, and, shortly after it came into effect, loopholes were discovered by the taxpaying public which made avoidance of the tax very simple.[18] The law accordingly failed in its two stated purposes of discouraging speculation in land and of raising revenue. By utilizing devices which the Land Betterment Tax Law did not reach, taxpayers were able to transfer interests in land free of both land registration fees and of the land betterment tax. Speculation continued but the transactions merely took on another form. These defects in the law were well known but for reasons which are not entirely clear it was not until 1963 that the law was changed to eliminate the loopholes.

In 1951 the Income Tax Ordinance was amended so as to impose a capital gains tax on profits from the sale of depreciable assets. The amendment also authorized the Minister of Finance, by order approved

17. II *Survey of Palestine* 546; Morag, pp. 107–108. Ironically, Nathan, Gass, and Creamer (pp. 610–611), apparently assuming that this proposed tax had already been enacted in 1946, praised it as a "constructive innovation," although suggesting that all capital gains should be taxed, as part of an integrated tax on capital gains, capital losses, inheritance, and income.

18. *First Annual Report on State Revenue*, pp. 197–180; A. Witkon and I. Neeman, *Dinei Misim* [Principles of Taxation] pp. 64, 271–272; Meir Heth, *The Legal Framework of Economic Activity in Israel*, pp. 37, 209.

by the Finance Committee of the Knesset, to subject other capital gains to tax. The loopholes in the land betterment tax could have been closed by such an order, which might have subjected to income tax gains from transactions which had avoided the land betterment tax. However, this was not done. In fact, application of the 1951 amendment to capital gains did not take place until 1964, following the recommendations of the Zadok Commission. By this time the Land Betterment Tax Law of 1949 had been superseded by the Land Appreciation Tax Law of 1963,[19] which closed the loopholes in the prior law for the first time in fourteen years.

The 1963 law applies to any transaction in land which in substance and legal effect accomplishes a transfer of an interest in the land, irrespective of the form which the transaction takes. The tax applies to the profit, defined as the difference between the value at the time of sale and the value at time of acquisition, after deduction of expenditures permitted under the law. Progressivity is achieved under the rate structure, the tax being 20 percent on that portion of the profit which is less than twice the original cost; 30 percent on that portion of the profit which is between two and four times the original cost; and 40 percent on the remainder. There is a credit against the tax based on the number of years during which the land had been held: for two to fifteen years it is 6 percent per year, and for over fifteen years it is 1 percent per year. Accordingly there is no tax on property held 37 or more years. Moreover, residences are given large exemptions.

Collections increased appreciably after the 1963 law was enacted, although they dropped again somewhat as a result of the economic slowdown of 1966–67 and the attendant drop in construction.[20] With subsequent improvements in economic conditions, collections have risen again.

Estate Tax

The third of the taxes enacted in 1949, the estate tax, has been of minimal importance as a revenue-raising measure. There are few large personal fortunes in Israel and those which have accumulated as a re-

19. Although the official English translation of the title of the Land Betterment Tax Law of 1949 is as given here, some have preferred to call it the "Land Increment Tax." At times it has also been referred to as the "Land Value Increment Tax." As mentioned in the text, the 1949 law has been superseded by a new law passed by the Knesset on August 26, 1963, and published in 405 *Sefer Hahukim* 145, on September 1, 1963. The new law, except for the date, has the identical title in Hebrew as the 1949 law. However, the official English translation designates it as the Land Appreciation Tax Law, 5723–1963. This illustrates some of the difficulties in translating Hebrew into English, or vice versa.

20. *Hitpathut Hamisim b'Eretz Yisrael*, pp. 154–155, 157; *Thirteenth Annual Report on State Revenue, 1966/67* (Hebrew), p. 85.

sult of expansion of the economy in recent years are in the hands of individuals who are still relatively young and vigorous. Accordingly, since death is a prerequisite to collection of the estate tax, it can hardly be expected to be a significant revenue-raiser for some time. Nevertheless, there are indications that more revenue could have been collected in past years than has been the case. In part, the failure to achieve even the modest budget estimates of past years can be attributed to a combination of defects in the statute and to lax administration.[21]

As originally enacted in 1949, the Estate Tax Law was an ingenuous attempt to combine estate tax concepts with inheritance tax concepts. The principal characteristic of an estate tax (or "estate duty") is that the estate is taxed as a unit, without regard to the manner in which it is to be distributed (except to the extent that deductions might be allowed, as for gifts to charity); whereas the inheritance tax (or "legacy duty" or "succession duty") is imposed upon individual legacies at effective rates which vary in accordance with the degree of relationship between the deceased and the heir.

The initial Israeli effort to hybridize these two concepts produced anomalous and clearly undesirable results. Three schedules of progressive rates were established, the first applying to the spouse, parents, and children, the second to relatives of the second degree, and the third to more distant relatives and strangers. All inheritances in the same category were combined and the rates applied to the sum of the inheritances in the group. As a result of application of the progressive rates to the combined inheritance, it could turn out that a higher rate of tax would apply to the individual shares of an estate going to each of several children than would apply to a share of the same size going to a single distant relative or stranger.

In addition to peculiarities of the rate structure, due to efforts to combine estate tax and inheritance tax concepts, the 1949 law was weak in its administrative provisions, most particularly those relating to the obligations to file a return, marshall the assets of the estate, and pay the tax. These weaknesses were recognized in the mid-1950's but it was not until 1964 that an amending statute was enacted [22] which both strengthened the administrative provisions and eliminated the inheritance tax features, by prescribing a single schedule of progressive rates applicable to the net taxable estate.[23] However, although the statute was strength-

---

21. *Nineteenth Annual Report of State Comptroller*, (Hebrew), pp. 125–130.
22. Estate Tax Law (Amendment no. 3) — 1964.
23. After taking the sum of all of the assets, various deductions are allowed, as for debts. Exemptions are also allowed for certain assets qualifying under the Law for the Encouragement of Capital Investments. Personal exemptions up to stipulated amounts are allowed for portions of the estate passing to the spouse, children, and parents, these being similar to exemptions provided in the original statute.

ened, the administration remained weak, and anticipated increases in collections did not materialize.

Foreign Travel Tax

This is a tax imposed upon residents of Israel traveling abroad. It must be paid with the purchase in Israel of tickets for foreign travel, whether by air or sea. Railroad tickets for foreign travel (there are now no railroads operating across Israel's borders) are also taxable.

The Foreign Travel Tax Law was enacted in 1950 as one of the measures, like the luxury tax, intended to shift the burden of taxation to that part of the population considered to be the more affluent. The Minister of Finance was authorized to prescribe the rate of tax, not to exceed a ceiling fixed by the statute. Initially, this ceiling was 50 percent of the cost of the ticket and increased to 100 percent in 1923. In 1961 the law provided for a further flat sum to be paid on each ticket in addition to, and irrespective of, its value.

For security reasons, Israelis traveling abroad were at times required to obtain an exit permit, for which there was also a fee. Under Israel's system of compulsory and universal military service, for both males and females, the ostensible purpose of the exit permit was to assure that individuals wishing to leave the country had either fulfilled their service obligations or were excused therefrom. In the interest of maintaining individual freedom of movement, the exit permit, which seems not to have deterred travel while it was in effect, has been eliminated.

The Israelis are great travelers for both business and pleasure. Government and industry have many interests abroad. Employees sometimes appear to receive the opportunity to travel abroad as a fringe benefit. Private travel is also considerable and understandable: the area of Israel is limited, and its land borders are sealed. With a highly cultured population, most of whom have families and interests abroad, it is natural that vacations would be spent by many outside the country.

Although, initially, one of the purposes of the foreign travel tax was stated to be the protection of local vacation resorts,[24] this no longer appears to be a significant factor in view of the very substantial increase in the number of foreign tourists in recent years. If anything, Israelis wishing to vacation in Israel might very well find that accommodations in their own country are scarcer and more expensive than the economical accommodations which they generally seek out when traveling abroad.

At any rate, the travel tax, high though it is, has not discouraged foreign travel by Israelis. It has therefore not achieved its stated purposes of discouraging expenditures for luxuries, preserving foreign exchange, and protecting the local resort industry. It remains, accord-

24. Morag, p. 193.

ingly, almost entirely a revenue-raising measure, in which respect it has become one of the most substantial of the taxes on expenditures.

Local Taxation

The system of local taxation which prevailed during the Ottoman regime was extremely involved. Almost every item, transaction, or activity which could be identified was subject to some form of tax or fee. The structure of local government was regularized during the mandate by adoption of the Local Councils Ordinance of 1921, followed by the Municipal Corporations Ordinance in 1934. Various ordinances dealing with local and municipal taxes, fees, and rates were thereafter adopted.[25]

The principal sources of municipal revenue during the mandate were taxes on buildings and land, fees, and licenses. These carried over into the Israeli regime. There is a general charge for municipal services (*Arnona Klalit*) imposed on all occupants of residences, industrial and commercial establishments, and occupied land, measured by the number of rooms or size of the area in use. There is also a charge on property (*Arnonat Rehush*), imposed on the owner, whether or not he is the occupant. This charge has, since 1968, been incorporated into the national property taxes for administrative purposes, although the proceeds are made available to the local authorities.

There are local occupational taxes of various sorts — annual license fees (as on vehicles and pets), taxes on display signs, entertainment taxes, and charges for specific services. Assessments are also imposed for improvements, such as paving, sidewalks, and sewage. There is a welfare levy, imposed upon guests in hotels, resorts, restaurants, bars, and night clubs.

The tendency has been for the national government to supply an increasing share of the revenue of municipalities and local councils, with the local taxes representing a correspondingly diminishing share. This trend has been particularly evident in respect of the local councils, which generally comprise one or more unincorporated settlements. In imposing their taxes, fees, rates, and charges, the several municipalities and local councils differ considerably from each other, since they are obliged to take their varying local conditions into account. The increasing participation of the national government in this process is recognition of the fact that the needs of some areas exceed their taxing capacity and that those with the greatest needs are frequently without the administrative skills and resources necessary to achieve maximum collections.

25. These are conveniently collected, as of the end of the British Mandate for Palestine, in A. B. Kandel, *Local Government in Palestine* (Jerusalem: Hamadpis Lipshitz, 1947).

Tax Incentives

One of the principal criticisms which the Jewish population of Palestine directed against the economic policies of the mandatory authorities was that they did not sufficiently foster the economic development of the country. This criticism carried over to the asserted lack of positive fiscal policy favoring local industry.[26] It was also contended that the tax burden fell disproportionately upon the Jewish population.[27]

Since establishment of the State of Israel, the economy has expanded at a rapid pace. Much of this growth was stimulated by positive measures taken by the government, both in the enactment of supporting statutes and in their execution. Included among these are a number of incentives incorporated in taxing statutes. These will be mentioned only briefly, since a full exposition would transcend the bounds of this study.[28]

In order to encourage immigration and to alleviate the absorptive problems of new immigrants, several measures were adopted. New immigrants were wholly or partially relieved from the burden of customs duties and purchase tax on their personal possessions. Housing acquired by them was wholly or partially free from property taxes for stipulated periods. Income, particularly that received from abroad, was exempted for stipulated periods. Immigrants (as well as others) settling in designated "development areas" were granted income tax reliefs. Thus, in addition to assistance which immigrants were given from official and quasi-official sources, various tax exemptions, remissions, and reliefs were afforded them.

The growth of industry has also benefited substantially from express provisions of the tax laws. The customs tariffs were revised at the outset to protect local industry, although the extent to which this was done has varied from time to time in accordance with changes in governmental economic policies. A Law for the Encouragement of Capital Investments, enacted first in 1950 and since substantially revised, particularly in 1959, was adopted. In addition to various privileges accorded to approved investors and to approved enterprises, there are a number of specific tax benefits in this law. These include deferment of land registration and land transfer fees, exemptions from national and local property taxes for stipulated periods, and exemptions from customs and purchase tax on goods imported or purchased for approved purposes. Among the income tax benefits are accelerated depreciation and a maxi-

26. Nadav Halevi and Ruth Klinov-Malul, *The Economic Development of Israel*, pp. 36–37; Nathan, Gass, and Creamer, pp. 319–320, 363–364, 575, *Palestine: Problem and Promise*.

27. Nathan, Gass, and Creamer, pp. 4, 346–347; Granovsky, chap. x.

28. The Harvard Law School International Tax Program has a study of Israeli tax incentives in process. See also Heth, *The Legal Framework of Economic Activity in Israel*.

mum 25 percent tax rate for five years on income derived from an approved enterprise, investment, or loan.[29] Approval, for purposes of receiving the benefits of the Law for the Encouragement of Investments, is administered by the Investment Center, an agency which operates in conjunction with both the Ministry of Commerce and Industry and the Ministry of Finance, although administratively under the supervision of the former.

Tax incentives have also been utilized to encourage savings. Income tax limits have been placed upon interest derived from deposits in certain approved savings plans administered by the banks. Interest on savings accounts deposited and retained in foreign currency has been exempted wholly or partially.[30] Tax ceilings have also been placed on interest derived from certain debentures issued or guaranteed by the government.

The shortage of certain technical and professional skills is recognized by the income tax law in the form of special inducements. To encourage women with particular skills, such as nurses, teachers, and others, to continue in employment after marriage, additional tax exemptions are accorded to working wives. Overtime pay and productivity bonuses are taxed at lower rates. Approved foreign experts are also taxed at lower rates. Certain classes of employees have been permitted to claim "business" deductions, sometimes without being required to prove that the amounts allowed were actually expended for the stated purpose. Some of these allowances to employees have been the product of protests and demands made by organized groups of workers as, for example, stevedores at the ports.

In some instances administrative practices have been responsive to, or influenced by, economic conditions. Laxity in administration may not have been intentional, but it has had its consequences. For example, working capital has always been in short supply and, in spite of usury laws, high rates of interest have been charged by lenders. To the extent that income tax assessments were not made promptly, or even after having been made were not collected promptly, the government, which

29. These income tax remissions have been taken into account in some of the double tax conventions which Israel has negotiated with other countries. Inability to arrive at a mutually acceptable treatment is also largely responsible for delays in adoption of a treaty with the United States, pending since 1959.

30. The purpose of this exemption was, in part, to encourage recipients of personal reparations from West Germany to transfer these funds to Israel while relieving them of the obligation to convert their foreign currency into Israeli pounds. For a time, this had been a problem because, technically, Israelis were immediately obligated to report and transfer their foreign currency holdings. Some reparations recipients resented these requirements and either refused to comply or, in some instances, even emigrated from Israel. Another, counterinflationary, purpose of the exemption was to induce owners of foreign currency not to convert their holdings into Israeli pounds, which would expand the currency in circulation.

at best could charge minuscule rates of interest on payments in arrears, was in effect financing many businessmen. The income tax administration went even further by enabling delinquent taxpayers to make government-sponsored bank loans, at reduced interest rates, to discharge their arrears. Such loans could not have been obtained otherwise. And, to the extent that assessment and collection were delayed, inflation and currency devaluations enabled taxpayers to discharge old debts with cheap currency. This put a premium upon delays and, in part, accounts for the large number of instances in which payment of assessments was deferred by the filing of appeals. Other instances of administrative forebearance had to do with delays in the imposition of administrative penalties authorized by law for substantial understatements of income and for unreasonable accumulation of earnings by closely held corporations. Deferments of customs and purchase tax could also be arranged. Although some of the instances mentioned in this paragraph may not have been intended as economic incentives, there is no doubt that the government had for some years been a far less pressing creditor than others to whom businessmen have had to respond.

Inaction in the legislative area may also be construed as indicating economic policy. Almost immediately after its enactment in 1949, the Land Betterment Tax Law was found to be so full of tax loopholes as to render it almost wholly ineffective. Yet these loopholes, although well known to the authorities, were not eliminated by amendatory legislation until 1963. The reasons for the delay are not entirely clear, but they seem to have included a certain degree of regret for the haste with which this tax law was enacted. By purporting to tax land speculation, its effect would have been to discourage the sale of land which was badly needed to provide housing for the rapidly expanding population. Similarly, although the Income Tax Ordinance was amended in 1952 to authorize the Minister of Finance to subject all capital gains to tax, the necessary ministerial order was not issued, and only capital gains on depreciable assets, which were explicitly taxed by the statute, were covered. It was not until 1965 that the law was amended to tax all capital gains, except those exempted by order of the Minister of Finance. This followed the recommendations of the Zadok Commission, which had proposed various changes in the income tax law, including a capital gains tax. However, extension of the capital gains tax to profits on the sale of securities, which was accomplished by an order issued in 1964, was a severe blow to the infant stock exchange [31] and although that

31. Morag, p. 114, n. 79. Dr. Morag suggests that some of the pre-1964 stock market activity was financed by unreported income, whose owners felt safe because some securities were issued in unregistered form and, as to others, the brokers would protect their anonymity. This hope was shaken by the possibility that the tax authorities might penetrate the veil of ownership, and the "smart money" went elsewhere. As to the effect of tax enforcement upon the channeling

order was rescinded in 1965 and stock exchange profits were exempted from capital gains tax by the 1965 amendment, the stock exchange did not fully recover.

On the whole, the economic philosophy which prevails in Israel is far from *laissez-faire*. The government takes an active role in fostering and controlling economic policies. The tax system is considered to be one of the available tools, and although not as sensitive or quick-acting as others, tax measures have been viewed from the start in terms of their economic effects.

Recent Tax Increases

From the beginning of 1966 until the introduction of the budget for fiscal year 1970–71, there were no substantial increases in tax rates and no new taxes were introduced. The reasons for this relative stability in the fiscal system involved a combination of economic and political considerations. A major change has since taken place, however, under compulsion of rising defense costs.

The stated purpose of the new economic policy of 1962 was to bring the economy under control by slowing down the forces which had contributed to the preceding galloping inflation. This would have required a considerable amount of belt-tightening, which the government was not quite prepared to compel.[32] The principal feature of the new policy was to be a freeze on wage increases. Prices were to be stabilized by removal of restrictions on imports of consumer goods and by reductions in customs and purchase taxes payable thereon, so as to force local producers to compete with imported goods by increasing their own efficiency, improving the quality of their products, exporting, and lowering their local prices.

The 1962 policy only partially achieved its purpose, and, by 1965, continuing inflation and the end of the wage freeze produced wage increases as high as 30 percent, in spite of signs of increasing unemployment. Further efforts at control of wages were accompanied by tax reductions and a promise by the government that taxes would not be increased. Early in 1966 more drastic economic restraints were instituted.

The 1966 revised economic policy put so effective a brake upon the economy as to be almost frightening. From a boom in 1962 the economy reversed itself to a near state of depression in 1966–67. The hitherto steady rate of increase of the gross national product dropped substantially. For the first time since 1954 there was large-scale unemployment.

Again, this situation reversed itself dramatically after the Six-Day War

---

of tax-evaded income, see also Amotz Morag, "Some Economic Aspects of Two Administrative Methods of Estimating Taxable Income," 10 *National Tax Journal* 176, 177–179 (June 1957).

32. Halevi and Klinov-Malul, pp. 268–269, 281–282.

of June 1967. The country has since been experiencing an economic boom, and inflation has once again become a serious problem. That inflation would have to be dealt with, by fiscal and other measures, was apparent fairly soon after the Six-Day War. Yet the government promised not to raise taxes [33] while attempting to hold labor to its commitment not to press for wage increases.

With the pressure of inflationary forces rapidly building up, however, the pressure for wage increases began to express itself again in the latter part of 1969 in the form of strikes by various groups of employees. These the leaders of the Histadrut (General Federation of Labor) had difficulty in controlling. Among the striking groups were the postal workers, stevedores at the ports, and even employees of the several tax administrations. By January 1970 it was obvious that substantial wage increases would be demanded from employers by the Histadrut. It was estimated that these wage increases, which would range between 6 to 8 percent for 1970, would produce total increased wages of between 600 to 700 million pounds.[34]

Although the economy turned around in the latter part of 1967, the stated policy of not increasing taxes was adhered to. Instead, an effort was made to soak up excess purchasing power by starting a drive for the purchase of government bonds on a voluntary rather than compulsory basis. These efforts to control inflation by voluntary means were obviously insufficient, but politically the government had little choice. By January 1969, when the budget for fiscal year 1969–70 had to be prepared, any effort to increase taxes would have been political suicide for the parties in power, because the quadrennial elections to the Knesset were scheduled to take place in October of that year. Meanwhile, the economy got further out of control, with inflation increasing and foreign currency reserves decreasing. It was clear that the new postelection government would have to take drastic measures in submitting its budget for the fiscal year 1970–71.

At the outset of 1970, a "package deal" was worked out among the government, the Histadrut, and representatives of private industry. Although wage increases were agreed to, a large portion of these was frozen in the form of a new compulsory loan, imposed upon both employees and employers (see Chapter 9). Additionally, the Compulsory Defense Levy was extended for two years and was increased by 50 percent. Then, in August 1970, a supplemental budget was enacted which, among other things, increased tax rates substantially. Additional increases in tax rates were enacted in the budget for fiscal year 1971–72, which commenced April 1, 1971.

33. *Shnaton Hamemshalah* [Government Yearbook] 5729–1969 (Jerusalem: Prime Minister's Office, 1969), p. 108.
34. *Maariv*, January 15, 1970, p. 1.

The effect of the tax increases since the beginning of 1970 is sharply illustrated by the ratio of revenue collections to gross national product. In fiscal year 1967–68, taxes absorbed 22.9 percent of gross national product; in 1968–69, 24.3 percent; and in 1969–70, 26.1 percent. By contrast, in 1970–71 taxes absorbed 37.7 percent (estimated) of gross national product; and, in 1971–72, budget estimates give anticipated gross national product as IL. 19.265 billion and revenue collections (taxes and compulsory loans) at IL. 7.750 billion, or 40.2 percent of gross national product.[35]

By these recent increases, Israel has catapulted itself into the forefront of the most heavily taxed nations in the world. This was done, however, with assurance that the revenue administration would be able to cope with the burden of collection and that the taxpaying public would respond affirmatively.[36] Conditions have indeed improved dramatically from the breakdown in administrative competence and taxpayer morale which, as Chapter 1 shows, had reached crisis proportions in the early 1950's. The confidence in the taxpaying public expressed by Minister of Finance Pinhas Sapir in introducing the budget for 1971–72 contrasts sharply with the tone of despair expressed twenty years before by Minister of Finance Eliezer Kaplan in his budget message for 1951–52, quoted in Chapter 1.

35. *Shnaton Hamemshalah* [Government Yearbook] 5731–1970 (Jerusalem: Government Printer, 1970), p. 45; Ministry of Finance, "Background Data for Consideration by the Finance Committee on Estimated Tax Receipts for 1971/72," (Hebrew), Table 5 (Jerusalem: Ministry of Finance, 1971).

36. *Budget Message of Minister of Finance for 1971/72* (Hebrew), p. 17 (Jerusalem, January 1971).

3 / Development of the Administrative Structure

Introduction

Israel's revenue collections have increased steadily and rapidly. In the State's first full fiscal year, 1949–50;[1] collections from taxes, fees, and licenses totaled about 35 million Israeli pounds. Twenty years later, in fiscal year 1967–68, collections totaled over 2,700 million pounds. Discounting for the several currency devaluations which took place over the twenty-year period,[2] this represents, in real terms, about a seventeen-fold increase in collections.[3] As mentioned at the close of the preceding chapter, revenue collections have risen even more precipitously since the beginning of 1970.

Collections of such magnitude would have been impossible without an effective revenue administration. Although much of what follows in this and succeeding chapters concentrates upon the maturation of the administration, it must also be emphasized that innovations and improvements in administrative structure and procedures had to interact with the readiness, willingness and ability of the general public to accept the heavy burden of taxation. At times, taxpayer attitudes prodded the administration into major changes, as happened in 1954. At other times, the administration engaged in activities specifically designed to improve taxpayer compliance, as for example, the public relations program, the criminal prosecution program, or the introduction of bookkeeping requirements. Although the administration had much to learn, so did the taxpaying public. Over the course of years, both administration and the public learned together, and by interacting helped to achieve substantial improvements both in administration and in the level of voluntary taxpayer compliance.

1. The State of Israel was established May 15, 1948. The government fiscal year runs from April 1 through March 31, following the precedent maintained during the British Mandate for Palestine since 1932. Granovsky, *Fiscal System of Palestine*, pp. 9–10.

2. Until 1952 the Israel pound was linked to the British pound sterling which, before its devaluation in 1949, was approximately £ 1 equals $4. As to Israeli currency, that rate was maintained only for soft currencies, the rate for hard currencies being IL. 1 equals $3. From 1952, a series of devaluations occurred and, at times, several official exchange rates were in effect simultaneously. The current (1972) exchange rate is IL. 4.20 equals $1. Thus, the Israel pound, in relation to the dollar, has depreciated to less than one-tenth of its 1948 value. See Robert David Ottensooser, *The Palestine Pound and the Israel Pound* (Ambilly: Les Presses de Savoie, 1955); Yaacov Neeman, *The Tax Consequences of Devaluation — The Approach of the Israel Law.*

3. *Shnaton Hamemshalah* [Government Yearbook] 5729–1969 (Jerusalem: Government Printer, 1969), p. 106.

Administration of the numerous taxes in effect in Israel is now distributed between two branches of the revenue administration.[4] These are the Income and Property Tax Branch and the Customs and Excise Branch. In name, at least, these are similar to the principal branches of the tax administration during the period of the British Mandate for Palestine and during the early years of the State. However, their responsibilities, scope of authority, and structures have changed considerably since 1948, and major changes are still going on. The Income and Property Tax Branch is still in the process of digesting administration of the property taxes, which were merged into the income tax administration with the abolition in 1968 of the Property Tax and Damages Fund Branch. The Customs and Excise Branch has undertaken a major reorganization, which entails a shift from divisions along substantive tax lines (e.g., purchase tax, excises, customs) to functional divisions such as audit, valuation, and assessment.

Significant changes have also taken place in the administrative hierarchy which overlays the two branches of the revenue administration. During the mandate, the tax administration was diffuse. When the State was established in 1948, the lines of communication were tightened, the Minister of Finance being given control over the several tax administrations. However, the tendency toward administrative diffusion continued, being evident particularly as new revenue measures were introduced. And when the office of Director of State Revenue was established by the first Minister of Finance, the early incumbents did not assert themselves as tax administrators. That changed in 1954 when a new Director of State Revenue took control.

In the course of time, the vertical integration which was accomplished by the strengthening of the office of the Director of State Revenue was reflected also in a horizontal integration of the several tax administrations. Independent administrations, which had existed alongside the two major branches, were absorbed into either the Customs and Excise Branch or the Income Tax Branch. For a time it appeared that a third branch, the War Damages and Property Taxes Branch, would survive, but it met its end in 1968, being merged into the Income and Property Tax Branch.

Accordingly, as of 1972, the Minister of Finance stands at the head of a three-level, bifurcated structure, consisting of himself, the Director of

4. Of the 2.7 billion pounds collected in 1967/68, 93 million were collected by other ministries. These other ministries are the Ministry of Transport, which collected fees for vehicle and drivers' licenses; the Ministry of Justice, which collected fees for court costs, registration of companies, land registry, and certain other legal fees; and the Ministry of Posts, which collects fees for radio licenses. Minor fees are charged by some other ministries, principally for services rendered. There are also local fees, rates, and licenses. Since these items are relatively minor in amount, and since their administration is relatively uncomplicated, they will not be dealt with further.

State Revenue, the Income and Property Tax Commissioner, and the Director of Customs and Excises. The latter two, in turn, are supported by their respective hierarchies, to be described later. First we must examine the structure of the revenue administration in mandatory days because it significantly influenced the course of subsequent developments.

Structure of the Revenue Administration

Under the British Mandate for Palestine (1920–1948)

The principal characteristic of the pattern of revenue administration established during the British mandate was that each tax had its own independent administration. This compartmentalization persisted for a number of years after the State of Israel was established.

During the mandate there were two areas in which the revenue administration was centralized. The first of these was the general control vested in the High Commissioner for Palestine, who, as the supreme executive, appointed the commissioners or directors of the various taxes and, through the Chief Secretary and the Executive Council, exercised administrative control over the several tax administrations. The other point of contact for some of the tax administrations consisted of the administrative hierarchy centering around the several District Commissioners.

For purposes of administration the country had been divided into districts, of which there were six in 1946. Each of these was under the control of a District Commissioner, responsible to the Chief Secretary. The District Commissioners, and one or more Assistant District Commissioners, were British subjects. Some districts were further subdivided and were placed under the charge of District Officers who might be either Palestinian Jews or Arabs, according to the makeup of the population in the subdistrict.

The various government departments functioned independently of the district officials, although they coordinated with each other. In the administration of property taxes the District Commissioner had specific functions as a revenue officer, for he and his assistants participated in the assessment of the property taxes and the hearing of appeals from disputed assessments. The District Commissioners and District Officers also executed the Taxes (Collections) Ordinance, which authorized them to take drastic measures to enforce payment from delinquent property and income taxpayers.

There were two areas, however, which were substantively independent of the district hierarchy. These were the customs administration and the income tax administration.

The customs were under the jurisdiction of the Director of Customs, Excise and Trade, who also administered the excise duties levied on tobacco, intoxicating liquors, salt, matches, and cement of local production. This was the major revenue department of the Palestine government, producing about 35 percent of the revenue in fiscal year 1944–45. The Collectors of Customs, at the customs houses, and the officers in charge of the other field offices of the customs and excise organization, were independent of the District Commissioners and their staffs.

The income tax headquarters staff during the mandate consisted of the Commissioner of Income Tax, two assistant commissioners, and requisite subordinate staff. The headquarters organization was small and its functions very limited in scope. In part, this was due to the concept of government administration generally followed during the mandatory period whereby administrative functions were largely decentralized.[5]

The pattern of administration established by the Income Tax Ordinance of 1941, which instituted the first income tax in Palestine, called for the appointment by the High Commissioner for Palestine of a Commissioner of Income Tax, Assessing Officers, and such other personnel as might be necessary. When the Income Tax Ordinance first went into effect in September 1941, the income tax assessing districts were generally defined to conform to the existing administrative districts. Five District Commissioners were also designated as the Income Tax Assessing Officers for their respective districts. For the Lydda District (which included Tel Aviv) two assessing officers were appointed: one of them, a Jew, was in charge of "non-Arab" assessees, and the other, an Arab, was in charge of all Arab assessees.[6]

This arrangement was short-lived, and in April 1943 the appointments were revoked and four other income tax assessing officers were designated. These new appointments were accompanied by a redrawing of boundaries and a major redefinition of the assessees for whose accounts the respective assessing officers were responsible, with a considerable extension of the lines of demarcation between Arab and Jewish taxpayers.[7] These organizational changes came into effect simultaneously

5. For an official description of tax administration during the British mandatory period, see I *A Survey of Palestine* 109–117; II ibid., 1065, 1069 (Palestine: Government Printer, 1946).

6. Notice regarding appointment of assessing officers, September 1, 1941, *Palestine Gazette* no. 1128, supp. no. 2, p. 1415, reprinted in Moses, *The Income Tax Ordinance of Palestine*, pp. 328–329. In essence, this division of authority amounted to a geographic subdivision of the Lydda District, for the Jewish and Arab populations generally did not reside in the same areas.

7. Notice regarding appointment of assessing officers, April 8, 1943, *Palestine Gazette*, supp. no. 2, p. 376, reprinted in Moses, ibid, second supp. 1943, pp. 137–138. See also, notice of October 1, 1941, *Palestine Gazette*, supp. no. 2, p. 1562. Collection responsibilities remained with the District Commissioners and District Officers, under the Taxes (Collection) Ordinance.

with major revisions in the Income Tax Ordinance, which reflected increases in rates and other changes designed to increase the yield of the income tax as a wartime revenue measure.[8] It appears that the new appointments reflected recognition of the greater difficulty in administering the income tax than was the case of other taxes.

The statutorily defined powers of the Commissioner of Income Tax in 1941 were somewhat restricted, whereas those of the assessing officers were quite broad. Essentially, the assessing officers had the responsibility of dealing with the individual taxpayers whereas the Commissioner and his staff were primarily concerned with planning, reporting, and interpretative functions. To a limited extent the Commissioner might become involved in an individual case, either because of its importance or in the exercise of certain powers pertaining to administrative review of disputed assessments.[9]

Before the end of the mandate in 1948, the Commissioner of Income Tax had shared the responsibilities of his office with two Assistant Commissioners, one of whom was responsible for technical or professional matters (interpretation, legislation) and the other for procedural matters (records, personnel, equipment, procedures). This functional division of responsibilities within the Commissioner's office has generally continued to the present time, although the scope of activity has broadened considerably and the headquarters staff is now greatly enlarged.

The Israeli Revenue Administration

Transition from the Mandate

When the State of Israel came into being in May 1948 several changes in the structure of the revenue administration were required. These paralleled changes in the structure of the government generally. When the High Commissioner for Palestine and other British members of the mandatory hierarchy departed, they left a void behind them; no effort had been made to hand over the administration to any official successors.[10] The void was rapidly filled, however, by the provisional government, which began to function under a blueprint prepared in anticipation of the end of the mandate.[11]

8. Income Tax (Amendment) Ordinance, 1943, and War Revenue (Income Tax) (Amendment) Ordinance, 1943, *Palestine Gazette* of March 30, 1943, supp. no. 1, pp. 7 and 14, respectively. The former, *inter alia*, increased the basic rates and the latter imposed a surtax.

9. I.T.O., 1941, sec. 49. This section became sec. 56 of the I.T.O., 1947, and is now (as amended) sec. 147 of the Revised Ordinance. Pursuant to sec. 49, I.T.O., 1941, the Commissioner could review or revise action taken by an assessing officer in a particular case.

10. Joseph, *The Faithful City*, pp. 112, 120–121; Sacher, *Israel: The Establishment of a State*, p. 112.

11. Ze'ev Sharef, *Three Days*, pp. 51–58; Marver H. Bernstein, *The Politics of Israel*, p. 21.

In the new system of government, the legislative and executive functions, which up to that time had been combined in the person of the High Commissioner for Palestine, were reapportioned. The legislative functions of the High Commissioner were vested in the Provisional Assembly which in turn, with the first elections, was replaced by the Knesset (Parliament). One of the first acts of the Provisional Assembly, the Law and Administration Ordinance of 1948, made it crystal-clear that thereafter the sole authority to levy taxes was to reside in the elected representatives of the people. Thereafter, although proposals for changes in the system of taxation originated in the executive branch, the legislature retained control over taxation.

The executive functions were vested in sixteen ministers, and the various mandatory government departments were reorganized into ministries.[12] Accordingly, the powers of the High Commissioner under the several existing taxing statutes were conferred upon the Minister of Finance, who in turn became the superior of the heads of the several tax departments.

The posts of Director of Customs and Excise and of Income Tax Commissioner were filled by the appointment of Jewish officials, neither of whom had previously served in the tax administration.[13] The property tax administration presented a special problem because the blueprint for the new government did not contemplate maintaining the district and sub-district pattern of administration in the form followed during the mandate.[14] To resolve the problem of maintaining administration of the property taxes and the Taxes (Collection) Ordinance, the individual selected to head the Collections and Property Tax Division was appointed, *pro forma*, as District Commissioner for each of the districts and parts of districts remaining within the boundaries of the State.

During the mandate, centralized control over the several tax administrations was maintained through the Chief Secretary of the government. With the establishment of several ministries, each headed by a minister, an office like that of the Chief Secretary could have no standing. Although an office of Secretary of the Government, attached to the

12. The number has since varied, mainly to accommodate coalition partners.

13. Although there were Jewish officials in both of these administrations with considerable experience, the tendency at the time was to view such officials with suspicion. Bernstein, p. 155; Edwin Samuel, *Problems of Government in the State of Israel*, p. 60. It was not until 1954 that several of these were promoted to top posts, in which they thereafter served with distinction.

14. Although the post of District Commissioner was retained, under control of the Ministry of Interior, the incumbent's responsibilities were more formal than actual. For example, some countries having diplomatic relations with the State of Israel did not wish to acknowledge the legal status of Jerusalem as the capital of the State. The District Commissioner for the Jerusalem District, whose legal status stemmed from pre-State mandatory legislation, became a convenient, albeit largely fictional, conduit for diplomatic communication with high officials in Jerusalem.

office of the Prime Minister, came into being, it did not take over the functions of the mandatory Chief Secretary. To fill these functions, insofar as control over the several tax administrations was concerned, the first Minister of Finance created the post of Director of State Revenue.[15] Initially, however, this was conceived of more as an advisory than as a supervisory office.

Accordingly, at the inception of the State, the chain of command consisted of the Minister of Finance, the Director of State Revenue, and under the latter, in a very loose fashion, the Income Tax Commissioner, the Director of Customs and Excise, the head of the Collections and Property Division, and the Director of Stamp Duties and Amusement Tax.[16] Effective control was achieved on a personal rather than a formal basis, since the Office of Director of State Revenue was occupied from 1948 until 1952, either in tandem or interchangeably, by the individuals who were simultaneously serving as Income Tax Commissioner or Director of Customs and Excise. Furthermore, the Director of State Revenue had no statutory standing and, technically, could not *require* the head of any individual tax administration to do anything.

Centralization of Control — The Office of Director of State Revenue

Beginning about 1953, signs of awareness of the need to strengthen the revenue administration began to appear. Recommendations for administrative improvements had been made by a United Nations expert.[17] A new, strong Income Tax Commissioner was appointed, and as he began to reorganize and build up his own headquarters the administrative weakness of the Directorate of Revenue became more apparent.

Various proposals for strengthening the top administrative levels were considered. One of these, which was dropped in 1954 at a point when it was almost about to be put into effect, was to divide the country into tax districts. Each tax district would be headed by a "district director of

15. The Hebrew title of this official — *Memuneh al Hakhnasot Ha-Medinah* — may be translated literally as "Officer in Charge of the Revenues of the State." Several of the incumbents of the post have preferred "Director of State Revenue" as the best English equivalent of their title, and that has been used in this work. Occasionally, the title "Director of Inland Revenue" has been used but this is inexact because the Director is also responsible for administration of the customs, unlike the British Board of Inland Revenue or the U.S. Commissioner of Internal Revenue.

16. Later, administration of the taxes enacted in 1949, and later, was assigned as follows: The estate tax to the Income Tax Commissioner; the purchase tax to the Director of Customs and Excise; the war damage compensation levy and the compulsory loan to the Director of Stamp Taxes; and the land betterment tax to the Land Registry in the Ministry of Justice and to the Collections and Property Tax Division. Many changes in these assignments subsequently occurred; see, e.g., Chapter 9.

17. Henry S. Bloch, *Revenue Administration and Policy in Israel* (New York: United Nations, 1953), hereinafter referred to as "I Bloch."

taxes" who would be in charge of the assessment and collection of all taxes within that district.

The proposed pattern may have been inspired by the mandatory district organization. Under this plan central headquarters staff would have remained small, consisting perhaps of the Director of Revenue, and the several tax Commissioners and Directors who would have comprised the "Board of Revenue" proposed by the United Nations expert. Their principal function, it appears, would have been to determine policy, with the administrative responsibility concentrated in the district directors of taxes, who would, in turn, supervise the local offices. The basis for this plan was a presumption that skills for the administration and execution of the several existing taxes were fungible, and that the problems and techniques of their administration were sufficiently similar so that they could be efficiently concentrated in a single office.

What might have happened if this plan had been adopted is a matter of conjecture. With the appointment in 1954 of a new Director of State Revenue from outside the tax administration, the proposed plan for creation of district offices was first deferred and then dropped. Almost immediately after the appointment of the new Director, the then Income Tax Commissioner, who apparently had hoped to be named to the Director's post, resigned. The three tentative nominees for the posts of district directors were shunted aside, and not long thereafter they also left the revenue administration.

The new Director of State Revenue proceeded to implement the recommendation of the United Nations expert, who had visited Israel a second time, for the establishment of an integrated revenue organization under a single head and at one location.[18] One of the first steps to achieve centralized control was the creation of a Revenue Commission (*Vaadat Hahakhnasot*). This consisted of the new Director of State Revenue, the new Director of Customs ar.d Excise, the new Income Tax Commissioner, the Director of Stamp Taxes, War Damages Compensation Levy, and Compulsory Loans, and the head of the Collections and Property Tax Division. Meetings of the Commission were to be held monthly in Jerusalem.[19] Staff assistants would attend, as required, although the assistants of the Director of Revenue were more or less permanent attendants. Other officials of the Finance Ministry would attend if the agenda related to their functions.

18. Henry S. Bloch, *Revenue Administration and Policy in Israel* (*Second Report*) 21 (New York: United Nations, 1955), hereinafter referred to as "II Bloch"; see also, *idem, Revenue Administration and Policy in Israel* (*Third Report*) 4, 33 (New York: United Nations, 1958), hereinafter referred to as "III Bloch."

19. Until Customs headquarters were transferred from Haifa to Jerusalem, communication with the Customs and Excise Branch remained tenuous. Establishment of the Revenue Commission was, therefore, an important step in achieving coordination with that branch.

The basic purpose of the Revenue Commission was to establish a unified administration by identifying common problems of the several branches and attempting to achieve a uniform approach to them. Items taken up at the meetings covered a broad scope — collections, physical accommodations, personnel, legislation, organization, and procedures. By 1965 the Revenue Commission had been discontinued, the office of Director of State Revenue having by then established effective direct control over the individual tax branches.

The trend toward establishment of centralized control at the level of the Director of State Revenue ran parallel to the strengthening of the central administrations of each of the still independent tax units. As the number and size of field offices increased, so did the need for expansion of the headquarters staffs. This was most evident in the Income Tax Branch, where the number of field offices (each headed by an assessing officer) increased from three at the inception of the State (Jerusalem, Tel Aviv, Haifa) to about twenty-five. During this period of expansion much of the attention of the office of Director of State Revenue was devoted to assisting in the establishment and administration of these field offices. Simultaneously, headquarters staffs of the branches were being built up and, perhaps unavoidably, some frictions developed between the offices of the Director of State Revenue and those of the several branch heads. These were no doubt the "growing pains" produced by the energetic pressure of the Director of State Revenue to achieve administrative improvements at a pace which was sometimes beyond the absorptive capacities of the individual administrations.

The concentration of the office of the Director of State Revenue upon increased collections and administrative improvements produced a number of significant changes in the role of that office. Initially, the functions of the office were defined as 1) proposing tax policy and 2) supervising execution of the tax laws. Over the years, the first of these has shifted to other officials in the office of the Minister of Finance, whereas the second has expanded considerably. This reflects a shift in the relative emphasis which the several incumbents of the office of Director of State Revenue have placed upon fiscal policy as compared to tax administration.

Role of the Revenue Administration in the Formulation of Tax Policy

The present role of the tax administrators in the decision-making process is principally that of technicians who, by virtue of their expert knowledge, are able to advise, first, as to whether or not a proposed measure is feasible from an administrative viewpoint and, second, as to the way the law should be formulated in order to be carried out effectively.[20] This process includes analysis of the ability of the existing organization to handle the additional administrative burden or to determine what changes would have to be made in the structure of the organization and its procedures to carry an additional levy into effect.

By contrast, in the early days of the State, the Director of State Revenue played a much more active role in the formulation of tax policy. Indeed, it appears that the office of Director of State Revenue, which did not exist during the mandate, was expressly created for the purpose of formulating tax policy rather than to supply centralized administrative control over the several existing tax administrations. The functions of that office have since evolved, so that its primary responsibility is now the formulation of "administrative policy" rather than "tax policy."

In the interest of clarity it would be appropriate to define the sense in which the term "tax policy" is used. Generally, it may be defined as the policy of the government with respect to the utilization of taxes as one of the means of achieving its political, social, and economic goals. In this sense, tax policy is a segment of fiscal policy, which, in turn, may be considered an aspect of public finance.[21]

Ultimate responsibility for the formulation of tax policy rests with the Minister of Finance, and, once policy has been formulated, it is the responsibility of the minister to implement it by securing the passage of a law which expresses the consequences of the policy in legal terms. The tax administration then executes the law, according to its terms, creating or modifying the administrative organization and procedures necessary to carry the law into effect. The process of execution also involves many policy determinations but these are at a different level and have different purposes.

The administrators take the law as they receive it. As technicians, their approach is essentially nonpolitical, regardless of their personal political affiliations. Thus, a distinction can be drawn between "tax policy," which is concerned with the reasons for enacting or amending a particular taxing statute consistent with government programs, and "administrative policy," which is concerned with the manner in which the administrative structure shall be organized to carry the law into effect.

This is not to say that the administrators do not participate in the formulation of tax policy. The facts are to the contrary. However, the

20. Simha Gafni, "Guidelines for Improving the Image of the Revenue Administration" (Hebrew), 1 *Quarterly Tax Journal* 14–15 (December 1965); compare Avraham Mandel, "Fiscal Policy and Administrative Tools for its Implementation," (Hebrew) 1 *Quarterly Tax Journal* 240–241 (April 1966); and see Moshe Neudorfer (currently Director of State Revenue), "Aspects of Tax Policy in 1969/70" (Hebrew), 4 *Quarterly Tax Journal* 130 (April 1969).

21. See, generally, United Nations Technical Assistance Administration, *Taxes and Fiscal Policy in Under-Developed Countries*, United Nations document ST/TAA/M/8, 1954.

nature and extent of that participation has varied over the years, sometimes because of prevailing conditions and sometimes because of differences in the backgrounds and personal philosophies of administration held by the incumbents of the office of Director of State Revenue and by their immediate staffs.

During the period 1948–1952, when the late Eliezer Kaplan was Minister of Finance, the heads of the two major tax branches — the Income Tax Branch and the Customs Branch — were individuals with whom the minister had long been closely associated in handling the economic affairs of the Jewish community of Palestine.[22] Both were economists rather than tax administrators, and their immediate and necessary concern was to keep the economy of the country on an even keel during a very critical period. The problems they faced were unprecedented, and it is entirely understandable that they should have been more involved in formulating fiscal policy than in the housekeeping problems of tax administration. Administrative policies of the several tax departments continued in the patterns which had been formulated during the mandate. Accordingly, serious problems in tax administration developed during this time which, had the attention of the top echelon not been diverted by more pressing issues, might have been anticipated and perhaps avoided.[23]

During the incumbencies of the first two Directors of State Revenue, the functions of that office were directed, almost exclusively, toward the policy-making concerns of the Minister of Finance. Since each incumbent also had time-consuming operating responsibilities, the first as Income Tax Commissioner, the second as Director of Customs, neither of them attempted to establish the office of the Director of State Revenue as the central control over the operations of the several independent tax administrations. Steps in this direction were not taken until 1954, when the then Government Secretary, Mr. Ze'ev Sharef, was appointed Director of State Revenue, while at the same time retaining his functions within the Prime Minister's office as secretary of the government.[24]

22. Finance Minister Kaplan was an engineer by training, but he had for many years previously been concerned with economic matters as Treasurer of the Jewish Agency for Palestine. *1952 Israel Government Yearbook* (Hebrew), p. 49 (Jerusalem, 1953).

23. This is not to say that top officials were unaware of the fact that unsolved administrative problems were accumulating. Their awareness is reflected in the first two reports of the United Nations Technical Assistance expert on his 1951 and 1953 visits to Israel. These reports deal with both economic and administrative problems. See I and II Bloch. However, action on the economic recommendations of the expert was taken sooner than on his administrative recommendations.

24. II Bloch, pp. 20–21. In September 1953, Mr. Sharef had been designated by Minister of Finance Levi Eshkol as chairman of a "Commission for Examining the Methods of Assessment and Collection of the Income Tax." This Commission's report, issued in March 1954, served as a blueprint for many of the administrative improvements undertaken in later years.

To a considerable extent the involvement of the Director of State Revenue in the formulation of fiscal policy was not only a response to the needs of the hour but also a reflection of the personal idiosyncracies, backgrounds, abilities, and interests not only of the person holding the office at the particular time but also of the person occupying the office of Director General of the Ministry of Finance. The Director General is the highest civil servant in an Israeli ministry, his office being comparable to that of a permanent secretary of a British ministry. The first Director General of the Ministry of Finance was Mr. David Horowitz, a brilliant economist, who has since achieved international renown as Governor of the Bank of Israel, the central bank of the State. In view of the numerous difficult economic problems which he faced during his incumbency as Director General (1948–1952), he did not concern himself with formalizing the structure of the revenue administration, leaving that to the Director of State Revenue. At the same time, as mentioned earlier, the Director of State Revenue, then also an economist, was almost completely involved with formulating fiscal policy, essentially as a member of the personal staff of the Minister of Finance and of the Director General.

This working relationship continued relatively unchanged after 1952, when the late Mr. Levi Eshkol [25] became Minister of Finance, and Mr. Pinhas Sapir [26] became Director General. If anything, immediate reliance by the new Minister of Finance and Director General upon the Director of State Revenue in the field of fiscal theory and policy might have been expected to be enhanced, because their inclinations were more to practical than to theoretical matters. The period from 1952 to 1955 was also characterized by serious economic problems — inflation, implementation of the "new economic policy" of 1952, an economic recession, flotation of a bond issue, industrialization of the economy, and integration of large numbers of recent, impoverished immigrants. These drew attention away from the internal needs of the tax administration.

Shift to Emphasis on Administrative Problems

The new Director of State Revenue appointed in 1954 was under a strong mandate to address himself to the administrative problems of the revenue system. These were already recognized as serious and for a time continued to worsen. By 1954, the essential legal framework of the tax system was already in being, and the basic problem at the time was how to get the various tax laws to work effectively rather than how to devise new and additional sources of revenue. In fact, emphasis upon stabilizing the fiscal system within the framework of existing law seems to

25. Subsequently Prime Minister.
26. Now again (since 1969) Minister of Finance, having previously also been Minister of Commerce and Industry, and occupied other key posts.

have been understood as a precondition to achieving administrative reforms over the long run. Accordingly, with few exceptions, additional
revenue needs (to the extent not satisfied by the increased collections attributable to economic growth and administrative improvements) were
either initially or eventually fitted into the existing structure. Underlying
this approach was the practical consideration that efforts to tap additional sources of revenue should utilize the existing revenue administration. Otherwise, as had happened before with such endeavors as the
Compulsory Loan, and as happened later with the Defense Levy, a temporary administration would have to be established which could not
complete the job effectively. The changes which began to occur in 1954
are significant because they reflected the end of a pattern of tax administration whose roots went back to the system of taxation which the
Jewish community of Palestine had imposed upon itself during the period
of the British mandate. The principal feature of that system was its
voluntary nature, both in the sense that there was no law to enforce it
and that assessment and collection were almost entirely handled by volunteers. Given the emergency conditions under which this system had
functioned, voluntary compliance was high, so that there were few cases
in which community pressures had to be brought to bear to compel payment by recalcitrant "taxpayers." This permitted the central organization
to be limited to a handful of full-time, paid, administrators, several of
whom carried over into the top echelons of the revenue administration
after establishment of the State.

When the Israeli government assumed administration of the mandatory tax laws, it was assumed that the idealistic spirit of self-sacrifice
which had been displayed by the entire Jewish population would carry
over into the more mundane area of compliance with the tax laws.[27]
Although this spirit of idealism and self-sacrifice manifested itself at its
highest levels several times during the short history of the State of Israel,
it was not sufficiently recognized in the early days of the revenue administration that taxpayer willingness to pay might ebb and flow in direct response to external conditions. Had this been recognized, perhaps
greater attention would have been paid in the early days of the State to
establishment of a strong revenue administration, capable of coping
immediately with the demands of independent statehood, and with the
novel problems arising from the sudden increase of the population and
the rapid expansion of the economy. Recognition of the realities of
the situation, when it finally came, shocked the authorities. By that time,
however, the damage which the administration had suffered required that
drastic measures be taken.

27. As well as the other laws of an economic nature, such as rationing, currency
controls, import and export controls, wage controls, rent controls, and so on. All
of these proved difficult.

It was perhaps unfortunate that the initial tendencies of some of the first group of tax administrators to rely upon an assumed high level of voluntary taxpayer compliance coincided with economy measures taken throughout the government in the early 1950's to reduce the number of civil servants. Underlying this move was an assumption that the initial rapid growth of the various government departments, and the rather haphazard way in which this had been achieved, might have produced some duplications of functions and redundancies of personnel. This was not the case, however, in the tax administration, which, if anything, was suffering from a serious lack of technically qualified personnel. It was difficult, however, to justify expansion of the tax administration at a time when pressure to reduce personnel was being applied everywhere else in the government establishment. In the interest of economy, therefore, the tax administration's staff had been kept at a bare minimum.

During this period of the early 1950's, the revenue needs of the State rapidly increased and, since they were not being met by existing tax measures, other revenue-raising measures were enacted. From the administrative point of view these displayed a similar characteristic — an effort to effect assessment and collection with a minimum of formal organization. This, in turn, reflected the administrative policy of those then in charge of the revenue administration, and this policy may now be traced, from what has been said before, to (a) the experience of the administrators with the pre-State system of voluntary taxes; (b) the assumption that voluntary compliance would continue at a high level; (c) reluctance to expand the tax administration in the face of a government-wide economy drive; and (d) involvement of the tax administrators in problems of fiscal policy, which diverted their attention from the growing inadequacies of the tax administration.

These last points can be illustrated by reference to several of the revenue measures which were enacted in the early days of the State. Three administrative patterns can be discerned: (a) creation of a new and independent administration, following the example of the mandatory tax laws; (b) tying the assessment and collection of the tax to some existing organization or procedure; or (c) efforts to recreate a voluntary organization similar to the pattern of the disbanded voluntary tax system.

It is noteworthy that, almost without exception, the administrative structure of the revenue measures adopted during this period was found to be faulty and had to be drastically revised. Experience proved that the assumptions upon which the administrative policy had been formulated were misconceived. It is to the great credit of the administration that, as these misconceptions became apparent, quick action was taken to change over to a more appropriate system of administration. This culminated in the concentration of the administration into two separate organizations — the Customs and Excise Branch and the Income and Property Taxes Branch.

Development of the Operating Branches

In sweeping across the historical panorama of revenue administration from British mandatory times to the present, one can discern the dynamic nature of tax administration by observing the continuous interplay between its organization and technique, on the one hand, and economic theory and the organization of the economy on the other. The two polar administrations in mandatory times were those of customs and excise taxes and the income tax. Between these stood the property taxes, both national and local. When the State of Israel came into being, the two polar administrations of mandatory times continued with new top personnel but substantially unchanged in their organizational patterns. The national property taxes, after a short period of confusion created by the effective elimination of the mandatory offices of District Commissioner and District Officers, also continued under a separate administration. Then, as additional taxes were enacted by the State of Israel in 1949 and subsequent years, the tendency until 1955 was to compartmentalize them either in an independent administration or to attach them to some other administration which was not part of either the Customs and Excise Administration or the Income Tax Administration.

Starting in 1955 a trend began toward combining the independent administrations into rational groupings. The present pattern of the Israeli tax administration consists of only two branches, each of which is responsible for the administration of a number of taxes.

All of the taxes which economists would classify as "indirect taxes" (or taxes on consumption) have become polarized in the Customs and Excise Branch, whereas all of the "direct taxes" are polarized in the Income and Property Tax Branch. From the administrative point of view there are practical differences between the taxes assigned to these two branches, but changes now taking place in the manner in which some of them are being administered, particularly in the Customs and Excise Branch, are beginning to blur these differences.

Administration of the Customs and Excise Branch

The Customs and Excise Branch administers the following revenue measures: i) customs; ii) excises, currently imposed on petroleum, tobacco, alcoholic beverages, and cement — in previous years, excises were also imposed on salt (abolished 1949), matches (abolished 1968), playing cards (abolished 1968), tires and tubes (abolished 1965); iii) purchase tax; iv) stamp taxes; v) amusement tax; and vi) foreign travel tax. Each of these has had its share of administrative problems.

The Director of the Customs and Excise Branch is assisted by a principal deputy and by deputies for valuation and classification, for operations, for audits, and for organization and administration.[28] The Director's staff includes the head of the Economic Unit and a legal adviser. There are also a number of functional units, responsible to the director or to one or more of his deputies.

The director, the deputies, and the legal adviser compose the principal staff of the branch. A secondary staff has also been created consisting of the principal assistants to the heads of the several units. From time to time other principal officers are invited to participate as consultants on subjects in which they have a particular competence. Among the assignments which the secondary staff has assumed are budgetary matters, administrative procedures, training programs, and the preparation of regulations appropriate to the taxes under the charge of the branch. One of the members of the staff functions as chairman, this position rotating at three-month intervals.[29]

Headquarters of the Customs and Excise Branch have been in Jerusalem since December 1957. Previously they had been in Haifa. The branch also has a number of field offices. There are customs houses at Haifa, Tel Aviv-Jaffa, Ashdod, and the Lod (Tel Aviv) airport. There are Customs and Excise stations at Eilat, Beersheba, Hadera, Nazareth, Netanya, Acre, Petah Tikvah, Safed, and Rehovot. Additionally, since the Six-Day War, offices of the branch have been established at Bethlehem, Hebron, Jericho, Gaza, Ramallah, and Shechem (Nablus). There are also district directors in Jerusalem (customs and excises, supervision and investigations), Haifa (purchase tax, supervision, and investigations), and Tel Aviv–Jaffa (purchase tax, excises, supervision, and investigations).

In 1948, when the State of Israel came into being, the Customs and Excise Branch had the good fortune to be staffed with a number of experienced Jewish officials who were able immediately to step into posts which had been vacated by the departing mandatory personnel. The office of Director was, however, filled from the outside by a member of the Economic Department of the Jewish Agency for Palestine. Over the years, this branch has maintained the reputation of being run very efficiently. It has therefore served as a manpower reservoir for the

28. David Peled (Director of Customs and Excise) "On the Revision of Traditional Customs Routines," (Hebrew), 4 *Quarterly Tax Journal* 242, 245–246 (July 1969); Ministry of Finance, *Proposed Budget for 1971/72*, Pamphlet E, 116 (Jerusalem, 1971).

29. David Peled, "Principal Administrative Developments in the Customs and Excise Branch," (Hebrew) 1 *Quarterly Tax Journal*, 231, 233–234 (April 1966).

staffing of important posts elsewhere in the government, particularly in the office of the Director of State Revenue. It has also been assigned special tasks on behalf of the entire revenue administration. For example, the Publications Unit at customs headquarters is responsible for editing and maintaining current the *Kovetz Dinei Misim* (Compilation of Tax Laws, briefly referred to as *"Kadam"*), which is the authoritative collection of all current tax laws and regulations. This is made available to all officials as well as to the general public.

For several years customs headquarters were permitted to remain at Haifa, and were not transferred to Jerusalem until December 1957. Removal to Jerusalem, essential to coordination with the other branches of the revenue administration, had been decided upon some time before, but had been delayed because of lack of suitable housing for the offices and for key personnel who would have to be relocated in Jerusalem.

The transfer to Jerusalem brought about several operational changes. Before the move, because of the contiguity of customs headquarters to the main seaport, headquarters staff was continually involved in matters pertaining to the relatively routine operations of the Haifa Customs House. Customs agents would by-pass, or go over the head of, the Haifa Collector of Customs. The move to Jerusalem put a stop to this. As other commercial ports of entry came into use in Eilat (1957) and Ashdod (1966) a more efficient relationship was established between headquarters and the several customs houses. The move also made it possible to tighten up other elements of the revenue administration, and it hastened the trend toward the ultimate consolidation of the administration into two branches.

Customs Administration

When the British officials departed the country at the end of the mandate, they handed over responsibility for the Port of Haifa, as well as the customs administration, to the mayor of that city. They did this because they recognized the mayor as a legally constituted official, whereas they did not acknowledge the existence of any successor national government. Very soon, however, control of the customs was revested in the new government of the State of Israel.

At the time, Haifa was the only major port of entry. There was a small port at Tel Aviv–Jaffa, but this could not accommodate seagoing vessels, which had to be unloaded by lighters. The airport at Lod (Lydda) was not yet the principal passenger port of entry, as it is now; and the present seaports at Eilat and Ashdod were then undreamed of.

The period of economic austerity which prevailed until 1955 created numerous enforcement problems for the customs authorities. As part of the new economic policy of 1952, strict controls were imposed on imports. Import licenses from the Ministry of Commerce and Industry were required, and goods imported without a license were subject to confiscation by the customs authorities. Devices of various sorts were used to circumvent these controls. A gray market in import licenses sprung up. Immigrants, of whom there were many during this period, were induced to bring in as their own possessions goods destined for others. Approved enterprises were entitled under the 1950 Law for the Encouragement of Capital Investments to import construction materials, equipment, and other goods customs-free. Some of them were found to have imported more than they needed, or even to have sold what they required themselves, being tempted by the high black market prices. Customs-free imports by certain exempt organizations were found to have filtered into commercial channels.[30] The latter problem, in particular, was resolved by a Procrustean law which, in 1957, abolished almost all customs, purchase tax, and excise exemptions, including those of the government and charitable institutions.[31]

Because Israel's land borders have been closed since 1948, smuggling at points other than the regular ports of entry has not been a major problem.[32] Accordingly, efforts at smuggling, to the extent it has existed, have concentrated upon getting relatively small, though valuable, items past the customs inspectors and police. The latter have been well trained to detect attempts at smuggling, whether by passengers or commercial importers. The authorities are also empowered to grant money awards for outstanding feats of detection by customs employees. The penalties for smuggling, aside from confiscation, are severe although there has been a tendency in recent years to resort less frequently to criminal prosecutions.

Relaxation of import controls (the product of improved conditions and changes in economic policy), as well as changes in the volume and source of immigrants, has eliminated many of the problems which the customs administration faced in the years from 1948 to 1957. Now almost all passengers enter at the Lod airport. Most are tourists who are passed without detailed inspection. Recent changes in procedures for imported goods will also simplify and accelerate their entry. Nevertheless, to the occasional importer, such as a recent immigrant bringing in his possessions from abroad, clearing them through customs can still be a painful experience.

Most imports into Israel are subjected to customs duties on an ad valorem basis. The standard of valuation employed is the price in the open market, as between unrelated buyers and sellers, i.e., the arms-

---

30. *Fourth Annual Report of State Comptroller, 1952/1953* (Hebrew), p. 85.
31. Customs, Excise, and Purchase Tax Law (Cancellation of Specific Exemptions), 1957.
32. This situation has changed somewhat since the Six-Day War of 1967.

length price.[33] In most cases, the invoice is the best evidence of the price, but there can be instances where it is not. If, for example, there is a special relationship between the foreign seller and the domestic buyer, the price agreed upon between them may differ substantially from the price in the open market. In such a case, when found, the customs authorities will adjust the price reflected upon the invoice so as to restore it to an arms-length price.

In order to assure consistency in the determination of prices in such instances, the customs authorities have prepared a questionnaire designed to elicit all of the details relevant to assessing value. Once supplied, this information is used as a basis for evaluating all similar goods received by the same importer, so long as no change has occurred in any of the relevant circumstances. This questionnaire is along the same lines — although somewhat abbreviated — of those in use by other signatories to the Brussels Convention on Customs Evaluations.

The practices and a substantial part of the procedures of the customs administration are now based upon current international standards. Israel participates in the Customs Cooperation Council and, gradually since 1958, has shifted its customs schedules to the Brussels Nomenclature for the Classification of Goods in Customs Tariffs.[34]

Excises Administration

The term "excise," as used in the mandatory period and in Israel, is an impost upon specified goods produced, processed, or manufactured in the country for sale in the domestic market. Currently, excises are imposed (in the order of their importance as revenue measures) on certain petroleum products (principally gasoline — called "benzine" in Israel), tobacco, alcoholic beverages, and cement. Other excises in effect at the inception of the State, or subsequently adopted, have been abolished.

The excises are generally required to be paid before the goods are removed from the manufacturers' premises. The number of Israeli manufacturers of products subject to excises is small. Following the practice in many countries, control was originally maintained in two ways: (1) by stationing excise officers on the manufacturer's premises to control the flow of raw materials into the plant, to check inventories, and to assure that goods leaving the plant were tax-paid; and (2) by the physical marking of tax-paid tobacco products and alcoholic beverages by a banderolle, or seal.

The plants producing excisable goods are required to be licensed.

33. A. Eilenberg, "Deliberations of the International Committee on Evaluation in Brussels," (Hebrew) 1 *Quarterly Tax Journal* 201 (April 1966).

34. Dov Weinman, "The Brussels Tariff Nomenclature" (Hebrew), 4 *Quarterly Tax Journal* 317, 234–235 (July 1969).

The possibility of being deprived of a license for failure to comply with the excise tax requirements is a potentially serious sanction. Moreover, the producers are fairly large industries which maintain accurate books of account. The trend over the past ten years has been to relax the physical controls and to rely to a greater extent upon audit of accounts and periodic returns as a basis for assessing the tax. Gradually, the excise officers stationed on the premises are being removed, and the stamping requirements have also been largely eliminated.

Administration of the excises has presented some problems of special interest. The tobacco excise, for example, was initially imposed, ad valorem, on the raw tobacco, by weight. This required detailed supervision of the crop in the fields and controlling its movement to the factory. In 1954, as an incentive to tobacco growers and to simplify administration, the tax was imposed on the finished products, mostly cigarettes. Also, three different rates of tax were imposed, the highest on Virginia tobacco (mostly imported) cigarettes, a lower rate on Oriental tobacco (locally grown) cigarettes, and a third, lower, rate on other forms of tobacco products. Cigarette smoking habits changed as a result, with many smokers shifting to Oriental tobacco cigarettes which were cheaper because of the lower tax. Thus, foreign currency was saved and a larger market created for the Oriental tobaccos grown by Israeli Arab farmers.[35]

During the period of austerity (until about 1956) when sugar had to be imported and was rationed, the black market price for sugar was much higher than the controlled price. Producers of nonalcoholic beverages were permitted to buy large quantities of sugar at the controlled price. Some of them were found to be diverting sugar into the black market.[36] This was promptly stopped and penalties were imposed. Improvement in conditions, and production of sugar in Israel from locally grown sugar beets, also helped to eliminate this problem.

Aside from such instances, the excises are relatively easy to administer. The sources of supply are few and they are readily controlled. This accounts for the relaxation in administrative procedures.

Purchase Tax Administration

Next to the customs, the purchase tax is the largest single revenue producer among the taxes administered by the Customs and Excise Branch.[37] In its initial form, as enacted in 1949, the tax was directed

35. *1955 Israel Government Yearbook*, p. 160; *1961/62 Israel Government Yearbook*, p. 151.

36. Some bakers and candy manufacturers were also found to be supplying the black market with sugar purchased at official prices. Artificial sweeteners were used instead.

37. In 1967–68, purchase tax collections were IL. 320.5 million, as compared to customs collections of 368.8 million; in 1968–69 they were IL. 472.6 million and IL. 551.1 million, respectively.

toward luxuries but since 1954 it has more nearly approached a general sales tax.

Structurally, the administration of the purchase tax consists of a headquarters staff in Jerusalem and three field offices, in Tel Aviv, Haifa, and Jerusalem. Since a substantial part (between a quarter and a third) of the purchase tax is collected on taxable imports, purchase tax personnel are also stationed at the ports of entry, although they are administratively controlled by the head of the local purchase tax office rather than by the Collector of Customs.

Until the recent reorganization of the Customs and Excise Branch along functional lines, control of the purchase tax was vested in a separate unit at headquarters, in charge of a Deputy Director of Customs and Excise. The dozen or so specialists who composed this unit will now, presumably, be reassigned. Similar realignments, along functional lines, will probably occur in the field offices of the purchase tax. Particularly affected will be those employees who have been concerned with audits and with classification and evaluation of merchandise. These are being merged with their functional counterparts in the several other tax areas administered by the Customs and Excise Branch.

The purchase tax, particularly as applied to goods manufactured domestically, has presented a number of administrative problems. These have accounted for changes in administration and for considerable experimentation.

In form, the tax is imposed ad valorem, at rates which are specified for particular categories of merchandise. The tax base is the price paid for the merchandise by the retailer. Initially, the administration attempted to control and collect the tax at the retailers' level, but this was soon found to be impracticable. Starting in 1953, the authorities shifted to requirements that goods manufactured in Israel be stamped and inspected at the place of manufacture, although retaining the measure of the tax as the price which would be paid by the retailer. Taken together with the requirement for payment of the purchase tax on imported goods at the time of release from customs, this substantially decreased the number of outlets required to be controlled. About 80 percent of the tax is now paid by about 20 percent of the taxpayers. Nevertheless, inspection of retail shops to assure that all merchandise on sale has been tax-paid continues.

Other techniques used initially to simplify procedures also had to be modified. One of these was the classification of certain taxpayers as "approved merchants" who were permitted to defer payment of the tax for a period of up to 90 days after sale, in recognition of the fact that it would take about that time for them to receive payment from their customers. This was a variation on the principal method of collection, which was based on the sale of purchase tax stamps to the manufacturers and their reporting monthly on the value of stamps used. However, it was discovered that the "approved merchant" procedure had been extended to some manufacturers whose accounts were unreliable. Many had to be removed from the approved list.[38] Later, as marginal producers were eliminated and bookkeeping procedures became more reliable, the trend was reversed, and some manufacturers were permitted to sell their merchandise without even affixing stamps, provided they maintained proper accounts.

Reliance upon accounts as the basis for imposing the tax requires a staff of auditors to check on the reliability of the periodic returns and of the account books themselves. The lack of sufficient auditing staff has been a perennial weakness of the purchase tax administration. In 1961, for example, the State Comptroller found that of about 900 enterprises assigned to the audit unit of 35 men, only 90 had been audited. Of these, 84 were found to have additional tax due.[39] In addition to expanding the audit staff, procedures were instituted to speed up the audit process by conducting abbreviated audits in some cases. Further improvements may be expected from the recent reorganization of the audit functions of the Customs and Excise Branch.

A maximum number of audits is essential to assure compliance, particularly since the most effective sanction was found to be the assertion of a "best judgment" assessment when the accounts were found to be unreliable. A best judgment assessment, on an estimated basis, may be made when the purchase tax authorities are convinced that incorrect information has been supplied as to the quantity or value of goods (Purchase Tax Law, sec. 19). Since such a determination would generally be made after the goods have been sold, the additional tax so determined cannot be passed on to the purchaser and to that extent the purchase tax effectively becomes a direct tax.

Best judgment assessments, and other determinations with which the taxpayer takes issue, may be appealed to an appeal committee consisting of three members designated by the Minister of Justice after consultation with the Minister of Finance. Each such committee consists of an advocate (lawyer) and two businessmen as associates. Decisions of this committee are final, unlike those of the Income Tax Advisory Committees.[40]

Aside from best judgment assessments, the purchase tax authorities may institute criminal proceedings in the case of flagrant violations.

38. *Fourth Annual Report of State Comptroller, 1952/1953* (Hebrew), pp. 86–87; cf. *Seventh Annual Report of State Comptroller, 1955/1956* (Hebrew), p. 93.

39. *Twelfth Annual Report of State Comptroller, 1960/1961* (Hebrew), pp. 60–61.

40. See Chapter 7. See also, for criticism of the manner in which the purchase tax appeals committees functioned in 1963, *Fourteenth Annual Report of State Comptroller, 1962/1963* (Hebrew), p. 95.

Penalties may also be imposed by way of compounding (administrative settlement) of criminal offenses (secs. 22, 25). As a condition to compounding the offense, the violator can be required to obligate himself to payment of a substantial additional sum if he is later convicted of another violation (sec. 25). This procedure has been found to be very effective in preventing recidivism by first offenders.

Stamp Duties and Amusement Tax Administration

The use of stamps as a revenue collection device is not novel. If the stamp tax is conceived of as an excise on the transaction which is evidenced by the document to which the stamp is attached, then the stamp is, in turn, evidence of payment of the tax. The revenue stamp, therefore, is not essential to the tax except as a means of collection. In Israel, the trend in recent years has been to change methods of collection of the stamp taxes, so that the stamp in many instances has become more of a symbol than a means of collection.

The Commissioners for Stamp Duty during the mandate were the Accountant General and the Administrator General. These officials were apparently selected because their duties included supervision of various institutions and activities which were likely to require documents subject to the stamp duty. For example, the Accountant General was also Examiner of Banks, and the Administrator General, in addition to administering certain estates, was also Registrar of Companies, Partnerships, Patents, and Official Receiver in Bankruptcy.[41]

Although posts corresponding to those of the mandatory Accountant General and Administrator General were established in the new government, in the Ministries of Finance and Justice respectively, these officials did not continue the functions of their predecessors as Commissioners of Stamp Duty. Instead, that responsibility was vested primarily in an individual who, before establishment of the State, had been involved in the unofficial tax system of the Jewish community. Several of these unofficial taxes had also been collected by means of stamps.[42]

Administration of the stamp duties remained in an independent unit until June 1956, when it was assigned to the Customs and Excise Branch. This transfer was part of a major reorganization of the State revenue administration which took place in that year. There had been three stamp duty offices, which were merged into the Customs and Excise Branch, whose field offices thereafter administered the stamp duties as an adjunct to their other functions.

41. I *A Survey of Palestine* 112–113; II idem, 1067 (Palestine: Government Printer, 1946).

42. M. Berger, *Kofer Hayishuv* [Redemption of the Jewish Community], pp. 24–31. As an aside, it is interesting to observe that these contributory stamps, notably those of the Jewish National Fund, were honored for postage until the new State could print and distribute its own postage stamps.

The stamp duties apply to almost every kind of legal document. Initially, the rates were relatively low, but they were increased substantially by amendments in 1954, resulting in collections almost doubling. In 1961 a revised law (Stamp Tax on Documents Law, 1961) was enacted, and the rates were again raised. Collections increased as the product of these increases in rates, in the volume of taxable documents, and improvements in administration.

The principal administrative improvement over the mandatory system has been in the methods of collecting the tax. The mandatory system required that a taxable document bear an adhesive stamp or be written on paper on which a stamp had been preprinted. The 1961 law permitted a stamp in the proper denomination to be imprinted by machine after the taxable document had been prepared. Substitution of an imprinted stamp for an adhesive stamp has overcome the temptation to refrain from paying the stamp tax until the document has to be submitted as evidence in court. Now, an unstamped document can more readily be identified and a penalty for nonpayment imposed.

Imprinting machines have been supplied to institutions, such as banks, which handle a large volume of taxable paper. This eliminates much running about to purchase stamps from the post office or approved dealers. It also saves the time of personnel required to account and provide safekeeping for a stock of stamps, and frees substantial sums of money which had to be laid out for an inventory of stamps. Others who prepare taxable documents less frequently have the choice of bringing their documents to the nearest stamp duty office for imprinting, or purchasing stamps at the post office.

Another simplification has involved payment of the tax on the basis of accounts, showing the number and denominations of taxable documents issued. This procedure applies particularly to bank checks and commercial receipts. In such instances the document simply bears the imprinted statement "Stamp Duty Paid." The number of enterprises and types of transactions converted to payment of tax on the basis of accounts is being expanded, and, gradually, the significance of the actual stamp is being diminished.[43]

The amusement tax, which has applied to admissions to places of entertainment since 1935, was initially a stamp tax. Most municipalities also imposed an entertainment levy on tickets of admission, also evidenced by a stamp. To simplify procedures, the Finance Ministry, in 1950, began to print the tickets of admission to cinemas showing both the amusement tax and the local entertainment levy. Then one-quarter of the total tax collected was paid over to the local authority where the cinema was located, another quarter was turned over to the Ministry of

43. Uri Schneider, "Stamping of Accounts with Adhesive Stamps or on the Basis of Turnover" (Hebrew), 2 *Quarterly Tax Journal* 180 (April 1967).

Interior for distribution generally among the local authorities, and the balance was retained by the Treasury. This arrangement continued until 1958. Then the amusement tax rates were reduced and the local entertainment levy rates were correspondingly increased. Nevertheless, because of two factors — increase in ticket prices and in attendance at cinemas — collections continued for a time to increase. However, the introduction of television in recent years has had the same effect in Israel as in other countries, and cinema attendance has begun to drop.

Foreign Travel Tax Administration

The foreign travel tax came into effect in 1951 pursuant to ministerial order and has continued since. The rates have varied from time to time in relation to fluctuations in the spread between the official value of the Israel pound and the black market exchange rate. It is obvious that this tax can easily be evaded by purchasing a ticket to the nearest point outside the country (say, to Cyprus) and then using foreign currency, sometimes purchased in the black market, to finance the rest of the trip. Accordingly, the rate of the foreign travel tax has been set by the authorities at a level which would make it cheaper to pay the tax than to pay the premium for acquiring foreign currency on the black market.[44] Of course, such considerations would not stand in the way of persons who by virtue of income tax evasion and other illegal transactions had accumulated funds which they had already converted into foreign currency in the black market. Nevertheless, even for such individuals the purchase of transportation subject to the foreign travel tax might have been attractive, first, because the rate at which the authorities permitted local currency to be converted into foreign currency was better than the black market rate, and, second, because such persons would deliberately avoid attracting attention to themselves by taking obviously long trips on short tickets.[45]

Like a number of other countries, Israel has sought to protect its foreign exchange position by limiting the amount of foreign currency which travelers may take abroad with them. This limitation has been evaded in various ways (sometimes explained by a fictitious wealthy relative abroad). One method was to take advantage of an exemption in the foreign travel tax which permitted railroad tickets for foreign travel to be purchased in Israel at the official rate, free of travel tax. In 1958, after it had been discovered that some of these railroad tickets were being converted abroad into foreign currency, the exemption was eliminated.

44. Morag, p. 194; *Hitpathut Hamisim b'Eretz Yisrael*, pp. 250–251, 253–254.
45. Valuable leads to possible income tax evaders might be obtained from examination of the lists of those traveling abroad. Reported income can be compared with estimated expenditures for long journeys. Additional information as to length of stay abroad could be obtained from passport control records.

The law contains other provisions to prevent evasion: it applies to transportation tickets received by way of gift, even from foreign donors who pay for it in foreign currency. Although the law provides for various exemptions, these have been tightened up to discourage evasion.

Another feature of the foreign travel tax, introduced to overcome to some extent its evasion by purchase of tickets to the nearest transfer point, was the imposition in 1961 of a flat rate per ticket on top of the percentage rate. This flat rate is the same irrespective of the value of the ticket.

All of these measures to prevent evasion of the travel tax are designed to assure that Israelis traveling abroad will purchase their transportation in Israel and pay the tax thereon. Aside from this, administration of the tax is relatively simple. The agencies from which tickets can be purchased are limited and well known. A ticket may not be sold unless the tax has been paid or unless exemption has been established. The airlines and steamship companies may not carry a passenger without a ticket. Accordingly, it is impossible to leave the country without having paid the tax unless legally exempted therefrom.

Administrative Trends in the Customs and Excise Branch

As a matter of administration, the taxes assigned to the Customs and Excise Branch are enforced by physical control, through inspection of the goods, services, or transactions to which they apply. Imported goods need not be released from the customs until they have been inspected and the duties paid. If they are subject to purchase tax, payment can be required before the goods are released from customs. As for locally manufactured goods, the purchase tax must be paid on sale by the manufacturer, and appropriate proof of payment affixed to the taxable items. If a document is subject to stamp duty, the absence of a stamp in the proper denomination is evidence of nonpayment. Excises can be controlled by stationing an agent on the premises of the manufacturer and by giving him a key without which the plant cannot be opened or locked. Items such as tobacco products or liquors can be required to bear a banderolle as evidence of payment of the tax. The amusement tax can be controlled by stamps affixed to admission tickets (printed by the administration) and by counting heads of audiences.

In practice, however, the administration of the Customs and Excise Tax Branch's array of taxes has turned out to be considerably more complex. Part of the complexity is the product of increasing efforts to encourage industrialization and the manufacture of goods for export. Raw materials or partially finished goods which are destined for export after manufacture are technically subject to immediate payment of the customs and purchase tax, but these are refundable on proof of the incorporation of tax-paid materials in an exported product. Over the years, a system of "drawbacks," instituted during the British mandate and expanded under the present regime, has developed. In its present form, the drawback system relieves most manufacturers of goods for export from paying all or some substantial part of the taxes. Instead, a system of documentary controls and bonds has been established whereby records are maintained both at customs headquarters and by the manufacturer to assure that goods released to the manufacturer under the drawback system would not find their way untaxed into the local market.

Relaxations of the "pay first" principle have also taken place in the administration of other taxes controlled by the Customs and Excise Branch. Some importers for local consumption have been permitted to release goods from customs without payment of taxes on posting acceptable security. This procedure developed because credit in Israel is costly and because the authorities recognize that a substantial period may elapse between import and ultimate sale. A similar change has occurred in the purchase tax administration, which has permitted manufacturers or importers whose books of account have been found to be reliable to be relieved of the obligation of affixing stamps (which must be paid for when purchased) to their taxable products. Instead, these "approved merchants" are permitted to file periodic reports and pay the tax in a lump sum based on actual sales during the period. Similarly, in respect of the stamp duties, the individual documentary stamp has in some instances (e.g. bank checks) been eliminated and the duty is computed on all of the taxable transactions reported for a specific period. In the case of excise taxes, also, there is a trend away from physical inspection and control. The banderolles formerly required to be affixed to certain excisable products, such as liquor and cigarettes, have been eliminated. Now the excise tax inspectors assigned to manufacturing plants are gradually being removed and more reliance is being placed upon the manufacturers' books of account.[46]

The changes in the pattern of enforcement of the taxes under administration of the Customs and Excise Tax Branch reflect a considerable advance in the structure of Israeli industry and commerce. One element of this advance is the reduction in the number of sole proprietorships which were characteristic of Israeli manufacture in the early years of the State. Few of these kept reliable books of account and, therefore, physical control of their products and transactions was the only reliable

46. *Eleventh Annual Report on State Revenue, 1964/65* (Hebrew) p. 76; Uri Schneider, "Stamping of Accounts with Adhesive Stamps or on the Basis of Turnover" (Hebrew), 2 *Quarterly Tax Journal* 180 (April 1967); Simha Gafni, "Our Plans — Some Comments About Ourselves" (Hebrew), 1 *Quarterly Tax Journal*, 389, 392–393 (October 1966). Schneider suggests that this administrative change may have the effect of converting the purchase tax into a gross receipts tax. See also Yaacov Arad, "The Unification of Purchase Tax Rates" (Hebrew), 1 *Quarterly Tax Journal* 331, 337 (July 1966).

means of collection. In recent years the small artisan has largely disappeared. If successful, his business has expanded, he has taken in outside investors, or he has merged with others to form a company. As the number of large enterprises maintaining reliable books of account has increased, the need for physical controls has diminished. The result has been a substantial shift in the pattern of administration of the Customs and Excise Branch.

The essential characteristic of changes in enforcement which have taken place in the Customs and Excise Branch is the greater reliance upon taxpayers' books of account as the basis for determining the tax due. To accomplish this change, it has been necessary for the branch to build up a staff of qualified auditors. These are hard to come by. With the development of Israeli industry, the demand for auditors and certified public accountants has outpaced the supply. As had been the case in the income tax administration, the Customs and Excise Branch found that it was losing its staff of auditors to outside industry about as fast as it could train them, because a qualified man could earn much more than his civil service salary on the outside.

This trend in the Customs and Excise Branch to shift from physical inspection of goods to audit of accounts has compelled a reorganization of the branch. Until this reorganization, announced in 1969, its structure was based on the separate administration of each of the several taxes assigned to the branch. Accordingly, there were three Assistant Directors — one for Customs, one for Excise, and one for Purchase Tax. Administration of the travel tax and stamp duties was under the Assistant Director for Excises.

At various times the structure of the customs and excise tax administration at the headquarters level was changed, but the administrative separation of the several taxes was maintained. This meant that, to the extent that control of any of them shifted from physical inspection to audit of accounts, each separate administration had to build up its own staff of auditors.

As this trend toward emphasis upon audit of accounts grew, it became apparent that the maintenance of separate audit staffs was inefficient from the administration's standpoint, and annoying from the standpoint of the taxpayer. There were many instances in which a taxpayer's books would be audited at one time by a customs auditor, checking to determine whether customs payments were due on raw materials which had been released under a drawback or other credit arrangement; again by a purchase tax auditor, checking to determine whether the return for a particular period was accurate; and again by a stamp tax auditor, checking the accuracy of a return reporting taxable transactions for a particular period.

This multiplication of audits was recognized as inefficient, and the 1969 reorganization of the Customs and Excise Branch placed all audit functions under one assistant director. This official plans and executes combined audit programs so that, in a single audit, all matters within the jurisdiction of the Customs and Excise Branch may be checked at one time.

Another functional duplication eliminated by the 1969 reorganization is in the classification and valuation of goods. Both customs and purchase taxes are imposed at varying rates, depending upon the classification of the goods, their quantity, and value. Each separate administration had to develop its own procedures and experts. These are now combined under an Assistant Director for Assessment and Classification. Other Assistant Directors are in charge of administration, operations, and enforcement.[47]

Insofar as the Customs and Excise Branch is concerned, its 1969 reorganization is a complete departure from the pattern of compartmentalization of individual taxes characteristic of the tax administration during the mandatory period and the first twenty years of the State of Israel.

Administration of the Income and Property Tax Branch

As presently constituted, the Income and Property Tax Branch is the product of a merger in 1967 of the Income Tax Branch and the Property Tax and Damages Fund Branch. The latter went through a number of changes before it came to rest in its present position. The combined branch now administers the taxes formerly assigned to the Property Tax and Damages Fund Branch, namely, property tax on land and buildings (including such taxes formerly administered by the municipalities), property tax on equipment and inventory, estate tax and land betterment tax. The Taxes (Collection) Ordinance, formerly administered by the Collections and Property Tax Division (the predecessor of the Property Tax and Damages Fund Branch) is also now administered by the Income and Property Tax Branch. The branch has also taken over administration of payments for reimbursement of damages caused by acts of war and drought, although the war damages compensation levy has been abolished as a separate item of collection and has been incorporated into the property tax.

The details of the changes which have taken place since 1948 in the administration of the property taxes are dealt with in Chapters 9 and 10. We are concerned here with the administration of the income tax.

47. David Peled, "On the Revision of Traditional Customs Routines," pp. 245–246. See also *Report of State Revenue Administration for 1967/8–1968/9*, (Hebrew), p. 44 (Jerusalem: Museum of Taxes, 1970).

Transition from Mandatory Income Tax Administration

The takeover of the income tax administration from the British was not easy. There were three income tax assessing offices in 1948 — in Jerusalem, Haifa, and Tel Aviv. The populations of both Jerusalem and Haifa were mixed, and the tax offices were located at the center of the fighting which broke out between the Arab and Jewish populations. This situation continued for months during the latter part of 1947 and through the middle of 1948.

In anticipation of the establishment of an independent State, the Jewish employees of the income tax offices were directed by the Jewish shadow government to protect the income tax files from destruction. At considerable personal risk, the Jewish employees managed to save the files in Haifa and Jerusalem so that assessment and collection of the income tax could proceed immediately on establishment of the State. The Tel Aviv files presented no problem insofar as possible destruction by the Arabs or departing British was concerned. The problem there, as in other cities, was to protect them from the Jewish underground movements which at various times considered destruction of mandatory government files as one of the means of producing chaos in that administration.

With the establishment of the State, the income tax offices began to function almost immediately. Since the income year 1947–48 had ended on March 31, 1948, income tax return forms for that year had to be distributed almost immediately. Moreover, many returns for previous years remained unassessed. This was due partly to the disruptions of the normal work of the offices and partly, it appears, to a deliberate effort of the Jewish inspectors to slow down assessments and collections in the latter days of the mandate, so that the funds would go to the new State. The administration had to operate under difficult physical conditions and with staffs that had been greatly depleted by the departure of British and Arab employees and by the absence of many Jewish employees who were serving in the armed forces. Accordingly, the administration started with a backlog, which continued to get worse for the next several years.

Expansion of the Income Taxpayer Network

Substantial increases in the tax rates, coupled with inflation and devaluation of the currency, had the effect of subjecting to tax many previously untaxed employees and self-employed individuals. Mass immigration also brought in many new taxpayers. One of the first problems of the administration was to assure that all who were liable to tax were identified and files opened for them so that they might be assessed. As the number of taxpayers swept into the network increased, the three original assessing offices could not handle the load. This was particularly true of the Tel Aviv area which doubled its population in the first five years and gradually became the industrial and commercial center of the country. The solution arrived at was to split the Tel Aviv area among several income tax offices. Additional offices were also established in other parts of the country. Each of these offices then proceeded to survey potential taxpayers in its district, sometimes by house-to-house canvassing and sometimes by reference to the population register and other public records. This procedure was ultimately regularized by the establishment of a central card index and mechanization of mailing of returns and follow-up procedures.

Some conception of the scope of the assessment load can be gathered from the number of taxpayers whose returns are subject to annual audit, comparing 1948, 1955, and 1968 for that purpose:

Table 1. Number of Active Income Tax Files

	1948	1955	1968
Self-employed	22,760	148,343	144,289
Companies and kibbutzim	3,800	8,325	16,006
Employees (active files)	62,000	304,572	86,601
Company directors	——	——	14,087
TOTAL	88,560	461,240	260,983

Sources: 1948: *Israel Government Yearbook*, 1952, pp. 110–111; 1955: *First Annual Report on State Revenue*, 1948–49 — 1954–55 (Hebrew), p. 71; 1968: *Israel Government Yearbook 5729–1969* (Hebrew), p. 110.

The 1948 figures reflect, essentially, the number of active files taken over from the mandatory income tax administration. The 1955 figures reflect the expansion of the network resulting from the activities just described. The 1968 figures show a substantial decrease in the number of active employees' files, a separate classification of "company directors," a decrease in the number of self-employed, and an almost 100 percent increase in the number of companies.

Actually, the number of employees subject to income tax increased substantially from 1955 to 1968.[48] However, changes in the law, regulations, and administrative procedures relieved many employees of the obligation of filing annual returns and also enabled the administration to make many assessments on the basis of returns, without further audit. By 1968, over 600,000 active employees' files had thus been eliminated.

The 1968 decrease in the number of self-employed's files is attribut-

48. Exact figures are not available but it can be reasonably estimated that in 1967–68 the number of employees subject to withholding was about 700,000. (Report of the Income and Property Tax Branch for 1967/68 [Hebrew], p. 50.) Of these, only about 87,000 were required to file returns.

able to several factors. Principal among these is economic development, which resulted in the elimination of many sole proprietorships and partnerships or their absorption into corporations. In this way many self-employed taxpayers shifted to the employee category as company directors. Reductions in tax rates and increases in personal exemptions also eliminated a number of marginal taxpayers. It was also found, on completion of the central index of taxpayers, that there were a number of duplicated files. These were eliminated. Overall, the trend has been toward an increase in the number of companies and a relative decrease in the number of self-employed. To some extent this trend has alleviated some of the compliance problems, for tax evasion is more difficult within the framework of a company required to maintain audited ac-counts than in the looser and less-controlled sole proprietorship. On the other hand, shift to companies has forced the administration to place greater emphasis upon the audit of returns of directors of closely held companies. These have been placed in a special category for audit purposes.

As to companies, although a 100 percent increase is indicated by a comparison of the 1955 and 1968 figures, the task of the administration in connection with the auditing of companies has increased to an even greater extent. Many companies listed for 1955 were in fact inactive. Included among them were a number whose sole function was retention of title to real property, with no income-producing activity. Such com-panies had been organized for convenience in transferring title to real property, in part to avoid the strictures upon the devise of *miri* land,[49] or to create a vehicle to avoid imposition of the Land Betterment Tax, prior to its amendment in 1965. Inactive companies are not included in the 1968 total. A significant change also took place in the quality and size of the active companies, as a product of industrial development. These quantitative and qualitative changes necessitated changes within the administration.

Reorganization of the Administration

There are now twenty-five income tax assessing offices, each headed by an assessing officer. This increase has resulted from subdivision of the three original assessing districts. The city of Tel Aviv itself has eight assessing offices, four of which perform specialized functions. One of them is the Assessing Office for Large Enterprises (*Pashmag*), estab-lished in 1955, which audits the more complex returns for the region.

49. *Miri* (rural) land could not, under the Ottoman intestacy law, which remained in effect in Israel, be transferred by will. Much of the rural land in Tel Aviv and other areas, although now urbanized, retained its *miri* classification. Shares in a company which owned *miri* land could, however, be devised. Thus the intestacy law could be circumvented. A 1970 statute finally abolished the Ottoman land law.

Another office concentrates on the current payment of income tax on wages of employees, conducting audits of employers for that purpose. A central office for the Tel Aviv area to deal with difficult collection cases has also been established. The officials in charge of criminal investigations in Tel Aviv and Haifa have also been designated as assessing officers.

Enlargement of the taxpayer network and increase in the number of field offices required an expansion in the structure of income tax headquarters. The initial organization, as in mandatory days, consisted of the Income Tax Commissioner, two assistants, and a few supporting employees. The first Israeli Income Tax Commissioner, who was also the first Director of State Revenue, was inclined to keep headquarters staff at a minimum. Organizational changes began to take place under the second Commissioner (1952–54). In 1955 and thereafter, the headquarters staff and functions were substantially enlarged, and the number of assistant commissioners and organizational units has increased.

Mid-1950 Problems

The income tax administration in the mid-1950's faced a number of outstanding problems:

a) Many potential taxpayers were not yet included in the tax rolls.

b) The organization had fallen far behind in assessing returns already on file.

c) There was good reason to believe that many of the returns on file were inaccurate (by error or design) and would require substantial revision upward during the assessment process.

d) Pressure of making assessments, coupled with insufficient qualified personnel, had resulted in as many as 80 percent of the assessments being objected to by the taxpayers.

e) Hearing and disposition of objections absorbed much time of senior personnel, interfering with their other functions.

f) The filing of objections deferred payment of the tax, so that increased assessments did not produce a corresponding increase in collections.

g) Even when assessments were agreed to, collections were slow because taxpayers found it difficult to pay the tax due to bunching of arrears and currently difficult economic conditions.

h) Efforts of the administration to meet these problems created frictions both within the administration and with the taxpaying public, these being exacerbated by the currently tense economic and political conditions.

It was apparent that a major overhaul was essential. Planning for this took time and, even after a plan could be adopted, it took years, in some instances, to put it into effect. Impatience with the slow pace at

which some of the reforms were carried out resulted, perhaps too frequently, in changes in top-level personnel, who were either forced out
of the administration or accepted employment elsewhere under pressure
of criticism from both within and without.

These problems, and the manner in which some of them were solved,
are the subjects of several of the chapters which follow.

Collection Procedures

Comparison of Direct and Indirect Taxes

Two interrelated fundamentals of effective tax administration are (1)
determination of the correct amount of tax due and (2) prompt collection. The techniques for achieving both of these vary in accordance with
the characteristics of the particular tax.

"Indirect taxes" are the easiest to assess and collect. They usually are
based upon the arms-length value of some physical good, asset, or service. Disputes which may arise over quantity, value, or price, are readily
resolved. Collection can also be immediate, for the movement of a taxable asset can be prohibited until the tax is paid.

The relative ease of administration of the indirect taxes accounts for
their popularity among those who determine fiscal policy, in spite of their
tendency to be regressive and to bear more heavily upon those least able
to pay.[50] In Israel, the customs and purchase tax have been used deliberately, not only to raise revenue but also as anti-inflationary measures, as means of regulating foreign trade, and for manipulating the
real rate of exchange of the Israel pound.[51] Thus the immediacy of collection of the customs and purchase tax (particularly on imports) has
made them suitable for use as economic tools.

On the other hand, assessment and collection of the income tax follow
the event, sometimes by several years. Collection may be deferred even
more, either by inability to pay, recalcitrance, or appeals (spurious or
otherwise). The main concerns with this tax have therefore been to
speed up and improve the quality of assessments and to devise procedures for accelerating collections.

Pay-as-you-earn — Income Tax Current Payments

The trend in Israel is to place as many income taxpayers as possible
on a pay-as-you-earn basis. This has been achieved by a combination of

50. Halevi and Klinov-Malul, *Economic Development of Israel*, p. 187; Morag,
p. 57.

51. Robert Szereszewski, *Essays on the Structure of the Jewish Economy in
Palestine and Israel*, p. 8; David Horowitz, *The Economics of Israel*, pp. 149–150.

requirements for withholding of the tax at source and for current payments.

Provisions for withholding taxes at the source were contained in the original version of the Income Tax Ordinance enacted in 1941.[52] Withholding applied to four types of payments. The most important of these from the standpoint of the revenue and the number of taxpayers affected was withholding of tax from wages. The other items subject to withholding at source since 1941 were dividends, debenture interest, and mortgage interest, paid to a person not resident in Palestine. The system has since been extended considerably, being now also applicable to capital gains, interest, authors' royalties, insurance agents' commissions, termination payments by provident funds, fees paid to artists, examiners, and lecturers, payments to building contractors, and payments for goods and services supplied to government agencies.[53]

The pay-as-you-earn system, particularly as applied to wage-earners, has been the major single source of revenue collection. In 1948–49, the first (partial) year of the State, withholdings from wages of employees comprised 28.3 percent of total income tax collections. The relative efficiency of the withholding system became apparent as the procedures were tightened up and as pressure was brought upon employers to comply. In 1952–53, wage-earners paid 55 percent of total income tax collections. The results of subsequent efforts to improve assessments and collections from companies and self-employed taxpayers are reflected in income tax collections for 1953–54, when the wage-earners' share of collections dropped to 49 percent. In subsequent years, it averaged in the low 40 percent range, but rose precipitously to over 50 percent in 1966–67 and 1967–68, when the economic slowdown produced sharp drops in collections from companies and self-employed individuals. Of total estimated income tax and compulsory loan collections for the fiscal year 1971–72, it is anticipated that 45 percent will come from wage withholdings and 8.2 percent from taxes withheld at the source from interest, dividends, and payments to building contractors and government suppliers.

The effectiveness of the pay-as-you-earn procedures, improvements in administration generally, as well as increased taxpayer compliance, are reflected in steadily decreasing costs of revenue administration. In 1968–69, administration costs averaged 1.9 percent of total collections; in 1969–70 they were 1.6 percent; in 1970–71 they were 1.2 percent, and, in 1971–72, it is estimated that they will go down to about one percent.[54]

52. Thus, withholding procedures were introduced in Palestine several years before they were adopted in the United States.

53. See Witkon and Neeman, *Dinei Misim* 219 ff.; and *Israel Government Yearbook* (Hebrew) 5731–1970, p. 46.

54. Budget Message of Minister of Finance for 1971–72 (Hebrew), pp. 33;

Although, in 1952, the current payment system was extended to companies and self-employed individuals, this did not yet put them on a par with employees. To effect the changeover, these groups of taxpayers were then required to pay advances (*Mikdamah*) toward the income tax liability which would be determined against them in the next year on account of the income currently being earned.[55] The advance payments were to equal 100 percent of the amount of the tax determined for the last previous year for which an assessment had been made. These advance payments were required to be made in four equal instalments. Later, individuals were required to make their payments in ten instalments.

The deficiencies in the advance payments system, as applied to companies and the self-employed, became apparent almost immediately. Even if their past assessments had been current, the system gave them an advantage over wage-earners. In a period of economic expansion and rapidly rising incomes, to measure the current payments by past earnings would naturally result in substantially less than the full amount of tax being paid. This disparity was aggravated by the fact that many companies and self-employed individuals had not correctly reported their incomes. Moreover, by contesting assessments made against them, they could defer payment of the tax for the years in dispute as well as minimize advance payments for the current year.

Some of these defects of the current payment policy applicable to companies and self-employed individuals are inherent in the system. Wage-earners have little room for manipulations of their incomes, although some employers were pressured into providing key employees with fringe benefits of various sorts. In some industries, particularly the building trades, under-the-table payments to skilled tradesmen were believed to be fairly common. In the main, however, the efficiency of the system as applied to wage-earners is apparent. It became even more efficient as the tax withholding tables, issued annually, were tailored to take into account personal exemptions, standard deductions, and fluctuations in wages. The accuracy of the system resulted in the release of many wage-earners from the obligation of filing annual returns.

As to companies and self-employed individuals, adherence to the concept that current payments should be based on the last previous assessment prevents these taxpayers from being placed completely on a

<hr />

supplement A thereto, pp. 92–93; *Annual Report of Revenue Administration, 1967/68–1968/69*, Table 12; *Israel Government Yearbooks* (Hebrew): 1950, p. 131; 1953–54, p. 132. See also Giora Gazit, "Deductions at Source from Income of Employees" (Hebrew), 2 *Quarterly Tax Journal* 352 (October 1967).

55. This awkward phraseology is due to the manner in which the tax was then assessed, a distinction being made between the "income year" and the "year of assessment." Following English practice, the tax for the current year was measured by the income of the previous year.

pay-as-you-earn system.[56] Nevertheless, some improvements have been introduced in an effort to have the advance payments approximate more closely the income for the current year. One procedure, authorized by law and effectuated annually by order of the Minister of Finance, is to require that the current payments be some prescribed percentage in excess of 100 percent of the last previous assessment. Since incomes have generally been steadily rising, the additional percentage increases in accordance with the time which has elapsed since the last assessed year.

This aspect of the system broke down in 1966 and 1967, when a new economic policy produced drastic drops in the incomes of companies and self-employed individuals, while incomes of wage-earners remained stable. The income tax rates had been raised for taxable year 1966, and these increases were reflected immediately in additional withholdings from wages. To balance this, advance payments required to be made by companies and the self-employed were also increased. These increases in advance payments produced a considerable outcry from taxpayers' associations, which objected more against the increases in advance payments than against the increase in rates. The fact is that incomes dropped precipitously in 1966–67 and in 1967–68, as reflected by reduced income tax collections from companies and self-employed individuals in those years. This was taken into account by the assessing officers, who are authorized to reduce the advance payments on receiving satisfactory proof that current income is lower than that of the year last assessed (sec. 180, I.T.O.).

A more significant factor in placing companies and the self-employed on a current basis was the drive to eliminate the arrears in assessments. As the lag between the end of the taxable year and the making of the assessments was reduced, collections were also speeded up. Many taxpayers were then faced with assessments which they were unable to pay. In 1954, when this situation became evident, the income tax authorities introduced a procedure whereby these arrears could be discharged by means of a bank loan which the taxpayer would obtain on the recommendation of the tax authorities. This arrangement continued for some years and even was extended to employers who had fallen behind in remitting the taxes which they had withheld from the wages of their employees. The latter practice was sharply criticized by the State Comptroller in several annual reports. That official has also criticized use of the bank-loan arrangement to enable taxpayers to pay up arrears in their advance payments.[57]

56. A study reported in 1966 that while almost 100 percent of wage-earners paid their taxes currently, advance payments by the self-employed covered only about 49 percent of the tax ultimately due (see Zvi Kessler, "Increase in Income Tax Advance Payments" [Hebrew], 1 *Quarterly Tax Journal* 257 [July 1966]).

57. *Twelfth Annual Report of State Comptroller, 1961* (Hebrew), pp. 57–48; *Fourteenth Annual Report of State Comptroller, 1963* (Hebrew), p. 94.

Administrative Trends

With the improvements in revenue administration which began to take place from the middle of 1954, several trends became apparent. One of these was the build-up of the office of the Director of State Revenue through the creation of a staff of professionals, who were at first attached to the Director as his personal staff, to advise and assist him in the performance of his functions. Then, as the administration matured, this staff expanded so as to provide centralized services for the several tax administrations. These services included economic analysis, legislative drafting, statistical analysis, computerization of functions (particularly income tax), and public relations.

Another change which took place simultaneously, and primarily at the behest of successive Directors of State Revenue, was the integration of the several tax administrations into more cohesive groupings. This trend was most recently reflected in the polarization of the various taxes into two branches — the Customs and Excise Branch and the Income and Property Tax Branch.

Increasing reliance by each of the Branches upon auditing procedures, coupled with perennial shortages of auditors, caused the revenue administration to begin considering, in 1965, the possibility of establishing an auditing staff which would serve all of the tax administrations. The thought was that simultaneous audits could be conducted for, say, income tax, purchase tax, and stamp tax purposes, with little more effort than might be entailed in an income tax audit alone.

This idea, although meritorious, met an immediate snag in the form of prohibitions against the disclosure of information contained in each of the several taxing statutes.[58] One such prohibition had already been eliminated so as to permit interchange of information between the income tax and estate tax authorities.[59] As the several statutes then stood, each tax administration functioned under a separate law which required that information obtained thereunder be kept confidential and used only for purposes of the tax for which it was obtained.[60]

Finally, in 1967, the relevant laws were amended to ease the interchange of information among the several tax administrations. This

58. See, e.g., Arye Dagan, "Purchase Tax on Services," (Hebrew) 2 *Quarterly Tax Journal* 78, 81–82 (January 1967).

59. For a time, until 1956, the same individual served both as Income Tax Commissioner and Estate Tax Administrator (*Israel Government Yearbook*, 1958, p. 230). This is again the case since 1968. Because of the secrecy provisions, he and his subordinates were in the ludicrous position of having to refrain from using, for purposes of either of these taxes, information which they had obtained for purposes of the other tax.

60. Zvi Kessler, "Relaxation of the Secrecy Requirements as between Tax Administrations," (Hebrew), 1 *Quarterly Tax Journal* 259 (July 1966); 2 *Quarterly Tax Journal* 266 (October 1967).

lifted the cloak of secrecy on information obtained by a particular tax authority relating to (1) returns or false information submitted with the intention of defrauding the revenue; (2) information which the authorities had obtained from sources other than the taxpayer himself; and (3) information in the possession of one tax administration which another tax administration would have been able to obtain by the direct exercise of its legal authority. The purpose of the 1967 amendment was to enable the several tax administrations to take consistent positions vis-à-vis a particular taxpayer and also to relieve taxpayers from the burden of duplicating for one administration information which they had already supplied to another.

The near future may see some major changes in the administrative structure. As noted in Chapter 2, the Minister of Finance announced, in his budget message for 1971–72, that enactment of a value-added tax was in prospect. The self-policing feature of this tax should simplify the administrative structure of the Customs and Excise Branch. If adoption of the value-added tax is accompanied by abolition of some existing levies, as has been indicated, the organization will be further simplified. Also in prospect is the enactment of a gift tax. This is not designed as a revenue measure. Instead, it is thought that a gift tax will aid in the administration of the income and estate taxes. Thus it becomes apparent that substantial changes in the structure of both branches can be anticipated for the fiscal year 1972–73.

4 / External Relations

Introduction

The tax administration does not function in a vacuum. As a governmental unit, it is necessarily responsive to other governmental agencies within the executive, legislative, and judicial branches. It also interacts with organizations outside of the government which have a legitimate interest in tax matters. It is also concerned with its relationships with the taxpaying public — recognizing that a taxpayer is not simply a file in the tax office but a human being, whose attitudes toward taxes and the way they are administered determine whether a satisfactory level of voluntary compliance can be achieved.

Interaction with Other Institutions

In its operations, the revenue administration interacts with and is responsive to many agencies both in and out of the government. These include the Knesset, the Cabinet, the Minister of Finance and various segments of his ministry, other ministries, the courts, international organizations, professional societies (lawyers, accountants, customs agents) and taxpayers' organizations.

The Knesset

The Knesset influences the revenue administration in several ways. Of course, legislation is the primary function of the Knesset, and there are a goodly number of tax measures, mostly amendments of existing laws, which are considered in the Knesset over the course of any year. The key item of fiscal legislation is the annual budget, which customarily is submitted by the Minister of Finance in January or February of each year. The budget-making process was at first haphazard but, with considerable assistance from foreign experts, it became standardized in the mid-1950's.[1] The revenue administration is a key participant in the preparation of the budget. With improvement in administration as well as in statistical techniques, the revenue authorities have been able to forecast collections under the proposed budget and the effects of proposed changes in the tax laws with greater accuracy.

After the budget or other revenue measure is submitted to the Knesset by the Minister of Finance and has had its first reading, it is referred to

1. For a full exposition of the development of the budget-making process in Israel, see Bernstein, *Politics of Israel*, pp. 247–265.

the Knesset's Finance Committee, which gives detailed consideration to every aspect of the bill. Officials of the Finance Ministry, including the Director of Revenue, the head of the particular branch, and their respective staffs, will be called upon to justify and explain particular features of the bill. Frequently substantial changes may be made as a result of this inquiry. The bill is then reported back to the Knesset for its second reading, accompanied by majority and minority reports of the Finance Committee. If the bill is approved on second reading, the third reading and final passage follow immediately; otherwise, the third reading will be deferred until necessary revisions are completed by the committee. Because of the technical nature of the subject matter and the speed with which tax legislation is sought to be enacted, the process is a grueling one for the tax officials and others concerned.

The State Comptroller

The State Comptroller has had a unique influence upon the development of public administration in Israel. Members of his staff are constantly reviewing the work of the various government departments to assure that the highest standards of administration are being maintained. The annual reports of the State Comptroller, which necessarily contain only a portion of the observations of his staff, nevertheless are the best single source of information on the progress of Israel's public administration.

Since the revenue administration is one of the agencies subject to control, many insights into the problems and achievements of that administration can be gleaned from the portions of the annual reports of the State Comptroller pertaining to the revenue administration. These reports point out deficiencies in administration which the State Comptroller considers to be serious enough to be made a matter of public concern. Each annual report is first submitted to the Minister of Finance who, in turn, is required to submit his comments to the Knesset Finance Committee. In due course, the Finance Committee will determine the extent to which inadequacies in administrative procedures have been corrected or continue. These are reported on to the full Knesset.

The State Comptroller was intended originally to function as the financial watchdog of the Knesset. This was the main thrust of the State Comptroller's Law, which was one of the first enactments in 1949. However, by amendments of the law [2] and expansion of the activities of his

---

2. A consolidated version of the State Comptroller's Law, incorporating amendments to date, was enacted in 1958. 12 *Laws of the State of Israel* (English translation) 107. A translation of the original 1949 Law will be found in 3 ibid. 23; see also Joseph Badi ed. *Fundamental Laws of the State of Israel*, pp. 73, 267, 322. The current Hebrew version is in the *Nineteenth Annual Report of the State Comptroller* (Hebrew), pp. 741–746 (Jerusalem, 1969).

office the State Comptroller has become the "conscience of the public." [3] In many respects he performs like the Scandinavian ombudsman, although this function of his office originally developed not because the law had expressly charged the State Comptroller with this responsibility but because his office was the most logical one to which complaints about unfair treatment by government officials could be addressed.[4] As to complaints which might be made against the tax authorities, the State Comptroller has stated that he will not intervene in matters of judgment, such as the correctness of an assessment, but will inquire into complaints about unfair or unlawful treatment.[5] Such inquiries, as well as the more technical matters raised by the office of the State Comptroller, are responded to immediately by the authorities and, to the extent possible, procedures are promptly corrected.

Other Ministries

In formulating legislative proposals the tax authorities must cooperate with other government departments. The ultimate responsibility for drafting of legislation in proper legal form is vested in the Ministry of Justice. Because of the volume of tax legislation, one of the assistants to the Attorney General specializes in the drafting of tax laws. Along with representatives of the tax administration, he participates in all stages of development of a tax bill, working closely with the staff of the Knesset Finance Committee.

Before a tax bill is submitted to the Knesset by the Minister of Finance, it will have gone through several preliminary steps. The initial proposal, especially of an amendment to an existing law, will usually originate in the branch responsible for its administration. It will be submitted to the Director of Revenue and, if approved in principle, will be put in the form of a proposal, drafted initially by the interested officials and the legal officers of the Directorate of Revenue and the affected branch. It will then be submitted to the Minister of Finance and, if he approves, cleared informally with the Ministry of Justice and with other ministries which may be substantively interested. In the field of tax legislation, the interested agency is most often the Ministry of Commerce and Industry. This would be particularly true of laws and orders which would vary customs, purchase tax, and excise rates. Other ministries might sometimes be directly concerned. For example, the Ministry

3. Bernstein, *Politics of Israel*, p. 266.

4. Office of State Comptroller, *State Control in Israel* (Jerusalem: Government Printer, 1965), pp. 9–10; Bernstein, p. 283. In April 1971, the State Comptroller was designated by law as the Commissioner of Complaints. This regularized his status as ombudsman.

5. Office of State Comptroller, *The State Comptroller of Israel and His Office* (Jerusalem: Government Printer, 1963), pp. 30–31.

of Interior (which controls the local authorities) was involved when the national and local property taxes were merged in 1968.

When a tax proposal is ready for submission to the Cabinet, it will be referred to the Committee of Economic Ministers. Then, if approved by a majority of the Cabinet, it will be drafted in final form in the Ministry of Justice and submitted to the Knesset.

The relationship between the Ministry of Finance and the Ministry of Commerce and Industry is particularly close. The concern of the latter ministry for the protection and development of industry, and the concern of both ministries in respect of economic and currency matters, require constant consultation in revisions of customs, excise, and other tax rates. The Ministry of Commerce and Industry, for example, is charged with the administration of the Law for the Encouragement of Capital Investments, which has a number of provisions pertinent to taxation. These include customs and purchase tax exemptions for approved enterprises, reduced income tax rates for investors, accelerated depreciation, and other tax inducements. Effectuation and control of these provisions requires close contact between these ministries.[6]

The Courts

The courts have also had considerable influence upon the administration. Provisions for appeals from disputed determinations have resulted in numerous court reviews of administrative action. These have tended to curb administrative arbitrariness.[7] On the other hand, court decisions have supported and confirmed administrative efforts to improve procedures or to raise the level of taxpayer compliance. For example, the courts have stressed the seriousness of tax evasion in their opinions and by imposing heavy fines and jail sentences. Bookkeeping requirements have been supported, while taxpayers who have maintained adequate books of account have been protected by the courts (as well as by statutory amendment) against arbitrary administrative efforts to ignore their books. As assessment techniques have improved, the courts have emphasized the greater burden which the taxpayer must sustain in attempting to overcome the presumption of validity of the administrative determination. This has been particularly true when the assessment had been reviewed by an Advisory Committee or had been based upon a standard assessment guide (*Tahshiv*).

Aside from hearing appeals from disputed determinations, the courts

6. During most of the State's history, the post of Minister of Commerce and Industry has been occupied by a member of the Labor Party. At times, the same individual has been both Minister of Finance and Minister of Commerce and Industry.

7. The late Judge Thurman Arnold is reported to have said, "Taxation without litigation is tyranny."

have not hesitated to assert themselves in matters in which administrative procedures clearly required correction, as, for example, the procedure with regard to income tax assessment notices. After the Supreme Court and the District Courts had observed a number of instances in which assessment notices did not supply the taxpayer with sufficient details to enable him to plead his case in court, the rules of court were amended in 1957 so as to require the tax authorities to file a responsive pleading which gave the taxpayer a reasonable explanation of the basis of the assessment.

In respect of other taxes, in which the appeal procedures are not so fully spelled out as for the income tax, taxpayers have been able to resort to the Supreme Court, sitting as the High Court of Justice, on applications for extraordinary writs calling upon tax officials to show cause why they should not be enjoined from performing acts which the petitioner claims to be unlawful, or why they should not be compelled to perform some act which they are allegedly required to perform under the law.

These functions of the courts have served over the years to clarify the roles of both the tax authorities and the taxpaying public in matters in which they have been in conflict. The existence of an independent and active judiciary has also had the *in terrorem* effect of bringing about the settlement of many disputes in anticipation of court decision.

Public Commissions

There have been times when the government has considered it necessary to form a public commission to examine a problem of broad scope which, for some reason, it did not desire to entrust solely to the officials directly concerned. Examples are the Commission for Examining the Methods of Assessment and Collection of the Income Tax, appointed in 1953, and the Sinai Commission, appointed in 1954 to examine charges that a Jerusalem baker had committed suicide because of income tax problems. Two other commissions reported in 1963. One of these was concerned with achieving improvements in administration of the national and local taxes on real property. This ultimately brought about a merger of administration of the local property taxes with the national property taxes. The other (Zadok) commission, reporting in 1963, was concerned with achieving equity in taxation, the effect of taxes on incentive, and the advisability of instituting a tax on capital gains.

Early in 1971 a commission was appointed to review the entire tax structure and to propose "tax reform." Under consideration are enactment of a value-added tax, elimination of compulsory loans, income tax reductions, return to the concept of a luxury tax in lieu of the purchase tax, and other major changes.[8]

8. *Jerusalem Post*, May 25, 1971, p. 15; *Maariv*, May 7, 1971, p. 16.

In choosing the chairman and members of these commissions, care is taken to assure that they should be leading persons whose reports would be given due weight by officials and public alike. The first of these (the Sharef Commission) was headed by Mr. Ze'ev Sharef, then Secretary of the Cabinet and later Director of State Revenue, Minister of Commerce and Industry, Minister of Finance, and now Minister of Housing. One of the members of his commission was Supreme Court Justice Alfred Witkon, who was later chairman of the Sinai Commission and the Real Property Tax Commission. The fourth commission mentioned above was headed by Knesset member Haim Zadok (later Minister of Commerce and Industry), and is referred to as the Zadok Commission. The 1971 tax reform commission is headed by Judge S. Asher.

Technical Assistance

Israel has been the recipient of technical assistance from abroad and, in turn has supplied technical assistance to other countries.[9] Specifically, it has received technical assistance in revenue administration from the United Nations [10] and from the United States Government, through the U.S. International Cooperation Administration, now the U.S. Agency for International Development. In addition to experts supplied to Israel from other countries, these agencies have also enabled many Israeli officials to receive training abroad. Several also participated in the Harvard Law School's International Program in Taxation. It has also obtained the services on a private contract basis of experts from abroad. It was in this capacity that the author served in the Ministry of Finance for three years (1954–1957) as adviser on tax law and administration.

The development experience of Israel has enabled it, in turn, to assist other developing countries in raising the levels of their tax administrations. Officials from abroad have visited Israel to observe its operations, and tax officials from Israel have been sent to other countries, either on a bilateral basis or under the auspices of international agencies (such as the International Monetary Fund) to advise on possible improvements in tax administration.[11] Israel has also supported a proposal for the establishment of an international center for tax administration.[12] It has

9. Leopold Laufer, *Israel and the Developing Countries* (New York: Twentieth Century Fund, 1967).

10. See, e.g., the three reports submitted by Dr. Henry S. Bloch under the United Nations Technical Assistance Programme.

11. See, e.g., Meir Lahav, "The Income Tax Department in Ghana" (Hebrew), 2 *Quarterly Tax Journal* 372 (October 1967); Yehuda Peleg, "How Uganda Adopted the Purchase Tax" (Hebrew), 4 *Quarterly Tax Journal* 104 (January 1969).

12. Proposed by Minister of Finance Pinhas Sapir at Third [1965] Rehovot Conference on Fiscal and Monetary Problems in Developing Countries, reported in *Haaretz*, August 10 and 18, 1965. The United Nations has shown some interest in this proposal.

also supplied information, on request, regarding its administrative experience to developed countries. For example, data supplied to the United States Government relating to the deterrent effect of prison sentences imposed upon income tax evaders were consulted by the United States District Court in Boston, Massachusetts, in imposing sentence upon an individual convicted of income tax evasion.[13]

Israel has also been active in bringing its customs tariffs and nomenclature in line with international standards. It has adopted the Brussels customs nomenclature, modifying its customs schedules accordingly. It has also recognized the importance of such nonofficial organizations as the International Fiscal Association, sending observers to annual congresses of that organization along with the representatives of the Israel branch.

Professional Societies

The licensing of lawyers and accountants is strictly controlled by law. The Bar Association and the Accounting Society have official status, in addition to the customary functions which organizations of this type perform. Both organizations are concerned with substantive and procedural aspects of tax administration. Many members of these organizations started their careers and received their basic training in taxation as employees of the tax administration. There is a great deal of interaction between the administration and these organizations.

The Customs and Excise Branch, in recent efforts to streamline its procedures, has been in consultation with the organization of customs agents. An objective is to raise the professional standards of these agents, tighten the procedures for licensing them, and otherwise assure their reliability. This is one of the keys to efforts of the customs and excise authorities to place greater reliance upon documents submitted by such agents.[14]

The Israel Branch of the International Fiscal Association has been quite active, both locally and internationally. Research facilities in both local and corporation tax law and administration are now being established by the recently organized Israel Tax Institute.[15] The Institute, in turn, is being assisted by the American–Israel Tax Foundation.

Taxpayers' Organizations

One by-product of the improvements in tax administration has been the establishment of numerous business and trade organizations which

13. *Boston Sunday Herald*, May 9, 1965.
14. Peled, "On the Revision of Traditional Customs Routines" (Hebrew), 4 *Quarterly Tax Journal* 242, 243–244.
15. See, e.g., Yaakov Neeman, *The Tax Consequences of Devaluation*.

function, as it were, as self-defense groups vis-à-vis the tax authorities. At first, the practices of some of these groups were rather crude, sponsoring such activities as taxpayer strikes and other forms of demonstrations against the authorities. In more recent years these organizations have become more sophisticated and function as pressure groups, both in relation to the administration and in political circles.

The tax administration has found these organizations to be useful in obtaining cooperation and understanding in connection with proposed improvements in procedure. They have been involved in the formulation of requirements for the keeping of books by particular groups of taxpayers. They have been called upon to recommend qualified individuals to serve as members of Income Tax Advisory Committees. They have been consulted in advance in connection with proposed changes in the law which might affect their members. They have also been consulted during the course of preparation of standard income tax assessment guides (*tahshivim*), although such consultations sometimes may result in a bargaining process which may affect the accuracy of the guide.

The Histadrut (General Federation of Labor)

About 90 percent of Israel's workers belong to the Histadrut, which is the only labor union in Israel. The Histadrut is also closely connected with the governing parties. Most government officials, of all grades, professional and nonprofessional, belong. They are represented within their ministries by workers' committees which exercise substantial control over hiring, firing, classification, promotions, demotions, and work assignments.

Although wages are fixed by agreement with the Histadrut, special groups of workers have taken to pressing for higher salaries, sometimes without the blessing of the Histadrut hierarchy. Among these have been professional and technical employees of the tax administration, who have participated in demonstrations or strikes in attempts to obtain higher wages or fringe benefits. These strikes have sometimes seriously interfered with the work of the tax administration.[16]

Taxpayer-Administration Relations

The stance which the administration and the taxpaying public have taken toward each other during the past twenty years has not been constant. Some variations were the product of national and international political forces over which the administration had little control. Others were the product of the interaction of changes for the better in the

16. *Tenth Annual Report on State Revenue, 1963/64* (Hebrew), p. 21.

makeup of the administration, on the one hand, and, on the other, the growing awareness by taxpayers of the relation between proper tax-paying and good citizenship. These changes did not come about easily.

The Development of Administrative Policy

The breakdown in tax administration which occurred in the first five years of the State manifested itself also in a breakdown of communications between the administration and the taxpaying public. This was particularly evident in respect of the income tax. When, beginning in 1952, vigorous steps were undertaken by the income tax administration to increase the level of assessments and collections, hardly any consideration was given to the effect which the new program would have upon taxpayer attitudes. The result was the generation of considerable opposition to the efforts of the administration: the assessing officers were swamped with objections to the proposed assessments; efforts at collection were resisted; and the quality of the administration became the subject of official investigation and political debate.

The Israeli tax administration was hardly prepared for the flood of public criticism which was directed against it in 1954. Such matters were, at the time, referred to the "Treasury spokesman," a largely mythical personage, for the response was generally assigned to whomever in the Treasury or in the affected administration might be handy or qualified to reply. Critical letters to the editors of newspapers (each political party had its own) were common, and the practice developed of the editor's transmitting criticisms of the tax administration to the Treasury, so that the letter and the reply by the "Treasury spokesman" could be printed simultaneously.

In 1955, the new Director of State Revenue emphasized the importance of establishing more cordial taxpayer-administration relations.[17] Taxpayers were invited to correspond directly with top officials in regard to any complaints they might have about their treatment by the tax authorities. For a time letters of complaint were turned over to the affected tax branch, which most often was the income tax administration. When it was found that there was a tendency for complaints to be set aside for an inordinate length of time, one of the clerks in the office of the Director of State Revenue was given the task of preparing replies for signature by the Director. When appropriate, the complainant was also afforded an opportunity to meet personally with the Director and such other officials as might be required to dispose of the complaint satisfactorily.

What began in 1954 and 1955 mostly as a reaction to stimuli from

17. Part of the Sharef Commission report (pp. 56–58) is devoted to a discussion of the subject. See also *First Annual Report on State Revenue* (Hebrew) p. 80.

outside the administration soon took on the form of an effort by the administration to adopt positive public information programs. For this purpose a public information officer was engaged in 1956 to serve on a full-time basis in the office of the Director of State Revenue. The importance of courtesy was impressed upon the staff. Thereafter, the "Treasury spokesman" ceased to respond on matters pertaining to revenue administration and, for several years, all such matters were handled through the office of the Director of State Revenue.

Since about 1960, each of the individual branches has been assigned an official who is directly concerned with maintaining satisfactory relations with taxpayers. This has resulted in a division of functions, with the public relations officer of the particular branch concerning himself with matters pertaining to his own branch, and the public relations director of the revenue administration concerning himself with supervision of the branch officers as well as problems of broader scope. Communications with the press and radio, whether by way of press releases, press conferences, or interviews, are the responsibility of the latter official. He also participates in all meetings of the top staff of the revenue administration, it being his responsibility to advise about the anticipated public reaction to new administrative and legislative measures which are under consideration, as well as to suggest programs for achieving public understanding and acceptance of them.

Public information policy of the revenue administration has gone through several stages since the public information office was established within the revenue administration. To some extent these changes have reflected the development of experience in public information matters as well as the differing philosophies of the incumbents of the office of Director of State Revenue.[18]

At first, emphasis was placed upon reminding taxpayers of their obligations under the revenue laws. A hard line was taken which emphasized the penalties to which taxpayers would be subjected for failure to meet their obligations honestly, fully, or on time. This was tied in with a program of publicizing criminal prosecutions and penalties.

Since about 1960 there has been a shift away from such hard-line publicity toward a greater emphasis upon public information. Less has been said about taxpayers' obligations and more about their rights.[19] This shift in direction is characterized by such recent developments as the issuance of a series of pamphlets entitled *Know Your Rights and Obligations*, containing basic information with respect to each of the

18. For an expression of the views of the former Director of Revenue, see Simha Gafni, "Guidelines for Improving the Image of the Revenue Administration" (Hebrew), 1 *Quarterly Tax Journal* 14 (no. 1, December 1965).

19. That taxpayers also had rights had not previously been overlooked. See, e.g., Harold C. Wilkenfeld, "The Juridical Guarantees of the Taxpayer vis-à-vis the Fisc: Israel," 33 *Cahiers de Droit Fiscal International* 78.

several taxes. As part of this series, the customs authorities have issued several pamphlets, in both Hebrew and English, containing information on the application of the customs to goods brought into the country by tourists, temporary residents, immigrants, and returning residents. In the same series, the income tax authorities annually publish a booklet of instructions to taxpayers to help in the preparation of their income tax returns. Additionally, during the annual period from the mailing of the income tax returns until their filing date (usually about a month and a half, ending on June 30)[20] special offices have been opened in ten key locations to assist taxpayers, without charge or identification, in executing their returns.[21] These were staffed with retired employees of the income tax administration. A further innovation was instituted during the income tax filing period in 1968 when a telephone advisory service was made available to taxpayers in the Tel Aviv area, replies being given to their questions by experts from the income tax staff. This service was expanded in later years.

These examples are only a few of the steps recently taken to remove some of the mysteries and misconceptions which had surrounded the various taxes. Other such steps, which are discussed in greater detail later, include the establishment of the Museum of Taxes which, in addition to maintaining exhibits open to the public, particularly to organized visits by students, has recently issued a number of publications dealing with taxes in Israel, notably the *Quarterly Tax Journal* which commenced publication in 1965. Another project, still in preparation, is the introduction at the eighth-grade level of a short course in Israeli taxes, including basic information on the filling out of an income tax return.[22]

A significant change in the attitude of the administration toward the general public can be seen in recent involvements of the public in proposed legislative changes. For years it had been the practice of the tax authorities to maintain absolute secrecy in regard to proposed tax legislation. The general public did not become aware of proposed legislation until it reached the Knesset in the form of a bill sponsored by the government. The bill would then become the subject of public debate, with all of its political overtones, in the forum of the Finance Committee of

20. In 1967, because of delays due to the June war, the filing period had been extended to July 31.
21. Simha Gafni, "Our Plans — Some Remarks about Ourselves" (Hebrew), 1 *Quarterly Tax Journal* 389–390 (October 1966).
22. An effort along these lines was made in 1956, using as a guide materials which had been supplied by the United States Internal Revenue Service. However, text materials were unavailable and the school system was not quite ready to adapt its curriculum to the inclusion of a unit on taxation. For the recent views of a member of the parliament on this subject see Shulamit Aloni, M. K., "On Education toward a Tradition of Taxes as a Rightful Obligation," (Hebrew) 3 *Quarterly Tax Journal* 205 (July 1968).

the Knesset. In 1962, when a major revision of the Land Betterment Tax Law was under consideration, a new approach was taken, and the public was given an opportunity to react to the proposed revisions of the law while they were still under consideration within the revenue administration. The opportunity which this afforded the administration to involve the public in the development of the law while it was still in its drafting stages was considered quite beneficial. Thereafter, in connection with several other legislative proposals, the public was again given an opportunity to express its views upon the proposed legislation before it was submitted to the Knesset.

Recently, in his budget message for 1971–72, Minister of Finance Pinhas Sapir announced that the Treasury was considering proposing adoption of a value-added tax, to become effective as of the fiscal year beginning April 1, 1972. He then stated his intention to consult with representatives of the general public before perfecting this proposal. He also announced appointment of a public commission to consider the overall subject of "tax reform." [23]

The Israeli taxpayer is highly vocal and taxes have been one of the favored and constant subjects of discussion. As before mentioned, the current policy is designed to involve the public in the taxing process as an active participant rather than as the object of administrative action. This approach could not be taken in 1954, when the administration was shaky and was viewed with "disdain" by the general public. It is, however, appropriate today, when improvements in the administration and in public attitudes both contribute to a considerable degree of mutual respect. This is also reflected in discussions currently taking place both within the administration and in the public press on such subjects as "voluntary compliance" and "self-assessment." [24] These subjects could not have been considered seriously ten years ago.

The efforts of the administration to anticipate the public reaction to new programs have not always been crowned with success. An interesting instance occurred in June 1968 as a by-product of the merger of the national and municipal real property taxes. The implementing legislation was introduced in the Knesset in February 1968, at about the same time as the budget for the fiscal year 1968–69. The burden of taxation during the previous fiscal year had been unusually heavy, to finance the expenditures leading up to and following the June 1967 war. The year before that had been a depression year, in which some increases in tax rates had generated considerable public opposition. Early in 1968 the Minister of Finance had on several occasions given assurance that the tax burden for 1968–69 would not be raised. Specifically,

23. 1971/72 Budget Message, pp. 33–34.
24. See, e.g. I. S. Ben-Meir, M. K., "Estimated Income Tax and Self-Assessment" (Hebrew) 2 *Quarterly Tax Journal* 331 (October 1967).

as to the property tax, the Knesset enacted a law in February 1968 which expressly provided that urban and industrial buildings should not be assessed for the taxable year 1967 at values higher than those at which they had been previously assessed. This may have been understood as intending that the *tax* for 1967 should not be higher than for previous years, but the law did not expressly so provide.[25] Consistent with the government's policy, the Directorate of Revenue, in February 1968, distributed a pamphlet to every householder entitled "Beginning in April You Will Pay Less." [26] The income tax authorities also announced that about 80 percent of the property tax bills would be lower than they had been in previous years. The public took these assurances seriously.

In late May and early June 1968, after enactment of the laws consolidating the national and municipal real property taxes,[27] tax bills were mailed by the Income and Property Tax Branch to all property owners. These were followed by an immediate outcry, for it turned out that about 20 percent of the property owners had received tax bills which were higher than those for previous years. There was an explanation for this increase which, however, was unacceptable to the affected taxpayers, who insisted that the Treasury had broken its word.

The explanation was this. In fixing the rate structure for the consolidated national and municipal taxes, nation-wide averages had been used. Application of the new rates to these averages produced estimated liabilities for the 1968–69 year whose total did not exceed the sum of the national and municipal property taxes collected in the previous year. However, the assessment and collection policies and procedures of the municipalities had not been uniform. Indeed, this lack of uniformity was one of the reasons for the abolition of the municipal property taxes and the establishment of a single national tax. But those taxpayers who before had been enjoying lower than average rates now found them-

25. The lack of clarity was undoubtedly the product of hurried legislative drafting. Although the text of sec. 2 of the Property Tax and Damages Fund Law (Temporary Provision) — 1968, referred to above, provides that the assessed value shall not be increased for 1967, its marginal note (which is not controlling) inconsistently reads "Freezing of *Tax* on Buildings" (emphasis supplied). Compare also sec. 3, which authorizes the Minister of Finance to freeze the *tax* on inventories. Obviously, the draftsman of sec. 2 had overlooked the fact that the new national rates were higher than some of the supplanted local rates.

26. About one-half million of these pamphlets were distributed. Although well received by the public, their issuance was objected to by some members of the Knesset who felt that the administration was committing the parliament to a fiscal policy before it had been legislatively considered and approved. Similar criticism had been made of the steps taken by the administration in making advance copies of proposed legislation available for public reaction.

27. Property Tax and Compensation Fund Law (Amendment no. 4) — 1968; Amendment of Municipalities Ordinance Law (Amendment no. 8) — 1968.

selves with a higher tax bill, even though no change had been made in the assessed values of their properties. In the face of strenuous objections from individuals and organized groups, the Treasury retreated, and, in spite of valid justification for the increases, those who had higher tax bills were reassessed at the level of the previous year.[28] Perhaps this situation should have been avoided, particularly since its net effect was a setback to the desired end of achieving national uniformity with regard to the real property taxes.

Frequency of Contacts with the Public

It seems axiomatic that one of the public relations objectives of the administration should be to reduce friction with taxpayers. Friction is generated if there are more contacts with taxpayers than are required for efficient administration or, even if contact is unavoidable (as, for example, for a traveler clearing through customs) if the circumstances of contact are unpleasant.

The speeded up activity of the Income Tax Branch tended to create frictions between the administration and many "small" taxpayers. The tax network was expanded very rapidly during this period, and many individuals who had not previously been subjected to income tax were swept into it for the first time. The number of individual income tax files increased from about 85,000 in 1948 to about 344,000 in 1953.[29] Many of these (aside from employees) were small shopkeepers, tradesmen, and artisans. The shock of being subjected to an income tax assessment, perhaps for the first time, was considerable. Furthermore, these assessments were during that period highly negotiable, because few of these taxpayers had any reliable books or records upon which a scientific assessment could be based, whereas the tax inspectors were naturally inclined to use their best judgment in favor of the revenue. The bargaining process which ensued was painful to both sides, and tempers tended to run high.

It became apparent by 1954 that the number of personal contacts between income tax officials and the general public was excessive and

28. In 1968 the Treasury was again faced with the need of raising revenue from internal sources. Being committed, however, to a policy of not raising taxes, it was prevented from using fiscal measures for this purpose. A compulsory loan, which many Israelis regard as the equivalent of a tax (see Chapter 10), was also considered to be objectionable. Accordingly, a voluntary Defense Loan Law was enacted, which is being administered in such a manner that for practical purposes it has become compulsory. In 1970 the voluntary loan was legally replaced by a compulsory loan.

29. *Israel Government Yearbook, 1952*, pp. 110–111. In about the same period, the Jewish population of the country increased from about 650,000 persons in May 1948 to about 1,466,000 in May 1953 — David Horowitz, *Calcalat Yisrael* [The Economy of Israel], p. 132.

that the assessment procedures (aside from criticisms on other scores) were a contributing factor. This was confirmed by an unpublished study of taxpayers' attitudes conducted in 1954 by the Israel Institute for Applied Social Research.

A number of measures taken by the income tax administration, from 1954 onward, to improve its own practices also had the effect of reducing the number of personal contacts with taxpayers. These measures are dealt with in detail in other chapters and will only be mentioned here. They included (1) improvements in assessment procedures so that there was less room for bargaining with the taxpayer; (2) issuance of regulations requiring specific classes of self-employed taxpayers to keep books, so that assessments could be based on actual facts; (3) implementation of requirements that assessment notices supply taxpayer with an explanation of the grounds for the assessment; (4) formation of the Advisory Committees and improvement of other procedures for the review of disputed assessments; and (5) raising the level of technical qualifications of the inspectorate by changes in recruitment practices and by intensive training programs.

As mentioned before, the Sharef Commission, in April 1954, recommended that the income tax Advisory Committee procedure be rendered operative "from the point of view of developing understanding with the taxpaying public." [30] This concern with the public relations effect of the Advisory Committees was further evidenced by their prompt implementation after the administrative crisis of October and November 1954. Establishment of the Advisory Committees was hailed in the First Annual Report on State Revenue (1955) as the most important public relations activity of the year.[31] The public relations function of the Advisory Committees has also been cited by an eminent jurist and teacher of tax law, who states that they were created against a background of growing criticism of the courts and a belief that the Committees would perform the decisional function more efficiently.[32]

To the extent that direct contacts between the taxpayer and the official remained necessary, a deliberate effort was made to find alternative means of communication (generally letter or telephone) which could substitute adequately for a personal visit. Also, although it took more time to achieve, an effort was made to break taxpayers of the habit of dropping in to the offices without appointment. This meant also, from the officials' side, that they should attempt to arrange their work schedules so that taxpayers with appointments, or those who had been requested to call, should not have to wait too long before being received.

30. *Sharef Report* (Harvard ed.), p. 20.
31. *First Annual Report on State Revenue, 1948/9–1954/5* (Hebrew), p. 80.
32. Witkon and Neeman, *Dinei Misim*, p. 230. In the first edition of his work, Justice Witkon expresses doubt as to whether this is an appropriate procedure for executing the law (p. 159).

Improvement of Physical Facilities

The provision of adequate office facilities for the several tax departments was a general problem which required solution as the work of
each department expanded. In making provisions for new facilities,
attention was also given, to the extent possible, to improving conditions
for reception of the general public.

The need for improvement of physical facilities was particularly
urgent in the income tax offices. As mentioned before, the increased
assessment activity starting about 1952 had generated a flood of taxpayers' visits to the income tax offices. The establishment of additional
assessing offices meant taking over whatever vacant office space happened to be available in the vicinity at the time. In Tel Aviv, for
example, where the original, single assessing office was split into several offices, one was housed in a former theater, which had just been
vacated by the Knesset when it moved from Tel Aviv to Jerusalem,
and another was housed in a former bank building. In the latter, what
previously had been the cashiers' area of the bank — a large open space
— had been filled with desks for the income tax inspectors. During
office hours there was a steady stream of taxpayers. With many conversations going on simultaneously, the general noise level was very
high, frequently penetrated by cries of anguish or outrage. Since this
was the period when many assessments were based upon guesswork
rather than provable facts, the general atmosphere was more like a
marketplace than a government office.

Conditions such as those just described were partially alleviated by
reducing the number of occasions for office visits by taxpayers. Improvements in the facilities for reception of the general public were
also achieved, by redesigning existing offices and by moving over-
crowded offices to better designed quarters.

Concern with proper office layout was reflected in the design of a
low-cost, one-story building, constructed at Hakirya in Tel Aviv and
completed in 1954. Designed under the direction of the then Assistant
Income Tax Commissioner for Administration, the building is now used
for several purposes. Principally, it houses the office and staff of the
Assessing Office for Large Enterprises, which was established in 1955.
A wing provides office space for the Income Tax Commissioner, his assistants, and other members of headquarters staff, for use during their
frequent (at least weekly) trips to Tel Aviv from Jerusalem. It also
houses a unit of special investigators attached to the Assistant Income
Tax Commissioner for Investigations.

This office deals with a relatively small, but important, segment of
the taxpaying public. They or their representatives generally come to
the office by appointment, to meet with a specific official. There is a

receptionist at the main door to guide visitors and announce their arrival. Each official has a small private office so that conferences can be conducted quietly and in a dignified manner, conducive with contacts with "large" taxpayers.

The problem of organizing the income tax offices to deal with the mass of small taxpayers was more difficult. Generally, a visit by a taxpayer to an income tax office will consume considerably more time than, say, clearance of the normal traveler through customs. Different facilities had therefore to be provided. In part to help solve this problem, as well as other problems of office organization and procedure, an arrangement was made with the United States Operations Mission to Israel whereby two specialists came to Israel at the end of 1954 to advise on matters of organization. One of their projects was to help in establishing a model income tax office, which they did, working over a period of a year in cooperation with the Assessing Officer for Netanya. Attention was given to such matters as providing an information clerk near the entrance, providing seats for taxpayers who were waiting to be received, improving internal office layout, and modernizing the filing system in part to eliminate delays in supplying inspectors with files needed for particular interviews.[33]

The premise underlying many of the physical changes in the offices was that if dignified surroundings were established for contacts with taxpayers, both the officials and the taxpayers would also conduct themselves with dignity. Experience proved this to be the case. Similar concern with improving physical facilities had been displayed by the Customs Branch, which also has to deal with large numbers of transients at the ports (both sea and air) as well as with merchants and customs brokers concerned with clearing shipments of goods.

Reduction of Contacts With the Small Taxpayer

Until fairly recently the approach of the revenue administration toward the taxpaying public was nonselective in the sense that little distinction was made in the administrative handling of the "small taxpayer, as compared with the large one. Accordingly, the small taxpayer was subjected to administrative attention which was far out of proportion to the revenue he produced. Perhaps this excessive preoccupation was necessary during the transition period, when the characteristics of each individual taxpayer were not yet sufficiently known to the authorities and when the apparently small man might, on close examination, prove to be much larger than he appeared. By 1968, however, it was concluded by the authorities that they could safely afford to relax their

33. Public Administration Service, "Project Completion Report on the Israel Income Tax Administration Project" (Tel Aviv, 1957 — mimeo).

grip upon the small taxpayer. This change in policy has already manifested itself in both the Income and Property Tax Branch and in the Customs and Excise Branch.

Income Tax

In June 1968 the Income and Property Tax Commissioner announced a new policy with regard to the administrative handling of self-employed taxpayers who are not required to keep books and whose taxable income for the previous year had been assessed at IL. 8,000 or less. There had been a tendency among these taxpayers, he stated, to report less than their full income, the reported figure being merely a starting point for negotiation with the income tax inspector. As a first step toward bringing this situation to an end, the Commissioner announced that about 80 percent of the returns filed by taxpayers in this group would be accepted as filed if, upon initial examination, the income reported thereon was consistent with the taxpayer's last previously assessed income for 1966 (or 1965, if 1966 had not yet been assessed). Of course, this announced policy is based upon the premise that the affected taxpayers would, in filing their returns for 1967, abandon their previous practice of understating their incomes and instead would come reasonably close to the correct amount. If this experiment proves successful,[34] which will not be fully known for about two years, it will result in a substantial reduction in the number of personal contacts between self-employed taxpayers and the administration, as well as in a substantial saving in manpower by both.[35]

Another development which will reduce administrative contacts with taxpayers — in this instance employees — is the abolition, as of April 1, 1968, of the taxation of the imputed income attributable to the rental value of the home which the owner himself occupies. This requirement, which had its origin in nineteenth-century British conceptions of the nature of income, may have had its primary impact, when the Palestine Income Tax Ordinance was first adopted, upon a relatively small group of well-to-do homeowners. In the course of time, however, the construction of rental housing became uneconomical in Israel, and almost

34. It must be mentioned that a similar effort in 1961 failed, but perhaps the developments of the intervening period will make a difference.

35. Taking the figures for 1965/1966, there were in all about 150,000 files of self-employed taxpayers. Of these 109,000 were not required to keep books, and 71,300 of this group had assessed incomes for 1961 of less than IL. 6,000 (*Twelfth Annual Report on State Revenue, 1965/1966* [Hebrew], Table 12, pp. 38–39). Estimating those whose incomes for 1966 would not exceed IL. 8,000 at about 80,000, and assuming that they would respond affirmatively to the Commissioner's announcement, this would mean that almost half of the returns of self-employed taxpayers would be accepted as filed. The Income Tax Commissioner also announced that if the experiment proved successful the IL. 8,000 ceiling might be raised (*Maariv*, June 28, 1968, p. 1).

all of the new housing constructed for the expanding population has been sold to the occupants. Thus, many employees are now home or apartment owners. Taxation of the imputed income attributable to home ownership had frustrated full utilization of the pay-as-you-earn system as a means of simplifying filing requirements and assessment procedures for wage-earners. The amount of revenue derived from the tax had been minimal in proportion to the effort and annoyance involved. Its elimination will substantially reduce administration contacts with this group of taxpayers.

Customs

Most of the personal contacts between customs officers and the general public involve tourists, returning residents, and immigrants; and most of these contacts take place at the Lydda airport. Relatively few travelers now come to Israel by sea, which would bring them to the Haifa port. Accordingly, almost all that travelers (other than immigrants) bring with them would be on their persons or in their hand baggage.

Since Israel depends heavily upon tourism as a source of foreign currency, the authorities are naturally concerned that travelers pass through the customs controls quickly and with a minimum of annoyance. On the other hand, although the import limits are fairly liberal,[36] attempts at smuggling have to be discouraged. Fortunately, the combination of vigorous past enforcement, improvements in local supply of previously scarce items, removal of import controls, reductions in tariffs on certain small items, and (perhaps not so fortunately) reduction in the number of immigrants,[37] has almost eliminated attempts at smuggling by all but the professional smuggler.[38] These circumstances have enabled the customs authorities to relax their examination of incoming travelers. Except on occasions when inspection of luggage is required for security reasons, it is estimated that average elapsed time from alighting from the plane to exit from customs need not exceed fifteen minutes.

Supplying Information to Taxpayers

A method which has been used with some success is the setting of public meetings with taxpayers in various parts of the country. These have taken different forms at different times. In the late 1950's, the Public

36. *State of Israel Customs Guide, Tourists* (Jerusalem: Department of Customs and Excise, 1968).

37. Immigrants are entitled to substantial exemptions for their household goods and, particularly during the mid-1950's, these exemptions were sometimes abused. There are now arrangements whereby immigrants may clear their possessions through customs before they are shipped. Also, few of the current immigrants are inclined to bargain away their exemptions, particularly since they now remain available for a three-year period.

38. These are generally identified by other means available to the authorities.

Information Administration in the Prime Minister's office conducted a series of public meetings dealing with various subjects of civic interest, taxes being among them. This gave the public an opportunity to meet with top officials and to hear explanations of policy and programs which were of public interest. The revenue administration itself organized such meetings from time to time during the early 1960's.

In 1966 a tax information office was opened in Tel Aviv on an experimental basis to answer questions pertaining to all of the taxes under the jurisdiction of the revenue administration. In addition to supplying technical tax information, it was proposed that the office would deal with taxpayer complaints. Only experienced personnel were assigned to this office.[39]

Another innovation instituted experimentally in Tel Aviv in 1968 is to invite groups of taxpayers to visit the local income tax office for the purpose of getting acquainted with the officials who would deal with their files and to receive instruction as to their rights and obligations. Consideration is also being given to the possibility of inviting "difficult" taxpayers to visit the offices in order to establish better relations with them.[40]

For the fiscal year 1968–69 the program for rendering assistance to taxpayers in the preparation of income tax returns was considerably expanded. Explanatory booklets, mentioned earlier, were prepared, containing answers to most of the questions likely to arise. Tax information offices in addition to the Tel Aviv office mentioned above, were opened in ten population centers.[41] A telephone service, manned by experts, was also provided in Jerusalem, Tel Aviv and Haifa during the filing period, and particularly during the evenings. To assure that taxpayers were receiving satisfactory service, the Commissioner announced the establishment of a Complaint Box, at the Post Office, to which any taxpayer could address comments, suggestions, or complaints. An Internal Inspection Division was also established, to improve procedures affecting taxpayer relations, and one of its assigned functions was to look into taxpayer complaints and to find means to correct them.[42]

Advisory Rulings

During recent years, the revenue authorities, particularly the income tax administration, have been requested by outside professionals to

39. Gafni, "Our Plans — Some Remarks About Ourselves," pp. 389–390.
40. Ibid., p. 394. A special assessing office was opened in Tel Aviv in October 1968 to deal with difficult collection problems.
41. Advertisement by income tax administration in *Maariv*, June 17, 1968, p. 15; *Report of Revenue Administration for 1967/68–1968/69* (Hebrew), p. 43 (Jerusalem: Museum of Taxes, 1970).
42. Y. Tamir, "1968 — Year of Events and Changes in Taxes" (Hebrew), 18 *Roeh Haheshbon* 145, at 151 (January–February 1968).

adopt a policy and procedure for the issuance of advisory rulings to tax-payers. This request was apparently stimulated by inclusion of the subject in the program of the Congress of the International Fiscal Association which was held in London in September 1965. In anticipation of this Congress, the Israel Branch of the I.F.A. intensively considered the subject, which aroused considerable interest among lawyers and accountants. The administration, on the other hand, rejected the proposal, although it is not entirely clear whether this was due to a feeling that the administration was not yet ready to undertake a program of this type, or to a policy decision to follow the lead of the British administration, which does not issue advisory rulings, rather than of the American administration, which does.[43]

There are indications that the subject of issuing advisory rulings to taxpayers is not entirely foreclosed. For example, recent issues of the *Quarterly Tax Journal* include a section entitled "What Would be the Law, If ——?", which contains technical questions submitted by readers of the *Journal*, and answers prepared by experts from *outside* the administration.[44] This appears to be a cautious step in the direction of a policy of making advisory rulings. The authorities have also adopted the policy of making available to the public "technical rulings" initially intended for internal use.

The Museum of Taxes

The idea of assembling in one place, for public display, items of interest which have accumulated during the course of a tax administration's activities is not new. The United States Internal Revenue Service, for example, has often placed on display such items as the 1865 income tax return signed by President Lincoln. Customs and excise administrations have tended to collect and display devices used by would-be smugglers or by illicit distillers. Until the Israel Museum of Taxes was established in 1964, however, the only comprehensive collection dealing with all types of taxes and incorporating materials relating not only to efforts at violating the law but, more significantly, to the manner in which the law is and has been administered, was that in Rotterdam, Holland.

The initial idea for the establishment of a Museum of Taxes in Jerusalem originated in 1958. It was known at the time that various items of interest had accumulated both within segments of the administration (particularly customs and excise) and in the hands of several individuals

43. International Fiscal Association, 19th Congress, London, 1965, Second Subject, "Advance Rulings by Tax Authorities at the Request of a Taxpayer," Vol. L(b) *Studies on International Fiscal Law* (*Cahiers de Droit Fiscal International*), London, 1965.

44. See 3 *Quarterly Tax Journal* 303 (July 1968) and subsequent issues.

who had made a hobby of collecting such items. There was concern, however, that unless rapid action was taken to preserve these materials, they might go astray or be destroyed. For example, valuable materials had accumulated relating to the unofficial tax system of the Jewish community of Palestine during the British mandate. This system, no doubt because of its voluntary and to some extent clandestine nature, had scattered its records, so that no complete picture of its history was available from a single source. One of the efforts of the organizers of the Museum of Taxes was to assemble, for preservation and for use by scholars, all of the materials which still existed.

Other materials relating to the place of taxes within Jewish history have also been the concern of the museum. Studies have been encouraged dealing with such subjects as the tax systems instituted by King David, King Solomon, and their successors through the days of the Second Temple; the systems of taxation of various Jewish communities in past centuries; and the tax systems in force in Palestine under the Ottoman Empire and the British mandate. Thus, the Museum of Taxes is concerned not only with assembling and putting on attractive display the exhibits which it has assembled, but also in publishing materials reflecting the results of research which the museum stimulated.

The public to which the museum seeks to make its appeal is very broad, ranging from the scholar, the professional who is seeking a precedent relevant to a client's case, and the interested adult citizen, through organized groups of school children or youth movements for whom special tours are arranged. A major purpose of the museum is to develop among the general public a better understanding of the role of the tax system and of the relationship between proper taxpaying and good citizenship.

Physically, the Museum of Taxes occupies part of the lower floor of the headquarters of the customs and excise administration building in the center of Jerusalem. Its displays are attractively arranged and instructively labeled. Visitors receive a catalogue and a collection of photographs of some of the more interesting exhibits. Visiting hours are, for budgetary reasons, limited to three afternoons during the week, but special visits by organized groups are encouraged and are arranged at other times.[45]

Publications

The use of official government publications as a means of communication between the administration and the taxpaying public started in a

45. Stimulated by a visit to the Museum of Taxes, the former United States Commissioner of Internal Revenue had a permanent tax exhibit installed in the main lobby of the Internal Revenue Service in Washington.

rather modest way but, by 1955, began to move ahead at an accelerated pace. Today, the revenue administration annually publishes a number of books, reports, pamphlets, and periodicals, designed to supply technical or general information to scholars, professionals, affected taxpayers, and the general public. Many of these are published under the auspices of the Museum of Taxes.

Newspaper Advertisements

In the early 1950's the administration began to publish, in the principal newspapers, notices to taxpayers announcing important changes in the law or calling their attention to due dates for the filing of returns or for the payment of taxes. This technique was used to the greatest extent by the income tax administration, which for a time published an "Income Tax Corner" (*Pinat Mas Hakhnasa*), generally weekly.[46] Later, the use of paid advertisements expanded into one, and sometimes two, pages devoted to articles dealing with timely tax subjects. These latter were prepared under the direction of the Public Relations Officer, serving under the Director of State Revenue. The use of paid advertisements as a regular means of communication diminished as other means of communication developed.[47]

Annual Income Taxpayers' Register (*Sefer Hanishomim*)

One of the 1952 amendments to the Income Tax Ordinance provided for the publication annually of a register of income taxpayers.[48] The first of these registers was published in mid-1955, and the last in 1958. The ultimate decision to discontinue publication was an acknowledgment that the basic premise underlying their publication had been erroneous. That premise was that by publishing the names of taxpayers and their reported incomes, those who had understated their incomes would be subjected to community censure. Thus, it was hoped, moral suasion could be applied and the attention of the authorities called to flagrant cases. It did not work this way. Although the registers created an initial

46. *First Annual Report on State Revenue* (Hebrew), p. 80.

47. There is some indication that the full-page advertisements also served to stimulate the press into giving greater coverage in their news columns to press releases issued by the information officers of the Directorate of Revenue and of the several tax branches. It took some time for the press to recognize that tax matters could be newsworthy, even when not controversial.

48. There are indications that the idea of publishing this taxpayers' list was stimulated by observation of such publications in Sweden. There are, however, important distinctions. In Sweden, there is a tradition of free public access to official documents, known as the "publicity principle." The official assessment lists, being public documents, are not kept secret. They are published, however, not by the tax administration but by newspapers and private firms. Harvard Law School, International Tax Program, World Tax Series, *Taxation in Sweden* (Boston: Little, Brown, 1959), pp. 50–51. In Israel, there is, if anything, a "secrecy principle," and official publication was resented.

sensation, the underlying concept was not well received by the general public. The feeling was that the administration should do its own work and not look to the public for assistance.[49] Traditionally, the informer is frowned upon by the Jewish community.[50] Informing to the tax authorities, whom many considered an adversary, went against the grain. Accordingly, as technical difficulties combined with essential failure of its purpose, the project was dropped.

Reports

Until 1956 there was no organized system for publishing reports on the operations of the revenue administration. At infrequent intervals one of the tax branches might publish a report on its own activities, but these were sporadic. It was not until the Office of Director of State Revenue had established centralized control over the several tax administrations that the practice was adopted of publishing an annual report covering all branches of the tax administration.

One of the difficulties which had to be overcome in preparing an annual report was the need for establishing systematic procedures for the collection, compilation, and analysis of statistical data. This need had already been emphasized in 1951 and 1953 by a United Nations expert and in 1954 by the Sharef Commission.[51] During 1955, under the general direction of an economist on the staff of the Director of State Revenue, and with the assistance of the Central Bureau of Statistics, guidelines were laid down for the compilation of statistical data by the several tax branches. These statistics were used for many internal purposes, aside from the annual reports.

In 1956 the First Report on State Revenue was printed, covering the fiscal years 1948–49 through 1954–55.[52] This contained text, statistical tables, and charts dealing with the fiscal system, with separate sections for each of the tax branches. Annually thereafter a similar report has been issued, covering developments during the year.[53] Content and

49. At the same time as these registers were being published, the Income Tax Advisory Committees were taking hold as an effective device for handling disputed assessments. However, members of these committees were selected for their presumed impartiality. They did not serve as witnesses or informants.

50. Dov Joseph, *The Faithful City*, p. 38; Christopher Sykes, *Crossroads to Israel*, p. 371; *Leviticus* 19:17, "Thou shalt not go up and down as a talebearer among thy people . . ."

51. See I Bloch, pp. 85–86; II Bloch, pp. 25–27, 40–45; III Bloch, p. 35; *Sharef Report*, pp. 6–7.

52. *Din v'Heshbon Rishon al Hakhnasot ha-Medinah*, Jerusalem, May 1956. This "first" report had been preceded by a July 1954 summary of collections for 1948/49 through 1953/54, prepared by the short-lived "Fiscal Statistics Service" in the office of the Director of Revenue. This was somewhat inaccurately entitled "Tax Developments" (*Hitpathut Hamisim*).

53. Publication fell considerably behind schedule after the 1967 Six-Day War. A combined report for 1967–68 and 1968–69 was published in January 1970.

format of these volumes have varied to some extent, with a trend, until 1967, toward greater emphasis upon the fiscal and economic aspects of the tax system than upon its legal and administrative aspects. This trend has been reversed in the combined annual report for the fiscal years 1967–68, 1968–69 which, reflecting the concentration of the then incumbent of the Office of Director of State Revenue upon problems of revenue administration, has shifted its emphasis in that direction. The change in emphasis is reflected in a change in the name of the annual report, which will hereafter be titled "Annual Report of the Revenue Administration."

Other relevant annual reports, although not issued by the Directorate of Revenue, should also be mentioned. The annual budget message of the Minister of Finance contains useful data, as do his statements to the Knesset in connection with proposed tax legislation. Since 1949 the *Israel Government Yearbook* has been published annually, in Hebrew and English editions, with a section on taxation in the chapter dealing with the Ministry of Finance. The annual reports of the State Comptroller have contained sections dealing with inadequacies in the tax administration deemed by the State Comptroller to be sufficiently serious to be called to the attention of the Knesset. The practice is for the Minister of Finance to respond to these criticisms, also in a report to the Knesset, which is published separately.[54]

Laws

Adoption by the State of Israel of the existing mandatory taxing ordinances as the basis for its taxing system meant that the official version of the law continued to be its English text. This was true of such laws as the several Customs Ordinances, Excise and Stamp Duty Ordinances, and the Income Tax Ordinance. Thereafter, amendments to these laws were enacted in Hebrew, which after establishment of the State became the official language. The result was that the official version of the law became a patchwork of English and Hebrew which even professionals found difficult to work with. Requests for Hebrew texts of the law were frequent but, as to those laws whose official versions were partly in English, a controlling Hebrew text could not be supplied until a new version was prepared in the Ministry of Justice and approved by the Knesset. Official Hebrew versions of the Income Tax Ordinance (1961), the Customs Ordinance, and of several of the excises have since been issued. Meanwhile, unofficial Hebrew texts, prepared by various translators, came into use.

54. See, e.g., *Nineteenth Annual Report of the State Comptroller*, (Hebrew) pp. 125–139 (Jerusalem, 1969), and *Responses of the Minister of Finance to Nineteenth Annual Report of the State Comptroller*, (Hebrew) pp. 29–57, (Jerusalem, 1969).

Amendments to many of the tax laws, notably the income tax, are adopted annually, if not more often. This presents difficulties to those who work with the law or who have occasion to refer to it, both within and without the government. In 1956 the Director of State Revenue decided to centralize in his office the task of compiling the various tax laws and of keeping them up to date. A loose-leaf format was decided upon, to enable easy substitution of pages containing current revisions. In late 1957 the work appeared in two volumes published by the Government Printer. It includes the current law, regulations, and orders. Loose-leaf revisions are issued from time to time, as needed.

Although this loose-leaf compilation of the revenue laws was undertaken principally for the use of employees of the tax administration,[55] it was decided to make the volumes available also to the general public. This was done on a subscription basis, through the Government Printer. The current version of the compilation of tax laws, known as "Kadam" (an acronym for *Kovetz Dinei Misim* — collected tax laws) is prepared in the Customs and Excise Branch rather than, as before, in the office of the Director of Revenue.

For some time before the preparation of this compilation there had been talk about the preparation of a tax code, similar to the United States Internal Revenue Code. Although there was general agreement that such a code would be desirable, several abortive efforts to produce one demonstrated that the task would take a long time. Meanwhile, the compilation of the several tax laws in convenient loose-leaf form has served some of the practical uses for which a code was desired.

The codification project was resumed in recent years under an arrangement with the Law School of the Hebrew University. As a first step, an effort is being made to achieve uniformity in the administrative provisions of the several tax laws, as proposed by the author of this book in 1956, and again in an address to the Directorate of Revenue in 1965.[56]

Instructions and Explanatory Materials

In connection with the mailing of income tax returns to all taxpayers in 1955, a four-page pamphlet, written in a conversational style, was attached to the return, explaining the various personal exemptions, deductions, and credits to which an individual taxpayer was then entitled. The approach taken by this pamphlet reflects somewhat the circumstances of the time. Many of the taxpayers had only recently been swept into the network, and this was the first income tax return they had been

55. Employees were supplied with those sections which were relevant to their work.

56. Harold C. Wilkenfeld, "Administrative Tribunals in Tax Matters" (Hebrew), 1 *Quarterly Tax Journal* 225, 226 (April 1966); Ze'ev Sher, "Codification of Tax Laws in Israel" (Hebrew), 1 *Quarterly Tax Journal* 129 (April 1966).

called upon to file. The pamphlet was obviously intended to soften the blow, and was therefore directed to the more "pleasant" aspects of the tax return. It contained no explanations for filling in the technical portions dealing with income and business expenses, which may perhaps reflect the fact that many in the class to which this pamphlet was directed were not then required to keep books of account. Perhaps consistent with the methods of assessment then in use, not too much confidence was intended to be reposed in the figures which the taxpayer might supply. This attitude toward taxpayers and, with it, this type of public relations approach were later discarded.[57]

Currently, the revenue administration issues a broad range of informational pamphlets, under the general heading of "Know Your Rights and Obligations." These summarize, in layman's language, the applicable law, regulations, and practices which would be of concern, for example, to tourists, immigrants, temporary residents, citizens returning from abroad, and importers generally. Notable among these are the highly useful pamphlets prepared by the Income and Property Tax Branch to assist taxpayers in the preparation of their annual returns for 1967 and subsequent years. These present a sharp contrast, in content and approach, to the 1955 effort just described.

Educational Materials

The revenue administration, as we have seen, has been following a long-range policy of seeking to raise the level of voluntary compliance by creating better understanding by taxpayers of the purposes of taxation, of what the tax laws provide, and of how they operate. In 1955 and 1956, stimulated by American experience, an effort was made to introduce a study unit on taxation into the secondary school curriculum. Discussions were conducted with officials of the Ministry of Education who, although pointing out that the curriculum was already heavily loaded, agreed to obtain the reactions of the affected teachers, principally those who taught the social sciences.

One of the recognized difficulties in putting such a program into effect was that it would be necessary to prepare suitable texts and classroom materials. Although samples of the materials prepared by the U.S. Internal Revenue Service for use in similar courses in American high schools had been supplied, they could not simply be translated, for they were unsuited to Israeli conditions. They did, however, offer a useful

---

57. This approach was reflected also in 1956 in a short motion picture, "Parashat Zippori" — The Zippori Affair — whose theme was the breakdown in public services which would result if taxes were not paid. This was sponsored by the Directorate of Revenue, with the assistance of the United States Operations Mission to Israel.

precedent. Meanwhile, for the interested teachers some materials could be supplied, because the First Annual Report on State Revenue was just then being prepared. Additionally, a pamphlet was prepared, for distribution to the teachers, which briefly summarized the substantive provisions of the several tax laws then in effect.[58] But at the time it was not possible to move further forward in the preparation of other materials specifically designed for classroom use. Therefore, the project, although accepted in principle, was temporarily set aside.

Efforts are now under way to take further steps in the direction of preparing classroom texts and other materials. Responsibility has been given to the director of the Museum of Taxes who for several years served as information officer of the Directorate of Revenue. A review of the Israeli tax laws, with statistical and other relevant data from 1948 to 1965, has already been published and is expected to be used for this purpose. Other materials expressly of interest to elementary and high school students have also been prepared by the Museum of Taxes, or are in progress.

Publications of the Museum of Taxes

In its program of publications, the Museum of Taxes concentrates on materials which are of scholarly interest, leaving to the other branches of the revenue administration publication of materials related to the technical aspects of the various taxes. The following are among its publications:

Rivon le'Inyanei Misim (Quarterly Tax Journal). This valuable, quarterly journal commenced publication in December 1965. Although its editors and staff are employees of the revenue administration, it has been established as a balanced forum for the publication of scholarly articles on the various aspects of taxation, in which free expression is given to views which may be critical of the administration, or which explore interpretations of the law or procedures which differ from those of the administration. Its contents include a survey of important developments since the last issue and articles on the general subjects of law and legislation, economics, administration and technical problems, and recent literature.

Seder Hahaarahah — 1963 (The Assessment Procedure). This is a reprint of the regulations pertaining to income and property taxes of the Jewish community of Mantua, Italy, originally printed in 1695.

Hilhot Misim b'Mkorot ha'Ivriim — 1965 (Principles of Taxation in

---

58. This pamphlet was later translated into English for general distribution. For the latest version see State Revenue Administration, *The Tax System of Israel*, as at 31st May, 1969 (Jerusalem: Museum of Taxes, 1969).

Jewish Sources), by Yaakov Bazak. The author, a judge of the Magistrate's Court in Jerusalem, assembles and explains the principles relating to taxation laid down by leaders of the scattered Jewish communities from the thirteenth through the nineteenth century.

Kofer ha'Yishuv — 1964 (idiomatically translated: The Redemption of the Jewish Settlement), and *Magbit haHitgaysut v'haHatzalah* — 1970 (Mobilization and Rescue Fund), both by Mordecai Berger. Compilations of the activities and accomplishments of the unofficial tax system of the Jewish community during the British mandate.

Hithamkut ve'Hishtamtut mi'Mas Hakhnasah — 1966 (Avoidance and Evasion of Income Tax), by Aryeh Lapidoth, published in both Hebrew and English. This is a comparative study of avoidance and evasion of income tax in both Israel and England, with discussion of some of the administrative aspects.

Hamediniut ha'Finansit be'Medinat Yehudah b'Yemei ha'Bayit ha'-Rishon veha'Sheni — 1967 (The Fiscal Policy of the Kingdom of Judah in the Days of the First and Second Temples), by Yehoshua Bar-Droma.

Hitpathut ha'Misim b'Eretz Yisrael — 1968 (The History of Taxation in Palestine and Israel). This is a useful survey, prepared by a group of economists in the revenue administration, of the taxes which had been in effect at the time of the establishment of the State of Israel and which since have been adopted. The origin of each tax is described, and its history is summarized up to 1965. Principal emphasis is upon the economic aspects.

Ikronot Mas Hakhnasah u'Mas Rivhei Hon — 1970 (Principles of Income Tax and Capital Gains Tax), by Aryeh Lapidoth.

Taxpayer Attitudes

Although complaints by Israeli taxpayers about the burden of taxation have been constant, the willingness to bear that burden, and, conversely, efforts at avoidance or evasion, seem to vary in response to internal and external political developments. The exact extent to which there is a correlation between political events and taxpayer willingness to pay cannot now be demonstrated. It would make an interesting interdisciplinary study. Some gross manifestations can be recognized, however.

During its first twenty years Israel had been involved in three life-or-death struggles with its Arab neighbors. The devotion and self-sacrifice of its citizens' army are well known. Similarly, before, during, and after each of these struggles, the general public has responded open-handedly, and at the outset even without being asked, to the financial needs of the government. Thus, these three events have in common the recognition by the general public that there is a direct connection between successful national defense and provision of the necessary funds. Yet, there have been interesting distinctions in the nature of the public response to the financial needs of these three events and in the reaction of the government thereto. These distinctions, to the extent that they bear upon the revenue administration, are worthy of examination.

The 1948 War of Liberation

In a real sense, this struggle may be said to have started in the late 1930's, when it became apparent to the Jewish population of Palestine that Great Britain, in its administration of the League of Nations Mandate for Palestine, had lost its initial enthusiasm for the establishment of "a Jewish home in Palestine." At the same time, stimulated to a large extent by Nazi propaganda, the relations between the Arab and the Jewish communities of the country continued to worsen. The conditions which culminated in the British abandonment of the mandate and the establishment of the State of Israel in May 1948 made it necessary for the organized Jewish community of Palestine to establish its own defense forces for protection against Arab attack and, in the case of some extremist groups, for action against the British. To finance these defense needs, as well as to maintain its system of public institutions, the Jewish community imposed upon itself a system of direct and indirect taxes which functioned parallel to the system of taxation maintained by the mandatory government. Administratively, the system was constructed upon a voluntary base, with relatively few paid workers. The sanctions, to the extent that any were needed, were mainly community pressure and, in rare instances, ostracism.

The essential characteristic of the fiscal measures which supported the War of Liberation was its voluntariness. Nevertheless, the response of the public by way of voluntary contributions had been generous.

The 1956 Sinai Campaign

In October 1955 the Israeli public became aware of massive supplies of arms flowing into Egypt. These were to be used, it was announced, "to drive Israel into the sea." Spontaneously there got under way in Israel a wave of contributions to finance the purchase of additional equipment for the Israeli defense forces. How this wave was first "organized" by the authorities and then converted into a compulsory levy is described in Chapter 10. In retrospect it would appear that the conversion of a drive for voluntary contributions into a compulsory levy may have had the effect of dampening some of the public's willingness to pay. This, however, was a political decision in which questions of administrative feasibility were perhaps considered to be of less weight than the immediate financial needs.

The 1967 Six-Day War

The manner in which the public, as taxpayers, reacted to the events leading up to and following the Six-Day War of June 1967 is in contrast to their behavior in the somewhat similar circumstances surrounding the Sinai Campaign of October 1956. These differences may have reflected major changes in taxpayer attitudes.

When the Israel army began to mobilize at the end of May 1967, reaction among taxpayers was immediate: there was a sharp increase in advance payments by self-employed taxpayers. Some paid their advances in full for the entire year; some made payments considerably in excess of the amounts due, which they asked to be credited against assessments which had not yet been made. A number of taxpayers who had filed objections to pending assessments withdrew their objections, explaining that although they felt their positions were reasonable, they preferred not to press them in the face of the government's obvious need for the funds. There were others who refused to accept refund checks.

There is an obvious similarity between this reaction to the fiscal needs of 1967 and the wave of contributions which preceded the Sinai Campaign of 1956. The important difference is that the public reaction of 1967 was channeled through the existing tax administration, whereas the contributions of 1956 ignored the existing structure and, in a short time, resulted in the enactment of the Defense Levy and the establishment of another, largely redundant, tax administration.

The 1967 Income Tax Amnesty

The foregoing description of the tax aspects of the crises of 1948, 1956, and 1967, and the differences in the reactions of taxpayers and administration, indicates improvements both in the revenue administration and in acceptance by taxpayers of their civic responsibilities within the framework of the tax system. But this must be considered along with the disappointing response to the income tax amnesty enacted in July and August 1967.

In the wave of jubilation which followed the Six-Day War and, particularly, the reunification of Jerusalem, the government proposed, and the Knesset promptly passed, a general amnesty. One of the motivations which led to the adoption of a tax amnesty, immediately thereafter, was an assumption that the overwhelming display of devotion to the defense of the country and the almost miraculous victory which had been achieved, would stimulate taxpayers who previously had evaded the law into desiring, once for all, to start a clean slate. This the general amnesty permitted; [59] and the Income Tax (Amended Returns) Law went even further by making it financially worth their while to do so.

59. If the crime could be rectified the amnesty did not apply unless the violator had taken the necessary corrective action. This would affect most tax crimes.

Yet the results of the amnesty were disappointing. Although the exact number of tax evaders is not known, it is the impression both within the administration and among outside professionals who are concerned with tax matters that there were many more than the 1,450 who took advantage of the amnesty. And although the exact amount of income unreported in previous years is also not known, the impression of informed persons is that it is several hundreds of millions more than the IL. 88.8 million which was disclosed.

The reasons for the poor response to this "once-for-all" opportunity for tax evaders to free themselves of the fear of prosecution, at bargain rates, have been the subject of some speculation. It has been suggested that the poor response was caused by lack of confidence in the administration — either in its ability to detect more than a few instances of tax evasion, or in its assurances that those who turned themselves in would not be given a hard time in the future.[60] It has also been proposed that the amnesty might have had a detrimental effect upon taxpayer morale, in that it may have supported the impression of some taxpayers that, in the long run, they would be better off financially if they consistently underreported their incomes.

Efforts toward Improving Compliance

What emerges from the foregoing summary of taxpayers' reactions to emergency conditions, on the one hand, and to the 1967 amnesty on the other, is that there remain some major discrepancies between the manner in which the authorities have anticipated that taxpayers will react and the manner in which they actually do react. The use of the strong arm, in the form of threats of prosecution, coupled with offers of immunity from prosecution and substantial monetary concessions, did not produce the expected result. There now appears to be some doubt, in administration circles, as to whether prosecutions and penalties are the most effective or desirable means of achieving better voluntary compliance, at least

60. Aryeh Lapidoth, "On Tax Amnesties," (Hebrew) 3 *Quarterly Tax Journal* 173, 177–178 (April 1968). Dr. Lapidoth suggests that the authorities might have stimulated a better response by instituting a number of prosecutions during the amnesty period. He overlooks, apparently, the obvious fact that such prosecutions would immediately have been frustrated by the defendants' taking advantage of the amnesty. The fact is that the "inventory" of cases in which charge sheets had already been filed, or which had been under investigation, was almost entirely depleted by the amnesty. The administration did proceed vigorously after the amnesty had terminated (in spite of the continued absence of officials on military service), but the time lag between the commencement of investigation and ultimate conviction is at least six months. Accordingly, the "first fruits" of the renewed program were not seen, in the form of convictions, until about June, 1968. See, e.g., *Maariv*, June 17, 1968 (failure to deduct tax at source on interest), and July 22, 1968 (evasion).

under conditions now prevailing in Israel.[61] There is a current trend toward offering financial inducements, by way of tax reductions, to those who comply with the law. This is reflected in a provision in the Property Tax Law granting discounts to those who pay their tax in full by June 30 or who make special arrangements on a pay-as-you-earn basis. It is further reflected in an amendment to the Income Tax Ordinance adopted in August 1968,[62] permitting the Minister of Finance to grant discounts in tax to those whose advance payments are made on or before the due date. Thus it appears that, in spite of the lack of response to the financial inducements offered by the amnesty, the authorities consider that inducements of this type will be effective in the future. Perhaps the distinction here is between tax evaders (for whom strong measures will still be required) and that portion of the taxpaying public which, although continuing to present difficulties, does not fall within the criminal class.

Some of the measures described above are trial-and-error efforts at achieving a more satisfactory level of compliance. There is a feeling both among administrators and taxpayers that there is greater acceptance of the obligations of paying taxes and that the public is complying more willingly with the law. However, this is more a matter of feeling than a scientifically demonstrated fact.

Though explanations are given for the misbehavior of the Israeli taxpayer, which has been said to be substantial,[63] the exact extent of tax evasion at any specific time is not known. And, to the extent that taxpayers' attitudes can be taken as a measure of the prevalence of voluntary compliance, or its antithesis — tax evasion — that, too, is not known except through the subjective impressions of the officials who are concerned with the problem.

In 1954 the Israel Institute of Applied Social Research was engaged by the Ministry of Finance to conduct a study of taxpayer attitudes. A statistically valid cross section of the taxpaying public was selected and the approximately 2,000 taxpayers who came within the sample were requested to reply to a carefully prepared questionnaire.[64] The study was conducted and its results analyzed by a psychologist of international repute. The results of the study have not been published [65] but, if and

61. See, e.g., Nahum Wermus, "The Problem of Compliance in Income Tax Administration" (Hebrew) 3 *Quarterly Tax Journal* 275 (July 1968). Wermus suggests that taxpayers could be induced to file returns and pay taxes on time and honestly if a system of discounts for prompt filing and payment were to be substituted for the penalties and interest now imposed upon delinquent taxpayers (ibid, 287–291). For a different view see Dan Bavli, "Trends in Taxation and Taxpayer Participation" (Hebrew), 1 *Quarterly Tax Journal* 496 (October 1966).

62. Sec. 111A. I.T.O., as implemented by Regulation, March 1969.

63. *Wermus,* above, n. 61.

64. *Sharef Report* (Harvard ed.), p. 58.

65. A tendency not to publish results of studies of tax evasion has been observed in other countries.

when they may become available, they may provide a base point from which to measure subsequent developments in taxpayers' attitudes.

In 1962, recognizing that the relationship between improvements in administration and in the attitudes of the public was a sociological phenomenon, the then Director of Revenue added a sociologist to his staff. In part, his assignment, although poorly defined,[66] was to advise the administration how to increase cooperation by taxpayers in assessing and collecting taxes. More recently, a sociologist was added to the public information and relations staff of the income tax administration. Some consideration is being given to conducting a sociological study of current taxpayer attitudes. If such a study is conducted, and its results published, it would help to measure the extent to which the empirical impressions of the revenue officials as to the current level of compliance are borne out by the facts as scientifically determined.[67]

66. Yehezkel Dror, "Public Administration: Four Cases from Israel and the Netherlands," in Paul F. Lazarsfeld, William H. Sewell, and Harold L. Wilensky, eds., *The Uses of Sociology*, pp. 418, 420–421.

67. A leading Israeli sociologist has expressed the view that a tendency toward a higher degree of tax evasion among middle-income groups is caused by a feeling that normally binding standards of behavior do not exist (S. N. Eisenstadt, *Israeli Society*, p. 187). Compare Halevi and Klinov-Malul, *The Economic Development of Israel*, p. 222.

5 / Men and Machines

Introduction

Building up the personnel of an administration is not simply a matter of creating a number of positions and filling them as quickly as possible. Such a hasty procedure is particularly risky when the administration is itself in a state of uncertainty. When improvements in administration began to take place — as in the income tax administration in 1955 — it was found that many positions had been filled by unqualified people. Stricter recruitment procedures had to be adopted, and training programs were instituted, both for existing and new personnel.

Over the years, many of the administrative procedures have become mechanized. At the outset, in 1948, almost everything was done by hand. Realizing that this was both costly and inefficient, the administration began to introduce what it considered to be the best available equipment. On occasion, mistakes were made, sometimes the result of poor initial choice of equipment and, at other times, because the demands and expectations of management exceeded the capacity of the equipment or of the available personnel. Generally, the administration was caught up in the contemporary world-wide rush toward computerization. On the positive side, this has culminated in the improvement of many operations through the most advanced mechanization. But this trend has also produced problems in adapting personnel and replanning procedures, as more and more sophisticated equipment has become available.

Personnel

Transition from the Mandate

Conditions might have been chaotic in 1948, considering that the mandatory power seemed to have been following the policy, in the last months of its administration, of dismantling its own organization without making any attempt to hand its operations over to a successor government.[1] Furthermore, when the new state was established it was already engaged in a war for survival with its neighbors. However, insofar as the processes of government were concerned, plans had been

---

1. Edwin Samuel, *British Traditions in the Administration of Israel*, p. 7; Joseph, *The Faithful City*, pp. 112, 120–121; Bernstein, *Politics of Israel*, p. 21.

carefully laid by the leaders of the Jewish population for an orderly takeover, and these plans were immediately carried into effect.[2]

For years before 1948, the Jewish community had a representative body, the Jewish Agency for Palestine, which was officially recognized by the mandatory government.[3] The Jewish Agency was supplemented by a National Council, the *Vaad Leumi*, which was elected by the Jewish population and had various legally recognized powers, including the levying of certain taxes. Additionally, there were elected both municipal and local councils which were responsible for the operations of local government.[4]

The experience gained in Jewish self-government, although on a limited scale, stood in good stead when personnel had to be recruited to staff the new government. Many of the ministers and other top-level personnel were recruited from this source. Included among these were the first Minister of Finance, the first Director General of the Ministry of Finance, the first Director of State Revenue, the first Income Tax Commissioner and the first Director of Customs and Excises. All of these had been active in the Economic Department of the Jewish Agency for Palestine. These individuals, in turn, brought along with them some of their previous staff to fill subordinate posts under their supervision.

Jewish self-government during the mandate had to be financed. Some of this was accomplished by a system of community-wide taxation authorized by mandatory law.[5] Additionally, there were organized fundraising activities conducted by the Histadrut and, mostly *sub rosa*, to finance the *Haganah*, the self-defense forces of the organized Jewish community. Several of the individuals who had been involved in these fund-raising activities were later appointed to posts in the new revenue administration. Noteworthy among them is a former administrator of one of these activities, *Kofer Hayishuv* (Redemption of the Community), who was initially appointed Commissioner of Stamp and Amusement Taxes, and later served as Deputy Director of Revenue. The second Income Tax Commissioner, before his appointment to that post, had been treasurer of the municipality of Tel Aviv, with experience in the collection of local rates. The fourth Income Tax Commissioner,

2. Sharef, *Three Days*, 51–57.

3. This was pursuant to specific provision of the League of Nations Mandate, which contemplated that such representative bodies would be formed by both the Arab and Jewish populations. The Arab community did not, however, choose to form an organization similar to the Jewish Agency. (Jacob Coleman Hurewitz, *The Road to Partition*, p. 23; Government of Palestine, I A *Survey of Palestine*, pp. 5, 21–22.)

4. I *Survey of Palestine*, 128 ff., 918–921; Kandel, *Local Government in Palestine*.

5. Moshe Burstein, *Self-Government of the Jews of Palestine since 1900*, pp. 261–278.

before entering the income tax service in the Jerusalem assessing office, had been concerned with the finances of the Histadrut.

The fact that the senior positions in the revenue administration were initially filled by individuals who had not been previously involved in the administration of the national system of taxation is not to be taken as indicating that there were no qualified Jewish personnel in the mandatory tax administration. On the contrary, a number of Jewish officials had been serving in that administration, some at high levels. This was the case particularly in the customs and income tax administrations. Some of these experienced individuals were later elevated to executive positions, but there was a lag of several years.

Several explanations for an initial reluctance to fill top positions with individuals having experience in the mandatory government may be suggested. Perhaps the leading one is that there was a tendency to view with suspicion those individuals who had been serving the mandatory government in any capacity. Even though most of these had cooperated fully with the Jewish shadow government (principally the Haganah), they were suspected of being susceptible to dual loyalties. As evidence of this suspicion, the new government did in fact appoint a commission to review the records of previous mandatory civil servants to determine whether they should be retained in the service of the new regime.[6] Meanwhile, the top posts had to be filled, and it was natural that the individuals selected should be among those who for years had been closest to the new Minister of Finance.

As conditions stabilized, the importance of specific technical qualifications in tax administration came to be recognized. By 1952, the Director of Customs and Excise and by 1955, the Income Tax Commissioner, were former mandatory civil servants. Their successors have also been promoted from within. This has been true, also, of recent appointments to the position of Director of State Revenue and of heads of branches. Thus it may be said that, insofar as the revenue administration is concerned, any early tendencies toward politicization or cronyism have been sublimated and the emphasis is upon technical ability. The same is true of middle management and of the lower ranks in the revenue administration.

At first, as was the case throughout the government, there were many jobs to be filled. Strict civil service procedures had not yet been laid down, and there was a tendency for the spoils system to operate, with jobs in a ministry going to loyal members of the political party to which the particular minister belonged.[7] Also, there was considerable pressure on all ministries to provide jobs for the large numbers of new

6. Bernstein, *Politics of Israel*, p. 157; Edwin Samuel, *Problems of Government in the State of Israel*, p. 60.
7. Samuel, *British Traditions*, pp. 25–26.

immigrants and for veterans who were being released from the defense forces. The result was that in the short period from 1948 to 1952 the government generally was found to be overstaffed. This was not true, however, of the revenue administration, which was, if anything, seriously understaffed. As a result, when in 1952 government-wide reductions in force were taking place,[8] the revenue administration was just beginning to embark on an expansion, particularly in the Income Tax Branch.

Unfortunately, educational and technical qualifications for employment in the Income Tax Branch had not yet been established. The result, which continued to plague the Branch for years thereafter, was that many of those who were released from other ministries, because of reduction in force, were rehired in the Income Tax Branch. Unavoidable though this policy may have been, under the conditions prevailing at the time, it contributed to some of the problems which culminated in the income tax crisis of 1954, related in Chapter 1.

From 1955 onward, the personnel situation improved considerably. Similar improvements were taking place throughout the Israeli civil service, stimulated by technical assistance supplied by the United Nations and by the United States Government.[9] Specifically, as they relate to the revenue administration, problems of organization, recruitment, training, supervision, and retention of personnel will now be discussed in detail.

Organization

In order to comply with both civil service and budgetary requirements, as well as to assure proper administration, each unit within the government is required annually to justify its plan of organization (called the *Teken*). This specifies the number of employees, their grades, functions, and assignments.

As of March 31, 1969, the office of the Director of State Revenue had 130 employees. There were 2,059 employees in the Customs and Excise Branch (including 201 temporary employees). Of these 332 were assigned to headquarters in Jerusalem; and the remainder were assigned to the customs houses in Haifa, Jaffa, Lod, Ashdod, and Jerusalem, customs stations in other localities, and other field offices of the excise and purchase tax, including 143 who were assigned to duty in the territories occupied since the 1967 Six Day War.

Also on March 31, 1969, the Income and Property Tax Branch had

8. *Tenth Annual Report of State Comptroller 1958/59*, 36–37.
9. F. B. Hindmarsh, *The Training of the Israel Civil Service*; *Technical Training for Israel in the United States of America* (Jerusalem: United States Operations Mission to Israel, undated); Edwin Samuel, "A New Civil Service for Israel," XXXIV *Public Administration* (London, 1956), 135, 140.

2,893 employees. Of these, 402 were assigned to headquarters in Jerusalem (including staff of the Investigations Unit); 2,080 were assigned to the 23 income tax assessing offices; and 411 were assigned to the 10 property tax field offices.[10]

Recruitment

Several sources from which the revenue administration recruited its personnel in the first few years have already been mentioned. These were mandatory government officials, employees of the Jewish Agency and other national institutions, the defense forces, political parties, and surplus employees of other government departments. The Customs and Excise Branch was able to put many new immigrants to work successfully in its various activities, after giving them a course in the Hebrew language and training them in such relatively routine posts as customs police, guards and inspectors. Many newcomers were also employed in the Income Tax Branch, particularly those who arrived with some education, as was true of many of the immigrants from Europe and some of the Arab countries. These were put to work initially in clerical and routine tasks. A few who had specific tax experience abroad proved to be particularly valuable.

By 1955 there were 1,670 employees in the Income Tax Branch and 1,372 employees in the Customs and Excise Branch.[11] The rapidity with which the Income Tax Branch had built up its staff indicates some lack of concern for the professional qualifications which the work of that branch demanded. The following figures showing fiscal year and number of employees illustrate the point:

1948–49	273
1949–50	284
1950–51	440
1951–52	563
1952–53	792
1953–54	1,352
1954–55	1,670

In 1948–49 through 1951–52 staff increases were minimal, in spite of the increased tasks of that administration. Then, beginning in 1952–53 the number of employees was suddenly inflated. Untrained and largely unqualified, they were given the task of making income tax assessments. Under the circumstances it was inevitable that the administration would break down, as in fact it did in 1954.

The haphazard recruitment methods of 1953 and 1954 were quickly

10. *Report of Revenue Administration 1967/68–1968/69* (Hebrew), 17–18.
11. *First Annual Report on State Revenue* (Hebrew), pp. 73, 199. These figures compare with 2,893 and 2,059 employees respectively as of March 31, 1969.

terminated. Realizing that knowledge of auditing procedures and other professional skills were essential, the administration sought to recruit people with the necessary experience or training. Efforts in 1954 to find such employees in other government departments and to induce them to transfer to the Income Tax Branch were unsuccessful.[12] Generally, auditors and other professionals were in short supply in the economy, and government salaries at the time could not compete with the higher salaries which even a beginner could command in the outside market. This compelled a change in the recruitment policies and procedures of the administration.

Without abandoning the search for professionally qualified individuals who could enter either the headquarters or field offices at relatively high levels of responsibility, the administration shifted to a policy of recruiting individuals who met prescribed educational standards and who were capable of being trained to perform technical tasks. In other words, the emphasis changed from trying to find individuals who were already trained to finding those who were trainable. To carry out this new policy, it was necessary for the administration to embark upon an ambitious training program.

Training

The need for professionalization of the Israeli civil service was recognized from the outset. To the extent that qualified people were available to fill positions, they were used; but there were many more jobs to be filled than there were qualified people to fill them. Accordingly, many jobs were initially occupied by officials who had good general educations but who did not have specific experience or training for their posts. Many officials were therefore self-taught, and the first few years were characterized by considerable improvisation.

In order to improve the capabilities of people already occupying senior positions, many were sent abroad for training and to observe how jobs similar to theirs were performed in other countries. This type of training was generally sponsored by the technical assistance programs of the United Nations and of the United States Government.[13] Several of the trainees spent a full academic year at the Harvard Law School's International Tax Program.

Other methods had to be devised for the training of the mass of the civil service. Specific recommendations for in-service training procedures had been made by experts assigned by the United Nations Technical Assistance Administration, and steps to implement these were undertaken by the Civil Service Commission.[14] Generally, these efforts

12. *Sharef Report* (Harvard ed.), pp. 67–70.
13. See, e.g., I Bloch 84–92.
14. Initially, control over the civil service was vested in the Ministry of Finance, but it was shifted in 1951 to the Prime Minister's office, under the direc-

have resulted in a greater professionalization of the civil service, although the degree to which this has been achieved is not uniform throughout the several ministries.[15]

Since the rather generalized approach of the Civil Service Commission toward training of government personnel did not meet the specific needs of the tax administration, the tax authorities instituted their own training procedures, though with the consent of the Civil Service Commission. The tax administration approached the problem of training on two fronts: First, recognizing that many employees already on the job were inherently capable of learning new skills, it offered them the opportunity to receive in-service training for higher-level positions. Second, examinations for technical positions were announced, with the understanding that applicants would have to undergo intensive further training and examinations before they received permanent appointments.

Courses for retraining of existing personnel and for training of new personnel began in 1955 and have continued since. Initially, these courses were conducted by the several branches of the revenue administration but, starting in 1956, there was a transition from particularized training for service in a single branch to a broader approach. At the beginning of 1958 a central training and planning unit was established in the Ministry of Finance. A Training Board was also established to coordinate training policy, advancement programs, promotions, and transfers of personnel to more responsible duties.[16]

A Treasury School was also established. This has since been expanded into a Central School for Public Administration, under Finance Ministry direction. Courses range in scope from short seminars of several days to intensive courses of up to six months. Those selected for the latter courses are paid full government salaries and are required to remain in residence for the duration of the course. These intensive courses are designed to develop special skills, such as auditors for the Income Tax and Customs and Excise Branches. They are not limited, however, to incoming employees. Even the heads of offices are required to undergo periodic retraining so that they may be able to keep pace with improvements in administrative procedures. In 1966–67, for example, 46 different courses were given for employees of the revenue

---

tion of the Secretary of the Government. A Civil Service Commission was then established and statutes enacted prescribing standards and procedures for government employment. In 1954 a new Civil Service Commissioner was appointed and the Commission was expanded. It has since been shifted back to the Ministry of Finance. See, for a critique of the early development of the civil service, Bernstein, chap. 6, pp. 153 ff.

15. Eisenstadt, *Israeli Society*, pp. 301–303.

16. Yosef Sharon and Moshe Weiss, "Training in the Treasury's Revenue Service" (Hebrew), *Sherut*, August 1959, p. 4.

administration. About 3,000 employees participated, representing about 60 percent of all of the employees of the administration.[17]

By now, there is hardly an employee of the revenue administration who has not taken at least one training course. The results are reflected in the makeup of the administration and in the current emphasis, in both branches, upon the greater use of audit procedures as the basis for assessments.

Although the administration could undertake, through its own training facilities, to develop skills such as auditing, or to maintain the abilities of already qualified personnel, it could not undertake to provide professional courses. Yet professional training was required to provide a staff of lawyers, economists, and public administrators. These needs were supplied by the universities, which have been producing an increasing number of graduates who have entered upon public service careers. This trend has gone hand in hand with, and is no doubt a product of, recognition by the administration of its need for professional skills.

Lawyers have been used in the formulation of legislation, in advising on statutory interpretation, and in the handling of tax litigation, both civil and criminal.[18] These functions are performed within each of the branches, in close conjunction with the Ministry of Justice, which also has specialists in tax legislation and litigation.

Economists are also involved at all levels of the administration. They assist in the formulation of fiscal policy, in formulating the budget insofar as it depends upon projections of revenue collections, and in the development of standards for guiding tax inspectors in achieving supportable assessments.

Both lawyers and economists take standard university courses which qualify them either to enter government service or to seek private employment. Courses in public administration, which are also offered by the universities, are already government-oriented. The impetus for the establishment of courses in public administration came from a recommendation in 1952 by a United Nations expert.[19] This was followed in 1955 and 1956 by two visiting professors from the United States, who came under United Nations auspices, to assist in the establishment of courses in public administration at the Hebrew University in Jerusalem. One of the courses offered at this time was a seminar in revenue administration. Then, encouraged by government interest, regular courses in public administration were introduced into the university curriculum.

17. *Thirteenth Annual Report on State Revenue, 1966/67* (Hebrew), p. 27.
18. See Harold C. Wilkenfeld, "Legal Services to the Revenue Administration — Proposals for Functional Organization," unpublished report (Jerusalem, 1955 — mimeographed).
19. Hindmarsh, p. 1.

These courses have contributed much toward the development of personnel who in time should succeed to the management of the Israeli government.

Supervision

One normally looks to the head of an office or unit to supervise his subordinates and this, naturally, is the role of the supervisor in Israel. However, supervision is in itself an art and, like others, does not come easily. Part of the training program for upper-grade personnel necessarily concerns itself with assuring that those in supervisory positions are skilled in that art.

The end product of most of the activities of the tax administration can be measured in terms of assessments and collections. Initially, greater emphasis was placed upon the quantity of collections than upon the quality of assessments. When it became apparent in the mid-1950's — particularly in the income tax administration — that this type of emphasis was counterproductive, generating as it did a mass of conflicts and criticisms, a major shift in the stance of the administration was required. The error of the initial emphasis upon increased collections, without regard to quality, was proved by the fact that improvements in the quality of assessments were accompanied by even larger increases in collections.

To assure both quality and quantity of assessments, the Income Tax Branch plans its activities each year, setting production goals to be achieved by headquarters and by each of the field offices. These goals are set out in a volume entitled "Work Program of the Branch," which is issued at the beginning of each fiscal year. Production reports are submitted to headquarters by each of the assessing officers and, if there is a substantial departure from the projections made at the beginning of the year, an effort is made to determine the cause and to eliminate it if possible.

Recognizing that individual assessments may vary in difficulty, no strict work norms are laid down for the individual inspectors. Nevertheless, weighted averages for particular types of cases have been compiled, and these help to measure relative productivity. Thus headquarters can gauge the efficiency of particular offices and even of particular inspectors.

To assure that standards are being maintained, there are frequent meetings of assessing officers with headquarters staff. Periodically, also, the Commissioner and other headquarters personnel — particularly the National Inspectors — will visit the field offices.

If a supervisor is dissatisfied with the work of an employee and is unable to induce an improvement, he has a difficult problem on his hands. The Israeli civil servant is very well protected by his union, the Histadrut, to which almost all employees, irrespective of rank, belong. Each organization has a workers' committee, which steps in vigorously to protect employees. Because of the close political links between the Histadrut and the government, negotiations with workers' committees cannot be conducted in an impersonal way. The unfortunate result is that the administration sometimes has to keep on its rolls individuals who are not carrying their proper share of the work.

On the other hand, the Israeli civil service is noteworthy for its high level of honesty. Instances of corruption are very rare and, when uncovered, are severely punished. Few taxpayers have attempted to bribe an employee of the administration. In those few instances which have occurred, the degree of revulsion displayed by the courts, the general public, and the civil service is the best evidence that bribery and corruption are not condoned. Nevertheless, to assure that there is no room for temptation, both branches of the revenue administration have internal inspection services which keep a close eye on their employees.

Retention

For many of Israel's civil servants, their roles in government represent as important a pioneering effort as draining swamps and building roads may have been to the generations of their fathers and grandfathers. But a man cannot live on idealism alone, and it is difficult for an outstanding individual to remain in the civil service when he knows that he can live much better by accepting a position in private industry. Accordingly, the ability of the government to induce its best employees to make a career of government service depends in large measure upon the salaries it is willing to pay, as compared to those available on the outside. It also depends, perhaps to a similar extent, upon the personal satisfactions which a capable person derives from his work. In both respects, if turnover of personnel is to be taken as a measure, there is still much to be desired.

Although salaries and grades of civil servants are provided by law, they are in turn the product of negotiation between government representatives and the Histadrut. There are, furthermore, professional and technical groupings within the Histadrut which negotiate special terms, conditions, and allowances on behalf of their members. Strikes against the government are not prohibited by law, and even when they may have been frowned upon by the leadership of the Histadrut they have taken place. Considering the continual inflation which has been characteristic of Israel's expanding economy, it is not surprising that the aspirations of civil servants should run counter to government efforts to put a brake on wages.

One factor other than inflation which contributed to dissatisfaction with salaries was a policy, partially abandoned in the mid-1950's, to pay employees in accordance with personal need rather than ability. This was reflected in a system of cost-of-living and family allowances as supplements to the basic wage. As a result of this system, a janitor with a large family could have a larger take-home pay, after taxes, than the highest-grade employee. In 1950, as a partial circumvention of this policy, high-level employees were given "representation" and "academic" allowances, as well as other perquisites such as residences, telephones, and chauffeur-driven cars. A new system of classification, with 17 grades, was introduced in 1951 and some of the special allowances were canceled, although they were restored for physicians in 1952 and for other professionals in 1953. Meanwhile, salaries outside of government were rising.

In 1953 the differential between the highest and lowest salary grades in the Israeli civil service was 1:1.54. This compared to 1:6 in Switzerland and 1:10 in the United States [20] (which was then itself far behind outside industry). Salary increases for government employees and increases in differentials between grades have been effected, but salaries still remain a subject of dispute.

Whether it is a matter of salaries, ambition, or the attraction of a greater challenge, turnover of personnel at all levels of the revenue administration has been relatively high. It may be of some significance that since 1948 there have been six Directors of State Revenue, six Income Tax Commissioners and three Directors of Customs and Excises. Turnover among deputies and principal assistants of these officials has also been high. In part, of course, these changes are indicative of the dynamics of Israeli society, in which many opportunities are available for persons of ability. However, each such change at a high level tends to throw the administration off balance, at least for a time.

Turnover among professionals has also been high. Lawyers have been attracted away by private practice, in which tax specialists are now able to command high fees. Economists and administrators have been lured away by the universities and private industry. Perhaps the most frustrating, from the point of view of the administration, is that many of the auditors whom it has trained at considerable cost and effort have left after a few years to go into private accounting practice.

It is only a slight consolation to the administration to realize that, largely through its efforts, the level of representation of taxpayers is now considerably higher than it was twenty years ago. Perhaps this is a compliment to the administration, for if its own level of competence had not risen there would be no demand on the outside for higher levels of competence among taxpayers' representatives.

20. *Tenth Annual Report of State Comptroller 1958/59* (Hebrew), pp. 40 ff.

Mechanization of Operations

When the British mandate terminated in 1948, all operations of the tax offices were still performed by hand. These ranged from maintaining registers of taxpayers to accounting, statistical analysis, and other necessary functions. Even typewriters were in short supply throughout the government.

The sheer increase in the volume of paper work which attended the enlargement of the taxpayer network made it impossible to keep up to date. Gradually, funds became available to purchase office machines and equipment, and with the help of experts supplied by the United States Operations Mission to Israel, one of the income tax assessing offices was equipped in 1955 as a model office to test out facilities which would be most suited to Israel's needs.[21] Cashiers were provided with recording cash registers; bookkeeping and adding machines made record-keeping and computations more efficient.

In particular, the Income Tax Branch could not maintain itself without mechanical aids. This became apparent when efforts were made to establish a central card index and to improve procedures for the mailing of annual returns and for the compilation of tax statistics. As the needs expanded, more sophisticated equipment became available. Ultimately, operations of the tax administration, particularly the Income Tax Branch, shifted to the use of computers. In turn, the availability, as well as the considerable expense, of computers made it necessary to centralize the operations to which computers are adapted. This centralization has occurred within the office of the Director of State Revenue.

The progression from hand operations to computers took place over a period of years, beginning with the central card index in the Income Tax Branch.

The Central Card Index

One of the first purposes intended to be served by the central card index was to mechanize the mailing of the annual income tax forms. Although each taxpayer was legally obligated to file his annual return by September 30, whether or not he had been requested to do so, by 1951 the practice had become established that the assessing officer would mail a blank tax form to each taxpayer listed within his district. The form contained a request, with the facsimile signature of the assessing officer, that the return be filed by a specified date (generally as fixed by the statute). The addressing of these tax forms was done by hand,

21. M. George Goodrick, *Management in the Government of Israel* (mimeographed report) pp. 93–94; Wayne F. Anderson, *Income Tax Administration in the State of Israel.*

which meant that, at mailing time, large numbers of the staff had to be diverted to this clerical task. Because this had to include also the checking of current addresses — no reliable system having yet been introduced to assure that they were up to date — the average number of forms addressed by a single clerk came to only one hundred or so per day.

The process of mailing tax forms in the early 1950's began in April, for the fiscal year which ended on March 30, and stretched out through October. A taxpayer who had received a form was required to file it within thirty days of receipt. Although those taxpayers who had not received one were required, in any event, to file no later than October 1, this deadline was largely disregarded since, in effect, the continued mailing of forms by the administration through October amounted to an extension of the time for filing by an additional thirty days beyond the mailing date, or as late as November 30.

It became apparent by 1951 that a new system for mailing the annual tax forms had to be instituted. The time-consuming task of hand-addressing disrupted the technical work of the offices, took up needed space, diverted the staff from more important work, and was costly in terms of the overtime pay for the regular staff and for additional temporary clerical help. Furthermore, try as they would, the staff could not complete the task in the seven months of April through October. In 1951, for example, the Tel Aviv office, with some 50,000 of self-employed taxpayers within its jurisdiction, had mailed out only 33,000 tax forms by September 15. Such delays in mailing produced corresponding delays in the filing of returns and in tax collections.

The 1951 recommendations of the United Nations expert were that the final date for filing returns be advanced and that the work of addressing the tax forms be mechanized, so that they could all be mailed during April, that is, within the first month following the end of the fiscal year. Both of these recommendations were adopted, the first by a 1952 amendment to the law. The second, which required considerable study and revision of existing procedures, as well as the acquisition of suitable equipment, took several years to carry into effect.

Some of the most difficult administrative problems were presented by the Tel Aviv assessing office. Since 1948 the Tel Aviv area had experienced an unusually rapid growth in population, as well as in financial and commercial activity. The single assessing office assigned to it was unable to keep pace with this growth. The result was that many potential new taxpayers had not been added to the assessment rolls, and for those already on the rolls the tasks of assessing and collecting the annual tax had fallen far behind. The 1951 delay in distributing the annual returns was only one aspect of the problem of administering the income tax in the Tel Aviv area. The decision was reached to split the area into several new assessing districts, each under a newly appointed assessing officer, with appropriate supporting staff. In fact, the United Nations expert suggested that establishment of smaller offices would make the need for mechanization less urgent, presumably because the hand-addressing of tax forms could then be shared among several offices, each of which would have a shorter list of taxpayers.[22] At about this time, additional assessing offices were established in other parts of the country. Meanwhile, mechanization of the process of addressing and mailing the returns was delayed.

In 1953, in apparent reliance upon the 1952 amendment which imposed the first administrative penalty for failure to file a timely return [23] (1 percent of the tax for the first month of delay and 3 percent for each additional month, with a minimum of IL. 10), and which emphasized the obligation to file a return without regard to whether one had been requested by the assessing officer, a decision was made to forego the mailing of tax forms that year. This proved to be a bad mistake. Only 10 percent of those liable to submit a return did so by the prescribed date. The 1954 Report of the Commission for the Examination of the Methods of Assessing and Collecting Income Tax (Sharef Commission) suggested that although this poor showing may have been due in part to the failure to mail the forms, it was really "the result of an attitude of disdain and general negligence." The Commission recommended:

1) that annual returns be mailed to all taxpayers, even though such mailing was not required by law;

2) that a public explanation program be put into effect before the final filing date; and

3) that a more severe and readily enforceable administrative penalty for nonfiling be enacted in place of the one introduced in 1952.[24]

Meanwhile, the income tax administration had begun to set up a central card index of taxpayers. This was intended as a means of assuring, by cross-checking with other lists — such as the population registry, social insurance accounts, and membership lists of professional and business organizations — that all potential taxpayers were included in

22. I Bloch, pp. 74–75, 81.

23. It was not until 1965 that an administrative penalty was enacted for failure of an employer to file an annual return of wages paid to, and income tax withheld from, his employees. In the fiscal years ending in 1963 and 1964, amounts withheld from wages comprised about one-half of total income tax collections. Until 1965, the only sanction available was a criminal proceeding which, as to standard income tax returns, had already proved to be ineffective more than two years previously. One of the earliest income tax criminal prosecutions had been of this nature. Yet, in spite of threats of prosecution, and a hard-working organization devoted exclusively to checking wage-withholdings, many employers persisted, as late as 1965, in delaying the filing of their annual wage-withholding returns. *Fifteenth Annual Report of the State Comptroller, 1965* (Hebrew).

24. *Sharef Report*, pp. 11–12.

the taxpayer network. Duplicate cards would indicate the existence of duplicate files with respect to the same taxpayer at two or more assessing offices. This was not an infrequent occurrence and a cause of no small amount of confusion, taxpayer complaints, and duplication of effort by assessing officers.

One of the advantages of a central card index of taxpayers was that all income tax forms could be addressed from one central point. It took several years, however, before this was achieved. So long as return forms still had to be addressed by hand, centralizing the list merely meant that the necessary clerical staff would be working at one point rather than another. The breakthrough could come only with mechanization, which involved, initially, placing the necessary data on punched cards and running them through machines which would do the addressing mechanically. This entailed the use of facilities of the special Agency for Office Mechanization which was established about 1952 as part of the Prime Minister's Office. This agency served all of the government departments, on a fee basis, and was ultimately responsible for the introduction of the most advanced techniques for automatic data-processing throughout the government.

At about this time, significant breakthroughs were occurring elsewhere in the world in the development and use of equipment for data storage, retrieval, processing, and analysis. The Israeli authorities, through the Agency for Office Mechanization and the Central Bureau of Statistics, sought to keep pace with the development of the art, constantly upgrading and modifying procedures within the several government departments to conform to the capacities of improved equipment, as it became available.

Sefer Hanishomim — Book of Taxpayers

Some of the difficulties encountered in shifting to a mechanized operation are sharply illustrated by problems encountered by the income tax administration in its efforts to publish *Sefer Hanishomim* (Book of Taxpayers) — an annual listing of taxpayers' names, incomes, and assessments. An amendment to the Income Tax Ordinance had been enacted in 1952, *authorizing* the publication of such lists. Then, in 1955 the law was amended to *require* publication no later than twelve months from the close of each taxable year." [25]

25. Until 1955, the Israel law, following the then British pattern, distinguished between "income year" and "assessment year." Thus, the income tax due for the "assessment year" 1953–54 would be measured, under the rates applicable to the "assessment year," upon the taxpayer's income for the previous year, 1952–53, which was the "income year." This caused numerous complications and misunderstandings, particularly in the application of the "pay-as-you-earn" system, which was based upon current income and current rates. In 1955, the law was amended to introduce the concept of "taxable year," which is identified by the

It had been thought that annual publication of these taxpayers' lists would have the effect of exposing tax evaders to public censure, thereby achieving a higher level of voluntary compliance with the law.[26] With this end in mind, the first issue of *Sefer Hanishomim*, comprising four volumes, was published in 1955 with considerable fanfare.[27] It was an immediate "best seller" and the subject of numerous newspaper articles, mostly critical both of the administration and of listed taxpayers belonging to political parties other than the one sponsoring the particular newspaper.

It did not take long for the inherent weaknesses of the first *Sefer Hanishomim* to be disclosed. First, the books had a number of errors, which caused undeserved embarrassment to some taxpayers and had to be corrected. Second, even though publication had been delayed until 1955, there were many assessments for 1952–53 (the year being reported) which either had not yet been made or which were actively being disputed. The law then in effect required that amendments to the originally published lists also be published. These published amendments were numerous and demonstrated the unreliability of the initial publication. In turn, the administration was exposed to criticism, either for delays or for making exaggerated assessments which later had to be reduced, or to charges of favoritism.

The second issue of *Sefer Hanishomim* was to pertain to the income year 1953–54 and should also have been published in 1955. However, it became apparent that this could not be accomplished, and in 1956 the law was amended, extending the publication date for a year and also providing that the obligation to publish corrections to the lists would apply only when the assessee expressly so requested.

Meanwhile, the revenue and income tax administrations had advanced considerably in perfecting their internal procedures for recording and analyzing statistical data. The economic staffs of both administrations had been expanded, and in May 1956 a landmark was established in the publication of the *First Annual Report on State Revenue* (Hebrew) covering the fiscal periods 1948–49 through 1954–55.

Mechanization of the income tax administration had also been advanced substantially, and the central index of taxpayers, on punchcards, was well on its way to completion. The rate of assessments had

---

calendar year in which the fiscal year begins. Thus, the tax for "taxable year 1954" was computed on the income for the fiscal year beginning April 1, 1954, and ending March 31, 1955.

26. *Sharef Report*, pp. 15, 17–18.

27. The list was divided by districts, under which about 115,000 self-employed taxpayers, companies, and kibbutzim were listed alphabetically, showing place of residence and assessed income. Also included were employees more than 25 percent of whose income came from sources other than wages (1956 *Israel Government Yearbook*, p. 209).

also been stepped up considerably so that, it was assumed, the second issue of *Sefer Hanishomim* would be much more accurate than the first. Unfortunately, this did not prove to be the case.

When the second issue was finally published in August 1956, it proved to be full of errors — in other words, a catastrophe. The machines were not at fault, of course, for they merely repeated the errors which had been fed into them. Errors aside, it was found that delays in effecting assessments for the report year, and further delays in communication between the assessing offices and the central card index staff, rendered *Sefer Hanishomim* undependable. It became apparent that publication of the taxpayers' lists, as originally contemplated, could not be achieved until assessments were more current and until more effective reporting and recording techniques could be introduced. Both of these problems, although subjects of continual concern, were not solved satisfactorily by the time publication of the third issue of *Sefer Hanishomim* was due in 1957.

It was finally recognized that the concept of the issuance of an annual register of taxpayers was unworkable. Furthermore, aside from the amusement which the press and the public were enjoying at the expense of the administration, it was also clear that the project had failed in its main purpose, which was to stir up public indignation against taxpayers who had grossly underreported their incomes. Accordingly, the requirement for the issuance of an annual register of taxpayers was eliminated from the statute.

Use of Computers

The establishment of a central card index, although it eliminated certain operations previously performed by hand (such as addressing of income tax forms, follow-up on filings, and preparation of advance payment booklets), was only a first step in utilizing the potential of mechanization for the assembling of information, the analysis of data, and as an aid in forming decisions. In order to abbreviate procedures in computing the tax, as well as to assure more accurate computation, plans were made in 1960 for the gradual introduction of mechanical computation of assessments. This in turn made it easier for the tax administration to secure data on the characteristics of the taxpaying public as well as the efficiency of the administration itself.

Success in mechanization of the assessment procedures suggested the use of mechanical means to follow up on the payment of the tax. In 1963, procedures were introduced to check on payments, but these were not considered successful, largely because the anticipated results were beyond the ability of the conventional equipment then in use. The desire to achieve a breakthrough was the basis for the decision reached in 1964 by the Directorate of Revenue to acquire a computer and to transfer to it all of the mechanical procedures pertaining not only to the income tax but to the property tax and customs.

In 1964, programming for the conversion of income tax procedures to the computer was begun. A guiding principle was that conversion should not interfere with normal office operations. It was decided that the changeover would be achieved in stages, and that during the conversion period the work would be done both by use of prior procedures and by the new procedures. Although this meant some duplication, it was considered worthwhile in terms of the end result.

The Jerusalem assessing office was the first one in which the new procedures were introduced. In the light of experience gained in that office, the program was revised before it was introduced in the next office, which was the one in Haifa. A special staff was established to feed data into the computer. The members of this staff were removed from their regular work assignments and were shifted to another place of work, so that they could carry out their new assignment without interference. When the work in Haifa was completed, the experience gained in the Jerusalem and Haifa offices was applied in converting the Tel Aviv offices to the computer.

The planning of the procedures for use of and conversion to the computer took several years. Each step was coordinated between the computer staff and the Organization Unit at income tax headquarters. Due consideration was given to the human element and the tendency of the employees to resist change. Before the conversion was actually carried out, training programs were conducted for both senior employees and those who were directly involved in the new procedures. A special unit was also established to supervise the work flow and to maintain liaison with the units which were concerned with the conversion procedures.[28] By 1967, eight income tax offices had been fully converted. These offices covered about two thirds of the companies and self-employed taxpayers. Four of these offices had been adapted to the computer during the previous year. A ninth office was in process and, when its conversion had been completed, three quarters of the population were expected to be covered. It was planned that all offices would be shifted to the computer during fiscal year 1968–69, and this was done.[29]

The computer program for 1968–69 contemplated that it would maintain accounts of all taxpayers with respect to the income tax (including employer and employee withholding accounts), property tax on inventory and equipment, and real property tax (both national and local).[30]

28. Josef Hahn, "Administrative Development in the Income Tax Branch" (Hebrew), 1 *Quarterly Tax Journal* 103, 104–106 (December 1965).

29. Y. Tamir, "1968 — Year of Events and Changes in Taxes" (Hebrew), 18 *Roeh Haheshbon*, pp. 147–148. (January–February 1968).

30. *Annual Report of Revenue Administration, 1967/68–1968/69* (Hebrew), pp. 45–56.

Increasing attention has been given to the statistical, economic, and administrative data which the computer might be able to supply.[31]

Although the computers contributed substantially to improvements in operations, the resources of the original equipment were limited. Consideration therefore had to be given to other equipment which would have to be obtained to meet the projected needs of the administration by the mid-1970's. The ability to plan ahead is limited not only by the anticipated needs and the availability of equipment to satisfy them, but also by the capacity of the administration to adapt itself to the new organization and procedures which more advanced equipment would require.

This effort by the Israeli Government to keep pace with the rapid development of data-processing equipment was accompanied by frustrations in which, no doubt, Israel is not alone. Costly equipment was often found to have become obsolete almost as soon as it was installed. Trained employees had to be continually retrained. Procedures adopted after extended planning had to be scrapped, sometimes before they could be put into effect, in order to make way for other procedures better suited to newer equipment which was on its way. Each change met with resistance from the employees whose task it was to supply and analyze the raw data which had to be fed into the machines.

Conversion to computer use was not achieved easily. At the outset, there was a considerable degree of administrative inertia. Although some officials were reluctant to accept the procedural changes which adaptation to the computer required, there were others, particularly in the upper levels of the administration, whose expectations were perhaps unjustifiably high.[32] Technical difficulties were also experienced.[33] Some of these were the product of faults in the original plan, which were corrected as they became apparent. Others were the product of human error, particularly during the conversion period, when both the previous and the new methods were in simultaneous use.

31. Meir Lahav, "The Computer in Tax Administration" (Hebrew), 3 *Quarterly Tax Journal* 373 (October 1968).
32. Meir Lahav, "Organizational Aspects of Conversion to Computer" (Hebrew), 2 *Quarterly Tax Journal* 97, 99 (January 1967), and "The Conflict between the Computer and the Organization" (Hebrew), 3 *Quarterly Tax Journal* 292 (July 1968).
33. See H. Cohen, "The Citizen and the Computer" (Hebrew), 17 *Roeh Haheshbon* 407 (July–August 1967).

6 / Improvement of Income Tax Assessment Techniques

Problems of Assessment

Israel does not have a self-assessment system. The function of determining the amount of income liable to tax belongs to the Income Tax Assessing Officer. The taxpayer's annual return should supply the assessing officer with the information which will serve as the basis for the assessment. If the return is acceptable, the assessing officer may accept it as filed and make a final assessment accordingly. If, however, it appears that the returned income may be inaccurate, the assessing officer may accept the return provisionally and require payment of the amount of tax due in accordance with the return. This enables the assessing officer to defer to a later date the final determination of the taxpayer's income. If further audit, or information obtained from other sources, establishes that the return is unreliable, the assessing officer may make what is termed a "best judgment" assessment. He may do the same if no return was filed if he is of the opinion that the affected person is liable to tax (sec. 45, Income Tax Ordinance).[1]

Resolution of the problem of how to make annual assessments for an ever-growing number of income taxpayers proceeded along several fronts. Changes in the rate structure as well as in the filing requirements relieved many marginal income-earners from the obligation of filing returns. Improvements in the withholding-at-source procedures, as well as elimination in 1958 of the imputed income attributed to use of a residence by its owner, enabled the Minister of Finance to exempt large numbers from the filing requirements. The toughest part of the problem was how to apply the assessing officer's "best judgment" most accurately in situations where it was required. This was tied to an even more important problem — how to induce taxpayers to file returns which were sufficiently reliable so that the number of best judgment assessments could be largely reduced.

The principal alternatives available to the assessing officer are either to base his assessment on the return as filed or to make an assessment in accordance with his best judgment. To choose between these alternatives, the assessing officer must make an initial judgment — whether the return is sufficiently reliable to justify its acceptance. The situation in the early 1950's was such that hardly any returns could be accepted as

1. Unless otherwise indicated, references to the Income Tax Ordinance are to the 1962 revised version, as amended.

filed. Even the returns of employees, whose wages were subject to deduction of tax at the source, were suspect. And, to make matters worse, many potential taxpayers had completely neglected to file returns — some for years. Best judgment assessments, in large numbers, were therefore a matter of necessity.

Some of the dimensions of the assessment problems facing the income tax administration in the mid-1950's can be seen by comparing the number of active taxpayers' files on hand when the State of Israel was established and at the end of the fiscal year 1952–1953. In 1948 the number of active income tax files were as follows: companies — 3,800, self-employed individuals — 22,700, wage-earners — 62,000. By 1952–53 the number of files had risen to 9,000, 121,000, and 222,000, respectively.

The sharp rise in the number of taxpayers from 1948 until 1953 (from 88,500 to 352,000) was the product of several factors, which differed somewhat with respect to each of the three main groups of taxpayers — companies, self-employed, and wage-earners. The assessment problems presented by each of these groups were to some extent related to the reasons for the respective increases in their numbers. Accordingly, it will be useful to examine some characteristics of each of these groups.

Companies

Israel company law divides companies (corporations) into two main classes — public companies and private companies. Public companies are generally (considering Israeli conditions) large enterprises whose shares are fairly widely distributed. Private companies, on the other hand, have by definition five or less shareholders and, in many instances, are for practical purposes either incorporated sole proprietorships or partnerships. Many of the latter, which had been organized in the early years of the State, did not really conduct any business, having been formed in many instances as vehicles for holding title to land. Others had been formed to avoid the sharp increase in individual tax rates as compared with the relatively low company rates.

Organization of a company is a matter of public record; companies are required to be officially registered. Unlike self-employed taxpayers and wage-earners, therefore, no real difficulty was encountered in identifying and sweeping companies into the "tax network." The main problem in respect of companies was in sorting out the active from the inactive files and in effecting procedures for the assessment of those that were active. Some of the latter companies were, of course, already identified and being dealt with from the outset. But, as the economy expanded, new companies came into existence, small companies grew, and the problems of auditing company accounts changed in quality. How these problems were dealt with will be described later in this chapter.

Self-employed Individuals

The self-employed group includes mainly professionals, contractors, brokers, farmers, shopkeepers, artisans, and tradesmen, operating as sole proprietors or as members of partnerships. The large increase in their number (as reflected by open income tax files) from 1948 to 1953 is due to several causes. Foremost among these is the fact that sharp increases in income tax rates, coupled with inflation, had drastically widened the income tax base, so that many self-employed whose earnings had been free of tax in 1948 had become subject to tax before 1953. It also appears that there were some self-employed individuals (how many cannot be accurately ascertained) who had successfully evaded inclusion in the mandatory tax lists, even though they may have then been subject to tax. Subsequent to the creation of the State, the ranks of the taxable self-employed were also swelled by population growth (through immigration) and by expansion of the economy, which created more opportunities for individual entrepreneurs.

Identification of self-employed individuals who might be subject to tax, but for whom active files had not yet been opened, was a difficult task, to which the administration vigorously addressed itself from about 1951 onward. The problem of how to assess them, once they had been identified, was less easily solved. Mass assessment methods, utilized principally in 1952 through 1955, proved undesirable. Some of the most significant improvements in assessment techniques took place in respect of the self-employed.

Wage-earners

From its inception in 1941 the Income Tax Ordinance provided for the withholding of income tax at the source from wages, thus preceding by several years introduction of this concept in the United States. This method of collection is relatively foolproof, except to the extent that an employer and employee might conspire to eliminate a particular employee from the payroll or to under-report (by omission or false entry) the amount of wages paid. Under Israeli conditions, such conspiracy was difficult, particularly after the National Insurance program, which was also tied to wages, came into effect in 1955. Another continuing problem was the tendency of some employers to delay prompt payment to the Treasury of amounts withheld from employees' wages, meanwhile using the funds for their own purposes.

Even assuming that all wage-earners were on the tax rolls, several problems had to be solved. These were (a) how to assure that the tax was properly withheld and promptly paid over by the employer; and (b) how to achieve the required annual assessment of each wage-earner, taking into account that in many cases the withholding at the source might not produce the correct amount of tax, either because of additional deductions to which the employee might be entitled (so that a tax refund might be due), or because of additional income (such as from part-time activities outside of his regular employment) which had not been subject to withholding but which was nevertheless assessable. Unlike the self-employed, many of whom had to be sought out by the authorities, most wage-earners automatically entered the assessment rolls by inclusion in their employers' withholding reports. The 1953 increase, therefore, is more a reflection of increased employment and wages than of increased administration effort. The problems of how to deal with the large number of wage-earners were solved — although it took some time — by changes in the law, by improvement of withholding and reporting requirements, and by internal reorganization of the income tax administration.

Development of Assessment Procedures

Israeli law and practice generally require that an assessment be made for each taxpayer for each taxable year, with certain exceptions recently enacted. This does not necessarily mean that the assessment must be made annually. In fact, backlogs of unmade assessments had accumulated to such an extent during 1948 through 1954 that, in spite of vigorous steps which were later taken to place assessments on a current basis, a backlog (although for more recent years and in smaller dimensions) still remains.

Efforts to clean up these backlogs sometimes sacrificed quality for quantity. This was particularly the case from 1952 to 1954 and, to a lesser extent, for a few years thereafter. However, as a staff of technically qualified personnel developed, coupled with growth of tax sophistication among the taxpaying public, the administration began to achieve a satisfactory output level both in terms of quality and quantity of assessments. This process took at least ten years, from about 1955 to 1965. Slow though improvement may have been, it was the product of administrative policy decisions made principally in 1954 and 1955.

Assessment of Companies

Companies are by law required to keep books of account, and they must attach to their annual income tax returns a balance sheet and profit and loss statement, certified by a public accountant (sec. 131). Although the standards maintained by the accounting profession in Israel are quite high, the number of certified public accountants has been limited. Until 1948, about the only way in which one could have qualified as a certified public accountant in Palestine was to qualify abroad, and then be admitted to practice by reciprocity.

With the growth of Israeli industry in recent years, the demand for qualified accountants has outpaced the supply. In part, the supply has been increased by the institution of local courses in accounting and by immigration of qualified accountants from abroad.[2]

However, given increased demand for accountants, there had been a tendency on the part of some members of the profession to spread their work rather thin, with the result that a thorough audit by the income tax authorities would sometimes disclose errors or irregularities in accounts which one might have expected to be uncovered by the taxpayer's accountant had he gone into the accounts in greater detail.[3] A good many audit reports, for a time, were so qualified in the accountants' certificates as to deprive them of any substantial degree of reliability.[4] When this became apparent to the income tax authorities, it also became evident that independent administrative audits would have to be made to assure that corporate incomes would be properly assessed.[5]

2. For a survey of the development of the accounting profession, see Eliezer Bavli, "Development of the Accounting Association in Israel" (Hebrew), 15 *Roeh Haheshbon* 354 (September–October 1965). The Accounting Society had about 60 members in 1949, 244 by the end of 1958, and 547 by the end of 1964 (ibid., pp. 355, 358). In recent years, about 100 additional certified public accountants have joined the profession annually. Remarks of S. Rovel, president of Association of Certified Public Accountants, 76 *Roeh Haheshbon* 52 (November–December 1966).

3. The question of the possible ethical conflicts between public responsibilities of the certified public accountant on the one hand, and loyalty to his clients on the other, had been the subject of much discussion among members of the profession. See, e.g., the views expressed by various participants in the 35th Congress (1966) of the Association of Certified Public Accountants in Israel, 16 *Roeh Haheshbon*, 58 (Lapidot), 84, 96 (Tamir), 88 (Stern), 89–90 (Shemer), 93–94 (Porat) (November–December 1966). The issue came into even sharper focus after the enactment in August 1967 of the Income Tax (Amended Declarations) Law, which permitted the reporting, without penalty, of previously unreported income. See Chapter 8, and M. Kane, "The 'Law' and the Accountant" (Hebrew), 17 *Roeh Haheshbon*, 465 (September–October 1967).

4. See Dan Bavli, "Accountants' Certificates for Specific Purposes" (Hebrew), 18 *Roeh Haheshbon* 152, at 158 (January–February 1968). Since the 1963 tax year, the law has specifically required that company income tax returns be certified by a qualified auditor and that the accounts be adjusted to conform with tax principles (sec. 131 [b], I.T.O.). Also, the assessing officer may require the auditor to report on the extent and results of his audit in connection with his preparation of the company's return (sec. 131 [B], I.T.O.). These provisions were enacted only after a sharp dispute between the tax authorities and the representatives of the accounting profession.

5. See remarks of then Income Tax Commissioner A. Givoni in 10 *Roeh Haheshbon* 136–137 (April–June 1960), explaining why the authorities were fre-

Largely as a result of the improvements in income tax audit procedures, the demand for accountants rose sharply and steps were taken to
enable qualified individuals to obtain training and certification in Israel.
Some obtained their training in auditing as employees of the income tax
administration, some as apprentices to accounting firms, and some in
accounting courses given originally at the Tel Aviv College of Law and
Economics (now incorporated into Tel Aviv University). Later, courses
in business administration (including accounting) were instituted at the
Hebrew University, Jerusalem, in 1957, with the assistance of the
United States Technical Operations Mission to Israel.

Administrative Need for Audit Skills

If qualified auditors in the early years were in short supply in private
industry, they were in even shorter supply in government. And since
companies, unlike the self-employed, were all required to keep books
of account, the authorities could not resort to empirical methods of
assessment as substitutes for technical audits. The administrative problem at all times, with respect to the assessment of companies, was how
to recruit, train, and retain manpower with a level of technical competence at least equal to that of the professionals available to outside
industry.

The most serious problems in the assessment of companies were
encountered in the Tel Aviv area. Jerusalem, even before the establishment of the State, had not been an important industrial center and,
after the boundaries of the State had been established in 1948, it was
so isolated from normal trade channels that commerce and industry
there withered; even while they were growing in other parts of the
country. On the other hand, when Jerusalem became the seat of government, its population growth reflected increased employment by the
government and other nonprofit institutions, such as the Jewish Agency,
the Hebrew University, and the Hadassah Medical Organization. The
number of taxpayers assigned to the Jerusalem office increased, but
their presence was reflected in the wage-earners and self-employed
(mostly services and small shopkeepers) categories. Even with a limited supply of auditors, therefore, the Jerusalem assessing office was
able to keep up with the task of auditing the relatively few companies
within its jurisdiction, with an occasional assist from the office of the
Income Tax Commissioner, which was also located in Jerusalem.

Haifa, on the other hand, had been an important industrial center
for years and continued to be so after establishment of the State. Even
though the Haifa assessing office also experienced a shortage of techni-

quently unable to rely upon the work of private accountants. See also *Fifth Annual Report of the State Comptroller, 1953/54* (Hebrew), 116–117.

cally qualified personnel, with a resulting diminution in both quality and quantity of company assessments, it was, relatively, a strong office. Accordingly, like Jerusalem, it was not thought to present an emergency situation.

Tel Aviv was much different. It had shot ahead of the rest of the country in population growth and had largely supplanted both Jerusalem and Haifa as the center of finance, commerce, industry, and tourism. Such remaining skilled income tax personnel as had not been attracted away by the greater financial and career opportunities outside of government service had been spread extremely thin by reassignment to newly established offices into which the former single assessment office for the Tel Aviv district had been divided. The result was that the assessing offices in the Tel Aviv area were unable to keep up with the task of assessing the companies assigned to them. And, after unsuccessful efforts had been made to find qualified auditors within government willing to accept assignment, even on a temporary basis, to these offices, it was concluded that other solutions had to be found.

The Central Audit Section (1953–54)

The need for reconcentrating available auditing skills was quickly recognized, and in 1953 and 1954 some of the auditors (officially entitled "inspectors") were transferred back to a central Audit Section whose task was to conduct audits of company files on behalf of the several assessing offices in the Tel Aviv area. The initial conception, it appears, was that this Audit Section would be a temporary expedient, to be used until additional skilled auditors could be trained and made available. Then each assessing office might be supplied with sufficient auditors of its own to handle company audits. Consistent with a plan to allocate taxpayers' files strictly on a geographic basis, responsibility for making company assessments remained with the local assessing office, even though the audit which was to serve as the foundation for the assessment would be made by the central Audit Section, which functioned independently of any one assessing office.

It did not take long to discover that this arrangement would have to be substantially improved upon. Its principal weakness lay in the split of authority, by which the Audit Section might lose contact with a case before the critical assessment stage. It was feared that an assessing officer, being under pressure from Jerusalem to increase collections, might abandon or compromise some of the technical issues raised by the Audit Section in order to reach a quick settlement with the taxpayer. Thus, much of the work of the Audit Section might go for naught. Furthermore, since it was up to the assessing officer to decide whether or not a company file should be referred to the Audit Section, many of the "easier" files were assessed without reference to the Audit Section

— the criterion often being the willingness of the company to agree quickly to a proposed assessment, without regard for its technical validity. The most vulnerable taxpayers were the ones most willing to settle quickly, before being subjected to detailed audit. Thus, the procedure was weak at both ends: (a) since there were no objective criteria for reference of cases to the Audit Section, many files were assessed without receiving the attention they required; and (b) return of the case to the local assessing officer after audit by the Audit Section meant loss of control over final disposition of the case in accordance with the results of the audit.

The Assessing Office for Large Enterprises (Pashmag)

The division of the Tel Aviv region into several assessing offices had been based upon the assumption that each office would be a self-contained entity, charged with and capable of handling all taxpayers within its geographic boundaries. By the fall of 1954 it had become apparent that this geographic approach would not work out with respect to companies, even with the staff assistance of the Audit Section. Audit personnel could not be developed in sufficient numbers to staff each of the assessing offices, as had been originally hoped; while experience with the Audit Section had already demonstrated that company audits could be conducted more consistently, efficiently, and economically by concentrating auditing skills in a central office. Accordingly, it was decided to establish for the Tel Aviv region a specialized assessing office to deal exclusively with the more difficult cases. This office, which was implemented in early 1955, took over from the other assessing offices in the region full responsibility for all taxpayers' files assigned to it. Criteria for selection of the more difficult files were established, taking into account such factors as the nature of the taxpayer's business, the type of business organization, the number of employees, annual turnover, and other such objective factors for identifying the more difficult cases. Specifically included at the beginning were financial institutions, large building contractors, enterprises with annual turnovers of 1/4 million Israel pounds and above, enterprises with over 30 employees, and large hotels.[6] Other categories were added later. These files were then transferred to the new office. The officer in charge of this new office was given the title of "Assessing Officer for Large Enterprises" and the office has come to be known as the "Pashmag," this being the acronym derived from the Hebrew title — *Pakid Shuma le'Mifalim G'dolim*.

The same principle of concentrating responsibility for the audit and assessment of the most difficult files was applied in the northern section of the country as well as in Jerusalem, although the pattern was different.

6. First Annual Report on State Revenue (*Din v'Heshbon Rishon al Hakhnasot ha'Medina*) 1948/49–1954/55, pp. 74–75.

In the north, industry and commerce remained largely concentrated in the Haifa area. The Haifa assessing office had been able to maintain a strong cadre of auditors and, unlike Tel Aviv, growth conditions had not been such as to require fragmentation of the Haifa office. And, although experience in Tel Aviv had indicated the desirability of concentrating the more difficult files in an independent assessing office, this was not considered either necessary or desirable for the northern districts. Instead, the assessing officer for Haifa was given the additional function of serving as the Assessing Officer for Large Enterprises for all of the northern districts, and all of the more difficult files in those districts were reassigned to the Haifa office. Jerusalem, in turn, continued to be responsible for the difficult files which were already within its jurisdiction, as its staff was considered both large and competent enough to deal with these, as well as with any additional enterprises which economic development of the Jerusalem district might produce.

Subsequent to the establishment of the Tel Aviv Assessing Office for Large Enterprises (and its Haifa and Jerusalem counterparts), recruitment and training procedures were instituted to supply the offices with the required auditing personnel. Over the years, their staffs were built up, both through retraining of existing personnel and through training of newly engaged and qualified personnel. The success of these specialized offices in substantially eliminating the backlog of unassessed company returns while maintaining high quality standards of assessment has indicated that the strict geographic allocation of taxpayers to assessing offices should be modified when dealing with taxpayers whose assessment problems require the application of specialized skills or techniques.

In summary, audits and assessments of companies depended upon the availability of technical personnel, qualified to audit the books and accounts which companies were required to maintain. In the absence of fraud (which called for specialized techniques) such audits, although technically difficult, nevertheless involved the application of standard audit procedures. With the recognition that the supply of sufficiently skilled personnel could be expected to remain short, the solution arrived at was to concentrate the skills within three specialized groups, in Tel Aviv, Haifa, and Jerusalem, thereby relieving the other assessing offices of the responsibility for assessing the more difficult cases, for which they were not and could not be adequately staffed.

Assessment of Self-employed Individuals

Self-employed taxpayers have continually been the most difficult group to deal with. Conversely, some of the most interesting administrative achievements have taken place in the development of techniques, discussed below, for assessment of the self-employed.

Empirical Assessment Techniques

It will be recalled that the number of active income tax files of self-employed individuals had increased from 22,760 as of May 15, 1948, to 121,516 as of March 31, 1953, or an increase of almost 100,000 known taxpayers in this class in five years. This increase produced, in turn, a massive backlog of assessments which could not be based upon the taxpayers' annual returns but in many instances required the exercise of the assessing officers' best judgment. The unfortunate fact was that many of these returns were unreliable. And, unlike companies, whose audits could at least take as a starting point the books and records which the taxpayers were required to maintain, self-employed individuals were not then subject to any such requirement. Consequently, given many returns which were unacceptable on their face, the problem in 1952 and 1953 was how to arrive at assessments which were more or less realistic. This problem was compounded by the fact that the income tax administration was badly understaffed, new recruits were largely unskilled, and mass assessment procedures had not yet been devised.

Lacking any better guides, many of the best judgment assessments made in 1952 and 1953 amounted to little more than "best guesses." Few of these were accepted by the affected taxpayers without protest and, as a result, the administrative review process became clogged with objections awaiting disposition. Taxpayer resistance to these often arbitrary assessments also produced pressures, which reached explosive proportions by 1954. Even proposed assessments which came close to being accurate were not accepted without protest, for it had become common knowledge among the taxpaying public that even these could be negotiated downward. Some objective criteria had to be devised whereby, even in the absence of books and records, assessments could be arrived at which were demonstrably consistent with the taxpayers' circumstances in the particular taxable year.

(1) "Tahshivim" — standard assessment guides

In 1954 the Income Tax Commissioner's office began a program of research regarding income and expenditure levels in specific businesses and agricultural branches. Based on this research, standard assessment guides — *tahshivim* [7] — were prepared, giving for specific occupations averages of gross incomes, expenditures, and net incomes per production unit or income-earner. These varied in accordance with the locale and other factors capable of objective measurement.

7. The Hebrew term *tahshiv* (pl. *tahshivim*) is difficult to translate literally into English. A literal translation might be "calculator," which does not accurately convey the sense intended. Accordingly, "standard assessment guide," a freer but more meaningful term, has been used.

Some of the earliest *tahshivim* were prepared for use in assessing incomes of farmers engaged in various agricultural activities. These *tahshivim* were prepared by experts in the Agricultural Branch at income tax headquarters. They helped in introducing uniformity in the assessment of farmers, who are inclined otherwise to be resentful of authority and very difficult to assess. The *tahshiv* technique, as applied to farmers, was also a great help in bringing the Arab farmers into the tax network on a fair and scientific basis.

Tahshivim had also been prepared by 1955 for various types of food producers, such as bakeries, noodle makers, ice plants; for various retail establishments, such as grocers, greengrocers, and fishmongers; for craftsmen, such as carpenters, plumbers, locksmiths, electricians, painters, plasterers, and building subcontractors; for service businesses, such as hotels, automatic laundries, and pharmacies; for transport, such as taxis. In agriculture, *tahshivim* of expenditures had been prepared for orange growers, vintners, vegetable growers, dairies, and poultry raisers.

The *tahshiv* of expenditures for orange groves, for example, specified the estimated number of work-days per *dunam* (approximately one-quarter acre) of grove, the wage per work-day, and the approximate annual wage cost per *dunam*. Also estimated were sums expended for irrigation, fertilizers, sprays, cultivation, tools, management and supervision, taxes, watchmen, depreciation, and other relevant factors. The standard grove for which these estimates were made was one producing between 60 and 90 crates of fruit per *dunam*, with guides for making adjustments in accordance with actual production.

As to groceries, since in 1955 rationing was still in effect, the annual estimated turnover was based upon the number of customers registered at the shop for rationing purposes; the estimated annual receipts per customer being based, in turn, upon the location of the shop, the numbers of employees, and the quality of the goods in the inventory. The gross profit percentage was set at between 13 percent and 15 percent of turnover, taking into account the balance between rationed and free goods. From this, allowable deductions were taken into account.

At first the *tahshivim* tended to be inflexible, both in their structure and in their application by the income tax inspectors. Rather soon, however, a staff of economists was organized at headquarters to gather scientific data for the construction of the *tahshivim*.

During the period that the *tahshiv* techniques were being developed, there was also imposed upon designated groups of self-employed individuals the obligation to keep books. The *tahshivim* therefore concentrated upon those groups of taxpayers who were not required to do so. Thus the *tahshivim* may be considered as a transitional technique which can be expected to diminish in use as reliable bookkeeping becomes more widespread.[8] Meanwhile, the *tahshivim* assure a greater degree of objectivity of assessment and conserve manpower. They also tend to diminish disputes between taxpayers and the authorities, for the advisory committees and the reviewing courts give greater weight to assessments based upon *tahshivim*.

Since the *tahshiv* is of necessity based upon averages, it can serve only as a *guide* to determine the taxable income of the individual taxpayer. Otherwise, it becomes a Procrustean bed which, if applied blindly, produces overpayments of tax by some and underpayments by others. This was understood by the Commissioner's office, which sought to impress upon the inspectors and assessing officers that the *tahshiv* was merely a presumptive method, and that the presumptions upon which it was based were subject to rebuttal by the taxpayer or the inspector, if able to present the actual facts. Nevertheless the tendency of the inspectors, particularly in the early years of the use of *tahshivim*, was to rely upon them heavily. Later, as the *tahshivim*, through improvement of the techniques for their production, became more sophisticated and accurate, corresponding improvements in the technical skills of the inspectorate, as well as in the compliance of the taxpaying public, brought about a higher degree of personalized application of the *tahshiv* to the particular taxpayer.

In selecting business groups for which *tahshivim* should be prepared, emphasis was placed upon those whose members were not obliged to keep books. This did not necessarily mean that none of them did, in fact, keep books; and some interesting problems arose where there was a conflict between taxable income as determined from the taxpayer's books and from the *tahshiv*. Some of the *tahshivim* had been prepared with the cooperation of representatives of the particular line of business and, when possible, their agreement to the *tahshiv* had been obtained.[9] This implied (and in actual practice, particularly in the early days of the use of the *tahshiv* became almost a mandate) that all members of the industry would be assessed upon the basis of the *tahshiv*. As might be expected, the industry representatives were less interested in scientific accuracy than they were in minimizing taxes for themselves and for other members of their group. The result, in some instances, was that these sources emphasized data relating to the marginal members of the group rather than the more efficient ones. By the same token, the

8. The essential conflict between the bookkeeping requirements and reliance upon *tahshivim* was pointed out by members of the accounting profession quite early in the game. See, e.g., Eliezer Turner, "The Standard Assessment Guides for Income Tax Purposes" (Hebrew), 6 *Roeh Haheshbon 5* (October–December 1955). See also Amotz Morag, "Some Economic Aspects of Two Administrative Methods of Estimating Taxable Income," 10 *National Tax Journal* 176, 181, n. 19 (no. 2, June 1957).

9. Naftali Birkenfeld, "Bookkeeping for Income Tax Purposes," (Hebrew) 2 *Quarterly Tax Journal*, 189, 191 (April 1967).

willingness of the tax authorities to accept data supplied by business groups had the effect of encouraging the formation of business organizations whose almost exclusive purpose was to negotiate a favorable *tahshiv* for the members of their group. Yet, given the circumstances at the time (about 1954–55), a *tahshiv* so negotiated, inaccurate though it might have been, was a sounder basis for assessment than the guessing game which had been practiced before. Greater accuracy, and less reliance upon negotiation with taxpayers' representatives, came with the formation by the Treasury of its own group of economists and with their development of expertise in the gathering of relevant business data.

Since preparation of a *tahshiv* involves a considerable degree of economic research into the characteristics of the particular business, only a few (five or six) can be prepared each year. In choosing a line of business for which a *tahshiv* should be prepared, principal concern is with the saving in administrative manpower which the availability of a *tahshiv* would make possible. Considering that there are now about 150,000 self-employed, low-income, taxpayers who are still not required to keep books, a *tahshiv* would generally be directed to a business branch which comprises several thousand such taxpayers. Another criterion for selection of a business branch for preparation of a *tahshiv* might be whether there is thought to be an unusual tendency for tax evasion among the members of the branch.

Attention is also given to new lines of business. For example, the development of the economy and the relaxation of controls upon the import of private automobiles resulted in a sudden increase in the number of driver-training schools. This required, in 1965, the preparation of a *tahshiv* for driving schools, the central element of which was the number of students taught to drive during the year. This, in turn, could be checked against the official records of drivers' licenses issued.[10] Another example of a new line of business for which a *tahshiv* was required, was salons for custom-made shoes. This business, like driving schools, was an offshoot of the development of a comfortable middle class which could indulge in luxuries. Initially, the key for the *tahshiv* for shoe salons was the number of cobblers employed, since the number of pairs of quality shoes which could be produced by hand by a single cobbler could be estimated with some degree of accuracy. The number of cobblers could, in turn, be checked against the wage records which each employer is required to maintain for tax purposes.

Once a *tahshiv* has been prepared for a particular business, it is kept up to date so as to be applicable in subsequent years. This involves a careful review of the changing characteristics of the business for each year. Sometimes taxpayers may vary their patterns of operation in order

10. This *tahshiv* was not accepted without protest by the affected taxpayers, who staged a "drive in" at the Finance Ministry, blocking traffic for hours.

to avoid the impact of a *tahshiv*. For example, in the case of shoe salons it was found that some proprietors, becoming aware that their incomes were being estimated for tax purposes on the basis of the number of cobblers employed, discharged their cobblers and sent their work out to independent contractors (frequently their former employees set up in another location). This required modification of the *tahshiv* to provide other guides for estimating income of salons resorting to this device.

Another example of modification of business methods in an effort to avoid the impact of a *tahshiv* occurred with respect to commercial laundries. The *tahshiv* for this business was based upon the quantities of water and electricity consumed. These quantities could be accurately determined by meter readings, which were in turn the basis for the charges for these items. It was determined, for purposes of the *tahshiv*, how much water and electricity was consumed, on the average, for each load of laundry handled by a machine. Soap consumption was also taken into account. It was later found that when laundry operators became aware of the criteria employed in assessing their incomes they modified their machines so as to use less electricity (as by eliminating heating of the water to high temperatures), or less water (as by recycling the water). The quantity of soap was also reduced by using more efficient detergents.

In a sense, the existence of the *tahshiv* stimulated changes in business methods but the latter, in turn, required modification of the *tahshiv* to assure accurate application of the criteria upon which it was based. Thus, annual updating of existing *tahshivim* by studying the changing characteristics of the businesses to which they related is essential to assure accurate assessments.

A *tahshiv* may also become obsolete as a result of changing economic conditions. This happened in the case of automatic, customer-operated, laundry machines. About 1953–54, a number of these coin-operated machines were imported. However, by about 1962 so many locally produced washing machines had been marketed for household use that many proprietors of coin-operated laundries had gone out of business. As a result, updating of the *tahshiv* for this line of business was discontinued.

By 1965 a fairly standard technique had been developed for the preparation of a *tahshiv*. One of the staff of economists in the revenue administration would be assigned to make a study of a number of files of taxpayers in the particular line of business. From these he would select a sampling of files which appeared to be characteristic and he would then visit the individual taxpayers to familiarize himself with the details of the business. The income tax authorities might be consulted in the choice of the samples. An effort would be made to select taxpayers who in fact kept books, although they were not required to do so (otherwise a *tahshiv* would be inappropriate). The purpose of the analysis is to identify one or more objective factors which have a direct relation to the level of income which a particular operator might realize. A draft *tahshiv* is then prepared for testing and criticism by income tax officials and other economists on the staff. After the draft is considered accurate and workable, it is submitted to the trade organization of businessmen in the particular branch for analysis and criticism. This involves a process of negotiation, in which the business representatives generally seek to minimize the impact of the *tahshiv* upon their members by attempting to demonstrate that industry averages are lower than those determined by the staff economist.

When this procedure was first followed, the administration was more inclined to adjust its figures downward, in order to obtain industry-wide acceptance of the *tahshiv*. This tendency produced some undesirable side effects, resulting in a *tahshiv* which would be more accurate for the marginal than for the efficient producer. It also created problems later for the more efficient producers who, having been underassessed, were hard put to it to explain increases in their personal net worths attributable to income actually earned but not taxed because of inaccuracies in the *tahshiv*.[11] These inaccuracies, which were beneficial to the efficient producer, had another undesirable side effect: Many of them did, in fact, keep books, although not required to do so; but they would not present them to the tax inspector, preferring to be assessed on the basis of the *tahshiv* which would impose a lower income assessment than the books would have shown.

Although negotiation of a *tahshiv* with industry representatives might produce concessions by the tax authorities — and resulting inaccuracies — it was considered, when the *tahshiv* procedure was first introduced, that the price in reduced revenues was worth paying in order to obtain acceptance of the *tahshiv* as a basis for assessment. Members of a trade whose representatives had approved the *tahshiv* would generally accept the assessment, instead of quibbling over each item. Of course, acceptance of the *tahshiv* by the industry has no binding effect upon the individual taxpayer, but if the trade organization has accepted it, it is more likely to be accepted by the individual. Additionally, the *tahshiv* is generally constructed so as to give the inspector some leeway to adjust for individual differences within ranges supplied by the *tahshiv*.

In recent years there has been less inclination on the part of the authorities to depart from economic assumptions established by the staff economists solely to obtain acceptance of the *tahshiv* by trade representa-

11. After passage of the Income Tax (Amended Declarations) Law of 1967, the Income Tax Commissioner expressed the opinion that such increases should be declared and tax paid thereon. This view was questioned by N. Gruenbaum in a letter to the editor in 17 *Roeh Haheshbon,* 534 (September–October 1967).

tives. This firming up is the product both of refinements in the methods of devising *tahshivim*, assuring their greater accuracy, and the growing tendency of reviewing tribunals (public committees and the courts) to affirm best judgment assessments based upon a *tahshiv*, particularly in the absence of acceptable records maintained by the taxpayer.

When a new *tahshiv* has been prepared, inspectors' meetings are held in the principal cities to explain its use. Inspectors attending are those who are charged with assessing taxpayers in the particular occupation covered by the *tahshiv*. Sometimes, also, one of the economists may for a time work along with an inspector to observe how the *tahshiv* actually functions. This may serve as the basis for further explanation or modification of the *tahshiv*.

The work to be done in preparing *tahshivim* and updating of those already in use is planned a year in advance by the Economic Unit at income tax headquarters. For example, the Work Program of the Income and Property Tax Branch for the fiscal year 1968–69 shows that five new *tahshivim* were planned for that year, and that thirteen were to be updated. The new ones were to cover nightclubs, public halls, garages for motorbikes, food stands, and dressmaking salons. Among those to be updated were pharmacies, florist shops, hotels, cafés, furniture shops, and others. Each of these was to be prepared in accordance with a time schedule, set out in the Work Program. It was also announced that several days would be devoted to training inspectors in the use of the *tahshivim* for taxable years 1966 and 1967.

(2) Net worth and expenditures methods

Even before the development of the *tahshivim*, which supply relatively accurate standards, taxpayers' apparent wealth and level of expenditures were used as a basis for estimating annual incomes. Until about 1955, when substantial improvements in methods of assessment began to be introduced (and even thereafter), many assessments of self-employed taxpayers had to be made on the basis of guesswork. To some extent a guess could be founded upon impressions of a taxpayer's level of wealth or expenditures. At the outset, however, this could hardly be described as a method, because the data were unreliable and the administration had not developed procedures for guiding the inspectors in the use of such data as might be available. However, in more recent years the assessing officers, relying upon statutory authority permitting them to require taxpayers to list their assets, have been able to obtain more reliable data regarding the assets and level of expenditures of a number of taxpayers. These data have frequently been used as a basis for assessment and, less frequently, as part of the evidence in criminal cases.

The net worth method of estimating income is based upon the premise that the increase in a person's net worth over a given period, adjusted for expenditures during the period and for non-income receipts (such as loans, gifts, or inheritances), should approximate the taxpayer's gross income during the period.[12] The expenditures method is based upon the premise that an individual does not normally spend beyond his income, and if he consistently does so he either has failed to report some of his income or should be able to furnish some valid explanation as to the source of the excess funds.

In its simplest form, the expenditures method is merely an extension of the impression received by the tax inspector from the standard of living maintained by the taxpayer and his family — the home, its furnishings, the food they eat, their clothing, the car, their social standing, and other such indices of the level of expenditures. Until more sophisticated methods of assessment came into use, a good many assessments in Israel were based on hardly more than the premise that one who appeared to be living well must have a good income. It was no secret that such factors were taken into account, and, it has been said, some taxpayers would deliberately put on their most ragged clothing before visiting the income tax office to try to bargain down an assessment.

To back up assessments derived from impressions of the level of expenditures maintained by taxpayers, the assessing officers sought to obtain statements from taxpayers with regard to their personal holdings. Even during mandatory days, such statements were occasionally submitted by taxpayers who had been requested to do so under the broad authority of the assessing officer to require the submission of information in support of the income reported in the annual return. Such requests were infrequent, however, and even when a specific request was made taxpayers were reluctant to supply information as to their wealth. Many statements of net worth submitted to the mandatory authorities were undoubtedly unreliable.

In 1949 a provision was enacted expressly authorizing the assessing officers to demand a statement of the assets of the taxpayer, his wife, and children dependent upon him for support.[13] In 1953, under this authority, all wage-earners were requested to add to their annual returns a description of any real property belonging to them. The purpose of this request, it appears, was to obtain information upon which to base an assessment of the imputed income, taxable (until 1968) under Israeli law, attributable to the rental value of the taxpayer's residence, if owned by him. This was, accordingly, only a limited use of the authority to require statements of net worth. It served, however, as the introduction to

12. See Discussion Draft, *Manual of Income Tax Administration*, pp. 300–305 (mimeographed), Harvard Law School, International Program in Taxation (New York: United Nations, 1967), for details of net worth method. See also A. Witkon and I. Neeman, *Dinei Misim* pp. 248–250.

13. Section 45, Income Tax Ordinance, 1947, now sec. 135 (1), new version.

a later request, addressed to all self-employed taxpayers, that they complete a special net worth form listing real property, bank accounts, cash, and other assets not necessarily related to their income-producing activities. These reports were to be submitted with the annual returns for the fiscal year ending March 31, 1954.

This 1954 request for the submission of net worth statements met with considerable resistance from taxpayers and may have been partly responsible both for delays in the filing of income tax returns by many taxpayers and for outright refusals by others to submit the requested net worth reports. Additionally, many taxpayers took advantage of ambiguities in the instructions in the net worth form and deliberately omitted assets which were not clearly specified.

Aside from the "attitude of disdain and general negligence" [14] which was then current among the taxpaying public, there was another reason for this reluctance to supply the authorities with accurate information as to one's assets. Only a short time before, the public had been subjected to a capital levy in the form of a compulsory loan and it was understandably feared that disclosure of all of one's assets (some of which may have escaped the compulsory loan) might serve as the foundation for another such capital levy. This fear was not alleviated by official assurances to the contrary. Accordingly, the 1954 effort to obtain full net worth statements from all self-employed taxpayers did not meet with any great measure of success.

In spite of this setback, the authorities did not give up. In 1955 a number of amendments to the Income Tax Ordinance were enacted, designed to aid in the enforcement of the law. One of these, although relating specifically to one of the criminal sanctions, nevertheless signaled an intention on the part of the authorities to resort to the net worth and expenditures methods for both civil and criminal purposes. The current version of this provision is as follows:

Where a person is charged with omitting or understating income under section 217, his guilt shall be deemed to be established *prima facie* if one of the following has been proved:

(1) that domestic or other personal expenditure incurred in the tax year exceeded the income of which a return has been made to the assessing officer;
(2) that his capital or the capital of his wife or his children under 20 years of age has increased in a particular period not exceeding five years by an amount exceeding the amount of the income of which a return or returns have been made to the assessing officer, after deducting the tax which has been paid.[15]

14. Sharef Report (Harvard ed.), para. 14, p. 11.
15. Section 223, Income Tax Ordinance, as amended, 1968.

By virtue of this provision, a rebuttable presumption is established, to support a charge under Section 217, which pertains to the filing of an incorrect return, without reasonable cause, omitting or understating income required to be reported, or otherwise supplying incorrect information affecting liability to tax.

The 1954 and 1955 amendments to the penal provisions of the Income Tax Ordinance anticipated the implementation of a full-scale criminal prosecution drive. However, recognition of the net worth and expenditures methods as support for criminal prosecutions gave them a respectable role as a basis for tax assessments. Training programs for inspectors included instruction in the use of the net worth method. With increasing frequency, individual taxpayers whose returns were believed to be substantially inaccurate were requested to supply net worth statements. To a considerable extent, increased understanding in the use of the net worth method was derived from several 1954 decisions of the United States Supreme Court, approving the use of these methods and defining the circumstances under which they were acceptable as measures of taxable income.[16]

The substantial reliance placed by the income tax authorities upon these methods of assessing income is reflected by a number of decisions of the Israel Supreme Court and the District Courts.[17] The expenditures method, in its pure form, was approved by the Supreme Court in 1959 in a case involving an individual who, in spite of having no apparent sources of income, was nevertheless found to be maintaining a fairly high standard of living for himself, his wife, and family of six small children. The assessments, for a three-year period, "were based upon what appeared to the inspector as the minimum living expenses necessary for the taxpayer to maintain himself and his family during the years in issue." The Supreme Court there declared:

This is one of the most difficult types of situations which the assessing officers encounter. They do not have the organization which would enable them to conduct intensive investigations of the financial status of taxpayers, their business activities and their standards of living; and this is regrettable, for the inescapable result is that the assessing officers are groping about in the darkness, at a time when they do not believe the taxpayer — and there are instances when an attitude of disbelief is not without support — and at such times they have no alternative but to base their assessments upon conjectures. . . . The taxpayer's principal argument is that the assessing officer is prohibited from assuming a source of taxable income if he is unable to identify such a source. In our opinion,

16. Witkon and Neeman, pp. 269–270. The American cases were *Holland* v. *United States*, 348 U.S. 121 (1954); *Friedberg* v. *United States*, 348 U.S. 147 (1954); and *United States* v. *Calderon*, 348 U.S. 160 (1954).

17. See, e.g., cases digested in 4 Boaz Nahir, *Moreh Derekh li'Psikat Mas Hakhanasah* [Guide to Income Tax Decisions], pp. 501–550 (Tel Aviv, 1962).

this argument is unacceptable. We believe that the assessing officer is definitely authorized to assume that generally, and by the ways of the world, an individual earns his bread by one of the sources of income which are caught in the income tax net. One who is an exception, whether unable to support himself by reason of illness, age, or similar reason; or whether his support is assured from other non-taxable sources, such as his wealth, capital gains [not then taxable], external support or gifts, is at least obliged to explain his special circumstances to the assessing officer.[18]

Although this case may appear to have given the assessing officers a blank check to base assessments upon "conjectures" derived from estimated expenditures, subsequent court decisions placed limits upon the use of this method. What appears to have occurred is that, as techniques for the use of the net worth method came to be perfected, both the administration and the courts realized that the expenditures method was primarily incidental to the net worth method. As an independent means of assessing income, the expenditures method involves so many "conjectures" as to become almost wholly unreliable as independent support for an assessment of income. The defects of the expenditures method were emphasized in a 1961 opinion of the Supreme Court involving best judgment assessments for a ten-year period based upon the expenditures method. In holding for the taxpayer, the Supreme Court concluded that, in order to use this method, the assessing officer is obliged "to show — perhaps even in a general way — what was the standard of living or, at least, that even at the most modest standard it would have been impossible to survive on the basis of the income reported" by the taxpayer.[19]

The net worth method proved to be more acceptable to the courts, particularly when the assessing officer was able to rely upon net worth statements submitted by the taxpayer covering the beginning and end of the taxable period.[20] Nevertheless, the Supreme Court emphasized that the taxpayer's net worth statement is primarily an aid to the assessing officer in making a best judgment assessment and, it was suggested, other available factors would also have to be taken into account.[21]

Once the assessing officer had demonstrated a net worth increase greater than could be accounted for by reported income, the taxpayer "remains silent at his peril" and, in the absence of evidence that the growth was not attributable to unreported income, it would be assumed

18. *Gabai* v. *Assessing Officer*, Civ. App. 194–58, 13 *Piske Din* 1258 (Sup. Ct., 1959), at 1259.
19. *Giltzer* v. *Assessing Officer*, Civ. App. 530/60, 15 *Piske Din* 1359, 1360 (Sup. Ct., 1961).
20. E.g. *Zilberstein* v. *Assessing Officer*, Civ. App. 237/58, 13 *Piske Din* 1435 (Sup. Ct., 1959).
21. E.g. *Melis & Lecker* v. *Assessing Officer*, Civ. App. 449/59, 14 *Piske Din* 306 (Sup. Ct., 1960).

to be such.[22] On the other hand, a taxpayer who had submitted a statement showing a nominal net worth in 1954, having been found not long thereafter to have assets many times larger than reported, was permitted to tender evidence to show that his opening net worth was in fact considerably more than originally reported.[23] Similarly, taxpayers whose combined expenditures and net worth were considerably out of line with reported income were permitted to show that, during the period, they had access to funds which were not taxable.[24]

Generally, the net worth and expenditure methods are less reliable than the *tahshivim* as means of estimating income. Nevertheless, where more accurate methods of assessment are unavailable, they have been used successfully to establish the *prima facie* correctness of best judgment assessments.

Bookkeeping Requirements

During the same period that the *tahshivim* came into use as aids in the assessment of incomes of taxpayers who did not keep books, the income tax authorities were engaged in a campaign to compel selected groups of taxpayers to keep books. The authority for this campaign was Section 43 of the Income Tax Ordinance of 1947, enacted in 1952 (now sec. 130), which authorized the Commissioner to require the keeping of books, generally or by a specified class of taxpayers, and to prescribe by regulation the bookkeeping principles to be followed. Such regulations were to become effective three months after their promulgation. Thereafter, the assessing officers were authorized to ignore accounts which were not based upon books maintained in the manner prescribed by the appropriate regulation.

The first such regulation was prescribed in 1953 and required that books of account be kept by members of certain free professions, namely, medical practitioners (physicians, dentists, dental technologists, and other related professions), lawyers, and engineers. In 1954 bookkeeping requirements were imposed upon building contractors.[25]

The books required to be kept by members of the free professions included a cash book for recording daily receipts and expenditures, and a

22. *Even* v. *Assessing Officer*, Civ. App. 182/60, 14 *Piske Din* 1308 (Sup. Ct., 1960).

23. *Rutenberg* v. *Assessing Officer*, Civ. App. 100/58, 14 *Piske Din* 1333 (Sup. Ct. 1960).

24. *Assessing Officer* v. *Weisl*, Civ. App. 458/58, 14 *Piske Din* 1621 (Sup. Ct., 1960); *Benedict* v. *Assessing Officer*, Civ. App. 286/60, 14 *Piske Din* 2235 (Sup. Ct. 1960).

25. The authorities continued for some years to have difficulty in assuring maintenance of proper accounts by building contractors. See, e.g., *Thirteenth Annual Report of State Comptroller* (Hebrew), p. 43 (1962); *Fifteenth Annual Report of State Comptroller* (Hebrew), pp. 87–88 (1964); *Eleventh Annual Report on State Revenue* (Hebrew), p. 41 (1966).

book of receipts, in duplicate, one copy to be given to the client or patient, the other to be retained by the taxpayer as a permanent record. Building contractors were required to maintain a cash book, a register of work in process with a separate sheet for each job, showing receipts and expenditures relative thereto, a wage register, and a register of all raw materials showing types, quantity, prices, sources of supply, and inward and outward movements of materials. It should be emphasized that the records so required were the minimum considered both necessary and practical to check the income tax returns of the affected taxpayers. They thus fell short of ideal bookkeeping standards.

The bookkeeping requirements imposed in 1953 and 1954 related to professions and businesses whose proprietors were presumably sufficiently educated to keep their own accounts or sufficiently affluent to hire a bookkeeper. A good many of them, experience showed, were already keeping books in one form or another. The purpose of the regulations, then, was to require that they *all* keep books and, as well, to prescribe the minimum standards under which they should be kept. Even so, the regulations were at first objected to and became the subject of negotiations with the representatives of the business and professional groups involved. In several instances these negotiations resulted in departures from the original requirements. Such special arrangements were made with the Israel Dental Association in 1953 and with the Israel Medical Association, effective as of April 1, 1959.[26]

Based upon experience of the administration in instituting the previously mentioned series of regulations, a new approach was tried in 1955 in advance of the issuance of regulations requiring the keeping of books by wholesalers, retailers with four or more employees, and by certain other retail establishments (hotels, incubator operators, furniture and jewelry shops, department stores and feed stores) irrespective of the number of employees.[27] It was anticipated that many of the taxpayers who would be affected by these regulations might encounter difficulty in complying with them, in spite of the relative simplicity of the records which were required.[28] To alleviate these difficulties, the administration undertook an educational program which had several facets. First, sample sets of records were prepared, after consultation with representatives of organizations whose members would be affected by the new requirements. Then, detailed sets of bookkeeping instructions were prepared, and these were initially tested in meetings with groups of affected taxpayers. Based on these preliminary contacts, adjustments

26. Joseph Stern, *Mas Hakhnasah* (Income Tax) (Haifa, 1962), pp. 61–63.
27. Income Tax Regulations (Bookkeeping by Wholesalers and Retailers), 1955; published March 31, 1955, amended June 12, 1958.
28. Some of these difficulties are described by Simha Fromer, former Deputy Income Tax Commissioner, in "The Bookkeeping Requirements for Wholesalers and Retailers" (Hebrew), 6 *Roeh Haheshbon* 53 (October–December 1955).

were made in the proposed regulations, in the instructions, and in the sample records. In this pretesting of the regulations, the authorities were assisted by one of a team of American tax experts then serving in Israel under a contract with the United States Operations Mission to Israel.

While this campaign was under way, the administration was engaged in a program of training its personnel to qualify for the task of auditing books of account. Meanwhile, it was relying more heavily upon stand-ard methods of assessment, such as the *tahshiv*, which required less technical ability on the part of the inspectors. It sometimes happened, during this period, that a taxpayer who had in fact kept books, although not required to do so, would find himself faced by an inspector who pre-ferred to ignore the books and to base his assessment upon his guess as to what he thought the taxpayer actually should have earned. This was contrary to instructions, unless the inspector could show specific reasons for considering the books unreliable.

Judicial support

At about this time, substantial encouragement to taxpayers who had kept books came from the Israel Supreme Court. One case, decided in December 1955, involved a physician who had for some years filed his returns on the basis of a cash book which he had maintained con-sistently. Just as consistently, the assessing officer had rejected the re-turns and, under pressure, the physician had agreed to increased tax liabilities for each of several years. Finally, when a similar increase was proposed for 1952–53, the physician refused to accept it, and took the matter to court. The case turned on the question whether the tax-payer had satisfactorily sustained the burden of proving that the assess-ment was excessive. The Supreme Court held that the books were sufficient *prima facie* proof of the accuracy of the return and, thereafter, the burden shifted to the assessing officer to prove that the books were unreliable. This the assessing officer attempted to do by reference to the taxpayer's prior agreement to assessments higher than those indi-cated by his books. This factor apparently induced the District (trial) Court to decide against the taxpayer, in spite of the taxpayer's explana-tion that he had agreed to the prior assessments not as an admission that his books were inaccurate but because he had neither the time nor the energy to dispute the relatively small increases then involved. The Supreme Court, in holding for the taxpayer, accepted his explanation and held that since the books were accurate on their face, they had to be accepted, in the absence of evidence that they were unreliable.[29]

Not long thereafter, the Supreme Court came even more strongly to the aid of a taxpayer whose return, based upon books, had been rejected by the assessing officer. This case, decided in June 1956, involved an

29. *Blumenthal* v. *Assessing Officer*, 9 *Piske Din* 1929 (Sup. Ct., 1955).

individual who made his living by preparing petitions at the courthouse door, recording his receipts in a simple notebook. The assessing officer, rejecting these records, made best judgment assessments for two years. The Supreme Court, obviously aware of some of the deficiencies in the income tax administration at that time, remarked:

The appellant (taxpayer) complains bitterly and says that "the respondent's procedure in making the assessment is arbitrary and illegal, causing a drop in taxpayer morale, disregarding records without explanation, and converting the assessment procedure into a bargaining and haggling process between the respondent (assessing officer) and the citizen." We must emphasize, to our sorrow, that there is support for much of these complaints. No one disputes that the citizen has the burden of convincing the assessing officer of the accuracy of the details contained in the return which he submits. But there is no irrebuttable legal premise that the citizen is a liar and that the documents which he submits are false. For this reason, that method is in our eyes invalid whereby the assessing officer increases the sum liable to tax, without any regard to documents which are submitted, and without consideration for the realistic grounds upon which he should make the assessment. The basis for this approach is the idea — also invalid in our opinion — that the citizen had reported less than his true income, that he is prepared to agree to an increase, that it is proper, therefore, that the assessing officer assess the income at an above-average level, which he will then be ready to reduce; and thus they will arrive, finally, after a bargaining process, to a sum which approaches, to the extent possible, the correct amount. We say that this method is invalid, because its consequence is that the negotiations between the citizen and the officials will be conducted from the outset on a basis of falsehood and lies, lack of belief, and mutual distrust. . .

In brief, the appellant produced before the respondent and the district court notebooks in which he recorded, he contends, all of his income, and he so testified under oath. He was cross-examined at length and on the whole gave credible answers. The notebooks were kept in a very simple, perhaps even primitive, manner, but it is not reasonable to demand from a citizen such as this appellant that he keep orderly books, arranged in accordance with the most advanced bookkeeping procedures. Also, he should not be expected to hire a bookkeeper or accountant. The notebooks are clean and neatly arranged. They contain no erasures and obliterations, nor have any omissions or false entries been proven. The appellant truly believes that this was the proper method of recording his taxable income. If he was mistaken, he does not know wherein, for neither the respondent nor the district court gave any explanation; and he is perplexed and does not know how to keep his books in the future so that the respondent may believe him. For this reason also it is desirable that reasons be given for rejecting evidence submitted by a taxpayer in support of his return. In our opinion the appellant has sustained the burden of proof imposed upon him by the law and we are accordingly obliged to hold for him.[30]

Although these two cases related to taxable years with respect to which neither of the affected taxpayers was under an obligation to keep books, the decisions of the Supreme Court were rendered after large numbers of self-employed professionals and businessmen had already become subject to the bookkeeping regulations. Others became subject to bookkeeping requirements thereafter. The effect of these decisions, which received widespread publicity, was to enforce the weight which the courts would give to tax returns based upon reasonable records, and to show that arbitrary disregard of taxpayers' books would not be condoned.

This did not end the matter, however. A best judgment assessment, being by its nature arbitrary, is easier to make than one requiring a detailed technical analysis of books of account. The inspectors are under pressure to produce assessments and, even when books of account are presented, some have been said to attempt to strike a bargain with the taxpayer without regard to his books.[31] Although this is not officially condoned and, in fact, is contrary to instructions, the practice is hard to eradicate unless the taxpayer stands firm upon his books; or unless the effectiveness of the tax inspector is evaluated on a basis which puts less emphasis on amount of assessments produced.

Administrative and statutory support

In general, the income tax authorities would prefer that all taxpayers keep books, to the extent consistent with the nature of their income-producing activities. Aside from the series of regulations imposing the obligation to keep minimal books upon specific trades, occupations, and professions, considerable weight is given both by the authorities and the courts to returns based upon books, even if kept by taxpayers who are not obliged to do so. If a taxpayer shows that his annual return is based upon and consistent with his books of account, the inspector is obliged to examine the books, and he must accept the return unless he can demonstrate specific inaccuracies therein which affect income or deductions. Otherwise, a best judgment assessment disregarding the books would be unwarranted. This would also appear to be the case in the event of a disparity between books of account and a *tahshiv*, in instances where one is applicable to the particular taxpayer. This could occur in the case of a taxpayer who keeps accounts even though not required to do so by regulation. The books of account would still control, unless, being guided by a discrepancy indicated by the *tahshiv*, the inspector is

30. *Lizra* v. *Assessing Officer*, 10 *Piske Din* 1032, 1034, 1036 (Sup. Ct., 1956).
31. See remarks of former Assistant Income Tax Commissioner Yitzhak Mann in 10 *Roeh Haheshbon* 139 (April–June 1960).

then able to demonstrate specific inaccuracies in the books of account.[32]

By November 1967, about 40 percent of the self-employed taxpayers were covered by regulations requiring the keeping of books. The administration proposes to continue with its efforts to extend the bookkeeping requirements to other groups of taxpayers not already subject to a specific regulation. This has entailed negotiations with representatives of taxpayers' groups and is being approached under a policy of persuasion rather than compulsion. The official position is that the type of books required, once a regulation is promulgated, should be adequate to assure proper reporting and checking of income.[33]

Consistent with this approach, and in response to complaints by some taxpayers that inspectors tend to disregard their records even if properly maintained, a new procedure was adopted in 1968 to apply in all cases in which an inspector proposes to disregard a taxpayer's records. Special review committees have been established in each assessing office and, before books may be disregarded, the case must be reviewed by the special committee. Perhaps of greater significance is the fact that in 1963 the law was amended to shift the burden of proof in court appeals onto the assessing officer, if the taxpayer has maintained records in the form required by the Commissioner (sec. 155, I.T.O., as amended). This provision may help to maintain public confidence in the good will of the administration's record-keeping requirements.

Bookkeeping problems of the purchase tax administration

It is important to mention that the income tax administration is not the only segment of the revenue administration which has an interest in the maintenance of records by taxpayers. In fact, almost all of the other taxes depend to some extent upon taxpayers' records. Of special interest in this discussion of problems relating to self-employed taxpayers is an experience of the purchase tax administration. In 1954 much of the furniture sold in Israel was produced in small carpentry shops. The tax on certain grades of "luxury" furniture was quite high. Evidence of payment of the tax was by stamps affixed to the article of furniture, in denominations based upon the value of the furniture. These had to be verified by a purchase tax inspector who would then cancel the stamps. The procedure was cumbersome and was much criticized by the artisans. At the same time there was widespread evasion of the tax. In an effort both to simplify procedures and to reduce evasion, the authorities printed sets of record books to be maintained by the furniture makers. There was an immediate outcry, and, encouraged perhaps by the success of previous demonstrations by organized groups of taxpayers, the artisans

32. Cf. *Assessing Officer* v. *Feiner*, 19 *Piske Din* 631 (Sup. Ct., 1965) further hearing 14/65.

33. Y. Tamir, "1968 — Year of Events and Changes in Taxes" (Hebrew), 18 *Roeh Haheshbon*, pp. 149–150 (January–February 1968).

announced their refusal to keep the required records. To emphasize this, marches upon the purchase tax offices were organized and large masses of the record books were contemptuously dumped on the office floors. In the face of this taxpayer opposition, the requirement to keep these books was withdrawn and other methods of collection and control were resorted to.[34]

Sanctions for failure to keep books

Before leaving the subject of bookkeeping requirements for income taxpayers, mention should be made of the sanctions imposed by law for failure to keep proper books. These sanctions are both civil and criminal.

Section 130(b) of the Income Tax Ordinance (new version) provides that the assessing officer may refuse to accept accounts not based upon account books kept in accordance with the regulations.[35] This provision could apply to a taxpayer who, having been required to keep accounts failed to do so, or to one who, although he may have kept accounts, did not maintain them in the prescribed manner. Furthermore, Section 33 of the Ordinance (new version), perhaps redundantly, provides that deductions otherwise allowed under the law shall not be permitted unless proper accounts are submitted to the assessing officer, together with a computation showing the assessable profits of the business or profession. In any event, if no accounts, or unacceptable accounts, are submitted, the assessing officer may make a best judgment assessment under Section 145 (new version), using for that purpose whatever presumptive method for assessing income he considers to be appropriate. The effect, therefore, of failure to comply with the bookkeeping regulations is that the taxpayer will find himself under the heavy burden of disproving the assessment; and, even if he kept books, of overcoming the considerations upon which the assessing officer relied for rejecting them as a basis for the assessment. On the other hand, if the taxpayer keeps books of account they may not lightly be set aside by the assessing officer; rather, the burden is on the assessing officer to establish substantial unreliability of the books before he can ignore them.[36]

The bookkeeping requirements are further enforced by penal provisions. Section 216(5) of the Income Tax Ordinance (new version) provides that every person who, without sufficient cause, fails to keep accounts in accordance with directions issued by the Commissioner or under Section 130(a) shall be liable to imprisonment for a term of up to

34. It should be mentioned here that the purchase tax on furniture was abolished in 1967, thus putting an end to this problem.

35. The taxpayer is authorized to appeal from this rejection of his books. It is not clear whether, on appeal, the burden of sustaining or disproving the assessment is upon the assessing officer or on the taxpayer. Cf. sec. 155, I.T.O., as amended.

36. *Aharoni* v. *Assessing Officer,* Income Tax Appeal 18/59, reported in 9 *Roeh Haheshbon,* 255 (April–June 1959).

six months, or to a fine of up to IL. 2,000, or both. Thus, irrespective of whether his income is correctly reported, and even if the failure to maintain accounts is without any intent to evade tax (cf. Sec. 220 — evasion), the mere failure to maintain required accounts, if without "sufficient cause," is itself punishable by fine and imprisonment. There have been, in fact, several prosecutions for this offense,[37] although the large number of best judgment assessments still made by the assessing officers would seem to indicate that prosecution for failure to keep accounts is used only as a last resort and in the most flagrant cases.[38]

As compared to mere failure to keep accounts, the preparation or maintenance of false books of account or records, when done wilfully and with intent to evade tax, is, under Section 220 (new version) subject to far harsher punishment. In the latter event, the penalty is imprisonment for a term of up to four years, or a fine of up to IL. 10,000, plus an amount equal to one and a half times the amount of income (not tax) sought to be concealed, or both these penalties. It is conceivable that the greater severity accorded to the keeping of false accounts, as compared to the failure to keep *any* accounts, has tended to discourage keeping of accounts by taxpayers who deliberately set out to evade tax. On the other hand, if no accounts are kept, particularly where they are required, a best judgment assessment, even if quite high, is likely to be made and to stand up under court review.[39]

Aside from the administrative and criminal sanctions just referred to, the administration has recently moved in the direction of imposing economic sanctions upon those who fail to keep proper books of account. For some time the Director of State Revenue had been urging that any person tendering a bid for the performance of a contract with the government be required to submit, along with his bid, a certificate of an accountant to the effect that the bidder is keeping books of account, as required by law. Upon recommendation of a ministerial committee, headed by the Minister of Justice, a decision to this effect was made by the government in 1968 and, hereafter, government contracts will be awarded only to those who keep proper books of account. Subsequently, the Director of Revenue suggested that the Ministry of Commerce and Industry similarly refrain from approving applications for import licenses unless the applicant submits an accountant's certificate that his books are being kept according to law.[40]

37. See, as to prosecutions against builders for failure to keep books, *Fifteenth Annual Report of State Comptroller* (Hebrew), pp. 87–88 (1964).

38. Cf. Simha Gafni, "Our Plans — Some Remarks About Ourselves" (Hebrew), 1 *Quarterly Tax Journal*, 389, 392–393 (October 1966).

39. E. S. Shimron and J. S. Zemah, "Selected Problems of Evidence in Income Tax Proceedings" (Hebrew), 1 *Quarterly Tax Journal*, 410, 414 (October 1966).

40. Simha Gafni, "Our Plans — Some Remarks About Ourselves," pp. 389, 392–393. Zvi Kessler, "From Issue to Issue" (Hebrew), 3 *Quarterly Tax Journal*, unnumbered preface (January 1968).

Changing trends in bookkeeping requirements

When in 1952 the income tax administration began to require record-keeping by specified businesses, professions, and occupations, many of those affected by the regulations had not been accustomed to keeping business records of any kind. Accordingly, the requirements were minimal, merely calling for the current recording, on a cash basis, of a few selected items of income and outgo. This was expected to assist the income tax inspector in checking the accuracy of the income reported by the taxpayer or in arriving at his own assessment of the taxpayer's income. These records did not represent "bookkeeping" in the scientific sense.

From the outset, the income tax authorities recognized that among those who, technically, were required to keep records, there were many small operators who could not satisfactorily comply with the requirements. Although in the early days of the criminal prosecution program, an effort was made to compel such taxpayers to comply with the record-keeping requirements by subjecting some of them to criminal prosecutions, the income tax authorities had found that such drastic measures were ineffective and that many of the small taxpayers could not, and therefore would not, keep records in the required manner. In recognition of the inevitable, the system of classification of returns for audit purposes now includes a classification (5.1) for self-employed taxpayers who are required to keep books but do not do so.

On the other hand, the dynamic quality of the Israeli economy has made it possible for many self-employed taxpayers who were marginal operators when the record-keeping requirements were first instituted, to expand their businesses to the point where they have now engaged accountants and bookkeepers to maintain, for their own internal purposes, double-entry sets of books. As to these taxpayers, their bookkeeping systems have outgrown the relatively simple record-keeping requirements of the income tax regulations. Yet, the income tax authorities have continued to insist upon the maintenance of records in the form originally prescribed by the regulations. The result is that some taxpayers are obliged to maintain duplicate sets of books — one set established and controlled by their accountants to provide management with information required for business purposes and — for presentation to the tax inspector — the relatively incomplete set of records required by the income tax regulations.

Recognizing that, for such taxpayers, the income tax record-keeping requirements may have become a Procrustean bed the income tax authorities recently, in conjunction with the Accounting Society, undertook a review of the regulations. One possible outcome of this review may be a revision of the specific record-keeping requirements and adoption of a general provision which would accept such system of books maintained by the taxpayer as has been installed by a certified public accountant, is appropriate to the needs of the business, fully reflects its operations, and is so certified by the accountant. As to those taxpayers whose businesses are still too small to permit the engagement of an accountant or book-keeper, the review of the record-keeping requirements is intended to determine the extent to which they can be simplified so that the taxpayer may be enabled to keep the necessary records without professional assistance.

In 1968 this review of the bookkeeping requirements was coupled with an educational campaign, directed to the smaller businessman, the purpose of which was not only to instruct him in the elements of simple bookkeeping but also to convince him that understandable records would assist him in conducting his business more efficiently and profitably. As part of this campaign, the income tax authorities issued a series of pamphlets, each one for a specific line of business, containing simplified, step-by-step explanations of the way to keep the records appropriate to that business.

Bookkeeping requirements of the Customs and Excise Branch

The experience of the customs and excise tax administration in regard to reliance on taxpayers' books and records provides an interesting contrast to that of the income tax administration. We have already mentioned the abortive effort of the purchase tax authorities to require furniture-makers to keep detailed records of their production. This happened at the end of 1954. The customs and excise authorities have since devised other means of controlling the proper reporting and payment of the series of taxes under their jurisdiction, while relaxing the system of physical controls over individual transactions which theretofore had been in use. As soon as Israel's commerce and industry began to expand, such physical controls became burdensome both to the taxpayers and the administration. Thus, a system which had worked quite well with a limited number of small businesses had to be reexamined as the economy expanded.

The customs and excise administration, because it deals with a much smaller taxpaying public than does the income tax administration, has found it possible to change its procedures for assuring the honest reporting and payment of its taxes by placing greater reliance upon books of account maintained in the ordinary course of the taxpayer's business. Thus, many manufacturers who are subject to the purchase tax have been relieved of the obligation of affixing stamps to each item manufactured by them and, instead, are permitted to file periodic reports of their sales, showing the tax due, which is required to be paid with the return.[41] The

41. See, e.g., Purchase Tax Regulations (Services) (Amendment), 1967, 1985 *Kovetz Hatakanot* p. 1191, referred to in 2 *Quarterly Tax Journal*, 149 (April

manufacturers thus relieved of the burden of purchasing the tax stamps and affixing them to the individual goods generally have trademarks or brand names on their products. Accordingly, if a purchase tax inspector should be conducting a physical check of the inventory of a retailer, he will pass those products which bear the brand name or trademark of a manufacturer who has been relieved of the obligation of affixing the tax stamps.

This trend of the customs and excise administration to rely upon books of account rather than upon physical control of the goods has also manifested itself with respect to other taxes under the jurisdiction of that administration. Control by periodic returns and audit of accounts has replaced the personal and continual supervision by employees of the excise tax units. Summary returns have also largely taken the place of the individual adhesive stamps required to be affixed to various taxable documents.[42]

Administration of the customs has also been moving in the direction of greater reliance upon taxpayers' records than upon physical control of goods. This has been particularly apparent in regard to raw materials or partially manufactured goods which are imported with a view toward manufacture and re-export. There has been in force since mandatory days a system of "drawbacks" which recognizes that such goods, although technically subject to customs duties upon import, should produce a refund when re-exported. With the development of Israel industry, there has evolved a rather elaborate system of conditional exemptions (which relates also to goods and equipment imported for use in "approved enterprises"), securities against goods destined for re-export which are released to the manufacturer without payment of duty, and drawbacks applying both to the previous instances and to goods re-exported after payment of duty on their prior import. Efforts to maintain control over such goods by physical means alone (such as special warehousing arrangements within the manufacturer's plant) proved to be unwieldy, and the recent trend has been to couple a relaxation of physical controls with intensive audit of the importers' or manufacturers' books of account.

The willingness of the customs and excise authorities to shift from physical controls to periodic returns and audit of accounts has been the product of the developing sophistication of Israeli business and its greater reliance upon internal records and accounting analyses as a means of keeping management better informed as to how the business is progressing.

1967); Yaacov Arad, "The Unification of Purchase Tax Rates" (Hebrew), 1 *Quarterly Tax Journal* 331, 337 (July 1966).

42. Uri Schneider, "Imposition of Stamp Tax through Adhesive Stamps or on Basis of Turnover" (Hebrew), 2 *Quarterly Tax Journal* 180 (April 1967).

This development has been coupled with a change in the type of tax-payers with whom the customs and excise administration has had to deal. For example, in the textile-weaving industry there has been a shift from a large number of small operators to concentration in a few large producers. This has made it possible to simplify administration of the purchase tax on textiles by eliminating the metal seals which previously had been required to be affixed to specified lengths of cloth. Only those small manufacturers who do not keep proper books are still required to affix the metal seals.

Similar changes have taken place in other branches of industry. The small artisan of fifteen years ago has either expanded his business, combined with others, or disappeared. The practice of keeping books of account has grown. The customs and excise administration, in respect of the various taxes under its jurisdiction, has attempted to convince the affected taxpayers that, by maintaining books of account appropriate to their own business needs, they can also satisfy the requirements of the tax administration and, through the filing of returns which thereafter are audited by the tax authorities, they can relieve themselves of some of the administrative burdens connected with the payment of the tax.

Thus, the trend within the customs and excise administration has been to encourage taxpayers to maintain that system of accounts which is most suitable to the needs of their business, these accounts serving at the same time as a means of complying with the requirements of the tax authorities. In adopting this approach the customs and excise authorities have in a sense outstripped the income tax authorities, who are still following the line of record-keeping requirements, which, though introduced as recently as 1952, now appears to have become outmoded.

Assessment of Wage-earners

A system of deduction at the source from wages and salaries has been in force since the initial adoption of the Income Tax Ordinance in 1941. This is, however, a method of advance collection of tax from a particular class of income rather than a method of assessment. Under the Israeli system, the general rule is that an assessment shall be made for each taxpayer for each taxable year. This assessment requirement applies, as well, to wage-earners. It has produced a number of problems, some of which will be discussed herein.

Assuming that wages are the sole income source, and assuming also that the annual wage-withholding tables prescribed by the authorities are accurately computed to take into account reasonable averages for various permissible adjustments to income and tax, the differential between tax withheld and tax finally assessed is likely to be small. This may, particularly, be assumed in the case of a taxpayer in the lowest wage brackets. This assumption provided the key to ultimate elimination of the requirement for separate assessments of wage-earners in the lowest tax brackets, whose sole source of income was from wages.

This problem was one of the many considered by the Sharef Commission in its examination of methods of assessing income tax. In its 1954 report, mention is made of a proposal to reduce the work of the income tax department by abolishing completely the requirement for making final assessments of taxpayers from whom the tax was collected mainly by deduction at the source from wages. This proposal was rejected by the Commission. The explanation given was that this would tend to place "on the shoulders of employed persons burdens that are not placed on those of self-employed persons," because "the monthly calculation of tax may be to the detriment of the taxpayer rather than to his advantage." Elimination of the final assessment might have had the effect of unjustly depriving some wage-earners of refunds to which they were entitled. To prevent this, the Commission proposed that, irrespective of any changes in procedure that might thereafter be instituted, the authorities should be obliged to make a separate assessment whenever a taxpayer requested that one be made.[43]

The 1954 Backlog of Unassessed Returns

Viewed as of 1954, the mountainous backlog of wage-earners' assessments which had been accumulating since 1948 appeared insurmountable. It would have relieved the administration of a vast burden had it been possible, as had been suggested to the Sharef Commission, to assume that the tax withheld from the wages of each wage-earner was exactly equal to the tax finally due. But this simple solution, aside from the injustices it might create in the cases of taxpayers who were, in fact, entitled to a refund, was otherwise not acceptable.

Given the breakdown of the Israeli income tax administration which had occurred since 1948, the system of withholding of tax at the source on wages was, perhaps, too efficient. Collection statistics for these years, during which unmade assessments of self-employed individuals and companies were also accumulating, showed that wage-earners, as a group, were paying about one-half of all income taxes collected. The peak was reached in fiscal year 1952–53, when collections from wage-earners by withholding comprised 55 percent of total income tax collections. This represented a sharp increase from fiscal year 1948–49, when collections from employees were 28.3 percent of the total. Even after introduction of an advance payments, or pay-as-you-go, system for self-employed taxpayers and companies, first enacted in 1952, the share of wage-earners in collections continued high, ranging in the vicinity of 40–45 percent of total collections.

43. *Sharef Report* (Harvard ed.), pp. 22–24.

In 1954, mutual recriminations between wage-earners and self-employed, heated by prevailing political developments, reached a peak. The administration was caught in the middle. It was hardly the time to adopt a procedure which, in effect, would have left hundreds of thousands of wage-earners' returns unchecked. Accordingly, the administration was compelled to address itself to the development of procedures which would dispose of the backlog of unassessed wage-earners' returns, while seeking revisions of the law and administrative practices so as to assure that, at least for the future, wage-earners' assessments would be maintained more or less on a current basis.

Classification of Wage-earners' Returns

Some proposals to achieve these results were made in the report of the Sharef Commission. These proposals were essentially carried into effect in a program of action developed by the National Inspector for Wage-earners in the office of the Income Tax Commissioner, after consultations in the summer of 1954 with the author of this volume. The essence of the plan for cleaning up the backlog for previous years was that all assessments would be made, but that the depth of the examination conducted prior to assessment would vary, depending upon such factors as whether the taxpayer had income from other sources, whether his wages exceeded a minimum established for each year, and, generally, whether there were administrative reasons to believe that special attention should be given to the particular taxpayer.

Before the actual work of assessment could be undertaken, the files had to be classified into two groups. Group A included those whose returns required detailed inspection, because their incomes were above a predetermined level or because they had income from sources other than wages; group B consisted of the remainder, whose returns were to be accepted as filed. This classification was an essential part of the program, and personnel assignments were to be in accordance with the relative difficulty of the files requiring inspection. Here the plan ran into an initial snag, which delayed the program for several months. Shortly before, a policy decision had been reached to redistribute the files of employees to the assessing officers for the districts in which the employees resided. Hitherto, following the practice of the mandatory administration, employees' files had been assigned to the assessing officer for the district in which the employer had his place of business.

Although it was recognized that there were administrative advantages to having the same assessing officer responsible for the files of both the employer and his employees, it had been concluded that there were more weighty reasons for shifting employees' files to the assessing officer at the place of residence. One reason was the assumption that if an employee had an additional source of income, this could be more easily ascertained by an office which was closer to his home. Another reason was that assignment to the place of residence would be more convenient for the employee in the event that he had to communicate with the assessing officer. The latter reason appeared particularly applicable to employees of the Government, of national institutions, or large firms, who might be scattered throughout the country. It also applied in the Tel Aviv area, which by then had been divided into several assessing offices, some of which covered the downtown business sections, while others largely covered the residential sections.

Later experience showed that administrative efficiency required reconcentration of employees' returns, particularly in the Tel Aviv area where they were ultimately assembled in one office, but, at the time with which we are now concerned — 1954 and 1955 — the fact that employees' files were in the process of being shifted among the assessing offices delayed the work of assessing their returns. The project thus lost some momentum.

The principal concern in assessing returns of wage-earners, from the standpoint of revenue, was to assure that those who had sources of income in addition to wages were being taxed thereon. This was a factor which could not be ascertained by checking the accounts of employers. The latter were required to keep detailed records as to wages paid to, and taxes withheld from, each employee. Additional, nonwage, income would not show up on the employee's records.

This is not to say that at this time all taxable compensation was necessarily being reported. In spite of the egalitarian wage policy which was then in force, skilled employees in short supply (such as construction workers) were able to demand either "under-the-table" payments, guaranteed "net" salaries after tax, "expense" allowances of various types, or other perquisites — such as free use of housing, automobiles, telephones, or interest-free loans. Such arrangements were also, for a time, common with respect to management-level employees.[44] However, these devices, which would be disclosed sooner or later on examination of the income tax returns of the employers, where they would generally appear as claimed deductions for expenses, were eliminated or controlled after a time. Special attention was also given to the possible existence of such items in checking the returns of company directors, who were given a special classification for audit purposes.

As indicated above, no amount of checking of employers' accounts could disclose additional sources of income which did not arise from the employment. Nor was it uncommon at this time for individuals who had full-time jobs to have rather substantial amounts of outside income. The economy was in a transitional stage, and many skills were in short supply. The working day for most employees began at 7:30 in the morning and, after at least one customary "tea" break, ended in the

---

44. *Fifth Annual Report of State Comptroller, 1953/54* (Hebrew), pp. 116–117.

early afternoon, with no intervening lunch period. Many enterprising workingmen, ambitious to establish businesses of their own or otherwise to augment their incomes, were able to find additional work during the remaining hours of the day. Much of the income from these sources was unreported until, in some way, the administration became aware of its existence.

Several methods of subjecting such additional income to tax were utilized. When many wage-earners were later relieved of the obligation of filing detailed returns, the simplified return form which came into use required a disclosure of whether the taxpayer had any income from sources other than wages. In such event, a full return had to be submitted. The system of classification of wage-earners' returns was also intended to subject nonwage income to tax. Classification into category A, which called for detailed inspection, might be based either upon information as to additional income supplied by the taxpayer himself, information obtained from other sources and inserted in the taxpayer's file, or the belief of the assessing officer or a member of his staff that the particular taxpayer might have additional income. It was this latter reason particularly which motivated the transfer of wage-earners' files to the assessing office for the place of residence.

Improvements in Pay-as-you-earn Procedures

In the long run, efficiency in the assessment of wage-earners was achieved by improvements in the pay-as-you-earn system. Withholding tables, supplied to employers each year, were adjusted so as to take into account all elements involved in applying the appropriate tax rates to a wide range of wage brackets, with appropriate guides for adjustment to the personal situation of the individual employee. Procedures were instituted permitting changes in rates of withholding to adjust for changes in the status of an employee (such as in his personal exemptions and allowances) which might take place during the year. As a matter of policy, the applicable tax rates were kept stable throughout the year. The objective was that the final tax liability should not vary from the tax actually withheld.[45] This made it possible to do away with the annual, separate assessments of the great mass of wage-earners.

Correlatively, substantial improvements were effected in the organization and procedures for checking the withholding accounts required to be maintained by employers. The administration revised the system of record-keeping, reporting, and payment required of employers, while improving the administrative procedures for auditing of employers' ac-

45. It was not until 1966 that the United States' system of withholding was adjusted in an attempt (still unsuccessful by 1971) to approach more closely the final tax liability, assuming wages subject to withholding to be the only taxable income and allowable deductions to fall within the standard range. On the other hand, the United Kingdom system (which was the model for Israel) had for some time before been adapted to achieve this.

counts. One of the key features of the system was the establishment of teams of external auditors who would periodically visit employers to check on the accuracy of the accounts being currently maintained. This external audit was in addition to, and a substantial control upon, the checking of the monthly and annual reports which employers were required to file. As this system developed, experience in the Tel Aviv area, particularly, showed that the necessary manpower could not be efficiently supplied to the individual assessing offices in the region and, several years ago, all of the work in connection with the wages withholding system in Tel Aviv was reconcentrated within a single assessing office.

Reduction of Employees' Returns

Substantial reductions in the number of employees' returns required to be audited annually have been effected by both legislative and administrative action. The Income Tax Ordinance authorizes the Minister of Finance to direct that individuals whose wages do not exceed an amount specified by him shall be free of tax on limited amounts of additional income (sec. 12) and, further, shall be relieved of the obligation of filing an annual return (sec. 134). Under this authority, large numbers of taxpayers had been freed of the obligation to file returns. The order applicable to taxable year 1968 exempted employees whose wages did not exceed IL. 18,000 (then equal to $6,000). The previous limit had been IL. 9,600. It was estimated that this would eliminate about 600,000 returns. The tax paid at the source by these taxpayers for fiscal year 1969–70 was estimated at 900 million pounds — about one-half of all income tax collections.[46]

Part of this substantial reduction in returns was due to another 1968 amendment to the law, which eliminated from the prescribed taxable sources of income the net annual value of a residence occupied by its owner.[47] This provision, which had been in the income tax law since its initial enactment in 1941, had its origin in an English conception of income as including the imputed income derived from the occupation of one's own residence. That conception has since been discarded in England. Its retention in the Israeli law had been the subject of much criticism, particularly because of apparent inconsistency with other laws pertaining to property.[48]

46. David Bar Haim, "From Issue to Issue" (Hebrew), 4 *Quarterly Tax Journal* 128 (April 1969).
47. Income Tax Ordinance Amendment Law (no. 13) — 1968, section 1, deleting subsection (3) from section 2 of the Income Tax Ordinance. See Y. Tamir, "1968 — Year of Events and Changes in Taxes," p. 147.
48. Aryeh Lapidoth, *Ikronot Mas Hakhnasah u'Mas Rivhei Hon* (Principles of Income Tax and Capital Gains Tax) pp. 147–152 (Jerusalem: Museum of Taxes, 1970).

Until adoption of this amendment, many employees whose only actual income was from wages were required to file returns and pay additional tax on account of the imputed income attributable to their homes. Elimination of the net annual value of the residence as a source of income not only relieved them of the tax but also relieved those who come within the wage level fixed by the Minister of Finance of the obligation of filing returns.

Classification of Returns

A significant development in improvement of assessment procedures was the classification of all taxpayers' files in accordance with their subject matter and difficulty of assessment. This made it possible to deploy technical personnel efficiently and to establish an order of precedence for the examination of taxpayers within selected classes. It enabled the administration to vary the depth of examination of files within a particular class, in accordance with estimates of compliance by its members and of anticipated revenue from the expenditure of additional auditing effort. It also made it possible to plan annual audit programs in advance and to evaluate the efficiency not only of the assessing offices but of the individual inspectors within each office.

To some extent the concept of classification of files by subject matter and relative difficulty is reflected in the concentration of complex corporate files and those of other large enterprises within the Tel Aviv Assessing Office for Large Enterprises (*Pashmag*). This occurred, as before mentioned, in 1955. It was also reflected in the establishment of special units for the assessment of wage-earners and, in Tel Aviv, in the eventual concentration of all wage-earners' files in a single office. However, the method of classification of files within each assessing office has represented a substantial advance in the use of the concept.

For assessment, statistical and other purposes, taxpayers' files have been classified as follows:

CLASS
1. Files to be closed, such as deceased taxpayers or emigrants.
2. Recipients of nontaxable income, such as pensions; or recipients of income not in excess of personal exemptions.
3. Company directors, 75 percent or more of whose income is from salaries and dividends.
4. Self-employed taxpayers who are not required to keep books. This is further divided into two subclasses.
    4.1. "Small taxpayers," with incomes below a stated level, e.g., IL. 6,500 in 1965.
    4.2. Taxpayers with incomes above the stated level, who do not keep books and are not required to do so. Included are certain agricultural settlements and farmers.

CLASS
5.   Taxpayers who are required to keep books and those, who although not required to keep books, actually do so. Class 5 is further subdivided.
   5.1.   Taxpayers required to keep books who, in fact, have failed to do so. Although technically this subclass should not exist, there have been a number of taxpayers who have been laggard in complying with the bookkeeping requirements.
   5.2.   Taxpayers who keep books whether or not required to do so.
6.   Companies. This is divided further into:
   6.1.   Housing companies, investment companies, and others whose income is solely from property, such as rents, interest, dividends.
   6.2.   Regular companies.
   6.3.   Large companies, assigned to *Pashmag* in Tel Aviv and to the units for large enterprises in Jerusalem and Haifa.
7.   Inactive companies, such as those organized solely to hold title to nonproductive land.

In addition, as before mentioned, employees are divided into two groups.

Within each assessing office there is a further grouping of files in accordance with subject matter. This method of classification is based upon the reasonable premise that an inspector who has accumulated experience in the assessment of a particular type of business — be it shoemakers or banks — will be able to handle the files of other taxpayers in the same line of business with greater facility.

The combination of these two methods of classification, by type of business and difficulty of assessment, enables supervisory personnel, both at the local offices and at headquarters, to program the work more effectively and to maintain a close watch upon production. The criteria for judging production are weighted in accordance with the numerical classification.

The numerical classification system has also made it possible to program, on a national scale, the task of disposing of the accumulation of assessments for past years.[49] Before this was done detailed studies were made of the characteristics of all self-employed taxpayers, based principally upon assessments for the taxable year 1955, which had been made by May 31, 1958. This study covered 87,597 self-employed taxpayers, out of a total of 118,145 subject to assessment for the year, leaving 30,548 (about one-quarter) for whom assessments had not yet been made by the report date. The purpose of the study was to show the distribution of taxpayers, the incomes, and taxes due, in accordance with income levels, economic branches, and geographic location, by assessing

49. The descriptive term for this accumulation was changed as the administration succeeded in reducing it to manageable proportions. At first, when the clean-up process required emergency measures, it was called "backlog"; later, as it began to come under control, it came to be referred to as "inventory."

offices.[50] A similar study was conducted for the taxable year 1957 with respect to wage-earners,[51] its principal purpose being to supply information as to the distribution of wage-earners in accordance with income levels, family status, sources of income other than wages, working wives, and other relevant data. Similar studies, although found to have been less reliable as a basis for administrative planning, had been conducted in prior years.[52]

The increased reliability of the statistical data as compiled for succeeding taxable years was attributed to a combination of several factors: improvements in the quality and quantity of the assessments, the development of staff experience in the gathering of statistical data and in its meaningful analysis, and the increasing availability of the most advanced equipment for storing and analyzing the data. The final breakthrough came with the electronic computer, which came into use in the Israeli tax administration, for computation of assessments and other purposes, almost as soon as these devices became available in the international market.

Public Advisory Committees

This discussion of improvements in assessment procedures would not be complete without mention of the involvement of members of the general public in the assessment process. The language of the statutory provision authorizing the establishment of Advisory Committees is broad enough to permit their use not only for the review of disputed assessments (as they are now used) but also, *ab initio*, in the process of making the assessment.

In some countries assessments are, in fact, made by members of the public. Officials of the Israeli tax administration, on travels abroad, had observed procedures in some of the Scandinavian countries, where assessments are made by public boards. Also, the origin of the Israeli Income Tax Ordinance could be traced to the British income tax law, which for many years had called upon members of the public, entitled General Commissioners of Inland Revenue, to assess their neighbors. However, considering the special needs of the Israeli administration at

50. *Din v'Heshbon Revii al Hakhnasot Ha-Medina, 1957/8* [Fourth Annual Report on State Revenue] pp. 198–295, 296–322.

51. In spite of the fact that self-employed taxpayers were already on a pay-as-you-earn system, the necessity for individual assessments with respect to them is reflected in the fact that while reliable data as to wage-earners could be supplied in 1958 with respect to taxable year 1957, the taxable year 1955 was the most recent available taxable year with respect to self-employed taxpayers; and even then about one-quarter of the assessments had yet to be made.

52. See, e.g., *Din v'Heshbon Shlishi al Hakhnasot ha-Medina 1956/7* [Third Annual Report on State Revenue], pp. 216–305 (self-employed), 306–314 (wage-earners); and compare First Annual Report on State Revenue, pp. 115–157.

the time, it was deemed inadvisable to rely upon members of the public to make the initial assessments.

In 1954, after considering the question, the Sharef Commission reported:

In accordance with Section 55A [now Section 146] of the Income Tax Ordinance, the Minister of Finance may appoint public committees to advise the assessing officer in the use of his powers. The cooperation of the public in certain aspects of income tax is very important in developing understanding on the part of the taxpayers, but in the present circumstances the Committee does not see any possibility of associating members of the public in the first stage of making an assessment.

We have come to the conclusion that there is no real desire on the part of professional people or of the leading figures in any particular branch of economic activity to assist in assessing the incomes of fellow members of their profession or vocation. Even if they were willing to do so it is doubtful whether many citizens could withstand the pressure that would be brought to bear upon them from various quarters in order to secure a reduction of the assessments.

Conclusions drawn from the experience of other countries are not relevant as far as Israel is concerned. These are based on the experience in countries where "tax morale" is high, "true" returns of income are the rule, and the concealment of income the exception. In Israel, the opposite is true — at least at the present time.[53]

Accordingly, when the Advisory Committees were implemented in 1954, their activities were restricted to participating with the assessing officers, in an advisory capacity, in hearing objections to assessments which had already been made. The manner in which they function in resolving disputes is discussed in Chapter 7. Noteworthy here is that in spite of the implication of the Sharef Commission Report, quoted above, to the effect that public members might be involved in the assessment process if conditions improved, there is no current sign of interest, among tax officials or taxpayers, in extending the Advisory Committee functions into the assessment area.

Statute of Limitations on Assessments and Objections

Until 1967 the law prescribed no time limit for the making of assessments. As long as there was no time limit, unassessed returns had a tendency to pile up. This had occurred from 1948 until about 1955, creating a large backlog which it took over ten years of intensive work to cut down to manageable proportions. By fiscal year 1966–67, the backlog had been sufficiently reduced so that the work could be considered as relatively current. This improvement made it feasible to enact an amendment to the Income Tax Ordinance limiting to five years

53. *Sharef Report*, Harvard ed., p. 20.

the period within which the assessing officer can make an assessment.[54] If it is not made within that period, the return is deemed to be accepted as filed.

Before enactment of this limitation upon the period for making assessments, it had not been uncommon for a taxpayer to be assessed simultaneously for as many as ten years.[55] Enactment of a five-year period of limitations did away with this. It also recognized the fact that by 1966 the number of returns which were acceptable as filed had increased. Although intensive audits of returns were still required, the revenue administration felt that the time had come to accept the discipline which a period of limitations imposed upon it. This meant that, to the extent that all returns could not be audited within the five-year period, those which appeared to be acceptable could be permitted to become final without further examination.

Adoption of a five-year period of limitations upon final assessments required a reorganization of the audit procedures in the assessing offices. This was based, in part, upon adoption of a five-year cycle for audits and revision of the procedures for the selection of returns requiring more intensive inspection.[56] One of the steps in this direction, announced in 1968 (before the close of the period during which returns for 1967–68 were due to be filed), was a policy of accepting as filed large numbers of returns of self-employed taxpayers with incomes under IL. 8,000. Further refinements of the processes for selecting returns for intensive examination are being developed. The same amendment which imposes a period of limitations upon assessments also imposes a six-month time limit upon disposition by the assessing officer of objections to assessments.[57]

54. Income Tax Ordinance Amendment Law (no. 11) 1967, 503 *Sefer Hahukim* 94 (July 20, 1967).

55. Zvi Kessler "Limitation of the Period for Assessments" (Hebrew), 1 *Quarterly Tax Journal* 259–260 (July 1966).

56. Simha Gafni, "Our Plans — Some Remarks about Ourselves," pp. 389, 390–391; see also Y. Tamir, "1968 — Year of Events and Changes in Taxes," pp. 145, 148.

57. The transition to strict statutory limits presented some interesting problems. In one case, a taxpayer had filed an objection to a proposed assessment in June 1963. The matter was still pending on July 20, 1967, when the law was amended to impose a five year limit upon assessments and a six-month limit upon disposition of objections. A hearing on the objection was held in February 1969 and a final assessment made a few days later. The taxpayer contended in the District Court that the assessment was void, in that it was made more than five and one-half years from the filing of the objection. The court held that as to objections filed before adoption of the amendment the six-month period for disposing of objections began with the date of the amendment. The assessing officer contended that the amendment gave him another five years in which to make the assessment. The court, holding for the taxpayer, voided the assessment, since it was not made within six months from adoption of the amendment. *Goldman* v. *Assessing Officer*, 2 *Kovetz Piske-Din Ezrahiim* 289 (Dist. Ct., Tel Aviv, March 30, 1969).

7 / Administrative and Judicial Resolution of Disputed Determinations

The Variety of Review Procedures

The Israeli taxpayer is far from complaisant. He is little inclined to accept a tax bill based upon the "best judgment" of the authorities. This tendency has been particularly manifest in regard to the income tax.

In his opposition to tax assessments not based upon provable facts, the taxpayer is supported by the law which, frequently in elaborate detail, lays down procedures whereby the taxpayer may contest the validity of the administrative determination. And even in those instances, such as the Customs Ordinance, where the taxpayer's rights are not fully spelled out, administrative and judicial practices have developed which afford the dissenting taxpayer an opportunity to be heard. As a last resort, if no other remedy is available, he can petition the Supreme Court, sitting as the High Court of Justice, for an order directing the administrator to show cause why he should not be directed to perform, or to refrain from performing, a particular act. This procedure is frequently resorted to and has proved most effective in curbing administrative arbitrariness.

Thus by law and practice the principle has been recognized that taxpayers must be given a fair opportunity to dispute determinations with which they do not agree. What is striking about the Israeli tax system, when the individual statutes are compared, is the multiple variety of procedures which have been provided. It would appear that when the several tax laws were originally enacted, whether under the British mandate or subsequently by the State of Israel, no effort was made to standardize a single procedure which would be applicable to more than the one type of tax then under consideration.[1] The Income Tax Ordinance, which of all the taxes produces the greatest volume of business for the courts, provides for a series of administrative reviews, and then, if an agreement cannot be reached, the taxpayer may proceed as a matter of right first to the District Court and then to the Supreme Court. A similar route is provided by the Estate Tax Law of 1949, as amended in 1964,[2] but, if the disagreement is over the valuation of an asset of

1. See Hannah Avnor, "Authority of the Court in Appeals from Decisions of the Assessing Officer" (Hebrew), 2 *Quarterly Tax Journal* 17 (January 1967); Ze'ev Sher, "Codification of the Tax Laws in Israel" (Hebrew), 1 *Quarterly Tax Journal* 129, 130 (April 1966).

2. Sec. 17; see also Stamp Duty on Documents Law, 1961, sec. 13; Defense Stamp Law, 1956, sec. 3.

the estate, the taxpayer may also, at his choice, have the valuation determined by an agreed upon or court-appointed assessor, whose decision then becomes final.[3]

A different set of patterns is prescribed by the Property Tax and Damages Fund Law, 1961. If (after appeal to the Director) the taxpayer disagrees with a determination relating to inventory or equipment, the appeal from the administrative determination is to the District Court, and further to the Supreme Court; whereas if the disagreement relates to real property, the appeal is to a review committee. The latter consists of three members designated by the Minister of Justice, of whom one is an advocate and one must have real property experience, neither of these being a government employee. The committee may decide substantive issues and is not limited to questions of valuation.[4] The decision of the review committee is appealable, but only on questions of law, to the District Court.[5]

By way of contrast, the Land Betterment Tax Law of 1963 also provides that an appeal from a disputed determination of the Director may be taken to a review committee (sec. 88), but this committee is constituted differently from the one prescribed under the Property Tax and Damages Fund Law. The land betterment tax review committee consists of a District Court judge, who serves as chairman, and two other members, one of whom shall be a public representative (sec. 89). Like the property tax and damages fund review committee, a further appeal can be taken only on issues of law, but in the case of the land betterment tax review committee, the appeal is to the Supreme Court rather than to the District Court (sec. 90). Presumably, the appeal to the Supreme Court is explainable by the fact that one of the committee members is already a District Court judge, but why there should be a different composition for two review committees performing essentially similar functions (indeed why there should be separate review committees for the two laws) is not easily explainable.

These procedural discrepancies, whatever may have been their historic origin, stand in the way of efforts to rationalize the structure of the revenue administration.[6] Perhaps some degree of uniformity will be

3. Secs. 18, 19, Estate Tax Law, 1929; cf. sec. 5, Purchase Tax Law, 1952, which provides for review by an appeals committee, whose decision is also final.

4. *Beit Yulus, Ltd.* v. *Director of Property Tax and Damages Fund*, Sup. Ct., 94/63, decided Oct. 8, 1963; summary at 1 *Quarterly Tax Journal* 154 (April 1966).

5. Property Tax and Damages Fund Law, 1961, secs. 26, 26A, 27, 27A, 29, as amended by Property Tax and Compensation Fund (Amendment no. 3) Law, 5727–1967, 21 *Laws of the State of Israel* 15 (Jerusalem: Government Printer, undated).

6. Harold C. Wilkenfeld, "Administrative Tribunals for Tax Disputes" (Hebrew), 1 *Quarterly Tax Journal* 225, 227 (April 1966).

achieved if the administrative provisions of the several revenue laws are ultimately codified.[7]

There are two essential threads which can be discerned in the variegated pattern of review procedures provided by existing law. One, which is characteristic of the direct taxes (income tax, inheritance tax, and the property tax on inventory and equipment), makes the administrative and judicial review procedures available to the taxpayer before the assessment becomes final and before he is obliged to pay the tax. The characteristic of the indirect taxes (customs, excises, stamp duty, purchase tax), on the other hand, is that the tax must be paid (or at least covered by adequate security) before the statutory review procedures become available. Nevertheless, by administrative fiat, informal procedures have been introduced whereby an indirect taxpayer may have his case referred to higher authority before being compelled to pay.

Although the procedural disparities have been of long standing, they did not become evident or irksome until recent years. As suggested before, the disputes which are least likely to be resolved at the outset are those which involve the exercise of best judgment by the tax authorities. The first tax with respect to which best judgment assessments were made in any substantial number was the income tax.[8] The flood of objections and appeals to the courts which were generated by the expanded activities of the income tax authorities produced a variety of problems and solutions. In the course of time, some of the experience gained in disposing of the thousands of income tax disputes may stimulate changes in the administrative and judicial review procedures applicable to other taxes. Accordingly, the balance of this chapter will concentrate upon the procedures under the Income Tax Ordinance and the experience which has accumulated thereunder.

Administrative Appeals under the Income Tax Ordinance

The administrative remedies available to a taxpayer who disagrees with a proposed assessment are expressly provided by law, unlike the American review procedures, which are supported only by administrative practice and regulations. Several procedures are prescribed, depending upon the nature of the determination and the official who makes it.

A procedure frequently resorted to by taxpayers is the formal objection to a preliminary notice of assessment issued by an assessing officer. The statute provides that within five years after the filing of a return

7. Sher, "Codification" pp. 132–133.
8. Best judgment assessments can also be made under section 19 of the Purchase Tax Law, in instances where the periodic returns and books of account are unreliable.

the assessing officer shall either (1) make a final assessment on the basis of the return, (2) assess the tax on the basis of his best judgment, if he has reason to believe that the return is inaccurate, or (3) make a tentative assessment on the basis of the return, but reserve the right to make a further assessment. If no return was filed the assessing officer may also make a best judgment assessment (Sec. 145).

If a taxpayer disagrees with a proposed best judgment assessment he may, within fifteen days after receiving the notice of assessment, file a written objection, stating his grounds and requesting the assessing officer to review and revise the assessment. In his objection the taxpayer can stipulate whether he elects to have the objection heard by the assessing officer alone, or that it be heard by him in consultation with an Advisory Committee of laymen (Secs. 150–152).

Once an objection has been filed the assessing officer must dispose of it within six months, or within five years after the filing date of the original return, whichever date is later. Otherwise the objection is deemed valid and the assessment must be modified accordingly (Sec. 152(c)). This period of limitation upon administrative action was imposed in 1967, simultaneously with enactment of the five-year statute of limitations on assessments, previously mentioned. Within the limited period, which cannot be extended by agreement, the assessing officer may either settle the dispute by agreement with the taxpayer or issue a final assessment, after a hearing either before the assessing officer alone or in conjunction with an Advisory Committee. If time permits and circumstances warrant, the assessing officer may also elect to conduct a further investigation. If the taxpayer disagrees with the final notice of assessment, he may appeal to the courts.

Although the bulk of disputes follows the administrative route which has just been described, there are several situations for which the statute prescribes other procedures. There are some determinations which, by law, are required to be made by the Income Tax Commissioner. These are (1) the manner of distribution of income among the stockholders of certain closely held corporations whose activities pertain only to buildings which they own (sec. 64); and (2) a determination by the Commissioner that undistributed profits of a closely held corporation should be taxed to the stockholders as though distributed as dividends (secs. 76–81). Although these determinations appears to be closely related, as to the first of these, the Commissioner's determination is immediately subject to judicial appeal (sec. 64), whereas the second requires that the Commissioner consult with a special committee of five (sec. 81) before exercising his authority to direct the assessing officer to tax the stockholders in accordance with his instructions (sec. 77). The committee with whom the Commissioner is required to consult in the latter instance is also different, both in its structure and method of appointment, from the Advisory Committee which is available in the case of the usual objection to an assessment.[9]

Another variation on these procedures applies when the assessing officer has imposed a deficiency penalty in the belief that a taxpayer's failure to file a return, or to disclose the full amount of his income upon a return which he has filed, was negligent or fraudulent. In such instances, if the taxpayer objects to the imposition of the deficiency penalty, the objection *must* be heard before an Advisory Committee drawn from the same panel as those who hear ordinary objections [10] (sec. 191[d]).

In addition to the prescribed procedures for administrative review of determinations of the assessing officer, the Income Tax Commissioner is also authorized, on his own motion or upon request of the taxpayer, to review the file pertaining to an assessment and to issue a new assessment notice. If the new assessment calls for an increase in the liability, the taxpayer must be given an opportunity to be heard (sec. 147).

Irrespective of the review procedures which may have been followed administratively in arriving at the final assessment, the taxpayer may, after having exhausted his administrative remedies, and without paying the tax in dispute,[11] appeal to the District Court and then, as a matter of right, to the Supreme Court.[12]

With minor exceptions, the procedures just described have been in the Income Tax Ordinance, substantially unchanged, since 1952. However, for some years the Commissioner did not exercise his authority to direct the assessing officers to treat undistributed profits of closely held corporations as dividends to their stockholders; and the Minister of Justice did not designate a panel of committee members to consult with the Commissioner in the exercise of that authority until 1964.[13] And although the provision for the imposition of deficiency penalties had

9. Compare sections 81 and 146. Among other things, the list from which the committee of five is selected is not the same as the one from which the Advisory Committee panels are selected. Two of the five may be government employees. Also, the Commissioner is *required* to consult with the committee in the case of the imputed dividend, whereas reference to the Advisory Committee, in the case of a taxpayer's objection to an ordinary assessment, is discretionary with the assessing officer.

10. In recent years, the number of taxpayers objecting to imposition of the deficiency penalty has been greater than those objecting to assessments.

11. Except in the case of a taxpayer whose tax is determined to be in jeopardy, because he is about to leave the country or for other reasons (sec. 194[d]). He must pay the tax first..

12. Sections 153–158. There are numerous other references to judicial appeals in the Income Tax Ordinance (e.g. secs. 30, 63(c), 85(e), 86(b), 87(2), 112(b), 130(b), 160(c), 167, 168, 173, 181, 194(d), (209), but these appear to be the product of redundant legislative drafting which might have been obviated by addition of a few words in the general appeal provisions.

13. *Fifteenth Annual Report of State Comptroller, 1963/64* (Hebrew), 84–85 (1964).

been in the statute since 1954, the assessing officers rarely applied it until expressly ordered to do so by the Commissioner, after sharp criticism by the State Comptroller.[14] Accordingly, experience with the use of public committees in these two areas has been limited until recently.

Income Tax Advisory Committees

The administrative appeal procedures just described had their origins in the mandatory Income Tax Ordinance as enacted in 1941 and as revised in 1947. Several Israeli modifications and additions to the basic procedures have been mentioned. The most significant of these is the establishment of the Advisory Committee procedure, for the hearing of objections to best judgment assessments. Because of the novelty of this procedure it merits detailed consideration.

The provision creating the Advisory Committee procedure was enacted in 1952.[15] In its current version it provides:

The Minister of Finance may appoint a committee, either generally or for a particular area or class of assessees, to advise the Assessing Officers in the exercise of their powers under sections 145(a)(2) [best judgment assessments where return is inadequate], 145(b) ["best judgment" assessments where no return was filed] and 150–152 [assessing officer's review of objections]; in appointing such a committee, the Minister of Finance shall have regard to different circles existing within the community.[16]

This provision was enacted upon the recommendation of a United Nations expert[17] and was apparently patterned upon institutions in use in the Scandinavian countries.[18] It should be observed that, as enacted, the provision contemplates that the Advisory Committees[19] could have been utilized to assist the assessing officers both in making best judgment assessments and in hearing objections to such assessments. It should also be observed that the establishment of the committees was permissive, not mandatory. When the provision was finally implemented in December 1954, the function of the Advisory Committees

14. *Fourteenth Annual Report of State Comptroller, 1962/63* (Hebrew, section on closely held companies [1963]).

15. Sec. 55A, I.T.O., 1947, as amended.

16. Sec. 146(a) I.T.O. (official translation).

17. See I Bloch, pp. 81, 103, and compare excerpt from budget address, ibid., p. 93.

18. Aryeh Lapidoth, "Trends in the Income Tax Legislation of Israel," in XVI *Scripta Hierosolymitana*, 325, 334, 337 (Jerusalem: Hebrew University, 1966).

19. When these committees were first put into effect, they were frequently referred to as "Public Committees" rather than "Advisory Committees."

was limited to the hearing of objections — they do not to any extent participate in the initial assessments.[20]

Implementation of the Advisory Committee Procedure

When, in 1952, the concept of involving members of the general public in the income tax assessment and review processes was first adopted, the administration was already in serious difficulty. The number of income tax files had increased from roughly 88,000 in 1948 to about 280,000 in 1952. The force of inspectors was hardly larger in 1952 than in 1948. The procedure for the inspection of income tax returns had not changed materially; it involved a slow, detailed review of each item in the return. The result was a heavy backlog of files waiting to be assessed. There were, additionally, many taxpayers who had never filed returns and who had not yet been swept into the network. The staff was unable to cope with the burden and, by 1952, the situation had reached emergency proportions.

In an effort to dispose of the assessment backlog, the number of best judgment assessments (often based on guesswork) were sharply increased during 1953 and 1954. These produced a corresponding increase in the number of objections filed against these assessments. It did not take long for the administration to realize that the speed-up process had been self-defeating, because the reduction in the backlog of unassessed returns had merely produced a corresponding backlog of objections awaiting disposition by the assessing officers. Furthermore, since the filing of an objection deferred payment of the tax, the speed-up was not reflected in increased revenue collections.

The arbitrariness with which assessments were made during this period may partially explain the two-year delay (from 1952 to 1954) in the implementation of the Advisory Committee procedure. The administration was unable to justify many of the disputed assessments. In this situation, it could not afford to disillusion the lay public further by exposing questionable assessments to review by public representatives serving on Advisory Committees. Instead, a new procedure was attempted, whereby objecting taxpayers were invited to appear before a committee of employees of the particular assessing office. Frequently, however, because of the shortage of technically qualified employees, only one member of the committee might be a qualified inspector and the others might be mere clerks, selected more because of their "judi-

20. In Sweden, lay boards make the initial assessment (Assessment Boards) and review disputed assessments (County Tax Appeal Boards). Harvard Law School, International Program in Taxation, World Tax Series, *Taxation in Sweden* (Boston: Little, Brown, 1959), pp. 575–578. For reasons later explained, the Israel authorities decided not to employ laymen in the assessment process and to limit them to an advisory capacity in the review process.

cial" appearance than because of their technical knowledge.[21] Then a bargaining process was resorted to in an effort to arrive at a figure agreeable to both sides. But, as a result of the shift to bargaining, the integrity of the administration suffered badly in the minds of the tax-paying public. The unfortunate repercussions of this period of almost three years, from the end of 1952 into 1955, continued to plague the administration for some years thereafter.

By the end of 1953, there were still officials within the administration who questioned some of the premises upon which the idea of establishing public Advisory Committees had first been based. They doubted the advisability of involving the lay public in the review process, at least until the backlog of past assessments had been cleared up; they were concerned about its effect upon the then shaky relationship between tax-payers and tax officials; and they questioned whether someone in the taxpayer's own line of occupation, who himself would likely be a tax-payer, would not be inclined to consider his own self-interest above that of the Treasury. These observations, it was felt, were particularly relevant if the Advisory Committees were to be used in the preliminary stages of making assessments (as the law permitted), as well as in the hearing of disputed assessments.

A strong recommendation that the Finance Ministry proceed with the organization of the Advisory Committees to assist in the review of disputed assessments was nevertheless made at the beginning of 1954 by the Commission for the Examinations of the Methods of Assessing and Collecting Income Tax (the Sharef Commission). After expressing the opinion (quoted in Chapter 4) that the then low level of taxpayer compliance made it inadvisable to involve members of the general public in the first stage of making an assessment, the Report continued:

On the other hand, it is the opinion of the Committee that public figures, leading members of various organizations and associations, would be ready to take part in committees dealing with objections to assessments, and this cooperation is most desirable from the point of view of developing mutual understanding with the taxpaying public.[22]

As a public relations measure, it cannot be doubted that appointment of the Advisory Committees could serve an important purpose. It will be remembered that in October 1954 the suicide of a Jerusalem baker, which some attributed to his income tax difficulties, had precipitated a strong public reaction against the income tax administration. Among

21. Israel Greenstein (Gal-Edd), "Developments in Assessment Procedures," in *Proceedings of Symposium on Income Taxation* (Hebrew), Hebrew University, Jerusalem, 1955, p. 24; see also Yosef Stern, 1 *Income Tax Law and Practice* (Hebrew) 283.
22. *Sharef Report* (Harvard ed.), p. 20.

the measures taken to restore public confidence was immediate implementation of the Advisory Committees, whose organization was announced in November 1954 and completed in December.[23]

The responsibility for compiling a register of qualified laymen was assigned to the Acting Income Tax Commissioner.[24] Candidates from throughout the country and from various fields of endeavor were selected either on an individual basis or on recommendation of various professional and trade organizations. The objective in formulating the register was to conform as far as possible with the statutory direction that, in appointing committees, the Minister of Finance "shall take into consideration the various sectors of which the public is comprised." This was construed as meaning that, so far as possible, an objecting taxpayer should have his matter considered by a committee which included at least one individual who had some familiarity with the type of business or other income-producing activity in which the taxpayer was engaged.

By December 1954 a general countrywide roster of 1,000 individuals considered qualified to serve on the Advisory Committees was published in the *Official Gazette* and, at the same time, the acting Income Tax Commissioner promulgated a set of rules setting forth the procedures to be followed by the Advisory Committees.

It is noteworthy that from the outset it was contemplated, both by the statute and the implementing regulations, that these committees should be advisory — to "*advise* the assessing officers in the exercise of *their powers*" (italics mine). The committees have no authority to make decisions which would be binding upon anyone. However, as a matter of practice, in order to deemphasize this limitation of the committees to purely advisory functions, the assessing officers were instructed by the Commissioner to refer directly to him any cases in which the assessing officers desired to reject the "advice" of an Advisory Committee. In most instances, however, the assessing officers have accepted the "advice." [25]

The advisory quality of the committees is reflected in their procedures. It was considered both permissible and desirable that the assessing officer — the person being advised — should have direct, *ex parte* contact with the committee. Thus, the procedure requires participation by the assessing officer (or his representative) in all deliberations of the Advisory Committee, without regard to whether the taxpayer is present or afforded an opportunity to be heard. Indeed, the statute permitting

23. *Haaretz*, November 21, 1954, p. 3; November 24, 1954, p. 5; December 2, 1954, p. 3.

24. The Commissioner who had been appointed in 1952 resigned in 1954, shortly after publication of the Sharef Report.

25. *Ten Years of Activity of the Income Tax Advisory Committees* (Hebrew) pp. 8, 10 (Ministry of Finance, Jerusalem, 1964).

establishment of the Advisory Committees makes no express mention of a hearing to be afforded the taxpayer. Nor did any of the functions of the assessing officer with relation to which the Advisory Committees were originally contemplated provide for an appearance by the taxpayer, as a matter of right. The right to appear is, nevertheless, assured by the regulations.[26]

Advisory Committee Rules of Practice

In prescribing regulations to guide the procedures before Advisory Committees, the authorities had to solve a series of problems not necessarily contemplated when the provision was enacted in 1952. With reference to the nature of the procedure to be followed before the Advisory Committees these included: whether it should be formal or informal; whether the hearing should be considered as adversary, with both sides treated equally as parties litigant, both to be present throughout, with no special advantage given to the assessing officer; whether there should be a written, reasoned decision submitted to both parties and made public. In other words, was an independent tribunal contemplated? The conclusions were in the negative.

The first rules governing Advisory Committee procedure were promulgated in November 1954. They have been revised from time to time as experience has required. The summary which follows is of the rules as in effect from 1964. A 1971 revision does not appear to have affected the pattern described below:

Organization of the Committee

An Advisory Committee consists of two individuals, selected by the assessing officer from the roster of committee members in his district. In organizing the committee, the assessing officer will take care that one member shall be, as far as possible, familiar with the characteristics of the taxpayer's line of business.

Notices of appearance

Taxpayers invited to appear before an Advisory Committee may be (i) those who requested such a hearing when filing an objection; (ii) those whose objections the assessing officer has himself designated to be heard before a committee, even though not requested by the taxpayer; and (iii) those who had objected to the imposition of a delinquency penalty. Notices to taxpayers to appear before a committee are given at least seven days before the hearing. If the taxpayer fails to appear, the meeting may proceed in his absence, but if he later supplies an acceptable explanation for his absence, the conclusion reached at the

26. Advisory Committee Rules, as in effect in 1964; see also Alfred Witkon and R. I. Neeman, *Dinei Misim*, pp. 230–231.

prior meeting will be set aside and another opportunity will be afforded him to present his case.

Hearing procedure

The assessing officer serves as chairman of the meeting, or he may designate a high-ranking member of his staff, who had not participated in making the assessment under review, to sit in his stead. If one of the panel states that he does not wish to deal with the matter of a particular taxpayer, the other committee member and the assessing officer officer may nevertheless proceed with the matter. If a taxpayer, before commencement of consideration of his matter, objects to the makeup of the committee, his objection will be recorded and the assessing officer will then determine whether to proceed, even in the taxpayer's absence, or whether to organize another committee to which the taxpayer will be summoned.

At the opening of the meeting, the assessing officer will supply the committee with the objections filed by the taxpayers whose matters are on the committee agenda and will also make their files available. Then the taxpayers are called in, one at a time, together with the inspector who dealt with the assessment. The taxpayer, or his representative, is permitted to explain in detail the reasons for his objection and may supply evidence orally or in writing. Then the inspector responds to the taxpayer's contentions, furnishing, in addition, affirmative support for his assessment.

After the taxpayer, his counsel, the inspector, and their respective witnesses have been heard, they leave the room and the committee considers the matter, with the guidance of the assessing officer. Summary minutes are made of the proceedings of the committee and of its conclusions.

Committee recommendations

The committee is authorized to approve the assessment or to recommend revision, upward or downward, as it sees fit. If both committee members are in accord, the minutes so indicating will be signed by both; if they are not, their views will be stated separately and each will sign only the statement of his own conclusions. Thereafter, the committee has no further contact with the case.

Amendment of the assessment notice — report to the Commissioner

If the members of the committee are in accord, and the assessing officer decides to accept their advice, he will issue an amended assessment notice accordingly. If the members are not in accord, and the assessing officer decides to accept the advice of one of them, he will issue an amended assessment notice accordingly, but will so inform the committee member whose advice had not been accepted. If the assessing officer does not wish to accept the advice of the committee members, whether joint or separate, he so advises the Commissioner in writing, attaching the relevant material and stating in detail the reasons for his disagreement with the committee. The Commissioner will notify the assessing officer of his own position in the matter, and this will be brought by the assessing officer to the attention of the committee, if the assessing officer, after consulting with the Commissioner, still decides to reject the advice of the committee.

Secrecy

The substance of the committee's proceedings and of any material supplied to a committee member in his capacity as such is secret, in accordance with Section 231 of the Ordinance. It is prohibited to furnish (without consent of the Minister of Finance) any information or document relating to the proceedings of the committee, under penalty, in accordance with Section 234, of two months' imprisonment or a fine of IL. 100.

Advisory Committee Membership

The initial list of about one thousand public members who had been selected to serve on the Advisory Committees remained effective for about ten years. By 1964 the roster had grown to approximately 3,300 members. These had disposed of about 100,000 cases over the ten-year period. During the fiscal year 1964–65 it was decided that thereafter appointments, which had been for an indefinite term, should be canceled, and, in consultation with the various affected professional, industrial, and commercial organizations, a new register of Advisory Committee members was issued. The announced purpose of this change was to strengthen the independent character of the Advisory Committees.[27]

The register of Advisory Committee members published in June 1965 throws some light upon the structure of the Advisory Committee as well as upon problem areas which the administration was then facing. The list is divided by assessing offices. Within each locality the list is further broken down into types of businesses, such as construction, artisans, shopkeepers, farmers, free professions, transport, hotel-keepers, food, and services. This distribution is in accordance with the directive of the statute, that committees be representative, so far as possible, of the makeup of the taxpaying public.

From this one can distinguish, in turn, which of the principal groupings of the taxpaying public served by the several assessing offices were

27. *Ten Years of Activity of the Income Tax Advisory Committees*, p. 8. *Eleventh Annual Report on State Revenue, 1964/65* (Hebrew), p. 37.

inclined to resort most often to Advisory Committees. For example, private farmers are perennial problems for the tax collector. Farmer-committee members are listed in many of the localities, indicating that private farming is rather widespread. In Israel a special problem is presented by the Arab farmer, with respect to whom, it appears, different approaches to assessment are employed from those used with the Jewish farmers. This is indicated by the fact that in several localities (Hadera, Netanya, Afula, Acre), where there are a substantial number of Arab farmers, there are separate lists of committee members under the heading of "farming" and under the heading "minorities," i.e. Arabs. On the other hand, in several other localities (e.g., Haifa, Jerusalem, Nazareth, Safed), which also have substantial numbers of Arab farmers, there is no separate "minorities" list, and in these localities Arab farmers are included in the "farming" list. The separation of Arab and Jewish farmers, where is exists, appears to be a relic of the method used in assessing Arab farmers during the mandatory administration. It appears that the Israeli authorities have not yet been able to replace it completely by more scientific methods of assessment. It is also an indication of the large numbers of private farmers to be found among the Arab population.[28]

The lists reflect other income-productive activities of self-employed taxpayers with whom the administration seems to have been encountering difficulties at the time. These include artisans of various types, construction contractors, tradesmen, and shopkeepers.

By 1965, when this revised list was published, there had been substantial improvements in the quality of record-keeping by many taxpayers and in the administrative procedures for accurately assessing annual incomes in many branches of business. To some extent these advances are reflected in the lists of Advisory Committee members. There is an emphasis upon those income-producing activities where, because of continuing difficulties in achieving accurate assessments, there continued also to be large numbers of disputed assessments.

The Business of the Advisory Committees

Experience demonstrated that the Advisory Committees have been most effective in situations where an informed guess had to be made of the amount of the taxpayer's income, because of the absence of more accurate means of assessment. This would usually occur in cases where there was no *tahshiv*, or not enough facts were known to use one.

28. In the first three years the number of Arab committee members was nominal. There was a sharp increase in 1957/58 and since then Arab members have comprised more than one-quarter of the total roster. See Table 1, in *Five Years of the Income Tax Advisory Committees* (Hebrew), p. 26 (Ministry of Finance, Jerusalem, 1960).

Having been given such facts as were available, and being guided by their general knowledge of the particular line of business, the committee members, in consultation with the assessing officer, would try to reach an assessment which was likely to be acceptable both to the taxpayer and to the assessing officer. At best, this method was a makeshift, which became less significant as the levels of sophistication of both administration and taxpayers were raised. Thus, the Advisory Committees have come to deal principally with taxpayers who have not kept books of account.

By their terms, the Advisory Committees are limited to the review of best judgment assessments. In 1954–55 objections were filed against more than one-third of all the best judgment assessments which were made. Of the more than 27,000 objections filed, about 80 percent were concluded by agreement with the taxpayer, and final assessment notices were issued with respect to the balance.[29] The Advisory Committees were operative during only a fraction of 1954–55, and then only in a few of the assessing offices. In the following year, although the available data are incomplete and difficult to correlate, it appears that no more than one-fourth of the objections to best judgment assessments were heard before Advisory Committees.[30] The annual reports for the next several years furnish no basis for analysis of the role of the Advisory Committees in the disposition of objections. There are indications, however, of a trend toward a decrease in the number of committee-reviewed objections disposed of by agreement.[31]

It should be observed that from 1955 onward there was a sharp increase in the number of cases appealed to the District Courts. From 1948 until the end of 1954, a total of 648 income tax appeals were filed. By comparison, in the first eight months of 1955 alone, 343 appeals were filed.[32] Since 1963 there have been as many as 1800 annually.[33] This represents about 1 percent of all assessments.

To some extent the increase in litigated cases has paralleled in both time and quantity the activities of the Advisory Committees. Yet these developments are not necessarily to be correlated, for it was another

29. *First Annual Report on State Revenue*, pp. 127–129.
30. See *Second Annual Report on State Revenue*, 1955/56 (Hebrew), pp. 46–47, 67–68, and Tables 22–24, pp. 109–111.
31. See, e.g., *Third Annual Report on State Revenue*, 1956/57 (Hebrew), p. 223. In that year, about one-third were disputed, as compared to one-fifth two years before.
32. E. W. Klimowsky, "Administrative and Judicial Appeals," in *Proceedings of Symposium on Income Taxation* (Hebrew), pp. 38, 39. Dr. Klimowsky also states that of over 87,000 objections filed by self-employed taxpayers from December 1, 1954, through May 31, 1955, only 5 percent had been disposed of by the Advisory Committees.
33. *Twelfth Annual Report on State Revenue, 1965/66* (Hebrew), p. 43; cf. Judge H. S. Lowenberg, Preface to Strauss and Neiger, *Mafteah Klali Lifsikat Mas Hakhnasah* (General Index to Income Tax Decisions).

factor, common to both of them, that was responsible, namely, the substantial improvement in the income tax administration and in the technical level of its personnel which began to take place in 1955 and which has since continued. This factor has affected the business of the Advisory Committees.

From the standpoint of a taxpayer who has kept proper books and whose income is reported on the basis of his books, resort to an Advisory Committee to resolve a dispute with the assessing officer as to the correct amount of his income is not likely to be helpful. In such instances the assessing officer has the judicially and legislatively imposed burden of explaining the particular respects in which he considers the taxpayer's books to be defective before he can ignore them and resort to a best judgment assessment. Although, at the outset, some taxpayers who had kept proper books nevertheless elected to have their objections heard before an Advisory Committee, experience often proved that the issues could be more satisfactorily resolved, on a technical basis, by requesting a hearing before the assessing officer, without a committee. Certainly, if an issue of law was involved, an Advisory Committee was not as likely to be qualified to pass upon it as the assessing officer, who often dealt with such issues.

The net result was that within a relatively short time after implementation of the Advisory Committee procedure — by the end of fiscal year 1956–57 — only about one-seventh of the objections were being heard by Advisory Committees, the balance being handled by the several assessing officers without the assistance of a committee. Experience had indicated that the Advisory Committees were being resorted to almost exclusively in cases where there were questions of fact to be resolved, not all of which were capable of ascertainment and therefore a best judgment (read "informed guess") was required. In such instances, the taxpayers seemed to feel (as shown by their choice) that the Advisory Committee would give them more favorable consideration than the assessing officer. On the other hand, even from the beginning, the Assessing Officer for Large Enterprises, all of whose clients were taxpayers of substance who were required to keep books, hardly ever had a dispute which was referred to an Advisory Committee. In general, also, few taxpayers who were represented by attorneys or auditors elected to appear before an Advisory Committee.

Statistics for recent years show that the highest ratios of objections to assessments occur among self-employed taxpayers who are not required to keep books (for 1965–66 more than half) and that, among these, almost two-thirds are filed by those whose assessed incomes are in the lowest brackets (Class 4).[34] The contrast is even sharper among

34. *Twelfth Annual Report on State Revenue, 1965/66* (Hebrew), pp. 36–37; *Annual Report of Income and Property Tax Branch, 1967/68* (Hebrew), Table no. 5, p. 85. For classification system see Chapter 6.

taxpayers who are required to keep books (Class 5), where objections are filed by more than half of those who are required to keep books and do not do so (Class 5.1) and by less than one-third of those who keep books, whether or not required to do so (Class 5.2). The ratio drops even lower, to about one-fourth, among companies (Class 6) and company directors (Class 3).[35] Clearly, the tendency to object to an assessment (and perhaps the ability to sustain an objection) is substantially lower among taxpayers who keep books and, conversely, highest among those whose assessments are most likely to be based upon estimates rather than provable facts.

In 1965–66, out of over 82,000 objections, only 11,700 (about one-sixth) were disposed of by the Advisory Committees; and of the latter more than 77 percent consisted of taxpayers whose incomes were finally assessed at less than IL. 9,000. Of the 11,700 objections heard by the Advisory Committees, the original assessment was reduced in almost 91 percent of the cases, increased in almost 2 percent, and confirmed in only 7.3 percent.[36] And, of those cases which have been reviewed by Advisory Committees in recent years, there has been a fairly consistent relationship among (1) the income originally reported, (2) the income as originally assessed, and (3) the income as determined by the Advisory Committee. The tendency has been for the income originally assessed (and objected to) to be somewhat over double the income shown on the return, and for the income as determined by the Advisory Committee to be less than half the difference between the two.[37] In other words, the committees have tended to "split the difference" between the taxpayer and the assessing officer, leaning more on the side of the taxpayer.[38]

The future may see a substantial drop in the number of objections heard by the Advisory Committees. In June 1968 the Income Tax Commissioner announced a new assessment policy, the result of which, if successful, will be the acceptance as filed of about 80 percent of the returns filed by taxpayers who are not required to keep books and whose incomes do not exceed IL. 8,000. This group comprises about one-half of all taxpayers other than employees. It has also accounted for more than half of the objections heard by the Advisory Committees.

35. The issues arising as to company directors are usually closely related to issues raised against their companies.

36. Derived from *Twelfth Annual Report on State Revenue, 1965/66* (Hebrew), Table 9, p. 36; Table 15, p. 41; and Table 17, p. 42.

37. See, e.g., Budget Message of Minister of Finance for 1971/72, Supplement E, p. 114.

38. This tendency is also characteristic of objections to the imposition of deficiency penalties. These are all required to be heard by Advisory Committees. For each of the years 1963–64 — 1965–66, the sum of the penalties finally determined has been about half that originally imposed (*Twelfth Annual Report on State Revenue, 1965/66* [Hebrew], Table 14, p. 40). Not surprisingly, objections had been filed against about three-fourths of the deficiency penalties imposed in each of these years (ibid.).

Acceptance of their returns as filed will eliminate their objections. A further reduction in the number of objections may also be anticipated, in coming years, as the number of taxpayers keeping books increases. As before mentioned, a relatively small percentage of taxpayers required to keep books (both individuals and companies) tend to file objections and, among these, very few elect to have their objections heard before Advisory Committees.

One can forecast that as the technical ability of income tax inspectors reaches a suitable level and as the majority of taxpayers begin to maintain adequate books, upon which their returns are based, resort to Advisory Committees as an aid toward the settlement of tax disputes will diminish.[39] Nevertheless, one cannot minimize the importance of the Advisory Committee procedure which, during the ten-year period from 1955 to 1965, at least, supplied an important medium for drawing fire from the embattled administration.

Reopening of Assessment by Commissioner

The Commissioner has the authority to reopen and revise an assessment even if it has otherwise become final. In the normal case he may do this within six years after the close of the year in which the return was filed. However, if the taxpayer has filed an erroneous return or has sought to evade the tax, the Commissioner may do so within ten or fifteen years, respectively, after the filing year (sec. 147, as amended). Until 1952, the provision then in effect [40] did not permit the taxpayer to request that his assessment be reconsidered by the Commissioner.[41] Until then the purpose of the provision was to permit an additional assessment to be made on the basis of newly discovered evidence, not to furnish the taxpayer with an additional opportunity for administrative appeal, or an avenue for granting a refund. In 1956, however, the law was amended to permit the assessment to be reopened "on the application of the assessee," as well as on the Commissioner's own motion. The effect of this amendment has been to make the Income Tax Commissioner available as a final arbiter of the action of the as-

39. See Harold C. Wilkenfeld, "The Rights of the Income Taxpayer" (Hebrew), 7 *Roeh Haheshbon* 287, 290–291 (May–June 1957); "Administrative Review of Objections to Income Tax Assessments" (Hebrew), 1 *Hed Hamishpat* 277, 278 (August 1957); and "The Juridical Guarantees of the Taxpayer vis-a-vis the Fisc (Israel)," *33 Cahiers de Droit Fiscal International* 78, 87–88. See also Dov Neiger, "Income Tax Objections and Appeals," 4 *Quarterly Tax Journal* (Hebrew) 257, 265 (July 1969).

40. For a more detailed statement of the origin and application of the present provision see Aryeh Lapidoth, "Revision of Assessments by the Income Tax Commissioner" (Hebrew), 1 *Quarterly Tax Journal* 27 (December 1965).

41. For the Hebrew text of section 56 of the Income Tax Ordinance of 1947 before and after its 1952 amendments, compare Avraham Fellman and Reuven Nohimovsky, *Dinei Mas Hakhnasah*, p. 88 (Tel Aviv, 1949), with Avraham Fellman, *Dinei Mas Hakhnasah be-Yisrael*, p. 202.

sessing officers. The taxpayer is entitled to a hearing before the Commissioner takes action to *increase* the prior assessment, but not if the proposed action is to *decrease* the assessment, even if the amount of the decrease is less than the taxpayer believes is due him. The Advisory Committee procedure is not available in a reopening by the Commissioner. And even though the reopening may be at the behest of the taxpayer, the Commissioner is not obliged to reopen the assessment, unless he is convinced that there is good reason to do so.[42]

Action by the Commissioner by way of revising an assessment may take place at any time within the periods of limitation prescribed by Section 147. Accordingly, such action may occur (a) while the assessing officer's preliminary assessment is pending on review pursuant to an objection; (b) after issuance of a final assessment but before expiration of the period during which an appeal could be filed in the District Court; (c) during the pendency of a court appeal; or (d) after an assessment has become final, whether as a result of the taxpayer's agreement thereto or as the result of an adverse court decision.

Procedural problems have arisen in connection with the Commissioner's exercise of his authority at each of these stages, and these have produced both litigation and amendments of the law. A number of potential questions remain to be clarified.[43] A problem which has recently arisen is whether the Commissioner can be compelled to reopen assessments that were based upon a Supreme Court decision which later had been reversed by the same Court.[44] Some have expressed the view that the reversal should not be applied retrospectively, and that the Commissioner is not obliged to reopen assessments which were made in accordance with the Supreme Court's previous decision.[45]

42. *Arazi* v. *Income Tax Commissioner*, 14 *Psakim* (Sup. Ct.) 269 (1954); compare Mishael Heshin, "More on the Commissioner's Reopening of Assessments" (Hebrew), 3 *Quarterly Tax Journal* 3 (January 1968).

43. Lapidoth, above, n. 43; Wilkenfeld; "Juridical Guarantees," 78; ibid. (in Hebrew) 7 *Roeh Haheshbon* 287, 292 (May–June 1957).

44. The issue was how to compute the taxable profit which an individual realized from the sale of an asset which he had acquired originally as an investment but which he had converted to business use before selling it. The Supreme Court had first held in *Ben Zvi* v. *Assessing Officer*, Civ. App. 20/63, 17 *Piske Din* 1963, that the basis for computing the taxable gain was the taxpayer's original cost. Not quite three years later, the Court reversed itself and held that the basis was the fair market value of the asset at the time it was converted to business use. *Cohen* v. *Assessing Officer*, Civ. App. 217/65, 20 *Piske Din* (part 2) 421. The panel in the *Ben Zvi* case consisted of three justices, whereas five sat on the reversing panel, as required by law in the case of reconsideration by the Supreme Court of a previous decision. For further discussion of the substantive issue see Aryeh Lapidoth, "Some Reflections on the British Rule in *Sharkey* v. *Wherner* with Special Reference to its Effects on Israel Tax Law," 2 Israel Law Review 270 (April 1967); and compare Yaacov Neeman, "Conversion of Asset from Investment to Business Inventory" (Hebrew), 1 *Quarterly Tax Journal* 427 (October 1966), with D. Cahana, "Self-Trade" (Hebrew) 17 *Roeh Haheshbon* 340 (May–June 1967).

45. See Heshin, above, n. 45, pp. 7–8; and see Lapidoth, above, n. 43, p. 36.

As a matter of practice, the number of instances in which the Commissioner exercises his authority to reopen an assessment is limited. There were about 500 such cases in fiscal 1967–68, most of them having been referred to the Commissioner by the assessing officers. Generally, these were cases in which, after issuance of a final assessment (which prevents the assessing officer from making a further assessment for the taxable year), further information had come to the attention of the assessing officer disclosing that the original assessment had been too low. These matters are handled, by delegation from the Commissioner, by the Assistant Commissioner for technical matters and the unit under his supervision.

Income Tax Appeals to the Courts

Mandatory Procedure

During the British mandate, appeals from disputed assessments would be heard by a British Puisne Judge sitting in Jerusalem. Hearings were conducted privately, in the judge's chambers. The decision of the judge was final unless, in his sole discretion, he should certify a question of law to the High Court, composed of three judges sitting as a court of civil appeal. In such event the judge who had rendered the original opinion might participate in the review.[46]

Present Procedure

The mandatory appeal procedure was completely changed by an amendment to the Income Tax Ordinance enacted in 1949 which established the appeal procedure that is still in effect. The provisions governing court appeals are now contained in Sections 153–158 of the Income Tax Ordinance.

The first stage of judicial review is to the District Court. Unlike the mandatory procedure, under which the decision of the court of first instance was final, the present procedure provides for an appeal, as a matter of right, to the Supreme Court. Furthermore, such appeals are not limited, as during the mandate, to issues of law, although in practice the Supreme Court has indicated reluctance to substitute its view of the facts for that of the trial judge.[47] In recent years a third possible

46. David Rosolio and E. W. Klimowsky, *Mas Hakhnasah b'Eretz Yisrael* [Income Tax in Palestine], pp. 49–50; Avraham Fellman, *Dinei Mas Hakhnasah b'Yisrael, 1952/53*, p. 115; Aryeh Lapidoth, "Trends in the Income Tax Legislation of Israel," in XVI *Scripta Hierosolymitana* (Hebrew University, Jerusalem, 1966), pp. 325, 328.

47. *Levitor* v. *Assessing Officer*, Civ. App. 98/56, 11 *Piske Din* 465; compare *Berger* v. *Director of Estate Tax*, Civ. App. 300/64, 2 *Piske Din be'Inyanei*

level of judicial review has been added. In unusual instances the Supreme Court may grant a rehearing on a matter originally decided by a panel of three justices. In event of rehearing, the reviewing panel consists of five justices.[48]

The taxpayer must have exhausted his administrative remedies and received a final notice of assessment before he can file an appeal. An appeal cannot be filed from a preliminary notice of assessment, which by law is reviewable only by the assessing officer (with an Advisory Committee, if requested) after the filing of an objection with the assessing officer. Neither can an appeal be taken from a tentative assessment which, by its terms, cannot differ from the taxpayer's income as reported on his return. A tentative assessment which purports, nevertheless, to increase the income is void.[49] Accordingly, the event which triggers the running of the 30-day period during which the taxpayer may file his appeal is the receipt of a final notice of assessment, issued after the administrative review procedures have been exhausted.[50]

When the pace of income tax appeals began to increase in 1955 and 1956, numerous complaints were heard from taxpayers, their legal representatives, and the courts that the form and content of the notices of assessment were insufficient to enable the taxpayer to understand the basis for the assessment. This frequently made it impossible for the taxpayer to sustain the burden, imposed upon him by law (sec. 155), of proving that the assessment was excessive. The Commissioner responded to these complaints by issuing instructions to the assessing officers requiring them to append to the notice of assessment and explanation of the grounds upon which it was based.

These explanations were also found to be unsatisfactory, and in 1957 the Supreme Court resolved the matter by amending the District Court Rules.[51] The procedure now is that the taxpayer files a notice of appeal which may be general in form. Within fourteen days after receipt of the notice of appeal, the assessing officer is required to file an answer which explains the basis of the assessment in detail. The supporting evidence

Misim, p. 46 (November 1967); and see Aryeh Lapidoth, "Imposition of Tax on Income from Trade or Occupation," (Hebrew) 2 *Quarterly Tax Journal* 243, 247 (October 1967). Similar reluctance has been expressed by the United States Supreme Court in *Dobson* v. *Commissioner*, 320 U.S. 489 (1943). The English House of Lords indicated a reverse trend in *Edwards* v. *Bairstow* [1955] 3 All E.R. 48, 1956, A.C. 14, where it accepted as a statutorily reviewable question of law an issue which American courts would be more inclined to consider a question of fact. Drawing the line among questions of law, questions of fact, and mixed question of law and fact, has always been difficult. It sometimes appears to be influenced by judicial policy, which may vary with the case load of the highest court in tax issues.

48. Henry E. Baker, *The Legal System of Israel*, pp. 200–201.

49. *Tempo* v. *Assessing Officer for Large Enterprises*. Civ. App. 33/63, 17 *Piske Din* 1785.

50. Sec. 153, I.T.O.; Rule 3, District Court Rules (Appeals in Income Tax Matters), 1941.

need not be disclosed. Then, within fourteen days after receipt of the assessing officer's answer, the taxpayer must file a reply, specifying the grounds of his appeal. The case is then at issue. If either party fails to comply with these pleading requirements, the court may decide the case against the delinquent party, or extend the time for filing the required pleading if good cause is shown.[52]

As soon as the appeal is perfected, the assessing officer is required to transmit the file to the Commissioner's office in Jerusalem. Thereafter, the government's representative in the appeal is the Solicitor General (State's Attorney) in the Ministry of Justice who, in turn, assigns the case to members of his staff in Jerusalem or in the field who specialize in tax matters. Much of the preparatory work is, however, done by the Legal Adviser to the Income Tax Commissioner or by a member of his staff. On occasion the latter may, on designation by the Solicitor General, also appear in court. The recent trend, however, has been for the Ministry of Justice to build up its own staff of tax specialists. This is considerably different from the way it was under the mandate and in the first years of the State. During the mandate the government was represented by a private law firm in the few income tax appeals in which it was respondent.[53] A similar arrangement was later made with a former Solicitor General who had since entered private law practice. This type of arrangement, for which there is English precedent, became impractical when, starting in 1955, the number of income tax appeals rose sharply.

The transition to the present procedure, in which the government is represented by its own staff of tax specialists, took several years. In 1954 the late Dr. Max Stein [54] was named to the new post of legal adviser to the Income Tax Commissioner, having previously been the assessing officer for Jerusalem. This appointment followed upon the recommendation of the Sharef Commission that special legal advisers be appointed in the office of the Commissioner and in each of the larger assessing offices. The Commission left open the question whether the government should be represented in the courts by lawyers from the income tax administration or from the Ministry of Justice.[55] For a time,

51. District Court Rules (Appeals in Income Tax Matters) (Amendment) — 1957.

52. Witkon and Neeman, *Dinei Misim*, pp. 255–258, and cases there cited.

53. Most of the cases were handled for the government by Dr. Alfred Witkon, who, as a Justice of the Supreme Court, chairman or member of various government commissions of enquiry, author, and teacher of tax law at the Hebrew University, has since been a major influence in the development of Israel tax law and administration.

54. To whom the author is indebted for much of his knowledge of Israeli law.

55. Sharef Report (Harvard ed.), pp. 43–44. The Commission recommended that, in "certain income tax cases," the Attorney General authorize appearances by income tax officials.

until the criminal prosecution program got under way (see chapter 8), it appeared that the trend was toward representation of the Income Tax Branch by its own legal staff. This was then, in fact, the pattern of representation of the Customs and Excise Branch, even in criminal cases. However, when the volume and difficulty of income tax cases, both civil and criminal, were assessed in late 1955, it was concluded that the responsibility for representing the government in both of these areas should be vested exclusively in the Ministry of Justice, with court appearances to be by the Solicitor General and members of his staff. Thereafter, Dr. Stein was transferred to the Ministry of Justice as Deputy Solicitor General in charge of tax litigation, and the arrangement for representation of the government by a private practitioner was in due course terminated.

The Ministry of Justice has since developed a staff of tax experts, both in Jerusalem and in the offices of the District Attorneys in Tel Aviv and Haifa, who appear in court in both civil and criminal tax matters. The division of functions, accordingly, between the Ministry of Justice and the legal staff of the Income Tax Branch is now clear, the latter being charged, among their other duties, with assuring that cases have been fully prepared before they are transmitted to the Ministry of Justice.

It is appropriate here to mention that at the same time the government was developing its staff of tax lawyers, a trend toward specialization in tax matters was also developing among members of the private bar. For several years students at the Hebrew University Law School had been offered a course in tax law taught by Dr. Alfred Witkon, a Justice of the Supreme Court with much experience in the field. Although it was not then customary for lawyers to be involved in the hearing of objections before the assessing officers,[56] perhaps in accordance with English practice, only lawyers could appear in court. When the volume of tax litigation increased, the Israel Bar Association sponsored several courses in tax law in which about one hundred lawyers participated. In 1955 the Hebrew University conducted an Income Tax Symposium, attended by 250 academicians, lawyers, accountants, and government officials.[57] This, in turn, stimulated definition by the governing bodies of the legal and accounting professions of their respective areas of responsibility in tax matters, with a view to avoiding overstepping by either profession of the legally defined jurisdiction of the

56. From about 1952 through 1955, although thousands of objections were filed, even accountants did not appear often. Instead, taxpayers frequently engaged as their representatives individuals whose only skill was their bargaining ability. These nonprofessionals have since been regulated, and the Commissioner may prohibit representation by an individual whom he does not consider to be qualified (sec. 236, I.T.O., as amended in August 1968).

57. See *Symposion le-Inyanei Mas Hakhnasah* [*Proceedings of Symposium on Income Taxation*] (Hebrew) (Jerusalem: Hebrew University, 1955).

other.[58] In recent years, the number of university courses in tax law has expanded, as have the number of technical articles on the subject in legal and other professional periodicals. Tax specialization is now common among members of the bar.

In the courts there has also been a tendency for particular District Court judges to specialize in income tax cases. Of the nineteen such cases decided from the inception of the State to the middle of 1952, all but two were decided by the same District Court judge,[59] who has since become the income tax specialist on the Supreme Court bench. This tendency toward specialization continued as the volume of income tax litigation increased. In a practical sense, therefore, it would appear that the Israeli court system has responded to the question whether tax appeals should be heard by judges who are generalists or specialists by providing within the framework of a general court system hearings by judges who are specialists in tax matters.[60]

This emphasis is especially noticeable at the trial court level, since the District Court judge hearing an income tax appeal is almost always a specialist in tax matters. At the Supreme Court level, however, where appeals are heard by panels of three justices out of the total complement of ten, the tendency toward specialization is somewhat diluted. For example, only two of the present justices were elevated to that court after having served as District Court judges specializing in tax matters. Therefore, although at least one of these tax specialists is likely to be designated by the Chief Justice to sit on a panel reviewing a tax case, his brothers will be generalists. The leading opinion, however, is most frequently written by the tax specialist on the panel. But this apparent deference to the specialist is somewhat modified, at the Supreme Court level, by the fact that a justice whose emphasis may have been upon tax cases when he sat at the trial level will, on the Supreme Court, participate in many non-tax matters.

Settlement of Appeals

A large percentage of the cases in which appeals are taken (85 percent in 1967) is disposed of by settlement without going to trial or decision by the court.[61] Settlement negotiations may be stimulated by

58. See closing remarks of Harold C. Wilkenfeld in *Proceedings,* above, n. 57, pp. 60–61.

59. Nohimovsky, *Mas Hakhnasah,* p. 71.

60. Compare Harold C. Wilkenfeld, "Administrative Tribunals in Tax Matters" (Hebrew), 1 *Quarterly Tax Journal* 225, 226–228 (April 1966); and Neiger, above, n. 39, p. 268.

61. During the calendar year 1967, of 1460 appeals which were closed in the District Courts, 1257 were settled (429 in court) and only 203 were decided by the courts (*Annual Report of the Income and Property Tax Branch, 1967/68* [Hebrew], p. 40).

the assessing officer, the Commissioner's office, the taxpayer, or by the judge when the case had been called for hearing.

Considering the large number of appeals which are filed annually it would be a practical impossibility for the courts to hear and decide all of them. In many there is some room for give and take, and these are susceptible to settlement. In others, one side or the other may be adamant, or a clear-cut issue of law may be involved which requires judicial disposition. As to these, there may be little choice but to have a full-scale presentation to the court.

In many cases there is reason to suspect that the appeal was taken principally for the purpose of delaying the ultimate payment of the tax.[62] A taxpayer is not required to pay that portion of the assessment which is in dispute. On the other hand, he is required to pay interest at the rate prescribed by the court from the date the tax was due until finally paid (sec. 185). Generally this rate is lower than what the taxpayer would be obliged to pay in the commercial money market. Accordingly, a taxpayer who is unable to borrow money elsewhere at an equivalent rate of interest (interest rates in Israel are generally very high) would find it to his advantage to delay payment of tax as long as he possibly could. This would include taking advantage of every kind of administrative and judicial review available to him.

However, deferment of payment of tax in dispute ends once the matter has been decided by the District Court. Accordingly, many cases which may be appealed to the District Court solely for purposes of delay will not go beyond that court.[63] Moreover, if the taxpayer is well aware that his case has no real merit, he may still, when the case comes to hearing, try to negotiate a last-minute settlement and, even if unsuccessful, hope that under some last-minute pressure from the judge the Commissioner may still be inclined to grant some final concession. Failing this, the taxpayer has no further alternative but to pay the tax.

An opportunity for, if not the necessity of, accelerated handling of disputes presented itself during the several months following the 1956 Sinai Campaign. As noted earlier, until 1955 there were relatively few income tax appeals filed with the District Courts. By October 1956 the situation had become quite different. When the Sinai Campaign began, and in the months thereafter, many of the income tax officials were in the army, and there was a shortage of skilled manpower. It seemed an appropriate time to review the cases pending in the courts to determine whether some substantial part of them could be disposed of with a minimum expenditure of administrative and judicial effort. Otherwise, the

62. Nahum Wermus, "The Compliance Problem in Income Tax Administration," (Hebrew) 3 *Quarterly Tax Journal* 274, 280 (July 1968).

63. In 1967, although the District Courts decided 203 cases, of which 80 percent were wholly (50 percent) or partially (30 percent) against the taxpayer, only 39 appeals were taken further to the Supreme Court.

backlog of undecided cases might have got out of hand.[64] Furthermore, the need for revenue was great, and cases pending in the District Court were completely unproductive.

Many of the assessments then on appeal had been made before the institution of more refined assessment techniques, by personnel who may not have been wholly qualified, and on the basis of administrative decisions that may not always have been the "best judgment." On the premise that sooner or later some settlement would have to be effected in these cases, the author, then Adviser on Tax Law and Administration to the Finance Ministry, proposed that a rapid survey be made of appeals arising from several key assessing offices to ascertain whether or not the percentage of cases susceptible of quick settlement was sufficiently high to warrant the introduction of an accelerated settlement procedure. This survey, which was conducted in the Jerusalem and Haifa offices and in several of the Tel Aviv offices, showed that there was sufficient doubt as to the accuracy of a number of the assessments under appeal to warrant administrative proposals for concessions in order to achieve rapid settlements.

On the basis of this survey, guidelines were laid down and a committee from the Commissioner's office met with most of the assessing officers to initiate negotiations with those taxpayers whose cases appeared to be susceptible of settlement. Within a relatively short time a large number of pending cases were disposed of without delay. The point was also rather forcibly made that it was the assessing officers who had the responsibility of making accurate assessments and that the judicial process was not to be utilized as a further opportunity for striking a bargain with the taxpayer. The essence of this procedure, temporary though it was, was to sift out many cases in which the assessments appeared to have been arbitrarily high and to shift the burden of closing cases on a reasonable basis back to the assessing officers.

Of course, 1957 was a transitional year during which both the administration and the taxpayers were moving away from the marketplace technique of assessment toward more technical understanding of the law and income tax determinations based on provable rather than supposed facts. The rapid settlement procedure adopted under pressure of the 1956 war with Egypt and its aftermath was only one element in this process of development. However, it was an appropriate demonstration that the period of arbitrary assessments was drawing to an end and that the integrity of the administration and of the courts required a policy of issuing final assessments which no longer were based on the assumption that the bargaining process was integral to income tax assessment procedures.

64. During the fiscal year ending March 31, 1957, 1,610 appeals were filed; 1,051 remained pending at the end of the year.

Burden of Proof and Presumptions

The law provides:

The onus of proving that the assessment is excessive shall be on the appellant: Provided that if the appellant has dealt with all the receipts and payments of his business according to such method, and in such manner, as the Commissioner has prescribed for the purpose the Assessing Officer shall have to justify his assessment.[65]

Although denominated as an "appeal," the proceeding in the District Court in a trial *de novo*, in which the taxpayer, as the moving party, has the burden of establishing a record by such evidence and testimony as may be in his possession, to prove the correct amount of his income.[66] It is reasonable to expect the taxpayer to bear this burden. He should be in possession of the facts; and if he is not, his inability to prove his case is generally due to his own failure to record the facts properly.

The situation becomes more difficult when the taxpayer has maintained records, whether or not required by regulation, or, if required, whether or not in full compliance with the regulations. The most difficult situation arises when he has kept records in apparent compliance with the regulations, but the assessing officer has nevertheless decided to ignore the records and to base the assessment upon other considerations.

There have been many cases involving such situations,[67] and they have evoked a feeling on the part of the courts that efforts by a taxpayer to maintain records appropriate to his business should be respected, and that the authorities should not lightly be permitted to base assessments on their own estimates, in total disregard to the taxpayer's records. The proviso to the burden of proof provision quoted above was enacted in 1961, in partial response to the emphasis placed by the courts on the obligation of the authorities to specify the inadequacies, if any, of the taxpayer's records. This proviso, and the related court decisions, have actually supported the long-range program of the administration to enlarge the number of taxpayers who keep books.

Taxpayers to whom regulations requiring the keeping of books do not apply, but who nonetheless have kept books, are not relieved of the burden of proof by statute; but even before enactment of the 1961 proviso, they were nevertheless, by court decision, effectively relieved of the burden. In several early leading cases (as the *Blumenthal* and *Lizra* cases, mentioned in Chapter 6) it was held that once the taxpayer

65. Section 155, I.T.O.
66. See E. S. Shimron and J. S. Zemah, "Selected Problems of Evidence in Income Tax Proceedings" (Hebrew) 1 *Quarterly Tax Journal* 410 (October 1966).
67. See also Witkon and Neeman, pp. 235–242, and B. Nahir, I *Guide to Income Tax Decisions* (Hebrew), "Bookkeeping" (Tel Aviv: Amihai, 1960).

had introduced his books in evidence and had demonstrated that his return was consistent with his books, the burden of proving the validity of the assessment shifted to the assessing officer.

There have been instances in which a taxpayer had kept books but had failed to produce them at the administrative level. The question then has arisen whether he should be permitted to submit them in evidence at the trial. The courts have been inclined to permit the books to be introduced but, taking into account the taxpayer's failure to produce them earlier, have somewhat discounted their value.[68] In several such instances the courts have referred the case back to the assessing officer so that he might further examine the matter in the light of the newly submitted books.

It would appear that the courts are seeking to impress upon taxpayers the importance of making a full presentation of their cases at the administrative level. On the other hand, since the court's decision must be based upon the court-created record, and since the taxpayer's burden is to prove "that the assessment is excessive," it would seem to be improper to exclude relevant and material evidence. But since the analysis of books is a technical and time-consuming task, reference back to the assessing officer seems an appropriate and fair practice. It is consistent also with the policy, which the Supreme Court has been seeking to impress upon the District Courts — that they should refrain from substituting their own assessments for those of the assessing officer.[69]

This brings us to the question of the relationship between the taxpayer's burden of proof and presumptions which the courts may apply in reaching their decisions. The underlying presumption, which derives logically from the statute, is that the assessment is correct unless the taxpayer proves otherwise.[70] In cases of appeals from best judgment assessments there has been a tendency to give greater weight to assessments based upon standard assessment guides (*tahshivim*) or arrived at after consultation with an Advisory Committee.[71] Yet, when the taxpayer's evidence, even though incomplete, has indicated that the assessment is so arbitrary as to require revision, the courts have not hesitated to set it aside.[72]

68. See cases digested in Nahir, IV *Guide to Income Tax Decisions* (Hebrew), "The Assessing Officers Considerations," (Tel Aviv: Amihai, 1963 semble), pp. 693–700.

69. See, e.g., *Assessing Officer* v. *Katz*, Civ. App. 62/58, 13 *Piske Din* 66 (Sup. Ct., 1959); *Assessing Officer* v. *Baron*, Civ. App. 13 *Piske Din* 947 (Sup. Ct., 1959); compare *Attorney General* v. *Levitor*, Civ. App. 11 *Piske Din* 465 (Sup. Ct., 1957).

70. See, e.g., *Moshe Feiner Co., Ltd.* v. *Assessing Officer*, on rehearing, Civ. App. 14/65, 20 *Piske Din* (part 1) 533 (Sup. Ct., 1966); *Assessing Officer* v. *Himelfarb*, Civ. App. 51/60, 14 *Piske Din* 888 (Sup. Ct., 1960); *Assessing Officer* v. *Weisl*, Civ. App. 458/60, 14 *Piske Din* 1621 (Sup. Ct., 1960).

71. See Witkon and Neeman, pp. 197, 207, 247.

72. See, e.g., *Feldman* v. *Assessing Officer*, Civ. App. 209/61, 15 *Piske Din* 2123 (Sup. Ct., 1961).

Several statutory presumptions which apply in certain criminal proceedings should be mentioned. A taxpayer who is charged (under Sec. 216 (4)) with failure to file a return has the burden of proving that he was not obliged to file one (Sec. 222(a)). One who is charged with destroying or concealing documents which are material to his assessment has the burden of proving that they were not material (Sec. 222(b)). And a company which is required to withhold the tax from dividends which it pays (Sec. 161), or a person who is required to withhold the tax from wages (Sec. 164), or from income payable to a foreign resident (Sec. 170), if he is charged with failure to withhold the tax (Sec. 218, as amended 1968), or with failure to pay it over to the assessing officer (Sec. 219, as amended 1968), has the burden of proving compliance with the law (Sec. 222(c)), as amended 1968). Furthermore, one who is charged with omitting or understating income on his return (Sec. 217) is presumed to be guilty as charged if the prosecution proves either (1) that his household or personal expenses during the taxable year exceeded the income which he reported, or (2) that his wealth, or that of his wife or children under age 20, increased in an amount which exceeded his reported income.[73] When a company is proved to have committed a criminal offense under the Income Tax Ordinance (Secs. 215–220), anyone who was active at the time of the commission of the offense as a director, partner, bookkeeper, responsible employee, trustee, or authorized representative, is also considered guilty of the charge unless he proves either (1) that he had no knowledge of the offense, or (2) that he had taken all reasonable steps to prevent the commission of the offense.[74]

There is an interesting contrast between civil appeals and criminal proceedings in regard to presumptions and the burden of proof: The burden of proof in civil appeals is generally upon the taxpayer. In criminal prosecutions, however, Israel follows the common law principle that the accused is presumed to be innocent until proved guilty. The only exceptions from this principle in the tax area are the statutory presumptions which have just been mentioned. The matter is complicated by the fact that in respect of several of the criminal offenses the

73. Sec. 223, I.T.O., as amended August 1968. It should be noted that this rebuttable presumption does not apply to sec. 220, which deals with the more serious offense of willful tax evasion. It has been suggested that this provision did not add materially to existing law, under which, in any criminal case, proof of substantial discrepancies between reported income and expenditures, or net worth increases, would in any event have established a *prima facie* case of guilt. See, e.g., Uriel Gorney, "Net Worth Increases and Burden of Proof in Criminal Cases Under the Income Tax Ordinance," (Hebrew) 6 *Roeh Haheshbon* 11, 18 (October–December, 1955); Wilkenfeld, "Juridical Guarantees," p. 78; Witkon and Neeman, pp. 269–270.

74. Sec. 224A I.T.O.; cf. sec. 224, which applies to one who knowingly assisted in the preparation of a false return or knowingly submitted false information as representative of a taxpayer.

fine which the court can impose in the event of conviction is, in part, measured by the unreported income or evaded tax which is the gravamen of the offense.[75] Therefore, the prosecution must not only prove that the crime was committed, but also the exact amount of the income or tax involved.

This brings to the fore another common law principle, also considered applicable in Israel, namely, that an individual cannot be compelled to incriminate himself.[76] In order to insure that the interests of a potential accused should not be affected during the course of a criminal investigation, the tax authorities had in 1955 adopted the policy of deferring normal assessment procedures in any potential criminal case at least until a decision had been reached as to whether or not a prosecution should be instituted. Deferring the assessment process meant, however, that the investigative authority of the assessing officer, for purposes of assessment and at the objection stage, could not be utilized.[77]

The question of the nature of the proof of income required in a criminal, as compared to a civil case, was presented in 1965. In a civil tax case as we have seen, the best judgment of an assessing officer is given great weight. It has been held, however, that in a criminal case best judgment is not enough: the assessing officer, when testifying as a witness in a criminal prosecution, must prove the basis of his determination of the taxpayer's income. Estimates are unacceptable unless shown to have been based upon solid facts. Accordingly, in criminal cases the presumption of the correctness of the administrative determination does not apply.

Use of Foreign Precedents

The Israeli Income Tax Ordinance, although enacted originally in 1941, in the period of the British Mandate for Palestine, bears less resemblance to the comparable law then in effect in Great Britain than does, say, the Companies Ordinance or the Negotiable Instruments Law. Its original source was the Model Income Tax Ordinance published by the British Colonial Office, modified by additions derived from the laws of India, Kenya, and Cyprus.[78] Neither does the Income Tax Ordinance contain a provision, as do some of the other laws enacted during the mandatory period, that, whenever necessary for purposes of interpreting the law of Palestine reference shall be made to the corresponding English law.

75. Secs. 217 (unreported income), 218 (unwithheld tax), 219 (tax withheld but unpaid), 220 (tax evaded).

76. But see Witkon and Neeman, p. 270.

77. This was solved by the enactment of sec. 227, I.T.O. permitting assessing officers to exercise the investigative authorities of police inspectors.

78. Nohimovsky, *Mas Hakhnasah*; Lapidoth "Trends in the Income Tax Legislation of Israel," pp. 325, 327–328.

Furthermore, since the income tax law is considered, even in England, to be in derogation of the common law, reference to the common law of England in seeking guidance to interpretation of ambiguous provisions of the Income Tax Ordinance was not considered obligatory under Section 46 of the British Order in Council of 1922. This prescribed, generally, that to the extent not inconsistent with existing law, the common law and equity of England should apply in Palestine.

In 1943, the opinion was expressed by the Palestine Supreme Court that it was neither necessary nor desirable that the Income Tax Ordinance be construed in the light of English income tax principles which, it was thought, were much too complex to apply to Palestinian conditions.[79] The fact is, nevertheless, that the Israeli courts, particularly the Supreme Court, have frequently referred to British decisions as guides to interpretation of similar provisions or concepts of the Israeli law. The courts do not, however, limit themselves to British precedents; they will consult decisions in other jurisdictions (as, for example, India or the United States) if they suggest a solution of the immediate problem that is relevant to Israeli circumstances. By the same token, the Israel Supreme Court has on several notable occasions expressly differed with the British House of Lords in its statement of relevant income tax principles.[80]

The judicial principle of *stare decisis* has been twice transformed in Israel. The Israel Supreme Court, in a series of early decisions, overruled several decisions of the mandatory courts which it considered to be no longer pertinent. This, for a time, was thought to lend support to the proposition that the Supreme Court would not consider itself bound by its own decisions. The Supreme Court rejected this proposition (although not unanimously), thereby choosing to follow the practice of the British House of Lords rather than that of the United States Supreme Court. The Knesset reacted to this firm rule by adopting a provision in the Judicial Courts Law in 1957, which now provides (Sec. 33) that a court shall be guided by rules of law decided by a higher court, and that decisions of the Supreme Court shall bind all courts but itself. Thus the Supreme Court was by statute freed to reverse itself.[81] It in fact did so in a recent tax case, indicating at the same time its disagreement with the House of Lords.

79. Gordon Smith, C. J., in *Horowitz* v. *Assessing Officer, Jerusalem*, Income Tax Appeal 9/42, 1943 Annotated L. Rep., p. 278; *idem* — A. M. Apelbom and B. Braude, *Palestine Income Tax Cases*, p. 43; see also Rosolio and Klimowsky, *Mas Hakhnasah b'Eretz Yisrael*, pp. 32–33.

80. For discussions of several such departures from principles expressed by the House of Lords see Lapidoth, "Some Reflections on the British Rule in *Sharkey* v. *Wherner* with Special Reference to its Effects in Israel Tax Law," and "Imposition of Tax on Damages and Effect of Tax Liability upon the Assessment of Damages" (Hebrew), 1 *Quarterly Tax Journal* 273 (July, 1966).

81. For a more detailed discussion, see Yehezkel Dror, "Some Recent De-

The Business of the Courts

In recent years, the number of income tax appeals filed annually in the District Courts has averaged about 1,800. Since approximately 180,000 assessments of companies and self-employed individuals are made annually, the court appeals average about one percent of assessments. Considering the fact that taxpayers are required by law to exhaust their administrative review remedies before they can appeal to the courts, the number of appeals seems quite high. By contrast, hardly any appeals were taken to the courts during the period of the British mandate (i.e., from 1941, when the Income Tax Ordinance was enacted) and in the early years of the State, through 1954.

It would appear that the large number of cases now being litigated is a reaction to the administration's resort to best judgment assessments in instances where there is a dispute over the facts. This is borne out by the large number of appeals which are settled in court. In these appeals the judge seems to perform the role of forcing the parties into a settlement which, presumably, they might have been able to reach at an earlier stage. *A fortiori*, the cases which are settled after the appeal has been filed but before the hearing has commenced could probably have been settled at an earlier stage.

Almost all of the cases which are settled, and a large number of those which are decided, involve questions of fact. In the course of time, as the interaction of improved assessment procedures and increased record-keeping by taxpayers make themselves felt, disputes over questions of fact are likely to be reduced. The anticipated reduction in the business of the Advisory Committees has already been discussed. The same factors should result in a decrease in the number of fact disputes which will ultimately reach the courts.

Although the Israeli income tax statute and procedures are of British origin, there is a major difference in respect of appeals to the courts. In England, appeals can be taken from the decision of the Review Commissioners only on questions of law. The facts must all have been submitted to the Commissioners, and the case is decided by the courts on the administrative record. In Israel, as in the United States, there is a trial *de novo*, both on the facts and on the law. Although the possibility of limiting appeals to questions of law has been discussed in Israel,[82] both the administration and the taxpaying public may not be ready for this change for some time.

Meanwhile, the opportunity which taxpayers have to resort to the

velopments of the Doctrine of Precedent in Israel," 5 *Scripta Hierosolymitana* 228 (1958); Guido Tedeschi, *Studies in Israel Law* (Jerusalem: Hebrew University Students' Press, 1960), pp. 129 ff.

82. See intervention of Harold C. Wilkenfeld in *International Lawyers Convention in Israel, 1958* (Jerusalem: Ministry of Justice, 1959), pp. 312–313.

courts for the resolution of their disputes with the administration has served several useful purposes. The courts are held in high regard in Israel, and their judgments are respected. Even in those cases which are settled, a settlement achieved under the aegis of the court seems to carry greater weight with both parties. The courts have also not hesitated to criticize the authorities when they have observed abuses and, with equal justice, have not hesitated to criticize taxpayers whose conduct has departed from the norm. To this extent, the courts have exercised a disciplinary function in helping both the administration and the taxpaying public to achieve desirable standards of conduct vis-à-vis each other.

8 / Overcoming Tax Evasion

Introduction

The story of Israel's use of an income tax criminal prosecution program as a means of raising the level of voluntary taxpayer compliance is a fascinating one. In previous chapters the reasons for the low level of income tax compliance in the early 1950's have been examined and administrative improvements have been discussed. In this chapter we focus upon what was undoubtedly the most difficult program undertaken by the tax authorities. Along with the simultaneous administrative improvements and the growing sophistication of the Israeli citizenry the success of the criminal prosecution program is evidenced by a very substantial improvement in taxpayer compliance and in the reduction of tax evasion to a minimum.

It was not easy for the tax authorities to decide that criminal prosecutions should be regularly instituted against income tax evaders. Indeed, it was not until 1955 that a clear-cut policy began to be formulated. Before then there were several attempts to institute prosecution programs, but they were short-lived. To some extent these false starts made it all the more difficult to adopt a permanent policy in 1955. To understand this, it would be well to review briefly what had happened in the enforcement area before 1955.

Early Enforcement Efforts

Among the measures taken in 1952 to bolster the income tax administration was the announcement of a "get tough" policy toward tax evaders. In fact, several prosecutions were instituted in 1953.[1] However, since no organization had yet been established for the routine investigation of tax crimes, those cases which were brought were more or less haphazard; nor did they necessarily demonstrate that the administration had acquired the skills necessary to uncover fraudulent schemes of tax evasion. Instead, most of these criminal charges involved "technical" offenses, such as failure to file returns, or failure of employers to

1. The first criminal charges under the Income Tax Ordinance were filed at the beginning of February 1953 (*Jerusalem Post*, February 3, 1953, p. 3). That same month several of the accused were fined by the Jerusalem District Court (Witkon, J.) for failure to pay over withholdings from wages or failure to file returns (*Jerusalem Post*, February 17, 1953, p. 3). Similar convictions followed: *Jerusalem Post*, March 1, 1953, p. 3 (Jerusalem); March 5, 1953, p. 2; March 10, 1953, p. 3 (Tel Aviv); November 19, 1953, p. 3 (Haifa); December 29, 1953 (Tel Aviv).

pay over taxes withheld from employees' wages. These were also violations of the law, of course, but announcement of a "get tough" policy, without a demonstration of ability to catch serious offenders, had the effect of confirming hard-core evaders in their belief that they were still safe from discovery.

There are indications that the few prosecutions which were instituted in 1953 were intended more as a single-shot warning to evaders than as part of any long-range prosecution program. In the first place, it was well known that the administration was not yet equipped to handle the normal civil functions of regular inspection and assessment of the mass of income tax returns — let alone the more difficult and specialized techniques of discovering and proving fraud. After five years of administrative breakdown, it was not surprising that threats of punishment would be received with considerable cynicism by the taxpaying public. And this reaction was confirmed by the announcement of a tax amnesty at the end of 1952 for those who came in voluntarily to straighten out their tax accounts.[2] The net result was that although a few hapless persons were convicted in 1953, the hoped-for improvement in taxpayer attitudes was not forthcoming.

One of the difficulties was that the law itself at that time tended to minimize the seriousness of income tax crimes. As originally enacted in the mandatory days, the Income Tax Ordinance had hardly any teeth, and even these lost their bite as the Israeli pound was devalued — since the penalties which the courts could impose were expressed more frequently in fixed money fines than in prison sentences. Furthermore, in the earliest income tax criminal cases the courts indicated a tendency to impose relatively light penalties, taking into account the fact that for some years the income tax administration had itself been lax.

A 1953 opinion by Supreme Court Justice Olshan illustrates the point. He said, in part:

> In view of the plague which has broken out among various circles in the country in regard to failure to meet their obligations to the State, which the Income Tax Ordinance has imposed upon its citizens, a plague which must be exterminated because it injures both the State and the citizen who fulfills his obligations honestly — because to the extent that evasion increases, the rate of tax imposed upon every citizen will have to increase — it is no surprise that the learned trial judge reacted severely to this crime.
>
> On the other hand, I am of the opinion that it is necessary to take into account that the appellant's crime relates to the year 1952, when the income tax authorities had not yet begun to insist upon the filing

2. *Jerusalem Post*, January 9, 1953, p. 5; January 18, 1953, p. 3; February 3, 1953, p. 3; February 17, 1953, p. 3. Compare the amnesty in 1967, discussed later.

of returns on time; therefore I am of the opinion that the fine should be reduced to IL. 100.[3]

The stop-and-go aspects of the early prosecution program may in part have reflected the difficulty of undertaking such a program before the more normal functions of the administration had been established. In the absence of an effective administration, threats of prosecution must have sounded hollow to the large segment of the population to whom they were directed. And, despite the vigor with which the income tax authorities seemed to be attacking the mountain of unassessed returns, the essential weakness of the administration was publicly exposed during 1953 and 1954.

The Bloch and Sharef Reports

In August 1953 the Income Tax Commissioner announced that a committee of experts had been appointed to propose more efficient income tax procedures.[4] In that month, Dr. Henry S. Bloch of the United Nations Fiscal Division was again serving in Israel as an expert appointed by the Technical Assistance Administration of the United Nations. In his second report, Dr. Bloch re-emphasized the importance of a system of penalties and prosecutions in "all cases of nondeclaration or nonpayment" and in all cases "where there is a serious suspicion of criminal fraud." [5]

Within the government, impatience with the work of the income tax administration was building up at this time. The March 1954 Sharef Commission Report made a number of recommendations for improvement of the structure and procedures of the income tax administration.[6] This report again focused public attention upon the broad extent of tax evasion,[7] the light penalties,[8] and the weakness of the administration in the area of enforcement.[9]

Among other things the Sharef Report proposed heavier judicial penalties, including jail sentences for tax crimes, and the imposition of an

3. Opinion of Supreme Court Justice Olshan in *Kahana* v. *Attorney General*, Crim. App. 276/53, 8 *Piske Din* 404, 408.

4. *Jerusalem Post*, August 5, 1953, p. 2. Among the subjects specified by the Commissioner as being within the ambit of the committee were 1) more efficient means of collection, 2) increased penalties for tax evasion, 3) establishment of tribunals to aid in making assessments and hearing income tax disputes, and 4) conditioning of import and export licenses on a prior clearance by the income tax authorities.

5. United Nations Technical Assistance Programme, *Revenue Administration and Policy in Israel (Second Report)*, p. 24 (ST/TAA/K/Israel/4, December, 1954).

6. See Chapter 1, n. 13.

7. *Sharef Report*, pp. 6, 9, 14–15, 28.

8. Ibid., pp. 12, 14, 18, 49–51.

9. Ibid., pp. 12, 13, 18–19, 54, 61.

administrative penalty for nonsubmission of the annual return of income.[10] The report stated that, as "the result of an attitude of disdain and general negligence," only 10 percent of persons liable to file returns in 1953 had done so by the prescribed date.[11] In advance of the increase in penalty for failure to file, the report suggested that "a final opportunity be given to those who have evaded inclusion in the network of taxpayers, to submit the missing returns (without foregoing, of course, the tax that is due).[12]

The "attitude of disdain and general negligence" of the taxpaying public became even more pronounced in 1954. Little attention was paid to the announcement, early in 1954, that the administration would not penalize taxpayers who voluntarily filed delinquent returns or otherwise sought to straighten out their tax accounts. Instead, the feeling seemed to prevail among some taxpayers that if they persisted in keeping the administration off balance they might succeed in obtaining some substantial remission of their past liabilities. Under these circumstances, talk about possible future penalties seemed to be futile.

Nevertheless, the Income Tax Ordinance (Amendment) Act of 1954 did substantially increase the administrative and judicial sanctions available against taxpayers who had failed to comply with the requirements of the law. But a serious lesson had been learned from the unsatisfactory experiences of the past several years, and although the desire to proceed vigorously against law violators continued, action was deferred until the income tax administration was adequately prepared for the task.

Transition to a Systematic Criminal Prosecution Program

Unfortunately, the abortive enforcement efforts of 1952–53 and the buildup of taxpayer resistance in 1954 made immediate implementation of a prosecution policy extremely difficult. It was recognized within the administration that short-range prosecutions, such as those of the previous years, might be more harmful to taxpayer morale than no prosecutions at all. For a while, prosecutions were suspended, until the tempers of 1954 could cool down. Meanwhile, vigorous steps were being taken to build up the internal structure of the income tax administration along more efficient, professional lines.

10. Ibid., p. 12. The penalty proposed was at the rate of 5 percent per month of delay, measured by the tax for which the assessee was liable in the last previous year for which he had been assessed, but not to exceed 25 percent of the tax finally determined for the year to which the delinquent return relates. For new assessees, the penalty would be IL. 50 per month, with the same percentage limitation.

11. Ibid., p. 11. The report also there suggests that the delay in filing may have been partially attributable to an "experiment made by the income tax authorities of not sending forms for a return of income to every assessee."

12. Ibid. See also p. 48.

In the prosecution area, almost all of 1955 and much of 1956 were devoted to formulating policy, establishing procedures, and creating the nucleus of an investigative staff.

At the outset, there were some officials who seriously questioned the advisability of undertaking a prosecution program, at least until the civil aspects of the reorganization had been completed. They felt that, to a large although immeasurable degree, the past weaknesses of the administration had invited infractions of the law. It was not fair, they felt, to make a public spectacle of a few transgressors when violations of the law had become the rule rather than the exception. Moreover, prosecution of all who had broken the law was an impossibility. Action should be postponed, they said, until the improved administration could demonstrate to the taxpaying public that all their evasive devices were futile. Then, when the mass of the public had returned to the straight path, if a hard-core of tax evaders still remained, the sanctions of the law should be directed against them with full vigor.

These arguments could not be lightly brushed aside. Recent experience had shown that random prosecutions had had little, if any, deterrent effect upon the behavior of the taxpaying public. Nevertheless, a firm policy was adopted in 1955 to institute criminal prosecutions as an integral part of the program to improve taxpayer morale. It was apparent that no advantage would be gained by deferring prosecutions until morale had already reached the desired level. Furthermore, it was anticipated that institution of a prosecution program would itself be an important factor in achieving the desired level of compliance with the law.

Teachings of the Previous Program

It was decided to move immediately toward the institution of a long-range prosecution program, but to proceed with caution in order to avoid the mistakes of the past. This in turn required an analysis of what had gone wrong before, as a guide to the formulation of the operating policy for the future. This analysis showed that the principal reasons for the failure of the earlier program and the lessons to be derived therefrom were:

Timing

The first five years, from 1948 to 1953, had been years of crisis, from the political, social, and economic points of view. Although some of these conditions had begun to stabilize by 1953, economic conditions were still very bad. There was considerable unemployment, and money was tight. Economic controls of all types were being stringently applied. There had been a sharp relapse from the former spirit of idealism and self-sacrifice. Political parties were vying for the support of the many new, politically uncommitted, citizens; and strong government was being pictured by some parties as an enemy of the people. It was hardly the time to add to public resentment by prosecuting a few persons for doing what, up to that time, almost everyone had taken for granted, as part of the normal way of life.

By contrast, conditions in 1955 were far better. The economy was again on the upgrade. Economic controls were being gradually relaxed, and future business prospects were bright. The results of the 1955 elections to the Knesset showed that the mass of the citizenry was politically mature and could not be led astray by extremists. The tax crisis of 1954 had been a catharsis which, once over, had cleared the air. Public spirit was being heightened by an increasing wave of acts of terror by infiltrators from across the hostile borders. The public seemed willing to be shown that compliance with the tax laws was preferable, as a general rule, to evasion.

Administrative Effectiveness

Until 1952, other more pressing problems of the State had diverted attention from the needs of the revenue administration. The income tax administration, particularly, suffered from neglect. Its inability to do a professional job in the tax assessment area was not conducive to creating respect for its activities. At worst, if one's income was understated — or not reported at all — some money settlement, in all likelihood at less than the correct figure, might ultimately have to be made.[13] This was no cause for fear. The situation by mid-1955 was, however, considerably improved and the time seemed ripe for a demonstration of strength.

Choice of Cases

The income tax criminal cases which had been prosecuted in 1953 and 1954 almost all involved technical offenses (failure to file returns, failure of employers to pay over taxes withheld from wages of employees). Moreover, the accused were mostly small taxpayers.

It was important, of course, that taxpayers should be taught that they had to comply with the technical requirements of the law, but the prosecution of only procedural offenses, the discovery of which involved no

13. Would-be evaders presumably took into account the risks of being caught. The prospect of settlement at low tax rates, if caught, must have been an inducement toward evasion. Those evaders who were able to hold out, undetected, until 1967 were able to settle their past accounts, if they chose, by payment of a flat 25 percent tax (without prosecution, penalty, or interest) upon previously unreported income. This was a result of the 1967 income tax amnesty, discussed later.

special technical skills, emphasized the lack of ability on the part of the administration to prove a case against the more sophisticated tax cheaters. However, as the administration built up skills on the civil side, there began to be some assurance that when a prosecution program was again introduced it could be expected to include at least some fraud prosecutions against the hard-core evaders.

Amnesties

At the end of 1952 the tax authorities announced a tax amnesty, which carried over to the beginning of 1953. Announcement of the amnesty was followed by a series of warnings that the administration intended to prosecute tax violators. The first criminal charges were filed early in February 1953, after the amnesty had already expired.[14]

It may be inferred that the strategy was to warn the public of the intended "get tough" policy, to give violators an opportunity to straighten out their affairs, and then to show by a series of actual prosecutions that the administration had really meant what it said.

It is difficult to say, in retrospect, whether the amnesty idea might have worked better in 1952–53 if a series of prosecution had first been instituted and an amnesty then announced. Perhaps this would have made a stronger impression upon tax delinquents and induced more of them to hasten to straighten out their tax affairs.

At any rate, the 1952–53 amnesty produced disappointing results. When the courts disposed of those of the 1953 criminal charges which had not been closed by compounding, the results were not particularly spectacular. Although convictions were obtained against some income tax offenders, the crimes of which they were convicted were, as before mentioned, almost all technical offenses and relatively nominal fines were imposed. By contrast, substantial jail sentences were being imposed for customs violations,[15] giving the impression that income tax crimes were not regarded as particularly serious.

At the outset of 1954, a similar amnesty was announced, with no less disappointing results. The occasion for this amnesty was the proposed amendment of the Income Tax Ordinance to sharpen the penalties against violators. However, as related in Chapter 1, these proposals become embroiled in the political maneuvers of 1954 and the taxpayer resistance which was characteristic of that year. Furthermore, this offer of amnesty was not even accompanied, as was the previous one, by a series of actual prosecutions.

In spite of the failure of these two tax amnesties, there were some who thought, when a long-range prosecution program was finally commenced in 1955, that another amnesty should be announced. On analysis, how-

14. *Jerusalem Post*, January 18, 1953, p. 3; February 3, 1953, p. 3.
15. *Jerusalem Post*, March 13, 1953, p. 3 (14 months in prison).

ever, it became apparent that to do so would endanger the desired deterrent effect of the program, which was dependent upon public realization that the empty threats of the past were not to be repeated. Furthermore, if amnesties were to become annual events, they would merely tend to encourage continuing contempt for the law.

Implicit in announcement of an amnesty is an admission that the administration is unable to cope with law-breakers. When, in mid-1955, attention was directed to building up a permanent enforcement staff, it would have been fatal to make another admission of weakness. Instead, it was resolved first to demonstrate the strength of the administration in the enforcement area and then to institute a policy which would still leave room for repentance — whether sincere or generated by fear of being caught. Consequently, instead of a further amnesty, a voluntary disclosure policy, later described, was proposed.

Settlement of Pending Cases

The Income Tax Commissioner has the statutory authority to terminate a criminal proceeding by compounding (settlement). Section 221 of the Income Tax Ordinance declares:

Where a person has committed an offense under Sections 215 to 220, the Commissioner may, with the consent of that person, take from him a monetary composition not exceeding the highest fine permitted to be imposed for that offense, and upon his doing so, any legal proceedings against that person in respect of that offense shall be discontinued; and if he is under arrest for it he shall be released.[16]

A substantial number of the criminal prosecutions which were instituted in 1953 were disposed of in this way, creating the feeling among some members of the public that the administration was more interested in the money than it was in obtaining convictions. This defeated the ultimate purpose of the prosecution program, which was to achieve a higher level of voluntary compliance. Offenders could reasonably assume that even if one were caught and charged with a crime, a settlement with the commissioner was always possible.

The fact that some criminal cases had been settled also produced some unfortunate results within government circles. The income tax inspectors and assessing officers began to question the wisdom of recommending prosecution — even in some of the most serious cases. The more flagrant the case, the more likely it was that the taxpayer, once he was

16. Almost all of the taxing statutes contain a provision authorizing the compounding of violations. See Ze'ev Sher, "Codification of the Tax Laws in Israel" (Hebrew), 1 *Quarterly Tax Journal* 129, 132–133 (April, 1966). More recent statutes expressly precondition the authority to compound, where criminal proceedings have already commenced, upon the direction of the Attorney General that the proceedings be terminated. See, e.g., Property Tax and Compensation Fund Law, 1961, sec. 60; Estate Tax Law, sec. 35, as amended 1964.

caught, would be anxious to close it out quickly by payment of the tax. The officials, being under constant pressure to increase assessments and collections, were naturally disinclined to divert such a case from its normal channels. The most flagrant cases generally involved the largest potential tax. When some of the assessing officers who had cooperated in the 1953 prosecution drive saw that these cases had ultimately been settled by compounding, they doubted their own wisdom in having recommended prosecution in the first instance. This attitude, bordering almost on cynicism, had to be overcome before a successful prosecution program could be instituted.[17]

The settlement of pending criminal cases also created some misunderstanding with the Ministry of Police and the Ministry of Justice. Some of the more serious such cases had arisen as a result of investigations conducted by the Economic Police. This branch of the Ministry of Police was concerned with the investigation of crimes against the economic controls which were in effect at the time. Not unexpectedly, investigation of a violation of the currency controls, for example, might also disclose an income tax violation. Since the income tax administration then had no investigative staff of its own, the Economic Police cooperated by investigating the income tax offense as well as the other offenses which had first brought them into the case. Then, if they concluded that there was sufficient evidence of violation of the Income Tax Ordinance, they would turn the case directly over to the Ministry of Justice for prosecution. If such a case were later compounded by the Income Tax Commissioner, the Police were left with the feeling that their work had been for naught and that they had been used merely as a means of frightening the taxpayer into a good settlement.

Similarly, compounding of cases in which charges had already been instituted produced a negative reaction in the Ministry of Justice. Traditionally, the Attorney General considered that it was his responsibility to evaluate a criminal case and to determine whether the interests of justice would be better served by prosecuting or by dropping the charges. Here there was a clash between the statutory authority of the Income Tax Commissioner and that of the Attorney General. Undoubtedly, the Commissioner was acting legally when he terminated a pending case by compounding, but this overlapping of authority seemed to require some accommodation between the two offices.[18] This was later achieved. By an interdepartmental agreement, both the Income Tax Commissioner

17. There are indications that, even as late as 1966, the assessing officers tended to ignore violations of the law, preferring to close the case by assessing and collecting the tax rather than forwarding it to the criminal investigators. See *Sixteenth Annual Report of the State Comptroller, 1966*, (Hebrew), pp. 94–95.

18. Compare the situation in the United States, where the Commissioner of Internal Revenue controls the case until it may be referred to the Department of Justice for prosecution, whereas the Attorney General controls it thereafter. There is no "compounding" of charges.

and the Attorney General undertook to refrain from unilaterally exercising their individual authority to terminate a case in which charges had already been instituted by the Ministry of Justice. In such cases, it was agreed, the two departments would consult with each other and charges would be dropped only by mutual consent.

Formulation of Prosecution Policy

The major problems encountered in previous efforts to proceed against income tax violators emphasized the need to move slowly and carefully in instituting a new, long-range prosecution program. The administration was not writing on a clean slate but in some respects the situation was better than if no attention had been given to tax crimes. At least there had been concern with the problem of evasion, and some steps to solve it had been taken.

Setting a Starting Point

One of the first questions to be considered in 1955 was whether to establish a cut-off date for past crimes. Although no accurate statistics were available as to the extent of past evasion, it was the informed belief of persons concerned with the problem that it had been very widespread. Undoubtedly, many instances of evasion would turn up as the enhanced inspectorial staff proceeded to clean up the backlog of unassessed returns, dating in some cases to 1948. Considering the anticipated number of such instances, common sense argued against opening criminal files for ancient crimes — even if not barred by the statute of limitations.[19] The infant investigative organization being formed in 1955 would have become so bogged down in attempting to follow cold trails that its efforts would have been frustrated at the very beginning. Within the administration, such a program would have encountered resistance from the assessing officers and inspectors, who were under heavy pressure to increase tax assessments and collections. Furthermore, the public would have reacted negatively (as it already had) to efforts to punish a few taxpayers for doing what almost everyone had been doing.

Consistent, then, with the underlying policy of the 1953 and 1954 amnesties, it seemed appropriate to deal with past violations strictly in terms of assessing and collecting the tax due, plus administrative penalties and interest wherever applicable. A cut-off date had to be fixed, because tax offenses are generally not discovered until the return is subjected to examination, and this may be several years after the crime has been committed.

19. The periods of limitation since 1967 are ten years after the close of the taxable year for evasion, and six years for other tax crimes (sec. 225, I.T.O., new version).

A number of circumstances suggested the fiscal year beginning April 1, 1954, and ending March 31, 1955, as the first taxable year to which the prosecution program should apply: the 1954 amnesty, having been retrospective, did not apply to this year; the Sharef Commission report, emphasizing the need for taking vigorous measures against tax evaders, had been issued in March 1954 and had received very wide publicity; at about the same time, amendments increasing penalties for tax evasion and other violations were being adopted; new personnel and organizational changes within the income tax administration were coupled with substantial, visible improvements in technical procedures; establishment of the public Advisory Committees at the end of 1954 signaled the eventual end of the guessing and bargaining techniques for making assessments, with greater emphasis placed upon assessments based upon the actual facts; and, generally, the income tax administration was taking on a more professional appearance in the public eye. By the fall of 1955, therefore, when income tax returns for the fiscal year ending March 31, 1955, were due to be filed, it should have been apparent to all taxpayers that the rules of the game had been changed and that tax evasion would no longer be condoned.

Initial Investigative Staff

Meanwhile, choice of the fiscal year ending in 1955 as the first one with respect to which the new prosecution program would apply gave the administration a breathing spell to organize its forces and to formulate operating police. A number of problems had to be resolved. One of the first was the question whether investigations should be conducted by the Economic Policy or whether the income tax administration should organize its own staff of criminal investigators. As to this, the Sharef Commission Report had concluded that "from the point of view of relations with the general public, it is preferable that these investigations be carried out by the [tax] Department itself." [20]

Implementation of this policy did not prove to be easy. What was required, obviously, was a staff of investigators who understood the technicalities of the income tax law and who had the ability and authority to gather the evidence necessary to convict persons charged with violations of that law. The first step which had been taken in this direction was the establishment of an Information Service, often referred to as the "*Shin Alef*," from the first letters of its Hebrew name, *Sherut Informatzia*. This organization, which existed from 1954 to 1958, was charged with two functions: (a) to gather information openly from various public sources which might be relevant to assessment of income of specific taxpayers, and to distribute this information, by way of information slips,

20. *Sharef Report* (Harvard ed.), p. 56.

to the relevant assessing officers; and (b) to conduct undercover investigations of taxpayers who were suspected of being engaged in law violations.

The first of these functions, which was largely clerical, is not of special interest here. The second, unfortunately, got off to a bad start. Perhaps because of the scarcity of qualified income tax inspectors who could be spared to participate in criminal investigations, the investigative staff of the Information Service was recruited from outside the income tax administration. Preferring to work independently of the assessing officers, the investigators of the Information Service were dependent upon leads which did not originate in the course of normal income tax audit activities.[21] This considerably narrowed the number of potential investigations. Furthermore, partly due to the aura of secrecy with which the Information Service surrounded itself, it inhibited reference to it of cases in which routine audits had indicated the possibility of criminal violations. Moreover, the methods of investigation utilized (sometimes paid informers) did not produce evidence worthy of submission to a court of law. Consequently, despite the existence of the Information Service, there remained a need for a group of investigators who would work openly alongside the assessing officers in the development of cases rather than independently of them.

In 1955, after an unsuccessful effort to modify its organization and procedures, it was concluded that the Information Service could not serve as the foundation for the type of technically qualified investigative staff which was needed to get the criminal prosecution program under way. Nor were later efforts to adapt it to the investigative needs of the income tax administration successful. By 1958, with the increasing success of the prosecution program, the Information Service was "reorganized" out of existence.[22]

Adoption of Operating Principles

By mid-1955, the following principles were agreed to as a basis for further action:

a) The Adviser on Tax Law and Administration (the author of this volume), then under contract to the Ministry of Finance and attached to the office of the Director of State Revenue, would guide the formula-

21. Actually, although the Sharef Commission Report had concluded (p. 55) "that investigations in connection with income tax [should not] be carried out by the Investigations Branch of the police force," the Information Service continued for some time to work in conjunction with the police.

22. Lapidoth, *Evasion and Avoidance of Income Tax*, p. 119. The Information Service was disbanded in 1958, simultaneously with the appointment of a Deputy Income Tax Commissioner for Investigations and Criminal Prosecutions. *Haaretz*, May 13, 1958. This was part of a general reorganization of income tax headquarters.

tion of prosecution policy and procedures for all of the several tax administrations. Emphasis was to be placed upon the income tax, which was in greatest need.

b) Responsibility for developing the prosecution program within the income tax administration would be vested in the Deputy Commissioner of Income Tax, Technical, to whom the Commissioner would delegate all of his authorities in this area. Legal matters, including weighing sufficiency of the evidence, would be dealt with by the Legal Adviser to the Income Tax Commissioner, in consultation, when necessary, with the Ministry of Justice.

c) A training program would be instituted to alert assessing officers, inspectors, members of headquarters staff, and others concerned to the purposes of the program and to instruct them in procedures for the identification and handling of potential criminal cases.

d) An investigative staff would be set up, under the direction and control of the Deputy Commissioner, Technical, its members to be recruited from among experienced income tax inspectors who had legal backgrounds and who were considered to be temperamentally suited for this type of work. These men would be stationed at the principal cities — Tel Aviv, Haifa, and Jerusalem — but would be detached administratively from any assessing office and would report directly to headquarters in Jerusalem.

e) The income tax assessing officers and inspectors would be instructed to maintain a watch during the course of audit for cases involving fraud, evasion, or other violations of the law. Such cases were to be referred to the Deputy Commissioner, Technical, or, as it later developed, to other officials designated by him.

f) Once a case had been identified as meriting criminal investigation, exclusive jurisdiction over it would be vested in the investigators, and normal civil assessment procedures would be deferred pending decision on whether to prosecute.[23] Although it was anticipated that this policy would encounter some resistance from the assessing officers, it was concluded that, at least at the inception of the program, preference should be given to the development of cases which might lead toward prosecu-

---

23. For conflicting opinions as to the validity of this policy in view of penalty provisions which were tied to the amount of the tax evaded, cf. Uriel Gorney, "Net Worth Prosecution and Onus of Proof" (Hebrew) 6 *Roeh Haheshbon*, 11 (October–December 1955) with E. Klimowsky, "Criminal Case or Civil Case, Which Comes First?" (Hebrew) 9 *Roeh Haheshbon*, 134 (February–March 1959). See also Harold C. Wilkenfeld, "The Rights of the Income Taxpayer" (Hebrew), 7 *Roeh Haheshbon*, 287, 296 (May–June 1957). This practice was inferentially endorsed in 1966 by the State Comptroller, who suggested, however, that the pendency of a criminal investigation should not deter civil collection proceedings for tax years which are not involved in the investigation. *Sixteenth Annual Report of State Comptroller*, 1966 (Hebrew), p. 95. A similar deferment policy is followed in the United States. See *Campbell* v. *Eastland*, 302 F. 2d. 478 (C.A. 5, 1962); certiorari denied, 371 U.S. 955.

tion, even though this meant delaying assessment and collection of the tax.[24]

g) The heads of the several tax units were to be requested not to exercise their compounding authority without clearance from the office of the Director of Revenue. This was designed to relieve the Income Tax Commissioner, particularly, of pressures to which he might be subjected once the prosecution program got under way. These pressures, it was felt, could be more firmly resisted at the level of the Director of Revenue.[25]

h) The final decision whether or not to prosecute a particular taxpayer would be made at headquarters, after investigation had been completed, and on the basis of a full written report summarizing the available evidence and giving the recommendation of the investigators, for or against prosecution.

i) A "selective" prosecution policy would be followed, in which the guiding principle would be to prosecute the most flagrant cases, which could be anticipated to produce the maximum positive effect upon taxpayer morale and voluntary compliance. This was a central element of the program.

j) Publicity would be controlled by the public relations officer on the staff of the Director of Revenue. No publicity would be given to cases in process of investigation. When charges were filed in particular cases, the attention of the press would be directed to this fact; but the only information to be supplied to the press would be that contained in the charge sheet, which was a matter of public record. When and if a conviction was obtained, a press release would be prepared limited to the facts of public record. In this way, it was hoped, "trial by newspaper" would be eliminated, and emphasis would be placed upon actual achievements of the prosecution program.

Comparison with Customs Prosecutions

While the foregoing principles were being formulated a survey was made of the investigative facilities and prosecution experience of each of the tax departments. By contrast with the income tax administration, it was found that the Customs and Excise Tax Branch was, if anything, too successful in its prosecution program.

Because goods subject to the customs, excises, or purchase tax had

24. Delay in assessment was limited only to the taxable years specifically under investigation. Assessments for other years could still be made. *Sixteenth Annual Report of State Comptroller*, 1966 (Hebrew), p. 95; but see *Nineteenth Annual Report of State Comptroller*, 1969 (Hebrew), p. 139, indicating that assessments for non-fraud years were still being delayed in some cases.

25. For some embarrassing consequences of a departure from this policy, see discussion of the *Olamit* case later in this chapter.

to flow through controlled channels, the opportunities for evasion were limited. And even if some goods sought to evade these channels, quite effective methods of detection had been instituted. Involved in these were the national police, the customs police, customs and excise inspectors at the points of entry or production, and staffs of special investigators within both the customs and purchase tax organizations. As a result, evasion was not easy and, when detected, was vigorously prosecuted.

Paradoxically, the relatively large number of prosecutions of violators of the customs and purchase tax and related laws pointed up the relative weakness of the income tax administration in this area. This disproportion, it was expected, would continue even after the income tax prosecution program could get well under way. Consideration was accordingly given to the possibility of achieving some sort of balance, without injuring the effectiveness of the customs and excise administration's enforcement activities. A review of these activities revealed that measures other than prosecution could be resorted to in some cases that would be equally, if not more, effective. Among these were confiscation of goods, administrative penalties, broader use of "best judgment" assessments, restriction or cancellation of import licenses to previous violators, bearing down on violators by more frequent checks and heavier controls, cancellation or nonrenewal of licenses of customs brokers who had broken faith with the administration, and other such measures available under the law.[26] In this way, it was felt, more routine violations could be punished by administrative means, while prosecutions in court could concentrate on the more serious violators or on recidivists.[27]

There was another important reason for seeking such a balance. Experience with the few income tax criminal prosecutions which had been instituted in 1952 and 1953 had shown a disinclination on the part of the courts to impose heavy penalties on the few hapless individuals against whom charges had been brought. The maximum penalties then permissible under the Income Tax Ordinance (until amended in 1954) were relatively low, and the courts did not even go to the limits of these light penalties. By contrast, the customs and purchase tax laws provided heavy penalties which the courts had been imposing quite frequently. Yet by 1955 there had already been a few instances in which magistrates (before whom most of these infractions were triable) had

26. For more economic sanctions, or for making the punishment fit the crime, see O. Oldman, "Controlling Income Tax Evasion," in Joint Tax Program of the Organization of American States, Inter-American Development Bank, *Problems of Tax Administration in Latin America*, (Baltimore: Johns Hopkins Press, 1967), a paper presented at a conference held in Buenos Aires in 1961.

27. It is interesting to observe that, by 1966, it was felt that too many income tax technical offenses were being prosecuted, and the State Comptroller recommended that administrative penalties be substituted for prosecutions in all but flagrant cases. The Income Tax Commissioner complied with this recommendation — *Nineteenth Annual Report of State Comptroller*, 1969 (Hebrew) p. 139.

imposed mere token penalties upon convicted customs and purchase tax violators. This seemed to indicate a reaction on the part of some magistrates to what may have appeared to them to be an overabundance of prosecutions for relatively minor offenses. This phenomenon, if continued, could have seriously affected the whole prosecution program.[28] What it indicated was some kind of application of the "law of diminishing returns" to tax prosecutions. The solution, it seemed, lay in sifting out the less important cases so that the flagrant ones would not be downgraded by association with a mass of lesser offenses.[29] The customs experience also indicated that the developing income tax prosecution program might run into difficulties in the courts unless it was designed to place emphasis upon serious violators rather than upon "traffic offenses." Indeed, this was demonstrated when the income tax prosecution program finally got under way in 1956 and 1957. Several of the early prosecutions involved shockingly gross violations of the law. Yet the sentencing judges were hesitant to impose heavy sentences, even though their opinions emphasized the seriousness of the crimes. Actual jail sentences, for example, were not imposed until 1959. In a sense the judges reflected the public mood in regard to income tax offenses. Leniency seemed to be called for until the public itself, by its attitude toward the income tax, showed that compliance with the law had become the accepted norm. This in turn was more a product of improvements in the administration on the civil side than in demonstrations of strength by prosecution of offenders. The latter could not have succeeded without the former.

Reinstituting the Prosecution Program

In proceeding toward the establishment of an income tax prosecution program, several realities had to be recognized. Principal among these were that:

— although improved audit procedures could be expected to uncover many instances of understatement of income or overstatement of deductions, sufficient to support additional tax assessments, much more intensive investigation would be required in order to prepare any such case for prosecution;

— even if an investigative staff were available (which it then was not),

28. A similar phenomenon was experienced in the United States during the prohibition era, when courts and juries also showed their annoyance with excessive prosecutions of minor offenders by imposing token sentences. The ultimate result was abolition of this unpopular law.

29. Compare *Sixteenth Annual Report of the State Comptroller*, 1966 (Hebrew), p. 95. This suggested further efforts to reduce the number of investigations and prosecutions of technical offenses so as to free the investigative force to handle the more serious offenses.

it would not be possible — and indeed would be inadvisable — to investigate every case in which fraud was suspected;

— bearing in mind the ultimate purpose of the enforcement program, which was to raise the level of voluntary taxpayer compliance, careful watch would have to be kept upon public reactions. Gauging these in advance, as could best be done by study of past experience and present conditions, it was felt that the volume of prosecutions should be kept low at the outset and should be permitted to expand *pari passu* with improvements on the civil side.

Although all indications pointed to a modest beginning for the prosecution program, it was also essential that those few cases which would signal the commencement of the program should make a heavy impact upon the taxpaying public. This meant proceeding first against violators whose fraudulent devices were so flagrant as to shock others who might themselves have been breaking the law. Since the general extent of evasion was then very high, it was felt that, at least at the start, there had to be a show of strength against the "big fish." If this could be done, the hoped-for reaction would be that the mass of taxpayers would fall back into line.

Thus, what later came to be called the "selective prosecution policy" really began without any choice. The cases which ultimately might be prosecuted had to originate with the inspectors and assessing officers. Unless they were convinced of the validity of the program, it would not move, and toward the end of 1955 prospects appeared discouraging. The reasons were understandable. The assessment and collection programs had been stepped up considerably, and the professional staff were under heavy pressure to meet and exceed their prescribed quotas. At least in the short run, recommending a case for criminal investigation would delay collection; and the more "juicy" the fraud case, the more additional tax it was likely to produce. Thus, there was a direct conflict between the collection program and the prosecution program.

Fortunately, there were a few assessing officers who were convinced of the need for an enforcement program and who were willing to give it another try. Notable among these was the assessing officer for Haifa. At first he, like the others, had been skeptical about the seriousness of the program but, once he was convinced that past errors were not to be repeated, he supported the program enthusiastically. As it happened, even before a central investigating staff had been established, the Haifa office had been able, on its own, to conduct fairly thorough investigations of several serious fraud cases. These Haifa cases were found to be of the type which could have some deterrent effect upon potential evaders. Also, it was felt, a renewed series of prosecutions might catalyze the other assessing officers into recommending further cases for prosecution. Accordingly, the decision was made to go ahead, even though there was the chance that an early start, before a series of follow-up cases were in the course of preparation, might detract from the desired continuity of the program.

The first of the new series of prosecutions was filed in late 1955 and was decided by the Haifa District Court in February 1956.[30] The defendants pleaded guilty to charges of fraudulent omissions of substantial amounts of income for 1951 and 1954 and the filing of false returns. The judge, while imposing very heavy fines upon the defendants, refrained from imposing a jail sentence. His thoughtful explanation of the sentence merits quotation at length:

First — Few criminal cases, if any, have been instituted until now in connection with serious violations, . . . and therefore no uniform sentencing policy has developed to serve as a yardstick whereby I may be guided, considering the circumstances of this case.

Second — It is well-known that violations of the income tax law are very frequent in the land. On one hand, this fact might weigh heavily in favor of a severe penalty, since it may help to eradicate the disease; but, on the other hand, I cannot close my eyes to the reality, known to all, that there is hardly a righteous man, in any level of the populace, who may have had an opportunity to evade payment of his correct tax and who has not sinned against this law in some amount, large or small. It is a fact (which I do not justify, but merely note) that an appreciable section of the public has considered the income tax as a decree which it is very difficult to bear; and it is an additional fact that for years there has been hardly any actual check on the amount of reported incomes — a matter which has eased, and even invited, violation of the law. The very fact that until now there have been hardly any, if at all, criminal cases involving serious violations of the Income Tax Ordinance shows that no serious and substantial effort has been made until now to overcome violations in this area.

Considering these facts, and other mitigating circumstances, I have decided, in spite of the seriousness of the crime, not to send the individual defendant to prison.[31]

This was a challenge to the administration which had to be met promptly in order to overcome the direct and implied criticisms expressed by the court. This meant that even while the investigative staff was being organized, at least some few additional cases had to be brought. Otherwise, the momentum of the first case would be lost, and the judge's criticism would be confirmed. To some extent it also meant, at the beginning, prosecuting almost any case which came along — and there were very few of these. How to get the assessing officers to feed

30. The timing of the decision was fortunate, for it came just before the end of the taxable year 1955–56.

31. *Attorney General v. Adi, Ltd., et al.*, Cr. 75/55, I *Kovetz Piske Din Pliliim* 16, 18, per District Judge Y. Cohen, Haifa District Court.

more cases into the investigative mill was a problem which still had to be solved. The approach taken toward its solution was to involve the assessing officers and principal inspectors in the process of formulating the investigative policy and procedures. Several national meetings of these officials were held during 1955 and 1956 at which all aspects of the prosecution program were thrown open to general discussion and analysis.[32] Top officials from headquarters, during visits to particular assessing officers, also included the subject in their agendas. Lesson units on methods of identifying frauds were included in training courses for inspectors. Gradually, the cases began to flow.

Organizing Investigative Staff and Procedures

Meanwhile, attention was being given to the organization of a professional investigative staff. The stated prerequisites were that candidates be experienced income tax inspectors with backgrounds of education in the law. There were all too few of these, and it was not easy to have them released from their current inspectorial duties. Two qualified men were found in the Tel Aviv area and one in Haifa. The decision reached at headquarters was to transfer the two men in Tel Aviv from their previous assignments, make them responsible directly to headquarters, and provide them with office facilities assigned to the Commissioner within the Assessing Office for Large Enterprises in Tel Aviv.[33] The Haifa man remained administratively responsible to the assessing officer at Haifa, with the understanding that his investigative functions would be given priority over any civil functions which might also be assigned to him. In Jerusalem, where the anticipated volume of potential criminal cases was the lowest, the program was placed under the personal direction of the assessing officer, who would then coopt such members of his staff as would be needed for particular cases. Cases originating in other offices were to be transferred to the closest of the three investigating offices. All investigations were under the general direction of the Deputy Income Tax Commissioner, Technical, and under the guidance, on evidentiary and other legal matters, of the Legal Adviser to the Commissioner.

The nucleus of an investigative staff having been established, the next step was to put it to work. Almost immediately a major defect was dis-

32. See discussion of tax prosecution policy by Harold C. Wilkenfeld, Attorney General Haim Cohen, Director of Revenue Zeev Sharef, Income Tax Commissioner T. Brosh, and others, reported in *Sherut* (Hebrew), July 1957, pp. 3–12.

33. One of the qualified Tel Aviv men had previously been devoting most of his time to the handling of estate tax cases. At the time, the Income Tax Commissioner also was occupying the post of Director of Estate Taxes. Most of the taxable estates were in the Tel Aviv area. The shifting of this official, who had been carrying the bulk of the estate tax load, was soon followed by a reorganization of the estate tax administration, which was thereafter concentrated in Jerusalem.

covered in the Income Tax Ordinance. This confined the investigative powers of the Income Tax Commissioner and the assessing officers within so narrow a compass as to prevent intensive investigations from being carried out. To have sought amendments of the law at that point to broaden the investigative powers was considered impolitic and, in any event, might have delayed the program for perhaps another year.

Fortunately, another solution was found. Just at this time conversations were being held with officials of the Ministry of Police in connection with effecting the decision to relieve the police of investigations of income tax violations. The police certainly had the necessary investigative powers. It occurred to the people concerned with this problem that it might be possible to confer the statutory investigative powers of police officials upon a limited number of selected income tax officials. This idea having been explored and found legally permissible, interministerial arrangements were made and about ten income tax officials, including the special investigators, were appointed by the Minister of Police as special police officers, with the assimilated rank of Police Inspector.[34]

It was at this point that one of the major differences between the operating methods of the newly organized investigative staff (for convenience, this will be referred to hereafter as the Investigation Unit) and of the *Shin Alef* (Information Service) became apparent. Unlike the *Shin Alef*, which operated like a "secret service," the Investigation Unit was to operate in the open. During the investigative process it was intended that the suspected taxpayer would be given notice that he was under investigation and, if he so desired, that he would be given an opportunity to explain his apparently irregular behavior. This procedure was to be part of the "voluntary disclosure" policy, later described. A taxpayer summoned in this fashion was to be advised that he had the right to consult and appear with his advocate.[35] Also, in utilizing the statutory powers of the police, the investigators would, before com-

34. A similar solution of a similar problem has been in effect in the Netherlands, where income tax criminal investigators also have been vested with special police powers. In Israel, the validity of this arrangement was sustained in *Attorney General* v. *Kunzman*, Crim. No. 180/56, Tel Aviv District Court, decided June 21, 1957; and in *Attorney General* v. *Jacobson*, Crim. No. 10135 (interlocutory motion to exclude confession), Tel Aviv Magistrate's Court. Any doubt as to the validity of this procedure was eliminated by amendments to sec. 80A of the Income Tax Ordinance, 1947 (now sec. 227, new version) providing expressly that the Minister of Police may empower an assessing officer to conduct investigations, searches, and seizures, and that an assessing officer so empowered shall have all of the authority of a police inspector under the Criminal Procedure Ordinance (Evidence). See also J. Stern, *Mas Hakhnasah* (Income Tax) 1965, p. 124 (Haifa, 1965). Similar provisions have been incorporated into other tax laws. See, for example, Sec. 48A of the Property Tax and Damage Law, as added in 1964.

35. A member of the bar in Israel is called "*orekh din*," translated as "advocate." Although in many aspects Israeli judicial practice follows the British, there is no diversification of lawyers into "solicitors" and "barristers."

mencing the interview (which was conducted under oath), expressly inform the witness that he was free to refuse to testify but that if he did testify any evidence which he might give could be used against him in a criminal proceeding.

It was recognized of course, that there were calculated risks in resorting to this procedure. Many prosecution cases could be built up without even interviewing the taxpayer in advance of the filing of a charge sheet. Documentary and other evidence could be assembled from third-party sources. The taxpayer's books and records could be seized under a search warrant. Indeed, much of the evidence sufficient to obtain a conviction might have been assembled even before the taxpayer would be approached. Why, then, communicate with him at all? The principal answer was that under the particular circumstances prevailing in Israel at that time, fairness to the taxpayer required that he be given an opportunity to explain away the evidence against him if he could. Similar opportunities were given to potential tax defendants in the United States and England, and, it was felt, the reasons for this procedure applied *a fortiori* in Israel.

Like England and the United States, Israel is a common law jurisdiction,[36] in which an accused is presumed to be innocent until his guilt has been proved beyond a reasonable doubt. Given the sensitive nature of the income tax prosecution program, particularly at its inception, it seemed far better that reasonable doubts be resolved at the administrative stage rather than in the courts. In fact, it was hoped, the evidence in the first few cases would be so overwhelming that the defendant would plead guilty rather than have the evidence against him exposed to public view. Indeed, the first several cases were so strong that pleas of guilty were entered.[37]

Although the desired deterrent effect of the prosecution program required public awareness of the fact that tax violators were being prosecuted on a regular basis, "show trials" were not considered essential. By giving taxpayers an opportunity to meet with the investigators, cases in which the accused might have a reasonable defense could be eliminated. This might mean foregoing some possible prosecutions (of which there were pitifully few at the start) but, on the other hand, it emphasized the purpose of the program to concentrate on the "hard-core" cases.

36. David M. Sassoon, "The Israel Legal System," 16 *American Journal of Comparative Law* 405, 406–407 (no. 3, 1968); Bernstein, *Politics of Israel*, pp. 93–94.

37. One can only guess at the reasoning which led to the defendants' decisions to plead guilty. Aside from the possibility that no defense may have been available, it was no doubt hoped that the sentencing judge would be inclined to be more lenient toward one who acknowledged his guilt, instead of protesting his innocence in the face of overwhelming evidence of guilt. In the early cases, the judges were indeed inclined to be lenient, although for other reasons. See quotation from *Attorney General* v. *Adi, Ltd.*, above, n. 31.

It was also recognized that even the most careful investigation might be so one-sided that evidence favorable to the taxpayer might be over-looked or disregarded. Also, in treading the indistinct line between "tax avoidance" and "tax evasion," [38] there might be technical arguments which would enable the taxpayer to raise reasonable doubts as to the existence of a prerequisite intent to violate the law. Fairness to investigatees seemed to require that, before prosecution proceedings were filed, they should be given an opportunity to dissuade the administrators if they could. This was in accord with the British dictum, very frequently quoted in Israel, that "it is not only essential that justice be done but that it also manifestly appear that justice is being done." [39]

Establishing the Integrity of the Program

There was another, perhaps unexpressed, reason for giving suspects notice that their cases were on the road toward possible prosecution. There had been much talk during the mid-1950's about *protekzia*, or protectionism, in government circles. Some of this talk had attached to the compounding of some of the earlier income tax prosecutions. It was essential to the integrity of the criminal prosecution program that the word filter out to the general public that *protekzia* was of no help to one whose income tax case was in the process of investigation. It was even more important that this be made clear to the assessing officers, because they could not be expected to refer important cases for criminal investigation unless they were convinced that their superiors would stand firm against any pressures which the taxpayer might try to bring to bear through his "connections." Otherwise, only the "little fish," who had no connections, would be prosecuted. Such an attitude would have crippled the program from the start.

Fortunately, one of the very first cases demonstrated that *protekzia* had no place in the criminal prosecution program. In December 1956 an important transport cooperative and one of its directors were convicted of income tax evasion by the Haifa District Court. The accused had pleaded guilty to charges of evading a total of IL. 37,500 of income tax over a two-year period. Fines totaling IL. 60,000 were imposed upon the cooperative and of IL. 15,000 upon the director.[40] An appeal from the severity of the fines was taken to the Supreme Court, sitting as the Court of Criminal Appeal. Promptly, in March 1957, the Supreme Court affirmed the judgment, saying, in part:

---

38. These terms are here used in the generally accepted sense, in which "avoidance" is within the permissible bounds of the law, and "evasion" is not.

39. See R. E. Megarry, *Miscellany at Law*, pp. 234–235.

40. *Attorney General* v. *Hanamal Hehadash Cooperative, Ltd., et al.*, Crim. No. 376/56, I *Kovetz Piske Din Pliliim* 27.

It is clear that the punishment is not of the lightest. Nevertheless, we see no reason to minimize the judgment. It is well that commercial organizations of substantial size should learn that it is not worthwhile to defraud the Treasury and to make prohibited profits at the expense of the public.[41]

This case was an important turning point in at least two respects: First, the fact that one of the country's most important transport cooperatives had been prosecuted made it clear to anyone who could read between the lines that there was to be no favoritism — political or personal. Second, it emphasized that the courts would stand behind the program and would impose heavy penalties (although some time was to pass before jail sentences would be imposed), which might even put the tax-payer out of business.

This early success gave a substantial impetus to the criminal prosecution program. Both within and outside the administration it demonstrated that the program was to be taken seriously. As the assessing officers began to see the deterrent effect which these early prosecutions were beginning to have upon the taxpaying public, they stopped holding back and began to feed additional cases into the investigation mill. As the number of referred cases increased, the elements of the projected selective prosecution policy could be given freer play.

Selective Prosecution Policy

By the end of 1955, reports on the results of field investigations began to reach headquarters in Jerusalem. A review committee was established consisting of the Principal Deputy Income Tax Commissioner (formerly the Deputy Commissioner, Technical), the Legal Adviser to the Income Tax Commissioner, and the Adviser on Tax Law and Administration, who served as *de facto* chairman. Other staff members were coopted from time to time, in part for the purpose of assuring continuity of the review process after initial policy had been formulated. There was also a clerk who recorded the decisions of the review committee, maintained registers of cases in process, and prepared statistical and other reports. As the volume of work increased, this committee held regular weekly meetings at which the reports from the field, which had been previously circulated among the members, were reviewed and decisions reached as to the disposition to be made of each case. In accordance with operating guidelines, which the committee formulated as its experience and exposure to actual cases increased, the selective prosecution policy began to develop.

41. *Hanamal Hehadash* v. *Attorney General*, Crim. App. No. 232/56, I *Kovetz Piske Din Pliliim* 29.

Selection Criteria

The central theme of the selective prosecution policy was that emphasis should be placed upon cases which were most likely to affect the behavior and attitudes of sizable portions of the taxpaying public. This meant that the administration had to identify particular problem areas in which a high level of evasion was thought to be currently taking place, and then, if possible, seek out several cases within this group where evasion could be demonstrated to have taken place in years for which returns had already been filed. In other words, to achieve maximum deterrent effect, with a minimum of prosecutions, it was necessary to demonstrate a degree of investigative expertise which would deter taxpayers from doing today what someone else was now being punished for having done several years before.

At the beginning of the program, when evasion was widespread, this was not too difficult, because almost any case would have some deterrent effect upon other taxpayers, and, in any event, there were not so many cases under active investigation as to permit any breadth of choice. However, after about two years, a backlog of cases in various stages of investigation began to build up, and the trial courts began to reach and decide the first of the cases in which charges had been filed.[42] This was felt to be an appropriate time at which to institute a greater degree of selectivity and to concentrate on special problem areas. Accordingly, the practice was instituted, which is still in force, to alert the assessing officers as to the particular trades, businesses, professions, or occupations in which a high level of evasion was suspected and to request them to concentrate on these areas in recommending cases for criminal investigation.[43] Of course, this did not mean that flagrant cases in other areas were to be abandoned: these still had to be referred to the Investigation Unit. But the purpose of these instructions was to invite attention to particular types of cases which were not being received in sufficient quantity. Among these, for example, were businesses in which cash transactions were prevalent, such as builders. Also, it was desired to give concentrated attention to "foci of infection," such as accountants and lawyers, where a negative attitude toward tax compliance, if it existed, could lead numerous clients astray.

Explaining the Program to the Field Officials

The problem of maintaining administrative support for the prosecution program had been difficult from the outset. Although those working

42. The Ministry of Justice and the courts cooperated in giving income tax criminal cases prompt attention. Delays in the courts would have been harmful to the program, particularly in view of the policy to refrain from publicity until after the cases were decided.

43. See *Eleventh Annual Report on State Revenue, 1964/65* (Hebrew), p. 41.

directly in the program were beginning to see encouraging results, other officials whose principal concern was with assessing and collecting the tax were still showing little enthusiasm. In December 1956 a national meeting of the senior officials of the revenue administration, including the heads of all field offices, was held in Jerusalem. An important part of the agenda for this meeting was a review of the progress of the prosecution program and a consideration of the problems which it still faced. As an aid toward involving these officials in the process of formulating policy, the following questions were drawn up by the Adviser on Tax Law and Administration:

1. Is it advisable to institute criminal proceedings in every instance where there is evidence of violation of the law? Does the law permit the tax administrator to select particular cases for prosecution? If so, what are the principles which should guide the policy for selecting cases for prosecution?

2. What is the relationship between the legal authority to compound a potential criminal case and the legal obligation to punish law violators by criminal proceedings? Is it advisable that the tax administrator voluntarily set limits to the exercise of his authority to compound? What should be the compounding policy in cases in which criminal charges have already been filed?

3. To what extent should the police be asked to assist in investigations of tax violations? What problems arise when the police are used, and how might this affect the policy of the tax administration?

4. When reaching a final decision whether or not to institute criminal proceedings against a particular taxpayer, what weight, if any, should be given to the following factors?

— The available evidence, that is, the chances of obtaining a conviction.

— The amount of tax evaded and, generally, the callousness of the offense.

— The degree of cooperation by the taxpayer with the tax authorities during the investigation and thereafter. Should the decision be different if (i) before any investigation of the taxpayer is commenced, he voluntarily discloses all of the facts in order to clear his name? (ii) after investigation has begun he cooperates fully and makes a complete disclosure? (iii) after the investigation is completed, the taxpayer admits the correctness of the evidence against him? (iv) after criminal charges have been filed, the taxpayer for the first time is prepared to admit his guilt and indicates his willingness to pay the tax on condition that the charges be dropped?

—The taxpayer's age and the state of his health.

— The reputation of the taxpayer and, particularly: (i) whether he had previously violated the tax or other laws; (ii) his standing in the community; (iii) his educational level; (iv) his political affiliations; (v) his social connections.

The effect which the filing of criminal charges and a conviction might have upon: (i) the morale of other taxpayers; (ii) innocent persons who have some connection with the taxpayer, such as business partners, family members, and public bodies.

5. Would it be advisable to announce a general amnesty for tax violators? Would an amnesty be more successful now, and would it be less likely to interfere with the administrative process than the amnesties of 1952 and 1954? [44]

Although put as questions, the broad outlines of the policy which was in process of formulation could be seen. A rather sharp reaction came from the Attorney General, who was present at the December 1956 meeting. He took the position that there was no room for selection of cases and that charges had to be filed whenever there was evidence that the law had been violated.[45] As against this position there was the explicit authority granted to the tax administrators to compound criminal cases, even after conviction. This reflected the recognition by the law-maker that tax crimes might differ from other crimes and that the administrator should have some discretion in deciding how they should be dealt with. The tax administrator stood firmly upon his authority to decide whether or not to institute criminal proceedings, even though this might imply special treatment of tax evasion as a "white-collar" crime.

Evolution of the Voluntary Disclosure Policy

Although it had been decided that the amnesties of 1952 and 1954 should not be repeated some recognition had to be given to the possibility that once a criminal prosecution program got well under way some taxpayers who had overstepped the law might want to clear their records in order to forestall possible prosecution. This was, in fact, one of the results which it was hoped the prosecution program might achieve. Aside from advantages accruing to the administration from "voluntary disclosures," Jewish tradition taught that one should not "close the door" in the face of one who desired to repent. This seemed to be from both the practical and traditional point of view a most appropriate attitude to take toward delinquent taxpayers whose consciences might be stirred by witnessing the punishments which had been meted out to others. The problem, at the outset, was how to express a "voluntary disclosure" policy which would be suitable to the Israeli conditions, and how to carry it into effect.[46]

44. Harold C. Wilkenfeld, "Prosecution or Compounding of Criminal Offenses" (Hebrew), *Sherut*, July 1957, p. 3.

45. *Sherut*, July 1957, pp. 4, 6.

46. Actually, it was not until 1962 that conditions were considered to be appropriate for the public announcement of a voluntary disclosure policy.

Preliminary Considerations — American and British Experience

By way of guides to the formulation of a policy, reference was made to the practice in England and the United States, both of which had vigorous criminal prosecution programs. In the United States there had been in effect from 1945 to 1952 a publicly announced policy of refraining from prosecuting any taxpayer who made a "voluntary disclosure" of his prior evasion. In order to qualify as a voluntary disclosure, the timing was critical: disclosure had to be made before the taxpayer's return had been assigned to an internal revenue employee for examination.[47] This rigid time requirement, and other aspects of the American voluntary disclosure policy, had given rise to so many problems that in 1952 it was abolished. Part of the difficulty turned on the question of the admissibility of incriminating evidence supplied by the taxpayer in the belief (at least he might so allege) that, by virtue of what he thought was a "voluntary disclosure," he had rendered himself immune from prosecution.[48] After several such cases, it became apparent to the American administration that the policy in its existing form was self-defeating. Its abolition became necessary in order to restore administrative freedom of choice.

In England the situation was found to be quite different. As in the United States, tax evasion seemed to have risen sharply during World War II, and there was a vigorous criminal prosecution program. But, by contrast with the "voluntary disclosure" policy in the United States, which did not apply after examination of a taxpayer's return had begun, the English had what might be called a "confession" policy. The publicly announced policy of the Commissioners of Inland Revenue, supported by express statutory authority, was that although they have a general power to accept "pecuniary settlements instead of instituting criminal proceedings in respect of fraud or wilful default alleged to have been committed by a taxpayer," they would "give no undertaking to a taxpayer in any such case that they will accept such a settlement and refrain from instituting criminal proceedings even if the case is one in which the taxpayer has made full confession and has given full facilities for investigation of the facts." Accordingly:

47. For a contemporaneous critique of the American voluntary disclosure policy see Charles S. Lyon, "The Crime of Income Tax Fraud: Its Present Status and Function," 54 *Columbia Law Review* 476, 491–496 (1954); see also Murray L. Rachlin, "Voluntary Disclosures in Tax Fraud and Evasion Cases," 25 *Taxes (The Tax Magazine)* 293 (1947), and J. P. Wenchel, "Tax Frauds and Voluntary Disclosures," 25 *Taxes*, 485 (1947).

48. Although the administratively announced standard was that disclosure had to be made before investigation (civil or criminal) had commenced, the question of admissibility of incriminating evidence supplied by the taxpayer turned, in several cases, on whether the taxpayer actually knew that an investigation of his tax affairs had started. See, e.g., *In re Liebster*, 91 F. Supp. 814 (E.D. Pa., 1950); and cf. *United States* v. *Lustig*, 163 F. 2d 85 (C.A. 2, 1947).

They reserve to themselves complete discretion in all cases as to the course which they will pursue, *but it is their practice to be influenced by the fact that the taxpayer has made a full confession and has given full facilities for investigation into his affairs and for examination of such books, papers, documents or information as the Commissioners may consider necessary* [49] [emphasis supplied].

The practical effect of this English policy was to invite "confession" and "cooperation" by a taxpayer even after he had been informed of the irregularities which the authorities had already discovered. On the other hand, the reservation just quoted prevented the policy from foreclosing prosecutions in flagrant cases of fraud, or in cases in which the "confession" was in bad faith and designed to mislead the authorities. In such cases, even after "confession" and "cooperation," criminal charges could still be brought and, by express statutory provision, evidence supplied by the taxpayer himself would still be admissible against him even though he was induced to supply it by having the policy of the Board of Inland Revenue called to his attention.[50]

On balance, the more lenient practice of the British appeared to be more appropriate to Israeli conditions in the latter 1950's than the American practice, even before abolition of the "voluntary disclosure" policy. The cut-off point for application of the American policy had been the assignment of the income tax return for examination. In the United States, only a relatively small percentage of returns (in recent years less than 5 per cent) were so assigned, this being a by-product of the self-assessment system there in force. In Israel, on the other hand (as in England), all returns (at least of companies and of self-employed individuals) were examined during this period.[51] In principle, therefore, almost all returns were destined for inspection as soon as they were received, it being only a matter of time until they would be reached by the particular inspector to whom they were assigned.[52] Taking into account, moreover, that the underlying purpose of the investigation and prosecution program was to induce straying taxpayers to return to the proper path, more leeway had to be provided to make this possible.

All of the details of this policy could not be finally worked out until

49. Answer given by the Chancellor of the Exchequer to a question asked in the House of Commons on 5 October 1944. A copy of this statement is supplied to taxpayers under investigation for fraud.

50. Finance Act, 1942, sec. 34; Income Tax Act, 1952, sec. 504.

51. In later years, certain returns, as of many employees and self-employed individuals with incomes below stated amounts, were accepted as filed.

52. Even in the case of a taxpayer who had not filed a return for a particular year (that in itself being an offense), his file, if there was one for him, would eventually be assigned to an inspector. Until 1967 there was no period of prescription upon the making of an assessment. In 1967 the Ordinance was amended by the Income Tax Ordinance Amendment Law (no. 11), vol. 503 *Sefer Hahukim*, p. 94, to provide that the assessing officer shall make the assessment within five years after the taxable year in which the return was submitted (sec. 145, I.T.O.).

there had been several more years of experience with the program. Until then, to the extent that particular taxpayers showed a sincere desire to clear their records, the disposition of these cases without prosecution was made on an ad hoc basis. Although the factors which might be taken into account were more or less indicated by question 4(c) of the agenda for the December 1956 meeting, the decision was to let future experience assist in determining the weight to be given to any one factor. Generally, however, some balance between the limits set, respectively, by the American and the English policies was achieved by an inclination to deal more leniently with a taxpayer whose admission of improprieties came early rather than late in the course of the investigation of his case.

Another problem was whether to extend an official and public invitation to taxpayers to come in to straighten out their tax affairs. Such official statements had been made both in the United States and in England, but on examination of the experience in both these countries, it could be seen that they sometimes created problems which became subjects of dispute in the criminal courts. Furthermore, the history of amnesties previously tendered to tax violators in Israel militated against such an announcement, for it might have been misconstrued by the public as merely a repetition of the past, with equally disappointing results. Instead, it was decided to let the program speak for itself. This meant deferring for several years, perhaps, the time when some accounts would be straightened out, but in the long run the decision to abstain from any official pronouncements was considered to be the soundest.

The Olamit Case

The absence of any publicly declared "voluntary disclosure" policy did not deter taxpayers from trying to dissuade the authorities from proceeding with a prosecution. One such case became a matter of public record in 1959 and indicated a certain lack of uniformity of policy at the time within the administration itself. The case involved a building supply company which, together with its directors (an aged father and two sons), was charged with evading tax on over one million pounds of income for the taxable years 1954 through 1956. After pleas of guilty had been entered in the Tel Aviv Magistrate's Court, pleas for leniency were made by counsel for the defendants. These pleas included a contention that both the Income Tax Commissioner and the District Attorney had given assurances that the charges against several of the individual defendants would be dropped, but that these assurances had not been honored. Meanwhile, after the fraud had been disclosed, one of the individual defendants committed suicide.[53] Fines totaling IL. 320,000 were imposed upon the company, and IL. 100,000 against one of the individuals. Appeals from these fines were taken to the Tel Aviv Dis-

53. The magistrate noted this suicide in his opinion and assumed that it was a result of the disclosure of the affair.

trict Court, sitting as a three-judge Court of Criminal Appeals. District
Judge Harpazi considered the matter of the alleged official assurances at
length in his opinion. He said, in part:

After the real books of the company were seized and the fraud fully
discovered . . . negotiations began between the taxpayers' advocates
and the Income Tax Commissioner and his Deputy. At the conclusion,
the representatives of the defendants requested . . . and the Income
Tax Commissioner gave his assurance that the criminal charges, if filed,
would be against the company only, and that the two directors . . .
would not be charged. The following morning, the Income Tax Commissioner informed the advocates that he was withdrawing this assurance. Afterwards, the matter was brought before the Attorney General
by the attorneys for the defendants, who contended that the original
assurance of the Income Tax Commissioner was binding; but the Attorney General rejected this contention, giving detailed reasons . . .

The representative of the appellants expanded on this matter . . .
and also spoke in a mysterious fashion about the intervention of a
"foreign influence" who has no official standing in this matter and on
whose account there was done what appears to be an injustice in the
eyes of defense counsel.

Consequently, it appears to me advisable to disperse the fog, to remove the imagined cloak of "mystery", and to clarify the extent to
which all this matter has any bearing in court. . .

True, we can associate ourselves with the regret expressed in the opinion of the Magistrate and, before then, in the letter of the Attorney
General, that persons in authority gave assurances which were not adhered to. And in order that this expression of regret should not be mis-
understood, let it be said immediately that we are far from any thought
of censure or criticism against the authorities, since they retracted their
assurances in time. And that "foreign influence," as it were, who interfered in the matter, was not a stranger to it at all, for it was the Director
of State Revenue, who is also the superior of the Income Tax Commissioner. He stood in defense of the interests of the State and of public
morals, and the Attorney General stood by his right hand. . .

It should be pointed out also that the assurances, when given, were not
for the purpose of obtaining anything from the defendants . . . which
might have adversely affected their position, such as making a confession.
The accused requested mercy, and the Income Tax Commissioner
promised them this, even though he was not so authorized, whether he
did so from pity or from other considerations. The assurances were
promptly withdrawn, when it was seen that a mistake had been made.[54]

The judgment of the Tel Aviv District Court was thereafter affirmed by
the Supreme Court, also sitting as a Court of Criminal Appeals.[55]

54. *Attorney General* v. *Olamit, Ltd., et al.*, Crim. No. 1136/59, decided by
Tel Aviv District Court, March 15, 1959.
55. *Olamit, Ltd.* v. *Attorney General* and *Attorney General* v. *Efron*, Crim.
Apps. 265/59 and 271/59, decided May 25, 1960, 14 *Piske Din* 910, rehearing
denied July 17, 1960, 14 *Piske Din* 1597.

Aside from the technical legal issues involved in this case, which are themselves of considerable interest,[56] it illustrates several matters of administrative importance. Early in the prosecution program, it had been determined that where there had been fraud in the conduct of a corporation, criminal charges should be instituted not merely against the corporation but also against those of its directors who had been responsible for the fraud. This policy seemed particularly appropriate in the case of a closely held corporation (referred to in Israel as a "private company"), which is substantially the alter ego of its director-owners. That was certainly the case here. To have brought charges against the corporation alone, while overlooking those responsible for its unlawful acts, would have been an empty gesture. Also, the amount involved was very substantial, the fraud was flagrant (including a false set of books), and the admission of guilt came very late, as District Judge Harpazi noted, "after the real books of the company were seized and the fraud fully discovered."

What the circumstances were which led the Commissioner to give his "assurance that the criminal charges, if filed, would be against the company only, and that the two directors . . . would not be charged," are not clearly shown by the record. It is suggested (as indicated by the opinions in the case) that these may have included the fact that one of the potential defendants had committed suicide, that the father was of advanced age, and that agreement had apparently been reached as to the amount of the additional tax liability, which was paid in full before the trial. These are, however, factors which a court might take into account in imposing sentence but of lesser significance to the administrator in deciding whether to prosecute a flagrant case.

It would be idle to speculate upon how this assurance against prosecution came to the attention of the Director of Revenue or upon what transpired overnight which led to the assurance being canceled. Undoubtedly, the decision to overrule the Commissioner was not easily arrived at. On the other hand, principles essential to the successful continuation of the criminal prosecution program seemed to have been at stake. Furthermore, there seems to have been a departure from the procedure, which had been in force at least until the middle of 1957, whereby the final decision as to what disposition to make of a case of this kind

56. The case also presented the question, dealt with at all three judicial levels, whether a fine measured by "treble the amount of tax for which he is liable" means only the tax resulting from the fraud or the entire tax. As to the company, it was held that it was proper to measure the fine by the entire tax (although, for technical reasons, the question was left open as to the directors). Coincidentally, the same conclusion was reached by the British House of Lords, under a similar provision, in *Inland Revenue Commissioners* v. *Hinchy*, [1960]1 All E. R. 505. The Israeli Magistrates Court had previously rejected the British lower court's opinion in the *Hinchy* case, which had been to the contrary. The *Hinchy* case did not long remain the law in England. The Finance Act of 1960 limited the penalty to the portion of the deficiency tainted by the fraud.

was to have been made in conjunction with the office of the Director of Revenue, rather than by the Income Tax Commissioner (or his staff) acting independently.

It is even more difficult to understand under what authority the District Attorney, acting apparently unilaterally, had later agreed to drop charges against one of the individual defendants. Aside from the merits of this agreement, whose reversal was approved by the Attorney General, there is no indication that the District Attorney consulted with the Treasury before agreeing to drop the charges. If he had failed to do so, he acted contrary to the operating arrangements between the Treasury and the Ministry of Justice in such matters.

Reorganization at Headquarters

Indications are that there had been some breakdown in the procedures and organization which began functioning in 1955. This may have been due largely to personnel changes. The *ad interim* chairman of the prosecution review committee had left the Treasury in the summer of 1957, upon termination of his contract. The Principal Deputy Income Tax Commissioner, who had participated in the work of the review committee and was to have taken over its direction, was concerned with other pressing matters and, indeed, did not remain in the Commissioner's office long thereafter. Other personnel changes at the level of Deputy Commissioner were also taking place at that time. The result was that perhaps less detailed attention was being given, toward the end of 1958, to the unsavory criminal prosecution files. In order to get the program back on the track a reorganization was necessary. In 1959, the Jerusalem assessing officer, after completing a program of study in the United States, was appointed as Deputy Income Tax Commissioner, in charge of investigations and criminal prosecutions. This meant for the first time that there would be a principal official in the Commissioner's office who would concern himself exclusively with these matters. This appointment was accompanied by other structural changes in the Commissioner's office which were to some extent the product of departures of top-level personnel.

Formal Announcement of Voluntary Disclosure Policy

The steadily increasing number of criminal prosecutions and the increasing severity of the punishments imposed by the courts had the effect which had been anticipated when consideration had been given in the early days of the program to the institution of a "voluntary disclosure" policy. By 1962 it was considered that the circumstances were appropriate for a public declaration.[57] On April 2, 1962, the newspapers carried the following statement by the Income Tax Commissioner: [58]

The Income Tax Commissioner will in the future continue to make arrangements as permitted by law in order to encourage taxpayers to file true returns.

Any taxpayer who has failed to report income and who will so inform the income tax authorities before a criminal file has been opened against him will not be punished, on condition that he pays the correct amount of tax for which he is liable.

Such announcements (as in Israel, England, the United States, and probably elsewhere) seem to reflect an empirical assumption by the tax authorities that vigorous enforcement activities will have a deterrent effect upon potential evaders. It is clear from their opinions that the Israeli courts have also made this assumption.

If general deterrence rather than punishment of the individual criminal is the purpose, selection of the most flagrant cases and imposition of particularly severe punishments would seem to be logically required.[59] This is the direction in which the Israeli courts and administration have been moving.

Prosecutions and Punishments

The tightening up of the structure and headquarters staff in the area of enforcement produced further results. By 1960 most of the birth pains accompanying the inception of the criminal prosecution program had been overcome. For the period from 1960 through 1964, prosecutions averaging 100 per annum were instituted in cases involving understatements of income, in addition to some 200 to 300 prosecutions annually

57. There are indications that a voluntary disclosure policy was already in practical effect in 1960. See remarks of Income Tax Commissioner A. Givoni in 10 *Roeh Haheshbon*, 137 (April–June 1960).

58. See *Attorney General* v. *Schreiber*, (Crim. No. 775/63), Haifa Magistrates Court, December 31, 1963. In convicting an accused who, after purporting to make a voluntary disclosure, still withheld important information from the authorities (by submitting a false net-worth statement), the Haifa Magistrates Court emphasized that the disclosure must not only be voluntary but complete.

59. See Shlomo Shoham, *Averot v'Onshim b'Yisrael* (The Sentencing Policy of Criminal Courts in Israel) pp. 67–68 (Tel Aviv: Am Oved, 1963). Dr. Shoham points out the conflict between consideration of the possible deterrent effect of the punishment upon the specific criminal and the deterrent effect upon other potential violators. In order to impress the latter, the punishment would have to be particularly severe and, possible, bear little relation to the circumstances and reform needs of the particular individual. He also suggests that unusually severe punishment may have a negative effect: hardening the recidivist tendencies of the individual while not deterring others, who may merely be induced to resort to more clever evasive devices.

in respect of technical offenses.[60] This reflects a phenomenon of considerable significance. It will be recalled that in February 1956, when the first of the new series of income tax prosecutions was decided by the Haifa District Court, the judge had expressly refrained from imposing a prison sentence. In so doing, he mentioned the frequency of tax evasion and criticized the administration for its past laxity in not having demonstrated a "serious and substantial effort . . . to overcome violations in this area." This criticism was seconded by one of the Supreme Court Justices, who was recognized as the country's leading authority on tax law.[61]

This judicially expressed reluctance to impose prison sentences upon convicted income tax violators continued for several years, during which the administration proceeded to demonstrate that it was making the "serious and substantial effort" which the courts seemed to expect. Perhaps more important was the fact that, aside from attention which was being given to the investigation and prosecution of income tax violators, the normal civil tax assessment and collection activities of the income tax administration had been showing major improvements. By 1960 it could no longer be said that the absence of "any actual check on the amount of reported incomes . . . has eased, and even invited, violation of the law." The administration had "passed the test" and, starting in 1960, the courts began to send income tax violators to prison.[62]

A review of the opinions and judgments in the income tax prosecutions for 1956 and thereafter shows a steady progression in the severity of the sentences which were imposed. At first only fines were imposed; then fines accompanied by suspended jail sentences, conditioned upon good behavior; and, finally, actual jail sentences in the most flagrant cases. The trend toward jail sentences was signaled by the Chief Justice of the Supreme Court, albeit by way of dictum, in connection with a petition for leave to appeal filed by the Attorney General in a case in which an appeal had already been heard by the District Court (three judges) from a sentence imposed by a Magistrates Court. The Chief Justice said:

60. The source of this information is a memorandum relative to the deterrent effect of prison sentences, supplied by the Israeli Director of Revenue and filed in the United States District Court for the District of Massachusetts in an income tax criminal case (*Boston Sunday Herald*, May 9, 1965). See also Chapter 4 above, n. 13.

61. See Alfred Witkon, *Mavo L'Dinei Misim* Introduction to Tax Law, 1st ed., pp. 155–156; cf. Witkon and Neeman, *Dinei Misim*, 3rd ed., p. 265.

62. In 1960, the maximum prison sentence for fraud was increased from two years (where it had stood since 1954) to four years. Income Tax Ordinance (Amendment) (No. 2) Law, 5720–1960, *Sefer Hahukim* No. 316 of August 18, 1960, p. 89, sec. 9. This increase had two effects: (1) it enabled fraud cases to be tried in the District Courts rather than the Magistrates Courts, thus emphasizing the seriousness of the crime; and (2) it stimulated the imposition of jail sentences, by emphasizing the concern of the Knesset with the prior leniency of the courts. See *Attorney General* v. *Litovsky*, Crim. App. No. 259/63, Sup. Ct., September 7, 1963.

From the point of view of the general question, namely, the imposition of actual prison sentences upon criminals of this class [tax evaders], I support the Attorney General; and I understand that this petition was submitted, and properly, because in the past the courts have not emphasized sufficiently the severity of offenses of this type, and have refrained from imposing jail sentences for the purpose of stopping, or at least reducing, this type of crime, which is becoming a national plague.[63]

Although, in the particular case, leave to appeal was denied, the message was clear. Thereafter, although somewhat hesitatingly at first, the lower courts began to send income tax criminals to prison.

The fiscal year 1964–65 was the tenth anniversary of the commencement of a serious criminal prosecution program. The annual report for that year is accordingly of special interest, reflecting as it does the fairly well-regularized activities of the criminal enforcement program. According to the report, principal attention was given to taxpayers in lines of business in which there was known to be a high degree of tax evasion. Among these were dealers and brokers in real property, building contractors, and professionals. Efforts were continued to convince the courts that long prison sentences should be imposed upon income tax evaders, particularly in the most flagrant instances. In fiscal year 1964–65, the courts decided 160 criminal cases. Of these, 48 involved tax evasion, 10 were for violation of withholding requirements, and 102 were for technical offenses.[64] In the tax evasion cases, which involved unreported income of IL. 3.2 million, fines of IL. 1.5 million were imposed. More significant, 160 months of actual jail sentences were imposed and 500 months of suspended jail sentences, conditioned upon good behavior. Obviously, the reluctance of the courts to impose jail sentences in criminal income tax cases had been overcome.

Deterrent Purpose and Effect

It should be noted that, in imposing prison sentences, the emphasis was placed upon the deterrent effect which such sentences would have upon other members of the taxpaying public who might also be tempted to violate the law. In the early days of the prosecution program, officials concerned with developing policy frequently summed up its purpose in the biblical phrase, "in order that Israel may hear and be afraid." Since the Bible is a common cultural bond of the population, irrespective of

63. *Attorney General* v. *Halpert*, Petition 38/60, 14 *Piske Din* 617 (1960).
64. Substantial offenses are defined as intentional evasion of tax by filing a false return or other document, keeping false books of account, or other fraudulent acts. Technical offenses are defined as failure to file a return or net worth statement, refusal to reply to inquiries by the assessing officer, failure to keep required books, and failure to pay over taxes withheld from wages.

the cultural overlay of their immediate countries of origin, the phrase was well understood.[65]

Later, when jail sentences began to be imposed more frequently, they were analogized by the Supreme Court to the "Mark of Cain" (*Genesis,* 4:15), as in the following opinion:

It appears to us that the learned President Judge did not give appropriate weight to the urgent and essential need not only to compel evaders to pay the income tax for which they are liable . . . but also (and in our eyes this is the essential point in this class of crimes) to place a mark of shame on the foreheads of those who defraud the country's treasury and become wealthy at public expense. The danger against which the courts are directed to stand in the breach is not merely or necessarily the great number of such violators, but the fact that among wide sectors of the public these crimes are still not considered as shameful. The general public has not yet accepted the proposition that robbery of funds destined by law for public purposes is no less serious than robbery of funds of an individual, if not more serious.

So long as this misconception is not torn up by the roots, the court is under an obligation to impose upon income tax evaders that punishment which alone among the available punishments clearly expresses, and is so understood by all, the shame which the court sees in this crime — and that is imprisonment.[66]

A number of court opinions dealt with this aspect of tax evasion. The deterrent purpose of prison sentences was well stated in a 1963 opinion of the Tel Aviv District Court:

In recent years, prison sentences have been imposed upon law violators found guilty of failure to report income with intent to evade tax, in addition to fines; and the court has continually warned that in the future it will be necessary to be even more severe. Even lawyers and accountants have not been found guiltless. . .

These crimes are of a type which injures the revenues of the State, and it is not necessary for me to say that this fact justifies deterrent punishments, which is the principal purpose in such crimes. . .

The strict attitude of the courts can also be explained by reasons which are not limited to the effect upon the revenue. Those who are involved in hiding income, wilfully and intentionally, resort to planned fraudulent procedures in order to cover their tracks; they submit false reports to the government, falsify balance sheets, book entries, bills of lading, receipts and other documents; involve a number of other citizens in their

65. The reference was to Deuteronomy 13:7–12. (See also Deut. 17:13; 19:20; 21:21.)

66. *Boneh-Yotzer Co., et. al.* v. *Attorney General,* and *Attorney General* v. *Dubovi,* Crim. Apps. 16/64, 126/64, 18 (2d) *Piske Din* 537, (Sup. Ct., 1964), per Justice Haim Cohen.

fraud; and seek hidden and illegal ways to use the unreported monies, so as to make additional profits.

Even from the point of view of public morals it is necessary to point out the negative effect. . .

It is also clear . . . that even though yesterday tax evaders did not go to prison, and today prison sentences are measured in months, it is not unlikely that in the near future prison sentences will be measured in years, in order forcefully to deter violators. For it will always be necessary to deter, even if the number of violators will decrease.[67]

Some of the other courts continued to be more lenient, but this tendency was put an end to by a series of reversals by the Supreme Court, which also emphasized the seriousness of tax crimes and the need for severe punishment.

The Income Tax Amnesty of 1967

The General Amnesty Law

The validity of many of the assumptions which have guided the formulation of administrative policy was recently put to the test by the passage, in August 1967, of the Income Tax (Amended Declarations) Law.[68] As an aftermath to the Six-Day War of June 1967, the Knesset enacted the Amnesty Law of 1967,[69] pardoning all crimes except genocide and treason and those other crimes subject to imprisonment of more than ten years.

Tax crimes were not excluded from amnesty. Accordingly, one who may have been convicted of tax evasion and sentenced to prison, or subjected to a fine which he had not paid by June 5, 1967 (the effective date of the amnesty), would be released from prison and relieved of payment of the fine.

The general amnesty law also directed the termination of any prosecutions which were in progress or contemplated. Most relevant to income tax violators was a provision conditioning the amnesty upon the violator's repentance, to be displayed by his correction of the wrong within three months after enactment of the amnesty law — that is, by October 14, 1967. This meant, for example, that an employer who, in violation of the Income Tax Law, had failed, prior to June 5, 1967, to pay over income tax which he had withheld from the wages of his employees, would not be prosecuted if he made the payment by the October date.

67. *Attorney General* v. *Ar-Kar Co., Ltd., et. al.*, Crim. No. 432/62, per Kennet, P. J.

68. 505 *Sefer Hahukim*, p. 102, of August 7, 1967; sometimes herein referred to as "the tax amnesty law."

69. 502 *Sefer Hahukim*, of July 14, 1967; herein referred to as "the general amnesty law."

The income tax administration, going a step further, announced, in the spirit of the occasion, that it would not impose any administrative penalties (under secs. 188 and 190) on any taxpayer who had corrected any default within the prescribed time. This included the remission of all administrative penalties which might have already been imposed. As to those violations which could not be corrected (such as past failure to keep books), no further positive acts were required of the violator in order that he might benefit from the amnesty. As to such violations as might have been the consequence of an improper income tax return or net worth report, the general amnesty law provided that these could be corrected by the execution of special forms to be prescribed by the Minister of Finance. These forms were required to be submitted within three months after issuance of the regulations prescribing them. These regulations were promulgated on August 7, 1967.

The Income Tax Amnesty Law

In the wake of the general amnesty law, it was urged that the time had finally come to permit the "cleansing" of "black capital," whose source was in previously unreported income. The question, as the Income Tax Commissioner expressed it, was not whether or when this "cleansing" should take place, but how to accomplish it.[70] Central to the solution which was adopted was the fixing of a flat income tax rate of 25 percent on all additional income reported in accordance with the Income Tax (Amended Declarations) Law. Since the normal tax rates progressed rapidly in the affected years to a 60 percent maximum, the flat rate represented a substantial concession. Furthermore, there was to be no criminal prosecution, penalty, or even interest, in connection with any such disclosure.

The reason for the adoption of this flat rate (which might be considerably below the tax bracket otherwise applicable) was stated by the Income Tax Commissioner:

This rate was selected to balance these counter-considerations: it had to be low enough to interest or attract those who wished to straighten themselves out, and yet high enough not to upset those members of the public who had meticulously complied with the law.[71]

The reduced rate applied to newly reported income for all taxable years through 1965. As to taxable year 1966, the returns were not yet due to be filed when the tax amnesty law was adopted in August 1967, but as to these, it was hoped, correct returns would be filed.

70. Y. Tamir, "The Amnesty Law and the Income Tax (Amended Declarations) Law — 1967, Background, Policy, and Execution" (Hebrew), 17 *Roeh Haheshbon*, 455, 457 (September–October 1967).
71. Ibid.

The privilege of filing amended returns and of enjoying the 25 per cent rate was limited to three months from the date of publication by the Minister of Finance of regulations prescribing the forms to be used by taxpayers for correcting prior omissions. Such regulations were promulgated on August 7, 1967, so that the filing date expired on November 7. The forms were designed to incorporate a net worth report as of March 31, 1967, and reports of additional (unreported) income for all taxable years through 1965. To the best of his ability, the taxpayer was expected to indicate the amount of his unreported income for each year, but if he could not do so, he could declare a round sum covering several years.[72] Payment of the additional tax was required by December 7, 1967.

It was recognized that a taxpayer desiring to file an amended declaration would not necessarily know what information might already be in the hands of the assessing officer regarding previously unreported income. Thus, questions might arise whether a disclosure was "voluntary," or whether it disclosed anything not already known. To avoid disputes, the tax amnesty law provided that the fixed 25 percent rate would apply to the excess of the income reported on an "amended declaration" over the income determined by the most recent assessment, made prior to August 7, 1967, with respect to the relevant taxable year. If no such assessment had been made for the relevant year, the additional income would be the excess of whichever was greater of (a) the income assessed for any previous year, or (b) the income reported by the taxpayer on his original return for the year. Other provisions were made for taxpayers to whom neither (a) nor (b) applied. As to a taxpayer who had filed no returns and had paid no tax, the amnesty would apply to all income reported pursuant to the tax amnesty law.

The effect of these provisions was to eliminate from consideration any information as to the taxpayer's undisclosed income which the assessing officer had already obtained from other sources — except that such information would, presumably, still be available as a means of checking whether the taxpayer's disclosure was indeed complete. If the assessing officer had information indicating the existence of additional income, and had issued an assessment notice to that effect, the additional income would be subject to tax at the usual rates; but if the assessing officer had delayed in the issuance of an assessment notice, the filing by the taxpayer of an amended return could freeze the tax rate at 25 percent.[73]

It will be remembered that it had been the policy to delay the issuance of assessments in cases which were under active investigation with a view

72. Since no "deficiency interest" was payable upon the additional tax due, and since the tax was computed at a flat, nonprogressive rate, apportioning the unreported income to a particular taxable year would not affect the amount to be paid.

73. Tamir, above, n. 70, p. 458.

toward possible criminal prosecution. In such cases, the amnesty law not only barred prosecution, but also nullified the already assembled evidence as to fraudulently unreported income. Thus, the taxpayer, by filing an amended return, would escape prosecution while paying his tax at a bargain rate. Others profiting from the bargain rate would be those whose returns had not yet been audited, of whom there were many.

Results of the Amnesty

Considering the fact that by August 1967 the investigative branch of the Income Tax Commissioner's office must have had a number of cases under investigation, administrative frustration attendant upon the amnesty must have been considerable. This accounts, perhaps, for the Commissioner's statement that the amnesty had no precedent and that "there will be no others like it." [74]

The reception which the amnesty had among members of the accounting profession was mixed. Although it could be viewed as consistent with Jewish tradition, which encourages repentance, it was also recognized as a gross departure from the principle of equality in taxation, in that the honest taxpayer was being taxed at higher rates than the dishonest one. Nevertheless, it was suggested, the amnesty was justifiable as offering an opportunity for taxpayers, once and for all, to straighten out their accounts with the income tax authorities.[75] On the other hand, there were some among the accounting profession who were troubled by the problem of their ethical responsibilities vis-à-vis a client who, unbeknownst to them, had been falsifying his accounts and then sought assistance in the preparation of an amended return in accordance with the amnesty law.[76]

The long-range effect which the granting of this tax amnesty will have upon the future of tax enforcement in Israel remains to be seen. Its immediate results, as stated by the Minister of Finance in response to an inquiry at a session of the Knesset, was that about 1,400 taxpayers took advantage of the opportunity to file amended returns, reporting thereon income previously unreported in the sum of about IL. 89 million.[77] Al-

74. Ibid., pp. 458–459. See also Y. Tamir, "1968 — Year of Events and Changes in Taxes," (Hebrew) 18 *Roeh Haheshbon*, pp. 148–149 (January–February 1968).

75. N. Freidkes, "The Tax Amnesty and the Taxpayer," (Hebrew), 17 *Roeh Haheshbon*, 460, 461 (September–October 1967).

76. M. Kanne, "The Law and the Accountant" (Hebrew), 17 *Roeh Haheshbon*, 465 (September–October 1967).

77. Of the about 1,450 taxpayers who took advantage of the amnesty, 6.8 percent were employees, 71.4 percent were self-employed, 3.5 percent were companies, and 18.3 percent were company managers. Of the about IL. 89 million additional income reported, 1.5 percent was reported by employees, 64 percent by self-employed, 9.2 percent by companies, and about 25 percent by company managers. These percentages support the administration's impression

though disclosures made on these amended returns are to be held in confidence, studies are nevertheless being made of the extent of prior evasion and of the types of incomes not previously reported, so that the administration may be aided in its future efforts to prevent evasion.[78]

Informed sources are of the opinion that many offenders refrained from taking advantage of the tax amnesty.[79] Lawyers and accountants have privately expressed the view that they were not able in good conscience to advise all clients who consulted them to take advantage of the amnesty. The administration also seems to be unhappy with the results, both because they were not as good as had been expected and because of the debilitating effect which it might have upon taxpayer morale. Furthermore, the amnesty deprived the administration of its inventory of investigations in process so that it was necessary to start all over again.

Ten years passed from the full start of the criminal prosecution program until it came almost to a full stop with the 1967 amnesty. Some time must elapse before its results can be fully assessed. Meanwhile, the income tax administration has reinstituted its criminal prosecution program.

In the two fiscal years 1967–68 and 1968–69 there were 54 convictions for tax evasion (sec. 220), 103 for technical offenses, such as failure to keep accounts (sec. 216), and 81 for failure to pay over tax withheld at source (sec. 219). The unreported income involved was somewhat over 3.5 million pounds. Prison sentences were imposed in 25 cases: in 10 up to three months, in 13 from four to six months, and in 2 for more than seven months. In addition, suspended sentences were imposed in 102 cases. Fines were also imposed in all 54 of the fraud cases, 19 of these receiving fines of less than IL. 5,000, 16 between IL. 5,000 and IL. 15,000, and 19 more than IL. 15,000. Fines, though substantially lower, were imposed on 204 of the less serious offenders.[80]

It would appear that the tax amnesty did not dry up the reservoir of tax evaders. Vigorous prosecution efforts still are necessary, and this is attested by the response of the courts in imposing heavy penalties upon the new crop of offenders charged and convicted after the amnesty.

---

that the principal tax evaders were to be found among the self-employed and manager-owners of closely held companies (see Y. Tamir, "1968 — Year of Events and Changes in Taxes," p. 149, n. 12; and Naftali Birkenfeld, "Implementation of the Income Tax Amnesty Law, 1967" (Hebrew), 3 *Quarterly Tax Journal* 168, 172 (April 1968).

78. Zvi Kessler, "From Issue to Issue" (Hebrew) 3 *Quarterly Tax Journal*, unnumbered preface (January 1968).

79. Aryeh Lapidoth, "On Tax Amnesties," (Hebrew), 3 *Quarterly Tax Journal* 173, 177 (April 1968).

80. *Annual Report of the Revenue Administration, 1967/8–1968/9*, 71 (Jerusalem: Museum of Taxes, 1970).

Conclusion

Criminologists are far from agreed upon the relevance of general and specific deterrent effects as factors in measuring the degree of severity with which particular crimes should be punished. And it is only in recent years that scientific attention has begun to be given to the nature, causes and cures of "white-collar" crimes, such as tax evasion.[81] The pragmatic insights of those immediately concerned with the problem have to be relied upon in the absence of any clear-cut scientific guidance.

The problem was particularly difficult in Israel because of the cultural diversity of its population. The adult population is still largely non-native-born, with diverse, and frequently negative, attitudes toward taxation. Even native-born adults reflect this cultural diversity. The immediate and long-range purposes of the enforcement program were to inculcate positive attitudes toward the tax laws. Punishment of tax offenders was viewed as a "shock-treatment" toward this end.

The Israeli tax enforcement program may be summed up as being founded upon the premise that criminal prosecutions are essential to maintain an acceptable level of voluntary compliance. Operating on this assumption, a steady flow of criminal prosecutions is maintained. But recognizing that not all violators can, or should, be prosecuted, a "selective" policy is followed. Simultaneously, through the "voluntary disclosure" policy, an avenue has been opened to tax violators who wish to "go straight." The courts seem to have accepted the premise that severe punishments, including jail sentences, would have a deterrent effect upon other, possible evaders. This might mean, in particular cases, that a heavier penalty might be imposed than might have been considered necessary, in other contexts, if the interests of society as directed to the individual criminal had been solely involved.

There has been much soul-searching about these attitudes toward tax crimes and their punishment. Some still question the fairness of prosecuting only a fraction of discovered tax evaders. Some question the nature of the penalties imposed — whether they are too lenient or too severe. Some question whether administrative penalties, to the extent available and imposed in fraud cases, are an adequate substitute for prosecutions and court-imposed fines and sentences where prosecution is not undertaken. These, and other issues, remain fairly frequent subjects of discussion.[82] However, for the present at least, the administration

81. See Herbert Edelhertz, *The Nature, Impact and Prosecution of White-Collar Crime*, a publication of the U.S. Department of Justice, Law Enforcement Assistance Administration (Washington, D.C.: U.S. Government Printing Office, 1970); cf. Edwin H. Sutherland, *White Collar Crime.* Although Sutherland's is the classical work in the field, Edelhertz points out (pp. 4, 5 *et seq.*) that economic growth and complexity since Sutherland wrote have raised many new questions which remain to be studied.

82. See, e.g., remarks of Income Tax Commissioner Yaacov Tamir, "The

is committed to continuing with the enforcement program as it has been described.[83] It remains for the future to tell, perhaps after sociological research techniques have been developed and applied to ascertain the real effect of the program upon taxpayer attitudes and behavior, whether the present policy should be modified and, if so, in what direction.

One thing is clear, and that is that in Israel the prosecution program is far from being an end unto itself. The program was instituted at a time when the tax administration was admittedly deficient in many respects. While the prosecution program was developing, the administration was undergoing major revisions which brought about substantial improvements on the civil side. A demonstration of strength on the criminal side was considered, during this period of development, to be both justified and necessary. The extent to which the prosecution program has been a factor in improving the level of voluntary compliance by the taxpaying public has not been demonstrated scientifically (if it is susceptible of such demonstration), but the judiciary, the public, and the administration feel that it has had a positive effect. Perhaps this feeling is sufficient to justify the program. However, to the extent that improvements in tax administration and in taxpayer morale may ultimately be achieved through the interplay of sound administration and good citizenship, perhaps the time will come when the deterrent purpose of the prosecution program will diminish in importance. When that time comes, a review of the program in terms of the prosecution policy of the administration and the sentencing policy of the courts may be necessary.

Attitude of the Tax Administration," (Hebrew) in "Symposium on Tax Planning," 16 *Roeh Haheshbon*, 76, 80–81, (November–December 1966). The Commissioner there stated that income voluntarily reported by self-employed taxpayers for the taxable year 1964 was substantially higher than that reported in previous years. He attributed this in large part to the rate reductions which came into effect in 1964.

83. There was a recent departure from the publicity policy which had been followed for some years, when the income tax authorities gave advance notice to newspapermen of early morning raids which they proposed to make on the homes and offices of evasion suspects, for the purpose of seizing their records (*Jerusalem Post Weekly*, May 9, 1972, pp. 7, 15). This procedure was editorially criticized (ibid., p. 16) and the Minister of Finance immediately informed the Cabinet "that tax-men in future would give the press no assistance that might enable them to intrude into the privacy of suspects of fiscal offenses" (ibid., p. 3). This aberration seems to enforce the previous policy.

9 / Administration of Taxes on Property

Introduction

This chapter and the one which follows are closely interrelated. Some of the most vexing problems in connection with the simplification of the revenue administration and the ultimate achievement of centralized control were presented by the taxes on property, dealt with mainly in this chapter, and the various forms of compulsory payments (some of which were based on property values), dealt with mainly in Chapter 10. Starting first with two separate administrations, there was a considerable amount of criss-crossing until, ultimately, all vestiges of the two original administrations were absorbed into the Income and Property Tax Branch.

The paths taken by these initially separate administrations were very tortuous. Yet, the history is worth examining because it portrays circumstances which are not likely to occur except in the context of a developing revenue administration.

There are several points to watch along the way. From the outset, the Collections and Property Tax Division followed the traditional administrative patterns established during the mandatory period, whereas the administration of the compulsory payments tended to follow the patterns of the voluntary, unofficial, system of contributions which supported some activities of the Jewish community during the mandatory period. The differing trends of these two administrations were influenced by the past experiences of the individuals who headed them, one having been trained in the mandatory district administration and the other having been a leader of the Jewish community's contributory system. The conflict between their differing philosophies of administration was reflected in the administrative structures of the compulsory payments and additional revenue measures enacted through the middle 1950's. This resulted in a split of jurisdiction over substantively related taxes and in an overlapping of functions. After considerable trial and error, a series of reorganizations culminated in abolition of both administrations.

Each step in the complicated story which follows in this and the succeeding chapter is best understood in the light of the prevailing conditions at the time. We start, therefore, with the transition from the mandatory property tax administration.

Achieving National Control after the Mandate

The government of the British Mandate for Palestine was headed by a High Commissioner who, as representative of the Crown, had very broad executive and legislative powers. The country was divided into districts (Jerusalem, North, and South), each under the administrative control of a District Commissioner, who was responsible directly to the High Commissioner. Within the districts there were subdistricts, under the charge of a District Officer. All but a few of the District Officers were British.

Under the Rural and Urban Property Tax Ordinances, the District Commissioners and District Officers had key administrative responsibilities in connection with the assessment and collection of these taxes. They were also responsible for administration of the Taxes (Collections) Ordinance which established the procedures for the collection of taxes which had fallen in arrears.

When the High Commissioner for Palestine and all other British mandatory officials left Palestine on or before the termination of the mandate (May 14, 1948), the posts occupied by the High Commissioner, District Commissioners, and District Officers were all left vacant. This left a corresponding void in the administrative organization for the assessment and collection of the rural and urban property taxes.

By contrast, the municipal rates on real property (imposed under the Municipal Corporations Ordinance, 1934, Secs. 101–117) were administered by the elected mayors and municipal councils, who were able to continue to exercise their statutory powers after termination of the mandate.[1] The continuing presence of the local authorities provided a convenient means to the departing British officials to turn over some of the functions of government, since they declined to recognize or help to establish any caretaker national government. Thus, one of the final actions of the British officials was to turn over responsibility for the control of the Port of Haifa and collection of customs duties at the port to the Haifa municipality. Similarly, the several municipalities were given the responsibility of collecting the national urban property tax for the fiscal year 1948–49, in addition to the municipal rates on real property.

After the Provisional Government of the State of Israel was estab-

1. Even so, problems could arise, for certain actions of a municipal council required approval of the District Commissioner and certain posts had to be filled by him. Nevertheless, those municipalities whose officials remained in office could continue to operate, at least temporarily, until suitable legislation was enacted by the new national government. For relevant laws and regulations during the mandate, see A. S. Kandel, *Local Government in Palestine* (Jerusalem, 1947).

lished as of May 15, 1948,[2] it was decided to permit collection of the national urban property tax to remain in the hands of the several municipalities for the fiscal year 1948–1949. Meanwhile, steps were taken to re-establish a national administration for the rural and urban property taxes. Within the year, as communications with the central government and its fiscal authorities improved, the organization of the national administration of the rural and urban property taxes reverted to a pattern somewhat similar to that which had existed under the mandate, except that the chain of command, insofar as fiscal matters were concerned, led to the Minister of Finance rather than to the High Commissioner — the latter office having ceased to exist on termination of the mandate.

As it happened, there had been one Jewish official in the Haifa District who had started serving as a Cadet District Officer at the beginning of 1947. By May 1948 he had received considerable training in the functions of a District Officer, including matters of property tax administration and general collections. Anticipating the void which would be created by the imminent departure of the British officials, he assumed the responsibilities of the Haifa District Officer. Later, as communications with the central government were established, this arrangement was formalized and extended. The organization which resulted vested responsibility for the property taxes and for enforcing the Taxes (Collections) Ordinance in a single, national official who, in turn, supervised the operations of a number of district and subdistrict offices.

The organization thus established was called the Collections and Property Tax Division. It combined the functions of assessment and collection of the property taxes with the more general function of servicing each of the other tax administrations (such as those for the income tax and purchase tax) in the collection of delinquent accounts. The latter function included sending demands for payment, attachment, seizure, and public sale of assets. In the exercise of these general collection functions the organization was frequently referred to as the "execution office."

In the first few years of the State, administration of the property taxes was beset with many problems. Most serious, perhaps, was the need for a general reassessment of all urban and rural properties. This was a massive undertaking, requiring skilled manpower which was unavailable. Accordingly, the organization operated as best it could with the facilities it had, directing most of its efforts to the collection rather than to the assessment functions, including the collection of arrears in taxes other than the property taxes.

2. The British mandate terminated at midnight on May 14, 1948. The following day was a Saturday. As this is the Jewish Sabbath, which commenced at sundown the previous day, many of the formalities attendant upon establishment of the State and its civil authorities either had to be accelerated or deferred until the close of the Sabbath.

Diffuse Administration of Taxes on Property

The weakness of the Collections and Property Tax Division in its ability to assess taxable properties ultimately resulted in a transfer of the property tax assessment functions to a different organization. The initial impetus for this transfer can be traced to the enactment in 1951 of the war damages compensation levy, requiring the payment of compulsory insurance premiums for the establishment of a compensation fund to reimburse property owners for damage suffered from enemy action. These payments (often referred to as the "Arnona") [3] were required of most owners of property that was susceptible to war damage. Principal among the affected properties were urban, agricultural, and industrial buildings, plantations (growing crops and groves), equipment, and inventories of merchandise.

War Damages Compensation Levy

There was sufficient overlapping of the war damages compensation levy and rural and urban property taxes to suggest that administration of the former might also have been vested in the Collections and Property Tax Division. This was not done. Instead, the War Damage Compensation Payments Law established a new administration under a new head.

The official appointed as administrator of the war damages compensation levy had participated actively in the drafting of the law and had otherwise seen it through the Knesset. At the time of his appointment he was serving in the Ministry of Finance as Director of Stamp Duties and Admissions Tax. His experience in tax administration had been gained as one of the administrators of the unofficial system of indirect taxes which the Jewish community in Palestine had imposed upon itself during the British mandate, to finance the defense and other needs of the Jewish community. Later, in 1953, the same individual was put in charge of the compulsory loan which, similar to the war damage compensation levy, was based upon the value of specified properties.

Initially, some effort was made to coordinate the activities of the war damages compensation levy (particularly in respect of payments due on buildings and plantations) with those of the separate property tax administration. For a time, the war damages office determined the amount due from the property owner, while the local property tax office made the collections and kept the necessary records. This division of responsibilities did not work well. It caused administrative duplication, breakdowns

3. This should not be confused with the *Arnona Klalit* (general municipal rate) or *Arnonat R'khush* (municipal property rate), both imposed by municipalities or local authorities under authority of the Municipal Corporations Ordinance, 1934, sec. 102, or the Local Authorities Ordinance, 1941, sec. 5.

of communication, and complaints from taxpayers, who had to conduct their affairs with different offices, depending upon whether they were concerned with assessment of the tax or its payment. Within a year, in June 1952, the war damages administration retrieved the function of collecting and recording payments on buildings and plantations.

Estate Tax and Land Betterment Tax

In 1949 the Knesset enacted two taxes which could involve valuations of property. These were the estate tax and the land betterment tax.[4] Administration of the estate tax was assigned to the Income Tax Commissioner, whereas administration of the land betterment tax was assigned principally to the Department of Land Registration in the Ministry of Justice. The Collections and Property Tax Division was thus again bypassed, except as to that fragment of the land betterment tax applying to taxable transactions in land which did not require recording in the land registry.[5]

Compulsory Loan

In 1953 another law was enacted which required valuations of property. This was the Compulsory Loan Law which was imposed upon property owners at rates based upon the value of their property as of April 1, 1953.[6] Generally, the classes of property affected were about the same as those which were subject to the war damage compensation levy, with the principal additions of land and vehicles.

Administration of the 1953 compulsory loan was assigned to the same official who had previously been charged with administration of the war damage compensation levy. Because of the similarities between them this was no doubt considered to be a logically related assignment.

One of the current concerns was to minimize, as far as possible, the hiring of additional personnel. The war damages organization, which itself had been staffed on a modest basis, was assumed to be capable of taking over the additional tasks of the compulsory loan. Indeed the policy of the administrator of the compulsory loan (who was also by this time in charge of the war damages compensation levy, stamp duties and admissions tax), opposed the establishment of an administrative hierarchy.

4. For more detailed discussions of these taxes and their administration see Chapters 2 and 3.

5. As a practical matter, this responsibility became insignificant, because taxpayers soon found a major loophole in the Land Betterment Tax Law which enabled them to avoid the tax completely by a rather simple device, approved by the Supreme Court. Civil Appeal 142/54, 8 *Piske Din* 1893. This loophole was not closed until enactment of the Land Appreciation Tax Law, 1963.

6. For a fuller discussion of the compulsory loan see Chapter 10.

This policy, which seemed to be derived from the administrator's prior experience in the unofficial tax system of the mandatory period, happened to coincide with the then policy of the government. Reduction of government personnel was a major concern at the time, and in 1952 and 1953 several programs were instituted to achieve this. Although new tax programs were undertaken, the official atmosphere at the time of their initiation was unsympathetic to establishment of the organizations essential to carry them into effect. As to existing organizations, such as the Collections and Property Tax Division, hiring of additional technical personnel was discouraged.

Collection Activities of the Collections and Property Tax Division

Lacking professional qualified property valuers, the Collection and Property Tax Division concerned itself principally with its general collection functions under the Taxes (Collections) Ordinance. These functions began to be called upon more frequently by the other tax departments, particularly in 1952–1954, as arrears in unpaid taxes increased. The collection responsibilities of the division at this time included all such activities in connection with the property taxes and the war damages compensation levy, supplementary collection services in connection with the compulsory loan, and an increasing volume of enforced collections of arrears.

Beginning in 1952 demands upon the Property Tax and Collections Division to assist in the collection of other taxes increased very substantially. Most of the increase was a reflection of the concerted assessment drive commenced by the income tax administration in that year. Delinquent income tax accounts collected by the "execution office" (as it was called) in fiscal year 1952–53 were more than three times those for the previous year (about IL. 2.4 million in 1952–53, as compared with IL. 0.7 million in 1951–52). Collections of delinquent income taxes almost trebled again in 1953–54 and doubled once more in 1954–55. By 1954–55, the execution office was also collecting substantial arrears of purchase tax, compulsory loan, war damages compensation levy, income tax advance payments (*Mikdama*),[7] and others. In all, enforced collections of taxes by the execution office rose from IL. 0.4 million in 1950–51, to IL. 1.68 million in 1951–52, IL. 3.8 million in 1952–53, IL. 10 million in 1953–54, and IL. 19 million in 1954–55.[8]

Beginning in 1953, public resistance to the payment of taxes began

7. Like the compulsory loan, this was a one-time advance payment based upon income, effective for fiscal year 1953–54. Its administration had also been turned over to the administrator of the Arnona and compulsory loan, rather than to the income tax administration, where it logically belonged.

8. *First Annual Report on State Revenue* (Hebrew), p. 319.

to become widespread. The result was a massive transfer of uncollected assessments from the income tax and other administrations to the Collections and Property Tax Division.[9] Many of the assessments transferred for collection were admittedly excessive (particularly income tax assessments), and were later compromised at substantially lower figures. Often, because suitable notification procedures had not yet been established, the execution office found itself making demands for payment of taxes which had either been paid already (without cancellation of the request for action by the execution office) or had been substantially reduced as a result of further negotiations of which the execution office had not been advised. This caused considerable resentment, which was directed against the organization collecting the tax.

In a way the Collections and Property Taxes Division became a whipping-boy during this period both for the tax administration and for the taxpaying public. To the extent that reluctance to pay taxes shifted the collecting function from the responsible tax administration to the execution office, the latter became the focus of attention. Its unpopularity increased as its activities expanded.

The procedure followed by the execution office was first to send a warning notice (demand for payment), followed in fifteen days by attachment of the delinquent's property. If the debt was not then paid or otherwise settled, the property was seized and, generally after a further delay of fifteen days, would be sold publicly. The proceeds of the sale were applied first against the tax debt and expenses of storage and sale; the balance, if any, was paid over to the former owner.

The extent of the contacts of the execution office with the taxpaying public during this period is illustrated by the following figures for the fiscal year 1954–55:

Warning notices mailed	222,480
Attachment authorizations	168,546
Attachments recorded	51,941
Notices of intended sales	24,276
Seizures of assets	1,045
Sales of assets	176 [10]

The sharp, progressive drop in these figures, and the relatively infinitesimal number of actual sales, are strongly indicative of taxpayer resistance during this period. It was, it would appear, more a matter

9. Collections of municipal and other local rates were also falling behind heavily during this period. *Sixth Annual Report of the State Comptroller, 1954/55*, pp. 282–289, 315–316. Collection of these arrears was not, however, within the jurisdiction of the Collections and Property Taxes Division (Municipal Corporations Ordinance, 1934, sec. 115).

10. During 1954–55, the enforced collection process produced a substantial share of total tax collections — about 10.4 percent, as compared to about 8.4 percent in 1953–54 (*First Annual Report on State Revenue* [Hebrew] p. 322).

of unwillingness than inability to pay. Perhaps more significant, this experience, which was repeated in several subsequent years, as shown by the Annual Reports, indicates a tendency on the part of several of the tax administrations (notably the income tax), to shift difficult cases to the execution office before their own administrative resources had been exhausted.

This tendency was partially reversed in 1956–57, when, on an experimental basis, the purchase tax offices throughout the country and the income tax offices in the Tel Aviv area began to send out the warning notices themselves, transferring delinquent files to the execution office only if the warning notices did not produce payment within fifteen days.[11] This procedure proved successful and, on its extension to all tax offices in 1957–58, the activities of the execution office (which in the interim had been separated from the property taxes) became concentrated upon the hard core of delinquent taxpayers.[12] In 1968 the establishment of a special income tax assessing office for hard-core collection problems concentrated that difficult function completely in the income tax administration.

Assessment of Property Values

Increasing concentration of the Collections and Property Taxes Division upon its general collection functions was not accompanied by development of professional staff and by activity in respect of the rural and urban property taxes. At best, administration of these taxes, up to at least 1955, was largely a holding operation, based almost completely upon the remnants of the assessment lists which had been carried over from the mandatory period.

Meanwhile, the population of the country multiplied as the result of mass immigration of Jews from the European concentration camps and from the Arab countries. This was reflected in the growth of the existing towns and construction of new towns in areas which, up to that time, had been largely or completely rural. Land values increased. By 1954 it became apparent that the rural property tax was no longer applicable in these newly developed areas, and the Minister of Finance, under authority of the Urban Property Tax Ordinance of 1940, commenced issuing a series of orders designating new and additional urban areas — property in which now became liable to the urban property tax.

The basis of liability for the urban property tax was completely different from the rural property tax, and this designation of new urban areas meant that many new assessments must be made. Because of a

11. *Third Annual Report on State Revenue, 1956/57* (Hebrew), p. 409.
12. *Fourth Annual Report on State Revenue, 1957/58* (Hebrew), p. 383.

scarcity of qualified assessors, the existing property tax administration was technically unequipped for this task.[13] And, owing to restrictions against the hiring of new personnel, the commitment of existing or new personnel to the increasing burden of collecting other delinquent taxes, and the duplication of certain activities by establishment of the separate war damages and compulsory loan administrations, the formation of a central staff of qualified property valuers became an urgent need which could not be satisfied within the framework of the existing organizations.

The Ministry of Justice had a small staff of land valuation experts in its Valuation Department, and occasional tax problems were referred to this staff. This improvisation, however, was not adapted to the everyday routine of the tax administrations. There were long delays in obtaining valuations because the staff was small and tax work had to be subordinated to the regular duties of the Ministry of Justice. The offhand way in which tax valuations had to be made was reflected in the quality of the work. Frequently, they could not stand up if contested; nor were sufficient details of the basis for the valuation supplied to the administrators so that they could make an accurate adjustment in cases where the initial assessment appeared to be excessive.[14]

Meanwhile, the two separate organizations which were handling taxes relating to property were essentially in competition with each other. After some efforts to eliminate duplication by dividing some collection functions between them, it was decided to transfer administration of the rural and urban property taxes to the war damages administration, forming a new Division of War Damages and Property Taxes as of April 1, 1955. This left the collection functions in the General Collections Division, as the remaining office was called.

It did not take long to discover that very little had been achieved by this reorganization, other than some change in lines of communication to a different administrator. The field offices of the General Collections Division could not be divested of any of their personnel, who were very busy with the collection of delinquent taxes. And, as before, the General Collections Division continued to handle current collections of the war damages compensation levy and compulsory loan. Although one of the stated purposes of the merger of the administration of these sev-

13. The municipalities were authorized by the Municipal Corporations Ordinance of 1934 to levy municipal rates on real property within their boundaries. It appears that they too suffered from lack of qualified assessors and, apparently for that reason, the Municipal Authorities (Supplement to Income Tax) Law of 1952 authorized municipalities to impose on their residents a 7.5 percent addition to their normal income tax. This was collected by the income tax administration and then divided among the municipalities. The problem continued until, ultimately, the national administration took over collection of the local property rates.

14. *Sixth Annual Report of the State Comptroller, 1954/55* (Hebrew), pp. 23–27.

eral taxes was to eliminate duplication, it took a long time before this was achieved.[15]

As an immediate goal, the new property tax administration sought to consolidate accounts of taxpayers who might own taxable properties in different sections of the country. Previously, a separate account had been maintained for each parcel of property, and this account was located at the property tax office for the district in which the property was situated. This meant that the owner of several properties might have to travel from office to office to handle his property tax affairs. Also, so long as the war damages compensation levy and the property taxes had been administered separately, a taxpayer owning property subject to both levies would have received a separate demand for payment of each of them. Through the consolidation it was hoped that billing, accounting, and collection procedures could be unified. Although, in principle, this objective appeared simple, it was not easy to carry into practice. The process took several years, during which mechanized procedures were substituted for handwritten accounts.[16]

Even more difficult was the problem of bringing the assessment lists up to date. The problem was only partially solved by training personnel in the techniques of real and personal property valuation. As valuation staffs began to function, it became apparent that the laws themselves were deficient. They prescribed varying standards of valuation which may have been appropriate to the conditions of the country in the 1930's and 1940's, but which had become irrelevant to the totally changed economy of the day. Moreover, the several laws prescribed disparate procedures for assessments, administrative review of assessments, and for judicial appeals from disputed assessments.

The need for a major revision in the basis of assessment of the several property taxes had become increasingly apparent as the reorganized War Damages and Property Tax Division began the task of bringing the assessments lists up to date. The principal difficulty, as noted earlier,

15. A study of the Arnona and Property Tax Division was made by the State Comptroller in 1956. He found that unification had not yet been achieved. One example given was that of the town of Kfar Ata, which several years before had been designated as an urban area by order of the Minister of Finance. This subjected property within the specified urban boundaries to the urban rather than the rural property tax. It was found that property owners still had to deal with two separate offices, because rural property tax accounts for the district, relating to liability for the period before urbanization, were maintained at the Acre office, whereas Arnona and urban property accounts were handled by the Haifa district office (*Seventh Annual Report of the State Comptroller, 1955/56* [Hebrew], pp. 94–96).

16. See and compare *Third Annual Report on State Revenues, 1956/57* (Hebrew), pp. 179–180; *Israel Government Yearbook, 5717* (1956) (Hebrew), p. 217; and *Israel Government Yearbook, 5718* (1957), (Hebrew), p. 230; with *Fifth Annual Report on State Revenue, 1958/59* (Hebrew), pp. 277–285; and *Seventh Annual Report on State Revenue, 1960/61* (Hebrew), pp. 139–144.

was that the several laws stipulating real property as the basis for assessment did not prescribe uniform methods of valuation.

For purposes of the present analysis, these laws may be classified into two groups: (1) taxes applicable to *transfers* of real property; and (2) taxes annually due on the *ownership* of real property. The taxes on transfers were (a) land registration fees; (b) land betterment tax; and (c) estate tax. The annual taxes on property were (a) the rural property tax; (b) the urban property tax; (c) the war damages compensation levy; and, although applicable to only one year, (d) the compulsory loan.

Transfer Taxes

Land Registration Fees [17]

These fees were based upon the fair market value of the land transferred, but this valuation, as a matter of practice, often was equated with the price stated in the contract of sale. An independent evaluation was not generally made by the authorities (the Department of Land Registration in the Ministry of Justice) unless the stated sales price was grossly out of line with known property values in the vicinity. In this event, some of the land registry recorders would refer the valuation to the Valuation Department in the Ministry of Justice (the Government Assessor), but this practice was far from uniform.

Land Betterment Tax [18]

This was imposed upon gains realized upon transfers of real property or of certain interests in real property, including shares in a company organized to hold title to real property. The measure of the gain was the difference between the original cost of the property (adjusted to reflect certain subsequent costs) and the price at which it was sold. If, however, the Director had reason to believe that the reported sales price was inaccurate, or if no return had been filed, he had the authority to assess the tax upon the basis of the fair market value.

Administration of the tax was divided. As to tax due on transfers required to be recorded in the Land Registry, collection and assessment were handled, like the land registry fees, by the Department of Land Registration in the Ministry of Justice. Since the latter fees were also, as a matter of general practice, based upon the reported sales price, avoidance of both the fees and the tax, by understatement of the selling

17. Imposed by the Land Transfer Rules (Fees), 1939. *Sixth Annual Report of the State Comptroller, 1954/55* (Hebrew), p. 26.
18. Imposed by the Land Betterment Tax Law, 1949, later the Land Appreciation Tax Law, 1963, 405 *Sefer Hahukim* 156 (September 1, 1963).

price, was not infrequent. As to transfers of interests in real property, of types not required to be recorded in the Land Registry (such as transfers of shares in a land company), administration of the land betterment tax was handled by the Collections and Property Taxes Division in the Ministry of Finance. When fair market valuations were required to be made by this office, it generally used its own assessors, whose standards of valuation frequently did not coincide with those employed by the Valuation Department in the Ministry of Justice.

Estate Tax

This tax applies to the fair market value of a decedent's estate. Value is defined (sec. 5) as the price which would be set upon each asset, as of the date of death, between a willing buyer and a willing seller, except that if the asset were actually to be sold at a lower price, in a bona fide sale, within one year after the appointment of the administrator of the estate, then the latter price would control. From 1949 until early 1956, administration of the estate tax was assigned to the Income Tax Commissioner, and it was handled by a few inspectors in the income tax assessment offices in Jerusalem, Tel Aviv, and Haifa. From June 1952, and even some time after establishment in April 1956 of a separate estate tax administration, responsible directly to the Director of State Revenue, the task of assessing particular assets, when required, was undertaken by the Valuation Department of the Ministry of Justice. This arrangement was terminated in December 1957, when the estate tax valuation work was transferred to the assessment units of the War Damages and Property Tax Branch, located in Jerusalem, Tel Aviv, and Haifa.[19]

This transfer reflected recognition of the increasing capacity of the property tax administration to conduct independent assessments as a result of the greater attention being given to the establishment of a professional staff of property valuers. Even more, it reflected the trend toward consolidation of the functions of the several tax administrations and the desire to cut across the artificial lines created by the separate statutes under which each tax was enacted. Estate tax collection functions were also delegated in 1957 to the General Collections Division,[20] thereby eliminating the need for a separate staff of tax collectors and cashiers. Practically, this permitted the estate tax administration to function with a very small staff. All other technical aspects of administration of the estate tax were concentrated in a single office at Jerusalem revenue headquarters, with a staff which averaged only eight employees as late as March 1965.[21] Because of the small volume of taxable estates,

19. *Fourth Annual Report on State Revenue, 1957/58* (Hebrew), p. 349.
20. *Third Annual Report on State Revenue, 1956/57* (Hebrew), p. 409.
21. *Eleventh Annual Report on State Revenue, 1964/65* (Hebrew), p. 71.

economy of operations was clearly called for, but greater efficiency was not achieved until recently.

Annual Taxes on Property

Unlike the transfer taxes just described, where the standard of assessment is expressed in terms of the classical definition of fair market value, the several annual taxes on property (until their merger in the Property Tax and Compensation Fund Law, 1961) prescribed varying standards which militated against efficient consolidation of the assessment procedures.

Rural Property Tax

This tax applied to real property (agricultural lands, fish ponds, plantations, and industrial buildings) which was not subject to the urban property tax. The Mandatory Rural Property Tax Ordinance, the provisions of which are long and complex, reflected the characteristics of the agricultural sector of the economy of Palestine at the time it was enacted in 1935. Changes in ownership, land use, and land values, which took place after 1948, rendered the basis of this tax largely obsolete and unworkable.

The underlying method of assessment of the tax on agricultural land was to classify the land in each village in accordance with fertility of the soil and the estimated value of the crop which it was capable of producing. This determination was made without regard to property lines. The rates varied with the location of the land, its quality, and the agricultural techniques employed in producing the crop. This resulted in lower taxes for the Arab farmers, who used more primitive methods. A determination of "net annual value," tied to assumed rental value, was made for industrial buildings subject to the rural property tax. Actually, however, a fixed rate per *dunam* (about one-quarter acre) was established for improved property without regard for the real value of the improvement. A general assessment was then declared for the village, and this was then divided among the individual property owners.

An elaborate assessment procedure was provided, involving an official assessor, the District Commissioner and Officer, and the village *mukhtar* (head man). There were administrative appeals to the official assessor, assessment appeal committees, committees of local residents appointed by the District Commissioner to apportion the tax among the several landowners, appeals from the apportionment to the District Commissioner, and further appeals on questions of law to the District Court. Provision was made for annual revisions of the land classifications and tax apportionments, with similar appeals available from these.[22]

22. Rural Property Tax Ordinance, 1942, secs. 11–24, 26–29.

In brief, the method of assessment of this tax had little actual relationship to the fair market value of the taxable properties. Furthermore, as land ownership and use changed after 1948, and as additional land was converted to agricultural use, the lack of maps and technical personnel resulted in a breakdown of the system. It was not until 1957 that steps were taken to update the agricultural cadaster and to carry out effectively the other detailed procedures prescribed by the law.

Urban property tax

This applied to land and buildings within urban boundaries, as specified originally by order of the High Commissioner for Palestine, and as supplemented in 1954 and in subsequent years by orders issued by the Minister of Finance. The basis of the assessment of this tax was the "net annual value" of the taxable property. As to buildings and tenanted land, this was the actual, or presumed, current rental value. A different measure — fair market value — was the basis for assessment of unoccupied urban land.

Aside from the difficulty of ascertaining current rental value, the concept became obsolete with the passage of time. When the ordinance was originally enacted in 1940 rental properties were commonly available, at rentals fixed by competitive market conditions. However, conditions during World War II, as well as the enactment of a Tenants Protection Law in 1941, which froze both tenancies and rents, made rents progressively less relevant as a factor in determining value. Rents became even more irrelevant with the continuation of the rent freeze during the period of massive immigration after establishment of the State. Hardly any rental housing was constructed after 1948. New construction was sold rather than rented to the occupants. As to rented properties whose tenants changed, "key money" paid on the quasi-purchase of the tenant's rights became much more significant than the nominal annual rent frozen under the Tenants Protection Law. To some extent this difficulty was avoided by resort to a provision which permitted the Assessment Committee to consider factors other than rent (such as size, quality of construction, age, number of rooms) if, in the opinion of the committee, the rent did not properly reflect the "annual value" of the property.

Nevertheless, the fact that a particular dwelling is occupied by rent-protected tenants remains a factor which significantly reduces the value of the property, as compared to similar properties which are free of rent controls.[23] Accordingly, even the 1961 Property Tax and Compensation Fund Law continues to recognize a distinction between rental properties subject to the Tenants Protection Law and those which are not.

23. See A. Witkon, "Tax on Transfer and Possession of Property" (Hebrew), 1 *Quarterly Tax Journal* 23, 25–26 (December 1965).

War Damage Compensation Levy

The taxable value of urban buildings and of industrial buildings in rural areas was arrived at for purposes of this levy by taking the "net annual value," as determined for purposes of the urban or rural property tax (whichever was applicable), and multiplying it by a factor which varied with the age of the building. The value of commercial or agricultural inventories was cost or fair market value, whichever was lower. Value of equipment was based upon historic cost less depreciation allowable for income tax purposes; but total depreciation deductions were limited to 50 percent of the original cost.

As to amounts due on account of equipment and inventories, reliance was placed principally upon periodic returns submitted by the taxpayers. The staff was insufficient to maintain physical control of these items, which — unlike real property — are transitory.[24] On the other hand, the administrator could fix a value other than the one reported by the taxpayer, and, if the taxpayer disagreed, an elaborate series of administrative and judicial review procedures became available. If the dispute was over the valuation of inventory, the taxpayer could request that a nonreviewable valuation be made by an official appraiser appointed by the Minister of Justice, rather than by the Minister of Finance, to whom the administrator was otherwise responsible.[25] Thus, the law itself tended to discourage the creation of a staff of appraisers within the tax administration.

Compulsory Loan

This was imposed in 1953 upon the value of land, buildings of all types (urban, industrial, agricultural), plantations, fish ponds, machinery and equipment, vehicles, animals, and inventories.[26] The premise

24. Similar control problems are, of course, encountered by the income tax administration. However, the income tax aspects of equipment and inventories are not as pressing annually as are the war damages aspects. If inventory is undervalued for income tax purposes, it may have an immediate effect of reducing income for the current year but, in some future year, the balancing effect of inventory accounting will bring the difference back into taxable income. At best, therefore, juggling of inventories achieves a shift of income from one year to another. However, for war damages purposes, an understatement of inventories achieved a permanent reduction in tax, if not immediately caught. Similarly, for income tax purposes it is to the taxpayer's advantage to record his depreciable equipment, whereas he might try to hide it for war damages purposes. These possible inconsistencies were eliminated when administrations of both were combined.

25. War Damage Compensation Levy Law, 1951, secs. 8–13, 21.

26. Imposed by the Compulsory Loan Law, 1953. The rationale for the adoption of this law, its legislative history, and an explanation of its provisions are set out in a printed report by its administrator. See Michael Landau, *Hok Milveh Hovah, 1953* [The Compulsory Loan Law], Government Printer (undated).

was that most of the necessary data for administration of this one-time levy would be derived from the war damage compensation levy files, and the administrator of the latter was also designated as the administrator of the compulsory loan.

The prescribed basis for the assessment of buildings and improved land was the number of rooms. The basis for assessment of equipment was its original cost (with no adjustment for depreciation), but equipment purchased before currency devaluations in 1952 and 1948 was assessed higher than more recently acquired equipment.[27] Commercial inventories were similarly assessed on the basis of cost, adjusted upward, with no alternative valuation on the basis of fair market value, if lower than cost. Other rules of thumb were prescribed for the assessment of other taxable properties. In the event of dispute, as well as for the purpose of valuing unimproved land, valuations were to be made by appraisers appointed by the Minister of Justice. Alternatively, appeals from assessments could be taken to a three-man appeals committee, appointed by the Minister of Justice, whose decision was not further appealable to the courts.

Achieving Centralized Administration

The foregoing survey of this series of complex laws illustrates an unfortunate tendency during the early years of the State to enact tax legislation without regard to achieving uniformity of administration. Although the shifts in administrative responsibility and the establishment of the War Damages and Property Tax Division in 1955 were intended to bring about administrative improvements, these were slow in coming. A direct result of the disappointment which this caused within the Directorate of State Revenue was the resignation of the head of the Division before the end of 1956. Simultaneously, he relinquished the post of Deputy Director of State Revenue to which he had been appointed in 1954. Administration of the stamp duties and of the entertainment tax were then placed under the jurisdiction of the Customs and Excise Branch; and the closing-out functions relating to the *Mikdamah* (income tax advance payments of 1953) and the compulsory loan were transferred to the Income Tax Branch. This signaled the end of efforts to maintain administrative organizations based upon the quasi-voluntary, unofficial, system of contributions utilized by the Jewish community of Palestine during the British mandate. Ironically, not long thereafter the head of the Collection Division (who had meanwhile been shorn of responsibility for the property taxes, for which he had been trained) also left to assume an executive post in another ministry. Perhaps this illus-

27. The purpose of this provision was, apparently, to adjust upward the historic cost of equipment purchased before devaluations of the Israel pound.

trates the futility of the creation of redundant hierarchies for essentially similar functions.

What was really at fault, it was later realized, was the underlying pattern of the various laws. Ultimately they had to be revised before some measure of administrative coordination could be achieved. In 1961 the Urban Property Tax Ordinance of 1940, the Rural Property Tax Ordinance of 1942, and the War Damage Compensation Levy Law of 1951 were repealed, and replaced by the Property Tax and Compensation Fund Law, which became effective April 1, 1961. This prescribed one tax on property [28] instead of three, and simplified the administrative procedures involved in the assessment and collection of the tax. The name of the responsible organization was then changed to the Property Tax and Compensation Fund Branch.

In 1963 further administrative improvements were effected. The Land Betterment Tax Law of 1949 was repealed and replaced by the Land Appreciation Tax Law of 1963. Several measures were introduced in the new law to tighten enforcement. To discourage transactions designed to avoid payment of the land registration fees, it was provided that in such cases an additional amount of land appreciation tax should be paid, equal to the amount of the land registration fee which would otherwise be payable (sec. 9[a]1). A major deterrent to evasion is a provision that the validity of a sale of land shall depend upon payment of the tax and compliance with the other requirements of the law (sec. 16).

The 1963 amendments were accompanied by changes in administration. Imposition and collection of the tax on land sales were transferred from the Land Registry Office in the Ministry of Justice to the Director of the Property Tax and Compensation Fund Branch in the Finance Ministry. In addition to the headquarters office, five field offices were established. These were staffed with real property assessors, who received several months of training in this work. The principal task of the assessors is to check the accuracy of the price reported by the seller and, if it is believed to be other than the true value, to fix the value properly. Ultimately, responsibility for administration of this tax, along with the other taxes which had been assigned to the Property Tax and Compensation Fund Branch, came to rest in the Income and Property Tax Branch, where the land betterment tax, being essentially a capital gains tax, logically should have been lodged from the beginning.

Administration of the estate tax — from the outset something of a stepchild — was also substantially improved. The Commissioner of Income Tax, who was originally appointed as Director of Estate Tax, was too busy to pay it much heed. From 1956 until 1968 the Estate Tax

---

28. Property now subject to this tax is generally land, buildings, plantations, inventories, equipment, and vehicles (including aircraft and vessels registered in Israel).

Unit was loosely attached either to the property tax administration or to the office of the Director of State Revenue.[29] In any event, it lacked strong direction. The need for improvement in the administrative structure became evident after the statute was amended in 1964. As a result of the spotlight which had been focused upon the weaknesses of the Estate Tax Unit by the 1969 Annual Report of the State Comptroller, it has recently been reorganized and shifted to the Income and Property Tax Branch.

A further step, proposed in 1963, was the consolidation of the administration of the municipal and other local rates on property with the administration of the national property taxes. It will be recalled that administration of the urban property tax for 1948–49, the first fiscal year of the State of Israel, had been handled by the several municipalities. Over the years, the successive improvements achieved in the administration of the national property taxes were not paralleled in the administration of the local property rates in at least some of the municipalities.[30] As the central property tax administration increased its efficiency, concern was expressed over the disparity of tax administrations among the municipalities and local authorities, some of which were falling behind in the assessment and collection of local rates.

In 1962 a Commission (headed by Supreme Court Justice Witkon) was appointed to investigate property tax procedures in the local authorities. Its mission included recommending means of "eliminating redundant administrative organizations," in the assessment and collection of the national and local property taxes and the municipal general rate. A subcommittee was directed to report on steps to be taken to permit unified assessment and collection of the several taxes, methods of prompt apportionment of collections among the local authorities and the central government, and the utilization of the manpower which would be freed if unification proposals were carried out.[31]

In August 1963 the subcommittee submitted a far-reaching report, the essence of which was a recommendation that assessment and collection of all of the national and local property taxes be vested in a central ad-

29. The occasion for the 1956 separation of the Estate Tax Unit from the Income Tax Branch was the establishment of the income tax fraud investigation unit. The official placed in charge of fraud investigations in Tel Aviv had until then been in charge of estate tax audits and doing a vigorous job. He could not handle both assignments, and when he was relieved of the estate tax responsibilities the Income Tax Branch could not find a replacement for him.

30. See Office of State Comptroller *Report on Audit of Haifa Municipality* (Hebrew), pp. 66–71, (Jerusalem, 1968).

31. Letter of appointment of October 17, 1962, reprinted in *Din v'Heshbon shel Havaada li'bdikat Darkhei Shiluv Hashuma v'Hagviya shel Misei Harekhush v'Haarnona Haklalit shel Hareshuyot Hamekomiyot v'Hamemshala*, [Report of the Committee to Examine Methods of Assessing and Collecting the Property Taxes and General Rates of the Local Authorities and the Central Government], p. 6, (Jerusalem, August 1963).

ministration, and that the individual local property tax administrations be abolished. Also, all property tax assessments would be based only on fair market value. It was estimated that these steps would make at least 1,200 employees superfluous, while achieving many systemic improvements.

The proposal to combine the national and local property tax administrations was received with little enthusiasm by the local authorities. In fact, those representatives of the municipalities who had been appointed to the commission withdrew from it while its work was in progress. Thereafter the interests of the municipalities were represented by an official of the Ministry of Interior, which supervises operations of the municipalities.

Meanwhile, officials within the revenue administration were looking critically at the property tax administration itself, pointing out that it seemed to have little reason for existence as an independent branch. In part, criticism centered upon relative costs of collection. In fiscal year 1964–65 the Property Tax and Compensation Fund Branch, with almost 600 employees, collected IL. 121 million. In the same year the Customs and Excise Branch, with about 1,800 employees, collected over one billion pounds, as did the Income Tax Branch, with about 2,200 employees. Average costs of collection in 1964–65 were: Property Tax and Compensation Fund Branch — 4.6 percent of amounts collected; Customs and Excise Branch — 2.1 percent; Income Tax Branch — 2.3 percent.[32]

In 1967 the income tax and property tax administrations were merged, and the Income Tax Commissioner was also designated as Commissioner of Property Tax. One of the first steps taken toward merger of the two administrations, in fact as well as in name, was the transfer to the income tax administration of the assessment of the property tax imposed upon equipment and inventory. The merger was expected to achieve economies in administration particularly through the elimination of duplicate field offices and the transfer of redundant personnel.[33]

From the point of view of the taxpayer, this reallocation relieved him of the necessity of filing separate returns, supplying substantially identical information to two separate tax administrations, and dealing separately (and sometimes inconsistently) with two different sets of officials. The merger had obvious advantages, but its achievement involved solution of a number of administrative problems. Not the least of these was the problem of personnel, which, under accepted Israeli labor conditions, had to be provided for even if rendered redundant by the merger. The

32. Giora Gazit, "Where Should the Property Taxes be Located?" (Hebrew), 1 *Quarterly Tax Journal*, 86, 87, 90 (December 1965).

33. Simha Gafni, "Our Plans — Some Comments About Ourselves" (Hebrew), 1 *Quarterly Tax Journal* 389, 390 (October 1966).

actual merger of the administrations was preceded by a series of legislative measures which became effective as of April 1967.[34]

In August 1967 the Minister of Finance appointed a committee, headed by the Director of State Revenue, to examine the various taxes imposed upon land. From the administrative point of view the principal recommendation of this committee, in conformity with its predecessors, was that the previously proposed merger of the national and local property tax administrations be hastened — to take effect, if possible at the beginning of fiscal year 1968–69.

A law merging the national and local property tax administrations was adopted in March 1968. This merger will eliminate technical differences not only between the national and local rates but also among the local rates themselves, which had varied substantially in different municipalities.[35]

As mentioned at the outset of this chapter, in 1948 the departing mandatory officials vested administration of the national property taxes in the local authorities. A generation later, the local property rates, and all of the other taxes on property, are being administered by a single national tax administration. Thus ends the tortuous course which administration of the property taxes has followed.

34. Property Tax and Compensation Fund (Amendment No. 3) Law, enacted March 29, 1967; Y. Tamir, "1968 — Year of Events and Changes in Taxes" (Hebrew), 18 *Roeh Haheshbon* 145, at 147 (January–February 1968).

35. Giora Gazit, "Background to Proposed Changes in Property Tax and Their Significance" (Hebrew), 3 *Quarterly Tax Journal* 142 (April 1968); cf. Alfred Witkon, "After Repeal of the Municipal Tax Rates" (Hebrew), 3 *Quarterly Tax Journal* 317 (October 1968). Dr. Witkon expresses concern over the manner in which nationalization of the local rates was achieved.

10 / Compulsory Payments

Introduction

The fiscal policy of Israel has come to regard taxes and related levies as among the means whereby the government can seek to control the economic development of the country. The intermixture of the classical conception that taxes are levied to finance government expenditures with more modern conceptions of the role of government in directing and controlling economic growth is reflected in a series of compulsory levies which were not denominated as "taxes." Some of these were explicitly imposed for economic purposes, principally to control inflation; others, which implicitly had the same purpose, were enacted ostensibly to provide funds to finance some emergency expenditure.

The legislative pattern for the imposition of these various levies and the avoidance of the "tax" label seem to have been designed to achieve acceptance by an already heavily taxed public. These levies, accordingly, were justified when enacted in terms of the stated needs to which they were directed. Emphasis was also placed upon their temporary nature, although several of them, by virtue of subsequent legislation, have tended to become permanent. The changing conceptions of the nature and purposes of these levies can be seen by tracing their development chronologically.

From the economic point of view, there is little practical distinction between those compulsory payments which are expressly denominated as taxes and those which, because of their temporary nature, specific purpose, or characterization as "loans" or "savings," are classified in other segments of the national income accounts. They all have the common element of being compulsory and of being destined for some essential governmental purpose.[1] Perhaps most significant from the standpoint of this study is the fact that they have all come to be administered by the revenue administration.

Compulsory Insurance

War Damage Compensation Levy

This is a compulsory, war risks, insurance levy which had its origin in conditions preceding the 1948 War of Liberation. Several foreign insurance companies doing business in Palestine had ceased to renew war damage clauses in their policies, whereas others unilaterally canceled such

---

1. Josef Gabai, "The Tax Structure of Israel" (Hebrew), in *Hitpathut Hamisim b'Eretz Yisrael*, p. 5. See also Morag, *Mimun Hamemshalah b'Yisrael*, pp. 255–258 (war damages compensation levy), p. 293 (social insurance).

coverage in policies already in effect.[2] A similar situation had occurred during World War II and had been alleviated by the enactment of the War Risks Insurance Ordinance of 1941.

To meet the situation in early 1948, the Provisional Assembly (*Minhelet Haam*) organized the Palestine Fund for Mutual Insurance Against War Damages, Ltd. The sponsors were the Jewish Agency for Palestine and various groups of property owners.

The impetus for organization of the Palestine Fund came from damages to property which had already resulted from activity of hostile Arab groups and which might result from the war with the surrounding Arab countries which threatened to break out on termination of the British mandate. The fund began to function in April 1948. Properties covered included vehicles, inventories, commercial and agricultural equipment, and plantations (orchards and growing crops). Buildings were added later. Although the fund had no legal authority to require that all affected property owners participate, it has been estimated that about 90 percent of the manufacturers and wholesalers participated in the first years, and about 50 percent of the home-owners. In all, there were about 30,000 insured. The premiums were fixed by the directors of the fund primarily on commercial standards, taking into account the relative degrees of war risk to which the various insured properties were exposed.

In April 1949 the Knesset adopted a resolution requesting the government to submit a bill that would impose a levy upon all owners of property which might be subject to damage from hostile activity. In February 1950 a bill was submitted, and on February 15, 1951, the Knesset enacted the War Damages Compensation Levy Law, effective as of April 1, 1951.

War damage compensation payments were required to be made with respect to urban buildings (these being also subject to the urban property tax), industrial buildings irrespective of location, business equipment and inventories, and plantations. Different rates were applied to different assets. Also, different procedures for measuring the "value" of the various taxable items were prescribed. In principle, the rate structure departed from the concept of insurance in that reduced rates were established for properties in high-risk areas.

After 1951 the War Damages Compensation Law was amended a number of times, and responsibility for its administration also underwent a number of changes. It is particularly noteworthy that this levy, which initially was conceived of as a compulsory form of insurance against war risk, has now lost its separate identity, and compensation for war damages is now funded exclusively out of property tax collections.[3]

2. Similar action was taken by the foreign insurance companies after the Arab riots of 1936 (see Morag, p. 256, n. 14).

3. The view that for all practical purposes the War Damages Compensation Levy was really a tax was shared by the late Dr. Amotz Morag, who for about

In 1961 the Property Tax and Compensation Fund Law was enacted, supplanting the Urban Property Tax Ordinance of 1940, the Rural Property Tax Ordinance of 1942, and the War Damages Compensation Law of 1951. This law eliminated the separate levy for war damage compensation purposes. A war damages compensation fund continued, but additions to it were to be derived from real and personal property tax collections. The property tax rates were accordingly increased to reflect abolition of the war damage compensation levy. Thus, although the principle has been maintained that property owners who suffer damages from enemy activity or from natural disasters shall be compensated by the national government, all pretense of a *quid pro quo* in the form of a presumed payment of premiums for insurance against anticipated losses has been eliminated.

Social Insurance

To a large extent, social insurance in Israel is privately organized and is financed through periodic membership payments. The Histadrut and other organizations have established sick funds, welfare funds, unemployment compensation funds, and various other insurance plans.

The only program established by law (Social Insurance Law, 1953) covers principally old-age insurance, death benefits, work injuries, maternity benefits, survivors' benefits (widows and orphans of insured workers), and, since 1959, benefits for families with four or more children under fourteen. Old-age insurance benefits become payable to covered workers at age sixty-five for men and age sixty for women. The benefits are uniform in amount for all recipients and do not depend upon the amount of contributions which the recipient has made to the fund. There is no means test for eligibility.

The social insurance benefits are funded by compulsory payments measured by the wages or incomes of all residents over the age of eighteen. Coverage for housewives is voluntary. Most of those covered are wage-earners. (In 1963 there were approximately 625,000 out of about 790,000 covered individuals.) By virtue of a floor and ceiling imposed upon the amount of wages or income subject to payment of the monthly charges, the social insurance tax is regressive in effect, falling disproportionately upon the lower-paid wage-earners.[4]

The social insurance program is administered by the National Insurance Institute, which began operations on April 19, 1954. Consideration was given early in the program as to whether contributions to the social insurance fund should be collected by the Institute or by the revenue ad-

---

ten years had been economic consultant to the Director of Revenue (see Morag, pp. 255–258).

4. Morag, pp. 287, 289, 293.

ministration. In 1955 the subject was studied by a tax expert attached to the United States Operations Mission to Israel. He concluded that the collections aspects of the program could be most efficiently administered by the income tax administration and he so recommended. Similar recommendations have been made over the years, but perhaps in an effort to divorce the compulsory social insurance payments from the appearance of being a tax, these recommendations were not immediately implemented. Nevertheless, collection of delinquent social insurance payments was made by the income tax administration, as the agency then vested with enforcement authority under the Taxes (Collection) Ordinance.

Meanwhile, the income tax administration had been improving its pay-as-you-earn procedures as it applied to wage earners. With the introduction of the use of the computer for this purpose, the obvious advantages to be gained by combining the two functions in one agency compelled the transfer of all collections of social insurance contributions to the income tax administration. This was finally accomplished in 1968.

Compulsory Loans and Savings

Successive Impositions

In 1952, in conjunction with the devaluation of the Israeli pound and adoption of a "new economic policy," [5] a compulsory loan to the government, at the rate of 10 percent, was imposed upon all bank deposits and banknotes (the latter being required to be exchanged immediately for new notes). A year later, a compulsory loan, at rates varying from 4.5 percent to 10 percent, was imposed by the Compulsory Loan Law of 1953 upon the value of real property, movable and fixed equipment, and inventories. The loan certificates, which were issued some time later, bore tax-free interest at the rate of 2.5 percent per annum and were redeemable by lot, over a fifteen-year period, beginning in 1957.[6]

Thereafter, pursuant to the Income Tax Advance Payments Law of 1953, individuals and companies were required to make advance payments (*Mikdamah*) against their income tax liabilities for future years, these payments to be made quarterly from July 1, 1953 through January 1, 1954. The measure was the last previous income tax assessment. These advance payments were converted into a "special national loan," to be repaid in instalments until 1979. Execution of the second of these

5. See Halevy and Klinov-Malul, *The Economic Development of Israel*, pp. 7–8, 230–231, 259–260.
6. For details, see *First Annual Report on State Revenue, 1948/49–1954/55* (Hebrew), pp. 191–195; and Asher Arian, "Compulsory Loans and Defense Levies" (Hebrew), chap. 2 in *Hitpathut Hamisim b'Eretz Yisrael*, p. 78 ff.

loans presented a number of administrative problems which are discussed later.

In August 1960 the Property Tax and War Damage Compensation Payments Advance Payments Law was enacted. Property owners whose liability for these taxes exceeded IL. 15 were required to make an advance payment equal in amount to their 1960 property tax liabilities with respect to buildings and land, and their 1959 liabilities with respect to other taxable property. Advances so paid bore interest at a net rate of 3.75 percent, and were applicable as credits to the extent of 20 percent per year against future property and war damage compensation liabilities for 1961 and subsequent years.

In 1961 an absorption loan was imposed by the Absorption Loan Law, the purpose of which was to finance the construction of residences for new immigrants. A similar absorption loan had been prescribed by a 1959 law, but the increase in immigration which had then been anticipated did not eventuate and the 1959 loan was not carried into effect. By October 1961, however, the rate of immigration was found to have exceeded prior estimates, and additional funds were required for immigrant absorption. The 1961 loan was specifically limited to that end.

The absorption loan was fixed at the rate of 6 percent of the 1961 income tax of each person, with certain exceptions. Individuals whose taxes were collected by withholding had their withholdings for the last half of the fiscal year increased by 12 percent. Companies were required to pay the loan in the form of two advance payments, on December 10, 1961, and March 10, 1962, respectively, the sum to be paid being measured by 7.5 percent of the income tax advance payments which the company was obliged to pay for 1961. Self-employed individuals were required to pay the amount of the loan by January 10, 1962. The loans were linked to the cost-of-living index and bore 4 percent interest, taxable at a flat 25 percent rate. The loan was to be repaid by the government in ten equal annual instalments, starting in 1967.

The Absorption Loan (Extension) Law of 1962, promulgated in April of that year, extended the absorption loan at the rate of 12 percent of the income tax liability for 1962. Since this loan, unlike the prior one, came into effect at the beginning of the fiscal year (April 1, 1962), wage-earners were placed immediately on a current basis. Self-employed individuals were required to make two equal payments, in June and December 1962, at the rate of 15 percent of the sum of the advance income tax payments which they were otherwise required to make during the year.[7] Companies, whose advance income tax payments are normally made in quarterly instalments, were required to pay an additional

---

7. The regular income tax advance payments by self-employed individuals are made in ten equal instalments. The requirement that the absorption loan be paid in two instalments apparently was induced by administrative considerations.

15 percent on each instalment. Other aspects of the loan, as to linkage, interest, and repayment, were similar to the prior loan.

In August 1962 the Compulsory Savings Law was enacted. Its purpose, like the 1952 compulsory loan, was to reduce the inflationary pressures which had been generated by the February 1962 devaluation of the Israeli pound.[8] Consistent with the anti-inflationary purpose of this measure, it was provided that the revenues should not be used for governmental purposes but should be retained in a special fund in the Bank of Israel until required to be repaid.

The basis for determining the amount to be saved was net income for 1962, after deduction of the applicable income tax. It applied only to individuals. The complicated rate structure was designed to produce compulsory savings of approximately 4 percent of the income as so adjusted. Advance payments to be made by self-employed individuals were based upon the last previous income tax assessment and were payable in three equal instalments. The "savings" thus collected were to be repaid by the government in four equal instalments, starting April 1, 1966. Meanwhile, the fund was linked to the cost-of-living index and bore interest at the rate of 4 percent, free of income tax.

In 1963 it was decided to combine the absorption loan and the compulsory savings, both of which were tied to the income tax, into one measure. This was accomplished by the Absorption Loan and Compulsory Savings Law, promulgated April 2, 1963. Generally, this law resembled the compulsory loan laws of 1961 and 1962. The principal difference was in the rates. Individuals were subject to an 18 percent rate, whereas companies (which had been exempt from the compulsory savings of 1962) were subject to a 12 percent rate. Wage-earners, as before, were subject to current withholdings. Self-employed individuals were obliged to make advance payments measured by 22 percent of their regular advances on their income tax; the comparable rate for companies being 15 percent of their income tax advance payments. This levy was repayable by the government in seven equal annual instalments, starting in 1968.

On April 1, 1964, a law was enacted extending the 1963 Absorption Loan and Compulsory Savings Law for 1964 and 1965. The provisions were similar to the prior law, except that repayments, in seven equal annual instalments, were to commence on April 1, 1970. On March 24, 1966, the Absorption Loan and Compulsory Savings (Extension) Law was enacted, applicable to 1966 and 1967. These loans were repayable in twelve equal annual instalments; the repayments of the 1966 loan were to commence in April 1, 1972, and the one for 1967 on April 1, 1973.

8. See Halevy and Klinov-Malul, *Economic Development*, pp. 9–10, 266–269. As to other measures undertaken to stimulate savings see ibid., pp. 214–219.

The premise underlying the imposition of this series of compulsory loans and savings was that in a period of continuing inflation they would soak up excess purchasing power. More drastic measures of economic control were taken starting about 1962, when the Israeli pound was substantially devalued. Thereafter, severe economic measures were adopted for the express purpose of cooling down the economy. This policy succeeded almost to a frightening extent and produced a sharp down-turn in the economy during the years 1964–67. Annual growth of the gross national product was sharply reduced, unemployment increased, and many businesses were forced to the wall. As a counterweight, the government announced a policy of maintaining taxes at existing levels, or even reducing them. This policy applied as well to the various forms of compulsory payments. Although the Absorption Loan and Compulsory Savings Law of 1963 continued in effect during the period of economic belt-tightening, collections during that period reflected the decreased incomes, particularly of companies and of self-employed individuals.[9]

The economy took a sharp turn for the better immediately after the June 1967 War. Until 1970, however, the government did not consider the situation called for a return to the compulsory savings or loan device as a means of economic control. Additional finances were required, but, having committed itself to a policy of maintaining taxes at existing levels, it had apparently been decided to maintain this policy at least for a time. This decision is reflected in the post-1967 war defense loan. Here, instead of making the loan compulsory, there was once again a resort to the pattern of public committees, wno were to seek subscriptions to the defense loan on a "voluntary" basis. Thus, after ten years of experience with compulsory loans, an effort was made to follow again the format of the voluntary, public committees which had to be abandoned after the unsatisfactory experience with the Defense Fund of 1955. The decision to resort to this method appears to have been motivated by political considerations.

Administration of the Compulsory Loans

The record of the administrative procedures provided for the foregoing series of compulsory loans reflects the development of Israel's revenue administration. The 1952 compulsory loan, which was imposed upon currency and bank deposits, was relatively simple to administer. The burden of collecting the loan fell upon the banks, to whom holders of currency or of bank accounts were tied. The other aspect of the compulsory loan, which a year later was imposed upon property owners by the Compulsory Loan Law of 1953, was much more difficult to administer. Responsibility for its administration was vested in the

9. *Thirteenth Annual Report on State Revenue, 1966/67* (Hebrew), p. 39, Table C/10, p. 53.

War Damage Compensation Levy Section attached to the revenue administration.

In order to fix the amount to be raised by the compulsory loan, as well as the rate structure, it was necessary to prepare a survey of all assets that were subject to the new levy. This was done by reliance, principally, upon the files of the War Damages Compensation Levy Section, as well as upon special studies which were undertaken for the purpose.

It was estimated that the total value of properties which would be subject to the compulsory loan was, as of April 1952, about 875 million Israeli pounds.[10] It was also estimated that the loan should produce about IL. 45 million, but only if all persons subject to the loan chose to treat it as such. In fact, the net sum of about IL. 29 million was collected. The reason for this difference was that the law provided that the "lender" could elect to waive his right to receive repayment, in which event his "loan" would be reduced by one-half. This choice was exercised by about two-thirds of the 50,000 persons subject to the levy, the result being that of the total collections (over a four-year period) of about IL. 29 million, approximately IL. 9 million remained as a loan, and the balance (about IL. 20 million) was converted by the payers into a nonrefundable levy.

In administering the compulsory loan, the War Damages Compensation Levy Section relied almost entirely upon temporary employees, divided into four branch offices in Jerusalem, Haifa, Tel Aviv and the central part of the country. The chief duty of this temporary organization was to assess the amount to be paid by each property owner who was subject to the compulsory loan. This aspect of the work was quickly phased out, although not without difficulties. These included numerous objections to the valuations placed upon subject properties. Another problem arose in connection with the distribution to the public of the certificates evidencing the amounts of compulsory loan ultimately to be repaid. This task was assigned to the income tax administration, which was then in the process of identifying and locating all income taxpayers in the country. This final task of the compulsory loan was tied in with the administration of the "special national loan" arising out of the 1953 Income Tax Advance Payments Law.

Generally, the experience in administering the series of compulsory payments arising out of the adoption of the 1952 new economic plan was unsatisfactory. Economic conditions in the country were on a downswing, and there was great public resistance to the various measures which the economic planners had undertaken. One of the by-products of the 1952 compulsory loan on bank deposits and currency was a tendency on the part of the public to avoid the banks and to convert their currencies into tangible assets. It took a long time for this distrust of bank

10. For further details as to problems resolved in fixing the rate structure, see *Hitpathut Hamisim b'Eretz Yisrael*, pp. 81–83.

deposits and of currency holdings to be dispelled. The government has apparently resolved not to resort to this type of levy again and, in fact, has not done so in connection with subsequent devaluation of the currency and issuance of new banknotes.

The pattern of the 1953 compulsory loan on real property, equipment, and inventories has also been avoided. The Property Tax and War Damage Compensation Payments Advance Payments Law of 1960, was tied directly to the tax liability which was already determined, and its administration was, logically, imposed upon the Property Tax and War Damages Compensation administration. This took place at a time when this administration was being reorganized and shortly before the several property taxes were about to be combined into one tax. It was apparently assumed that the administrative improvements about to be carried into effect would eliminate some of the problems which the 1953 compulsory loan had encountered, and this proved to be the case.

The concept of a compulsory advance payment, measured by an existing tax liability but to be credited against future liabilities, had already been instituted in the pay-as-you-earn structure of the income tax. Wage-earners had been subject to current tax payments by deductions of the tax at source by the employer since first enactment of the income tax in 1941. It was not until 1952, however, that a system of advance payments was adopted with respect to self-employed individuals and companies. Even so, the pay-as-you-earn system continued to operate much more efficiently in the case of wage-earners than for other taxpayers. Under the system, tax withholdings from wage-earners were measured by current incomes, whereas advance payments by self-employed individuals and companies were measured by their last previous assessments. The result was that wage-earners would be paying close to the full amounts of their tax liabilities for the current year, whereas advance payments by other taxpayers were considerably less than their current tax liabilities. The principal reasons for these discrepancies were (a) the unreliability of tax returns filed by self-employed individuals and by companies; (b) the administrative delays in making final assessments of these taxpayers; and (c) the continuing erosion of the value of the currency which placed a substantial premium upon delays in payment of prior and current tax liabilities.

Given these conditions, any one of the several compulsory levies which were tied to current income tax payments would have the natural consequence of falling more immediately and more heavily upon wage-earners than upon self-employed individuals and companies. Even as administrative assessment procedures improved and the backlog of unassessed returns was cut down, the discrimination continued.[11] It was

11. For a fuller treatment of the idiosyncracies of the Israeli pay-as-you-earn system, see Morag, pp. 99, 130–148.

only partially alleviated by the adoption of provisions in 1957 requiring self-employed taxpayers (but not companies) to make their advance payments in ten rather than four equal instalments; and by other provisions, first instituted by regulation and later confirmed by law, measuring the required current payment by a stipulated percentage in excess of 100 percent of the last previous final assessment, depending upon the relative recency of the taxable year for which the last final assessment had been made.

In spite of the built-in defects of the Israeli current income tax payments system, the authorities have continued to rely upon it as a basis for collecting subsequent compulsory loans. As time went by, it was assumed, apparently, that assessments of companies and self-employed individuals had become sufficiently current so as to justify a compulsory savings surcharge measured by current payments. The actual facts have been to the contrary. Although the assessment backlog has been steadily reduced, it has continued as a serious problem of the administration. Its existence may, at least in part, explain why the Absorption Loan Law of 1959 was never actually carried into effect. There are indications that the Absorption Loan Laws of 1961 and subsequent years and the similar Compulsory Savings Laws, have also presented difficult administrative problems. These were not unanticipated, but it appears that the decision to impose these compulsory loan and savings provisions, in spite of the administrative problems involved and the inequalities which they might produce, was motivated by a policy designed to combat inflationary forces by sopping up excess purchasing power. These are instances then, where the economic planners prevailed over the administrators.

Another instance of policy considerations being permitted to override considerations of administrative efficiency was the adoption of the defense loan after the June 1967 War. Instead of following the pattern of compulsory loans which, by that time, were well-established precedents, it was decided to put the defense loan on a voluntary basis and have it raised by public committees. As of the end of 1968, the amount realized by this loan barely reached original estimates. This can be taken as a relative failure, since 1968 was a boom year in which income tax collections far exceeded original estimates. Nevertheless, the decision to resort to voluntary contributions rather than to a compulsory loan seems to have been adopted because of the oft-repeated promises of the government not to raise the existing level of taxation. Thus it appears that political considerations dictated the use of fund-raising techniques which had already proved to be less efficient than revenue procedures.

At the beginning of 1970, inflationary pressures induced widespread demands for increases in wages, which had been frozen for several years. One feature of the "package deal" agreed to by government, industry, and the Histadrut, was the conversion of the defense loan from a voluntary to a compulsory basis, at 7 percent of taxable income. A substantial part of the wage increases was also soaked up, under the "package deal," by another compulsory savings loan, measured by 4 percent of gross salary (with certain adjustments) and payable by both employers and employees. Self-employed workers and companies are also subject to the compulsory savings loan. Both the compulsory defense loan and the compulsory savings loan are tied to the cost-of-living index and bear interest at the rate of 5 percent per annum. These loans will continue past the fiscal year 1971–72.

The experience with former compulsory loans remains fresh in the minds of the planners. The recent compulsory loans are not measured by the "lender's" money, property, or previous income tax assessment. Instead, they are based upon current income — in effect, an income tax surcharge. The decision to use current income as the loan base is largely governed by administrative considerations.

Administrative difficulties with the prior absorption loan have been considerable, both in terms of computing the amount of the loan (which is based upon the last previous income tax assessment, except for wage-earners who are on a current payment basis) and because of clerical errors, which have resulted in some 12,000 to 14,000 cases in which individuals liable for the absorption loan cannot be identified because their personal identification numbers, upon which the computers depend, are either missing or erroneously reported. The administrators, therefore, pressed for a form of compulsory loan which would be more directly tied to current income and with respect to which the loan certificates could be issued immediately, particularly to employees.

Defense Financing

A substantial part of Israel's budget goes toward the financing of defense activities. Currently, it is estimated, defense expenditures equal about one-fourth of gross national product. Revenue collections finance a large part of the internal expenditures for defense purposes. Among the revenue-raising measures, there were several which were expressly labeled as being for defense purposes. These were the voluntary Defense Fund, the Defense Levy, and the Defense Stamps. Numerous problems were encountered in their administration.

The Defense Fund (*Keren Magen*), 1955–56

In 1955 the uncertain state of equilibrium which had been established between Israel and its Arab neighbors was shaken by the announcement of an agreement for massive supplies of arms by Czechoslovakia to Egypt. Many Israelis reacted spontaneously by offering contributions for the purchase of arms.[12] In October 1955 the then Prime Minister, Moshe Sharett, proposed that all citizens should give voluntarily to this end. Shortly thereafter a public committee was named with the object of raising IL. 25 million within seven weeks, later extended to three months, or to the end of March 1956. The fund to be raised in this manner was called the Defense Fund (*Keren Magen*).

The pattern of administration adopted for this fund was a throwback to the voluntary system of taxation which the Jewish population of Palestine had imposed upon itself during the period of the British mandate. A public committee was organized, headed by one of the heroes of the Haganah, the Jewish self-defense force of those days. An effort was made to recreate the collection organization which had existed during the mandate, but it was quickly realized that, in spite of the public recognition of the need, the goal could not be accomplished with volunteers. The spontaneous and completely voluntary contributions were impressive but insufficient. Furthermore, there were many who held back or who made only token contributions. A quota system worked out among representatives of the various organizations of workers, businessmen, professionals, and industrialists created inequities, because the response of the workers was found to be much greater, proportionately, than that of the companies and self-employed individuals. The latters' reluctance to contribute reflected the financial problems which these sectors of the economy were then experiencing and their generally expressed resistance to efforts to extract money from them by compulsion or otherwise. In all, the contributions or pledges to the Defense Fund, totaling about IL. 19 million fell substantially short of the IL. 25 million goal. It soon became obvious that the social sanctions upon which the public committee relied were ineffective. Accordingly, the Defense Fund was quickly supplanted by the Defense Levy Law of 1956, which supplied the element of compulsion.

The Defense Levy (*Yahav Magen*)

By February 1956, when it became clear that the voluntary program would fall far short of the funds required for upgrading Israel's defense needs, consideration was given to imposing compulsory levy to finance arms purchases. In May 1956 the Defense Levy Law was enacted. The objective of this law was to raise the sum of IL. 55 million in the fiscal year 1956–57, less the sums already contributed to the Defense Fund. The pattern of the levy was twofold, consisting of a direct tax on incomes (intended to raise about IL. 44 million) and indirect taxes on various services and commodities (intended to raise about IL. 11 million).

12. Mordecai Berger, *Neshek l'Yisrael* [Arms to Israel] (Jerusalem: Museum of Taxes, 1968).

When the defense levy was adopted in May 1956, to replace the Defense Fund, the administrative pattern adopted was a hybrid, consisting of a small staff of officials supplemented by a voluntary organization, substantially similar to that of the Defense Fund. As originally enacted, the levy was to be in effect only for the balance of the current fiscal year, which ended March 31, 1957. The time was short, and the administrative problems were many.

The Defense Levy Law of 1956 created a new post — the Director of the Defense Levy — to be appointed by the government. The creation of this post might be attributed to several causes. The defense levy was originally conceived of as a one-year proposition, whose proceeds were intended to be absorbed into the defense budget rather than into the regular budget. Its sponsors may have felt that the defense levy might encounter public resistance if it was too closely identified with the existing tax structure. Furthermore, the prevailing pattern of the revenue laws was to establish a separate administration for each tax. Nevertheless, the person appointed as the Director of the Defense Levy was then also serving as Deputy Director of State Revenue, in charge of the admissions tax, stamp duties, compulsory loan, and war damages compensation levy. During the mandate, he had been one of the officials who had directed the voluntary system of taxation adopted by the Jewish community; and it was clearly intended that the defense levy organization, as had been the case with the Defense Fund organization, should follow the pattern of the previous voluntary tax system.

The authority of the Director of the Defense Levy was limited, however, being shared with a Defense Levy Council appointed by the President of the State. Most of the work of the Council, which met ten times during its ten months of existence, was performed by subcommittees which dealt with the rules of procedure for executing the defense levy. This somewhat tied the hands of the director.

The Defense Levy Law of 1956, recognizing that its income tax aspects, at least, would produce a number of disputed determinations, established a system of appeals committees differing in material respects from the advisory committees which had just been instituted successfully by the income tax administration. For example, members of the appeals committees were appointed by the Defense Levy Council rather than by the Minister of Finance; and their rules of procedure were prescribed by the Minister of Justice rather than by the Director. Considering that 404 committees were established, each consisting of three members selected from a list of 2,172 eligibles, and that 22,000 appeals were heard over a period of eight months, the duplication of effort hardly seems justified.

The major part of the defense levy was in the form of a direct tax, based upon current income for 1956–57. Collection from wage-earners presented no particular problem, as it was effected by the employers, at the prescribed rates, when the wages were paid. As to companies and self-employed taxpayers, however, the exact amount of the 1956–57 income could not be determined until it was finally assessed. Even in the normal course this would take several years. To overcome this delay, the Defense Levy Law provided that all taxpayers other than wage-earners would pay their 1956–57 defense levy in the form of advances, measured by the income assessed for the fiscal year 1953–54. This year was selected because, it was presumed, most of the income tax assess-ments for that year had already been made. Unfortunately, many of the income tax returns which had been filed for 1953–54 were unreliable, many assessments had not yet been made, and many of those which had been made were being disputed by the taxpayers and were in process of administrative or judicial review. Thus the premise upon which this aspect of the defense levy was based proved to be unreliable.

Another aspect of the Defense Levy Law of 1956 which created difficulty was the provision that the portion of the levy based upon income should be credited with the amount which the taxpayer had previously contributed to the Defense Fund. As to wage-earners whose previous voluntary contributions had been collected by deduction from their wages, this provision presented no particular problem because the proof of contribution was readily available. However, in order to ascertain the amount of credit to be afforded a company or self-employed individual, the process became much more complex, for the records of the Defense Fund organization appear to have been incomplete, unreliable, or both.

In retrospect, the assessment and collection problems produced by the defense levy could have been avoided by anticipating the problems men-tioned above and by turning over its administration to the existing revenue organization instead of creating a new administration, no matter how modest. In practice, this was done immediately with respect to the indirect tax aspects of the defense levy imposed upon certain commodi-ties and services. However, the most complex and, from the standpoint of revenue, the most significant, aspect of the defense levy — i.e., the levy on current incomes — was retained for a time in the defense levy administration and not delegated to the income tax administration where it logically belonged.

The Defense Stamp (*Bul Bitahon*)

The Defense Levy Law of 1956 was, by its terms, intended to be closed out as of the end of the fiscal year 1956–57, i.e., by March 31, 1957. However, relations with Egypt continued to worsen, culminating in the Sinai Campaign of October 1956. It became obvious that sub-stantially larger sums would have to be raised to cover the cost of arms and other defense needs.

The Defense Stamp Law of 1956, which came into effect as of November 30 of that year, somewhat overlapped the indirect levies imposed by the Defense Levy Law of 1956, while imposing stamp duties on other items not covered by the defense levy. The administrative defects of the 1956 Defense Levy Law, as well as the duplications with the defense stamp, were eliminated when the Defense Levy Law of April, 1957, was enacted. The indirect aspects of the defense levy were absorbed into the defense stamp; the income tax aspects were converted into an income tax surtax, at graduated rates. The separate defense levy administration then was terminated.

The income tax aspects of the defense levy were abolished in 1958, and the rates were reduced accordingly. In fiscal year 1959–60, a number of the items which had been subjected to the defense stamp, and which were also subject to customs or excises, were eliminated from the Defense Stamp Law (whose term had meanwhile been extended), and were absorbed into the appropriate customs or excise provisions. This left the defense stamp in force on a few items — such as transportation tickets, telephone service, electricity, and motor vehicles — whose collection was the responsibility of agencies outside of the revenue administration.

Much of the administrative confusion illustrated by this and the preceding chapter was part of a costly and annoying learning process. It has become clear from these experiences, that the needs of the hour, no matter how urgent, cannot be met by ad hoc measures. Although Israel's needs to finance its activities, to expand its economy, and to control inflation, continue at a high level, it is doubtful that it will repeat the mistakes described in these chapters.

Bibliography   Index

Bibliography

Readings in English

Anderson, Wayne F. *Income Tax Administration in the State of Israel.* Tel Aviv: U.S. Operations Mission to Israel, 1956.

Apelbom, A. M., and B. Braude. *Palestine Income Tax Cases.* Tel Aviv: Palestine Law Publishing Company, 1945.

Badi, J., ed. *Fundamental Laws of the State of Israel.* New York: Twayne Publishers, 1961.

Baker, Henry E. *The Legal System of Israel.* Jerusalem: Israel Universities Press, 1968.

Bentwich, Norman. *England in Palestine.* London: Kegan Paul, 1932.

Bergmann, Arthur. "Aspects of Fiscal Policy and Taxation," *Jerusalem Post,* February 12, 1953, p. 9.

Bernstein, Marver H. *The Politics of Israel.* Princeton: Princeton University Press, 1957.

Bloch, Henry S. *Revenue Administration and Policy in Israel.* New York: United Nations, 1953.

—— *Revenue Administration and Policy in Israel* (second report). New York: United Nations, 1955.

—— *Revenue Administration and Policy in Israel* (third report). New York: United Nations, 1958.

Blough, Roy. *The Federal Taxing Process.* New York: Prentice-Hall, 1952.

Burstein, Moshe. *Self-Government of the Jews of Palestine Since 1900.* Tel Aviv: 1934.

Dror, Yehezkel. "Public Administration: Four Cases from Israel and the Netherlands," in Lazarsfeld, Paul, Sewell, H. William, and Harold L. Wilensky, eds., *The Uses of Sociology,* 418. New York: Basic Books, 1967.

—— "Some Recent Developments of the Doctrine of Precedent in Israel," 5 *Scripta Hierosylimitana* 228 (1958).

Eisenstadt, S. N. *Israeli Society.* New York: Basic Books, 1967.

Fein, Leonard J. *Israel: Politics and People,* 2d ed. Boston: Little, Brown and Company, 1968.

Goodrick, M. George. *Management in the Government of Israel.* Tel Aviv: U.S. Technical Assistance Program, 1968, mimeo.

Government of Palestine. *A Survey of Palestine.* 3 vols. Palestine: The Government Printer, 1946.

Granovsky (Granott), A. *The Fiscal System of Palestine.* Jerusalem: Palestine and Near East Publications, 1935.

Halevi, Nadav, and Ruth Klinov-Malul. *The Economic Development of Israel.* New York: Frederick A. Praeger, 1968.

Harvard Law School, International Program in Taxation. *Manual of*

Income Tax Administration (Discussion Draft). New York: United Nations 1967.

—— World Tax Series, *Taxation in India.* Boston: Little, Brown and Co., 1960.

—— World Tax Series, *Taxation in Sweden.* Boston: Little, Brown and Co., 1959.

Heth, Meir. *The Legal Framework of Economic Activity in Israel.* New York: Frederick A. Praeger, 1967.

Hindmarsh, F. B. *The Training of the Israel Civil Service.* New York: United Nations, 1956.

Horowitz, David, and Rita Hinden. *Economic Survey of Palestine.* Tel Aviv: Economic Research Institute of Jewish Agency for Palestine, 1938.

—— *The Economics of Israel.* London: Pergamon Press, 1967.

Hurewitz, Jacob Coleman. *The Road to Partition.* New York: W. W. Norton and Company, 1950.

Hyamson, Albert M. *Palestine under the Mandate, 1920–1948.* London: Methuen and Company, 1950.

International Fiscal Association. *Advance Rulings by Tax Authorities on the Request of a Taxpayer* (Second Subject) L (b) *Studies on International Fiscal Law.* London: 1965.

International Lawyers Convention in Israel, 1958. Jerusalem: Ministry of Justice, 1959.

Israel Government Yearbook (English ed.). Jerusalem: Government Printer, various years. For Hebrew edition, see *Shnaton Hamemshalah.*

Joseph, Bernard (Dov). *British Rule in Palestine.* Washington, D.C.: Public Affairs Press, 1948.

—— "Palestine Legislation Under the British," 164 *Annals of the American Academy of Political and Social Science*, 39. Philadelphia: November 1932.

—— *The Faithful City.* London: Hogarth Press, 1962.

Kandel, A. S. *Local Government in Palestine.* Jerusalem: Hamadpis Lipshitz, 1947.

Kraines, Oscar. *Government and Politics in Israel.* Boston: Houghton, Mifflin and Company, 1961.

Lapidoth, Aryeh. *Evasion and Avoidance of Income Tax.* Jerusalem: Museum of Taxes, 1966.

—— "Trends in the Income Tax Legislation of Israel", XVI *Scripta Hierosolymitana* 325. Jerusalem: Hebrew University, 1966.

Laufer, Leopold. *Israel and the Developing Countries.* New York: Twentieth Century Fund, 1967.

Laws of the State of Israel. English translations of selected enactments of the Israeli Parliament, generally issued annually. Jerusalem: Ministry of Justice.

Lazarsfeld, Paul F., William H. Sewell and Harold L. Wilensky, eds. *The Uses of Sociology.* New York: Basic Books, 1967.

Lowdermilk, Walter Clay. *Palestine, Land of Promise*. New York: Greenwood Press, 1968.

Megarry, R. E. *Miscellany-at-Law*. London: Stevens and Sons, Ltd., rev. 1956.

Morag, Amotz. "Some Economic Aspects of Two Administrative Methods of Estimating Taxable Income," 10 *National Tax Journal* 176 (no. 2, June 1957).

Moses, S. *The Income Tax Ordinance of Palestine* (and supplements). Jerusalem: Tarshish Books, 1942.

Nathan, Robert R., Oscar Gass, Daniel Creamer. *Palestine: Problem and Promise*. Washington, D.C.: Public Affairs Press, 1946.

Neeman, Yaakov. *The Tax Consequences of Devaluation*. Tel Aviv: Israel Tax Institute, 1969.

Nowak, Norman D. *Tax Administration in Theory and Practice: With Special Reference to Chile*. New York: Frederick A. Praeger, 1970.

Oldman, O. "Controlling Income Tax Evasion", in Joint Tax Program of the Organization of American States, Inter-American Development Bank, *Problems of Tax Administration in Latin America*. Baltimore: Johns Hopkins Press, 1967.

Ottensooser, Robert David. *The Palestine Pound and the Israel Pound*. Ambilly: Les Presses de Savoie, 1955.

Palestine Gazette. Official Register of the Government of Palestine. Various issues.

Patinkin, Don. *The Israel Economy, The First Decade*. Jerusalem: Maurice Falk Institute, 1967.

Public Administration Service. *Project Completion Report on the Israel Income Tax Administration Project*. Tel Aviv, 1957 — mimeographed.

Quarterly Tax Journal (Rivon l'Inyanei Misim). See listing under "Readings in Hebrew."

Report of the Commission for Examining the Methods of Assessment and Collection of the Income Tax. Jerusalem: Ministry of Finance, 1954. English Translation, Cambridge: Harvard International Tax Program, 1962. (mimeo), Martin Norr, ed.

Sacher, Harry. *Israel: The Establishment of a State*. London: Weidenfeld and Nicolson, 1952.

Safran, Nadav. *The United States and Israel*. Cambridge: Harvard University Press, 1963.

Samuel, Edwin. "A New Civil Service for Israel," XXXIV *Public Administration* 135 (London, 1956).

—— *British Traditions in the Administration of Israel*. London: Vallentine, Mitchell, 1957.

—— *Problems of Government in the State of Israel*. Jerusalem: Rubin Mass, 1956.

Sassoon, David M. "The Israel Legal System," 16 *American Journal of Comparative Law* 405 (No. 3, 1968).

Sharef, Ze'ev. *Three Days.* New York: Doubleday and Company, 1962.

Sharef Report. *See Report of the Commission for Examining the Methods of Assessment and Collection of the Income Tax.*

State Comptroller, Office of. *State Control in Israel.* Jerusalem: Government Printer, 1965.

—— *The State Comptroller of Israel and His Office.* Jerusalem: Government Printer, 1963.

State of Israel. *Customs Guide, Tourists.* Jerusalem: Department of Customs and Excise, 1968.

State Revenue Administration. *The Tax System of Israel* (as at 31st May 1969). Jerusalem: Museum of Taxes, 1969.

Sutherland, Edwin Hardin. *White Collar Crime.* New York: Dryden Press, 1949.

Sykes, Christopher. *Crossroads to Israel.* Cleveland: World Publishing Company, 1965.

Szereszewski, Robert. *Essays on the Structure of the Jewish Economy in Palestine and Israel.* Jerusalem: Maurice Falk Institute, 1968.

Tedeschi, Guido. *Studies in Israel Law.* Jerusalem: Hebrew University Students' Press, 1960.

United Nations Technical Assistance Administration. *Taxes and Fiscal Policy in Under-Developed Countries.* New York: United Nations, 1954.

United States Operations Mission to Israel. *Technical Training for Israel in the United States of America.* Jerusalem: undated.

Wald, Haskell P. and Joseph N. Froomkin. *Agricultural Taxation and Economic Development.* Cambridge: Harvard University Press, 1954.

Wedderspoon, William M. "Simplifying Taxes in East Africa", 6 *Finance and Development* 51 (Washington, D.C., March 1969).

Wilkenfeld, Harold C. "Legal Services to the Revenue Administration — Proposals for Functional Organization," Unpublished report (mimeo.) Jerusalem, 1955.

—— "The Juridical Guarantees of Taxpayers vis-a-vis the Fisc," (national report for Israel) 33 *Cahiers de Droit Fiscal International* 78. Rome: International Fiscal Association, 1956.

Wilkenfeld, Jonathan, "The Irgun Zvai Leumi in the Israeli Independence Movement," unpublished Master of Arts thesis. Washington: George Washington University, 1966.

Zidon, Asher. *Knesset, the Parliament of Israel.* New York: Herzl Press, 1967.

Readings in Hebrew

Aloni, Shulamit. "On Education Toward a Tradition of Taxes as a Rightful Obligation," 3 *Quarterly Tax Journal* 205 (no. 11, July 1968).

Annual Reports on State Revenue. See Din v'Heshbon al Hakhnasot Hamedinah.

Arad, Yaacov. "The Unification of Purchase Tax Rates," 1 *Quarterly Tax Journal* 331 (no. 3, July 1966).

Arian, Asher. "Compulsory Loans and Defense Levies" in *Hitpathut Hamisim b'Eretz Yisrael*. Jerusalem: Museum of Taxes, 1968.

Avnor, Hannah. "Authority of the Court in Appeals from Decision of the Assessing Officer," 2 *Quarterly Tax Journal* 17 (no. 5, January 1967).

Bar-Droma, Yehoshua. *Hamediniut Ha-Finansit be'Medinat Yehudah b'Yemei ha'Bayit ha'Rishon veha'Sheni* [The Fiscal Policy of the Kingdom of Judah in the Days of the First and Second Temples]. Jerusalem: Museum of Taxes, 1967.

Bar-Haim, David. "From Issue to Issue," 4 *Quarterly Tax Journal* 128 (no. 14, April 1969).

Bar-Yosef, Y. "Memories of an Assessing Officer During the Mandate," *Sherut*, nos. 8–9, p. 3 (August 1958).

Bavli, Dan. "Accountants' Certificates for Specific Purposes," 18 *Roeh Haheshbon* 152 (nos. 169–170, January-February 1968).

—— "Trends in Taxation and Taxpayer Participation," 1 *Quarterly Tax Journal* 496 (no. 4, October 1966).

Bavli, Eliezer. "Development of the Accounting Association in Israel," 15 *Roeh Haheshbon* 354 (September-October 1965).

Bazak, Yaakov. *Hilkhot Misim b'Mekorot ha-Ivriyim* [Taxation in Jewish Sources]. Jerusalem: Museum of Taxes, 1965.

—— "Payment and Evasion of Taxes According to Jewish Law," 17 *Roeh Haheshbon* 372 (nos. 163–164, July-August 1967).

Ben-Meir, I. S. "Estimated Income Tax and Self-Assessment," 2 *Quarterly Tax Journal* 331 (nos. 7–8, October 1967).

Berger, M. *Kofer Hayishuv* [Redemption of the Jewish Community]. Jerusalem: Museum of Taxes, 1964.

—— *Magbit Hahitgaysut v'Hahatsala* [The Mobilization and Rescue Fund]. Jerusalem: Museum of Taxes, 1970.

—— *Neshek le'Yisrael* [Arms to Israel]. Jerusalem: Museum of Taxes, 1968.

Birkenfeld, Naftali. "Bookkeeping for Income Tax Purposes," 2 *Quarterly Tax Journal* 189 (no. 6, April 1967).

—— "Implementation of the Income Tax Amnesty Law, 1967," 3 *Quarterly Tax Journal* 168 (no. 10, April 1968).

Cahana, D. "Self-Trade," 17 *Roeh Haheshbon* 340 (May-June 1967).

Cohen, H. "The Citizen and the Computer," 17 *Roeh Haheshbon* 407 (nos. 163–164, July-August 1967).

Dagan, Arye. "Purchase Tax on Services," 2 *Quarterly Tax Journal* 78 (no. 5, January 1967).

Din v'Heshbon al Hakhnasot haMedinah [Annual Report on State Revenue]. Jerusalem: Ministry of Finance. Issued annually (with few exceptions) since 1956, in which the first report covered the period 1948/49 — 1954/55.

Din v'Heshbon shel Havaada Li'bdikat Darkhei Shiluv Hashuma v'Hagviya shel Misei Harekhush v'Haarnona Haklalit shel Hare-

shuyot Hamekomiyot v'Hamemshala [Report of the Commission to Examine Methods of Assessing and Collecting the Property Taxes and General Rates of the Local Authorities and the Central Government]. Jerusalem: Ministry of Finance, 1954.

Din v'Heshbon shel Havaada Li'vhinat Shitot Hahaaraha v'Hagviya shel Mas Hakhnasa [Report of the Commission for Examining the Methods of Assessment and Collection of the Income Tax]. Jerusalem: Ministry of Finance, 1954.

Din v'Heshbon Shnati Shel M'vaker Hamedinah [Annual Report of the State Comptroller]. Jerusalem: State Comptroller, various years.

Eilenberg, A. "Deliberations of the International Committee on Evaluation in Brussels," 1 *Quarterly Tax Journal* 201 (No. 2, April 1966).

Fellman, Avraham. *Dinei Mas Hakhnasa be-Yisrael.* (Tel Aviv, 1952).

—— and Reuven Nohimovsky. *Dinei Mas Hakhnasa.* (Tel Aviv, 1949).

Firmanim be-Inyanei Misim b'Eretz Yisrael me-ha-Shanim 1560–1585. (Tax Proclamations of the Ottoman Regime in Palestine During 1560–1585). Jerusalem: Museum of Taxes, 1965.

Freidkes, N. "The Tax Amnesty and the Taxpayer," 17 *Roeh Haheshbon* 460 (September-October 1967).

Fromer, Simha. "Reasonable Cause," 6 *Roeh Haheshbon* 288 (Nos. 40–41, July-August 1956).

—— "The Bookkeeping Requirements for Wholesalers and Retailers," 6 *Roeh Haheshbon* 53 (October-December 1955).

Gabai, Josef. "Comparative Levels of Taxation in Israel and other Countries," 4 *Quarterly Tax Journal* 176 (No. 14, April 1969).

—— "The Tax Structure of Israel," in *Hitpathut Hamisim b'Eretz Yisrael.* Jerusalem: Museum of Taxes, 1968.

Gafni, Simha. "Guidelines for Improving the Image of the Revenue Administration," 1 *Quarterly Tax Journal* 14–15 (no. 1, December 1965).

—— "Our Plans — Some Remarks About Ourselves," 1 *Quarterly Tax Journal* 389 (no. 4, October 1966).

Gazit, Giora. "Background to Proposed Changes in Property Tax and Their Significance," 3 *Quarterly Tax Journal* 142 (no. 11, April 1968).

—— "Deductions at Source from Income of Employees," 2 *Quarterly Tax Journal* 352 (October 1967).

—— "Where Should the Property Taxes be Located," 1 *Quarterly Tax Journal* 86 (no. 1, December 1965).

Givoni, A. "Remarks," 10 *Roeh Haheshbon* 136 (Nos. 81–82, April-June 1960).

Gorney, Uriel. "Net Worth Increases and Burden of Proof in Criminal Cases Under the Income Tax Ordinance," 6 *Roeh Haheshbon* 11 (October-December 1955).

Greenstein (Gal-Edd), Israel. "Developments in Assessment Procedures," in *Proceedings of Symposium on Income Taxation.* Jerusalem: Hebrew University, 1955.

Hahn, Yosef. "Administrative Developments in the Income Tax Branch,"
1 *Quarterly Tax Journal* 103 (no. 1, December 1965).

Heshin, Mishael. "More on the Commissioner's Reopening of Assessments," 3 *Quarterly Tax Journal* 3 (no. 9, January 1968).

Hitpathut Hamisim b'Eretz Yisrael [History of Taxation in Palestine and
Israel]. Jerusalem: Museum of Taxes, 1968.

Horowitz, David. *Calcalat Yisrael* [The Economy of Israel]. Tel Aviv:
Masada Press, 1954.

Income Tax Administration. *Sefer Hanishomim* [Book of Taxpayers].
Jerusalem: Ministry of Finance, 1955, etc.

Kahan, H. "Income Tax During the Mandate, the Transition, and in the
First Days of the State," *Sherut*, nos. 8–9, p. 5 (August 1958).

Kanne, M. "The 'Law' and the Accountant," 17 *Roeh Haheshbon* 465
(September-October 1967).

Kessler, Zvi. "From Issue to Issue," 3 *Quarterly Tax Journal*, unnumbered preface, (no. 9, January 1968).

—— "Increase in Income Tax Advance Payments," 1 *Quarterly Tax
Journal* 257 (no. 3, July 1966).

—— "Limitation of the Period for Assessments," 1 *Quarterly Tax
Journal* 259 (no. 3, July 1966).

—— "Relaxation of the Secrecy Requirements as between Tax Administrations," 1 *Quarterly Tax Journal* 259 (no. 3, July 1966).

Klimowsky, E. W. "Administrative and Judicial Appeals," in *Proceedings of Symposium on Income Taxation*, 38. Jerusalem: Hebrew
University, 1955.

—— "Civil and Criminal Action in Income Tax Cases," 7 *Roeh Haheshbon* 26 (nos. 42–43, September-October 1956).

——"Criminal Case or Civil Case, Which Comes First," 9 *Roeh Haheshbon* 134 (February-March 1959).

Kovetz Dinei Misim. (Kadam). Ministry of Finance, Jerusalem Loose
leaf — compilation of tax statutes, regulations, and orders.

Kovetz Hatakanot. Official Register of Regulations and Orders.

Lahav, Meir, "Organizational Aspects of Conversion to Computer," 2
Quarterly Tax Journal 97 (no. 5, January 1967).

—— "The Computer in Tax Administration," 3 *Quarterly Tax Journal*
373 (no. 12, October 1968).

—— "The Conflict Between the Computer and the Organization," 3
Quarterly Tax Journal 292 (no. 11, July 1968).

—— "The Income Tax Department in Ghana," 2 *Quarterly Tax Journal*
372 (Nos. 7–8, October 1967).

Landau, Michael. *Hok Milveh Hovah, 1953* [The Compulsory Loan
Law]. Government Printer, undated.

Lapidoth, Aryeh. *Hithamkut ve-Hishtamtut mi-Mas Hakhnasa* [Avoid-
ance and Evasion of Income Tax]. Jerusalem: Museum of
Taxes, 1966.

—— *Ikronot Mas Hakhnasa u'Mas Rivhei Hon* [Principles of Income
Tax and Capital Gains Tax]. Jerusalem: Museum of Taxes,
1970.

—— "Imposition of Tax on Damages and Effect of Tax Liability upon the Assessment of Damages," 1 *Quarterly Tax Journal* 273 (no. 3, July 1966).

—— "Imposition of Tax on Income from Trade or Occupation," 2 *Quarterly Tax Journal* 243 (nos. 7–8, October 1967).

—— "On Tax Amnesties," 3 *Quarterly Tax Journal* 173 (no. 10, April 1968).

—— "Revision of Assessments by the Income Tax Commissioner," 1 *Quarterly Tax Journal* 27 (no. 1, December 1965).

Lipavski-Halifi, I. "The Self-Employed and Income Tax," 7 *Roeh Haheshbon* 87 (nos. 44–45, November-December 1956).

Lipkin, O. "Opening of an Office during Military Occupation," *Sherut,* nos. 8–9, p. 12 (August 1958).

Loewenberg, H. S. "Assessment and Judgment," 11 *Roeh Haheshbon* 89 (nos. 87–88, December 1960-January 1961).

Mandel, Avraham. "Fiscal Policy and Administrative Tools for its Implementation," 1 *Quarterly Tax Journal* 240 (no. 2, April 1966).

Mantua Jewish Community. *Seder Hahaarahah* [The Assessment Procedure]. Jerusalem: Museum of Taxes, 1963.

Ministry of Finance. *Budget Messages of the Minister of Finance.* Jerusalem: Ministry of Finance, various years.

—— *Five Years of the Income Tax Advisory Committees.* Jerusalem: 1960.

—— *Responses of the Minister of Finance to Nineteenth Annual Report of the State Comptroller.* Jerusalem: 1969.

—— *Ten Years of Activity of the Income Tax Advisory Committees.* Jerusalem: 1964.

Morag, Amotz. *Mimun Hamemshalah be-Yisrael* [Public Finance in Israel]. Jerusalem: Magnes Press, 1967.

Nahir, Boaz. *Moreh Derekh li'Psikat Mas Hakhnasa* [Guide to Income Tax Decisions]. 4 vols. Tel Aviv: 1962.

Neeman, Yaacov. "Conversion of Asset from Investment to Business Inventory," 1 *Quarterly Tax Journal* 427 (no. 4, October 1966).

Neiger, Dov. "Income Tax Objections and Appeals," 4 *Quarterly Tax Journal* 257 (no. 15, July 1969).

Neudorfer, Moshe. "Aspects of Tax Policy in 1969/70," 4 *Quarterly Tax Journal* 130 (no. 14, April 1969).

—— Remarks before Institute of Certified Public Accountants 19 *Roeh Haheshbon* 373 (nos. 185–186, May-June 1969).

Nohimovsky, Reuven. *Mas Hakhnasa* [Income Tax]. Tel Aviv: Ayin, 1952.

Peled, David. "On the Revision of Traditional Customs Routines," 4 *Quarterly Tax Journal* 242 (no. 15, July 1969).

—— "Principal Administrative Developments in the Customs and Excise Branch," 1 *Quarterly Tax Journal* 231 (no. 2, April 1966).

Peleg, Yehuda. "How Uganda Adopted the Purchase Tax," 4 *Quarterly Tax Journal* 104 (no. 13, January 1969).

Proceedings of Symposium on Income Taxation, see *Symposion le-Inyanei Mas Hakhnasah.*

Quarterly Tax Journal (Rivon l'Inyanei Misim). Jerusalem, Museum of Taxes. Published quarterly, commencing December, 1965. Cited herein for convenience under English titles, generally as given in the English index to each issue, although the articles cited appear in Hebrew only.

Report of Income and Property Tax Branch. 1967–68.

Report of the Commission for Examining the Methods of Assessment and Collection of the Income Tax. See *Din v'Heshbon shel Havaada Li'vhinat Shitot Hahaaraha v'Hageviya shel Mas Hakhnasa*, and see above title in Readings in English.

Rivon l'Inyanei Misim (cited as *Quarterly Tax Journal*). Jerusalem: Museum of Taxes. First issue, December 1965.

Rosolio, David and E. W. Klimowsky. *Mas Hakhnasa b'Eretz Yisrael*. (Income Tax in Palestine). *Jerusalem*: 1944.

Salonika Jewish Community. *Sefer Avodat Masa*. (Achieving the Goal). Jerusalem: Museum of Taxes, 1964.

Schneider, Uri. "Stamping of Accounts with Adhesive Stamps or on Basis of Turnover," 2 *Quarterly Tax Journal* 180 (no. 6, April 1967).

Sefer Hahukim. Statutes of Israel, official Hebrew text, in numerous volumes.

Sharef Report. See *Din v'Heshbon shel Havaada Li'vhinat Shitot Hahaaraha v'Hageviya shel Mas Hakhnasa*; and see English readings.

Sharon, Yosef, and Moshe Weiss. "Training in the Treasury's Revenue Service," *Sherut*, (no. 11, August 1959), p. 4.

Sher, Ze'ev. "Codification of the Tax Laws in Israel," 1 *Quarterly Tax Journal* 129 (no. 2, April 1966).

Sherut. Publication for personnel of the State Revenue Administration. Superseded by *Quarterly Tax Journal*.

Shimron, E. S., and J. S. Zemah. "Selected Problems of Evidence in Income Tax Proceedings," 1 *Quarterly Tax Journal* 410 (no. 4, October 1966).

Shnaton Hamemshalah. (Israel Government Year Book). Jerusalem: Prime Ministers Office. Published annually since 1950. Also available in English translation.

Shoham, Shlomo. *Averot v'Onshim be-Yisrael* [The Sentencing Policy of Criminal Courts in Israel]. Tel Aviv: Am Oved, 1963.

State Comptroller, Annual Reports. See *Din v'Heshbon Shnati Shel M'vaker Hamedinah*.

State Comptroller, Office of. Report on Audit of Haifa Municipality. Jerusalem: 1968.

Stein, M. "Memories from Days of Destiny," *Sherut*, nos. 8–9, p. 10 (August 1958).

Stern, Yosef. *Mas Hakhnasa Halakhah u-Maaseh* [Income Tax Law and Practice]. Loose leaf, 2 vols. Tel Aviv: Gvilim, 1956.

Strauss, Israel and Dov Neiger. *Mafteah Klali Lifsikat Mas Hakhnasa* [General Index to Income Tax Decisions]. Tel Aviv: Israel Accounting Society, 1965.

Symposion le-Inyanei Mas Hakhnasa [Proceedings of Symposium on Income Taxation]. Jerusalem: Hebrew University, 1955.

Tamir, Y. "1968 — Year of Events and Changes in Taxes," 18 *Roeh Haheshbon* 145 (nos. 169–170, January-February 1968).

—— "The Amnesty Law and the Income Tax (Amended Declarations) Law- 1967, Background, Policy and Execution," 17 *Roeh Haheshbon* 455 (September-October 1967).

—— "The Attitude of the Tax Administration," 16 *Roeh Haheshbon* 76 (November-December 1966).

Turner, Eliezer. "The Standard Assessment Guides for Income Tax Purposes," 6 *Roeh Haheshbon* 5 (October-December, 1955).

Vatikei ha'Mekhes b'Namal Yafo Mesaprim [Old Timers of the Customs at Jaffa Port Tell Their Stories]. Jerusalem: Museum of Taxes, 1967.

Weinman, Dov. "The Brussels Tariff Nomenclature," 4 *Quarterly Tax Journal* 317 (no. 15, July 1969).

Wermus, Nahum. "The Problem of Compliance in Income Tax Administration," 3 *Quarterly Tax Journal* 275 (no. 11, July 1968).

Wilkenfeld, Harold C. "Administrative Review of Objections to Income Tax Assessments," 1 *Hed Hamishpat* 277 (no. 15, August 1957).

—— "Administrative Tribunals for Tax Disputes," 1 *Quarterly Tax Journal* 225 (no. 2, April 1966).

—— Haim Cohen, Zeev Sharef, T. Brosh. "Discussion of Tax Prosecution Policy," *Sherut*, no. 5, July 1957, pp. 3–12.

—— "Prosecution or Compounding of Criminal Offenses," *Sherut*, no. 5, July 1957, p. 3.

—— "The Rights of the Income Taxpayer," 7 *Roeh Haheshbon* 287 (nos. 50–51, May-June 1957).

Witkon, A. "After Repeal of the Municipal Tax Rates," 3 *Quarterly Tax Journal* 317 (no. 12, October 1968).

—— *Mavo Le-Dinei Misim* [Introduction to Tax Law]. 1st ed. Tel Aviv: Schocken Press, 1956.

—— and R. I. Neeman. *Dinei Misim* [Principles of Taxation], 4th ed. Tel Aviv: Schocken Publishing House, 1969.

—— "Tax on Transfer and Possession of Property," 1 *Quarterly Tax Journal* 23 (no. 1, December 1965).

Index